D1165529

Russia and Globalization

Russia and Globalization

Identity, Security, and Society
in an Era of Change

Edited by Douglas W. Blum

Woodrow Wilson Center Press
Washington, D.C.

The Johns Hopkins University Press
Baltimore

EDITORIAL OFFICES

Woodrow Wilson Center Press
Woodrow Wilson International Center for Scholars
One Woodrow Wilson Plaza
1300 Pennsylvania Avenue, N.W.
Washington, D.C. 20004-3027
Telephone: 202-691-4010
www.wilsoncenter.org

ORDER FROM

The Johns Hopkins University Press
Hampden Station
P.O. Box 50370
Baltimore, Maryland 21211
Telephone: 1-800-537-5487
www.press.jhu.edu/books/

2 4 6 8 9 7 5 3 1

This publication was made possible in part by a grant from Carnegie Corporation of New York.
The statements made and views expressed are solely the responsibility of the author.

Library of Congress Cataloging-in-Publication Data

Russia and globalization : identity, security, and society in an era of change / edited
by Douglas W. Blum.
    p. cm.
Includes index.
ISBN 978-0-8018-8842-7 (cloth : alk. paper)
    1. Russia (Federation)—Economic policy—1991.   2. Globalization—Economic
aspects—Russia (Federation)   3. Russia (Federation)—Foreign economic relations.
4. Russia (Federation)—Economic conditions—1991.   5. National security—Russia
(Federation)   I. Blum, Douglas W.
HC340.12R828 2008
337.47—dc22   2007049366

**Woodrow Wilson
International
Center
for Scholars**

The Woodrow Wilson International Center for Scholars, established by Congress in 1968 and headquartered in Washington, D.C., is a living national memorial to President Wilson.

The Center is a nonpartisan institution of advanced research, supported by public and private funds, engaged in the study of national and world affairs. The Center establishes and maintains a neutral forum for free, open, and informed dialogue.

The Center's mission is to commemorate the ideals and concerns of Woodrow Wilson by providing a link between the world of ideas and the world of policy, by bringing a broad spectrum of individuals together to discuss important public policy issues, by serving to bridge cultures and viewpoints, and by seeking to find common ground.

Conclusions or opinions expressed in Center publications and programs are those of the authors and speakers and do not necessarily reflect the views of the Center staff, fellows, trustees, advisory groups, or any individuals or organizations that provide financial support to the Center.

The Center is the publisher of *The Wilson Quarterly* and home of Woodrow Wilson Center Press, *dialogue* radio and television, and the monthly newsletter "Centerpoint." For more information about the Center's activities and publications, please visit us on the web at www.wilsoncenter.org.

Contents

Tables and Figures   ix

Acknowledgments   xiii

1   Introduction: Russia and Globalization—A Historical
    and Conceptual Framework   1
    Ulf Hedetoft with Douglas W. Blum

Part I. Globalization and Domestic Processes

2   The Russian Demographic Crisis in Cross-National
    Perspective   37
    Andrey Korotayev and Darya Khaltourina

3   Globalization, Regional Change, and the Territorial
    Cohesion of the Russian Federation   79
    Michael Bradshaw

4   Russian Identity and Siberia's Self-Identification:
    Historical Traditions in a Global World   111
    Evgeny Vodichev and Vladimir Lamin

5   The Transformation of the Russian System of
    Higher Education   139
    Gennady N. Konstantinov and Sergey R. Filonovich

6   The Russian Defense Industry in the Age of Globalization   153
    Alla Kassianova

7   Integration from Below? The Disappointing Effort to
    Promote Civil Society in Russia   181
    James Richter

Part II. Globalization and Foreign Policy

8   Going "Relativistic": The Changing Vision of "Just
    International Order" in Russian Foreign Policy   207
    Mikhail Troitskiy

9   Socializing Baltic Sea States into a Security Community:
    Aspects of Globalization   233
    Erik Noreen

10 Chechnya, the Council of Europe, and the Advocacy
    of Human Rights in the Toughest of Cases   259
    Rick Fawn

11 Russian Geopolitics in the Context of Globalization   287
    Eduard Solovyev

12 Globalization, Identity, and Changing Understandings
    of Security in Russia   307
    Alexey Fenenko

13 Conclusion: Links between Globalization, Security, and Identity
    in Russia   329
    Douglas W. Blum

Contributors   365

Index   369

Tables and Figures

Tables

2.1 Regression Model of Male Life Expectancy Factors
for Countries with Total Fertility Rate below Two
Children per Woman   60

2.2 Regression Model of Factors of Female Life Expectancy
in Countries with Total Fertility Rate below Two Children
per Woman   62

2.3 Regression Model of Factors Affecting the Difference
between Male and Female Life Expectancy, for Countries
with a Total Fertility Rate below Two Children per Woman   64

2.4 Regression Model of Factors Affecting the Total Fertility
Rate in Countries with a Total Fertility Rate below Two
Children per Woman   65

2A Summary of Mortality Rate Dynamics, 1990–94   71

3.1   Top Ten Exporting and Importing Regions in Russia, 2002   88

3.2   Top Ten Recipients of Foreign Direct Investment in
       Russia, 2000–2 and 1995–2002   96

5.1   Answers to the Question "What consequence of Russia's
       adopting the Bologna Process do you fear most?"   146

Figures

1.1   Model of the Relations between Globalization and
       Four National Nodes   5

2.1   Dynamics of Birthrate and Mortality Rate in Russia,
       1978–2003   39

2.2   Answers to the Question "Generally speaking, was this year
       better, worse, or the same as the previous one?" for the
       Period 1996–2004   40

2.3   Per Capita Gross Domestic Product in Estonia, Russia,
       Georgia, Armenia, and Uzbekistan, 1990–94   41

2.4   Dynamics of Mortality Rates in Estonia, Russia, Georgia,
       Armenia, and Uzbekistan, 1990–94   42

2.5   Mortality Rates for Children under Five Years Old in
       Estonia, Russia, Georgia, Armenia, and Uzbekistan,
       1990–94   43

2.6   Infant Mortality Rates in Estonia, Russia, Georgia,
       Armenia, and Uzbekistan, 1990–94   44

2.7   Mortality Rates for Males Age Twenty to Twenty-Four
       Years in Estonia, Russia, Georgia, Armenia, and Uzbekistan,
       1990–94   46

2.8   Mortality Rates for Males Age Twenty-Five to Thirty-
       Nine Years in Estonia, Russia, Georgia, Armenia, and
       Uzbekistan, 1990–94   47

2.9   Mortality Rates for Males Age Forty to Fifty-Nine Years in
       Estonia, Russia, Georgia, Armenia, and Uzbekistan, 1990–94   48

2.10   Mortality Rates for Females Age Twenty to Twenty-Four
       Years in Estonia, Russia, Georgia, Armenia, and Uzbekistan,
       1990–94   49

2.11   Mortality Rates for Females Age Twenty-Five to Thirty-

Nine Years in Estonia, Russia, Georgia, Armenia, and
Uzbekistan, 1990–94   50

2.12 Mortality Rates for Females Age Forty to Fifty-Nine Years in
Estonia, Russia, Georgia, Armenia, and Uzbekistan, 1990–94   51

2.13 Life Expectancy at Birth in Russia, Georgia, and Uzbekistan,
1990–94   52

2.14 Difference between Female and Male Life Expectancy in
Industrially Developed Countries with Alcohol Consumption
of More Than 9 Liters of Pure Alcohol per Adult per Year   56

2.15 Birthrate, Mortality Rate, and Alcohol Consumption in
Hungary, 1960–95   58

2.16 Birthrate, Mortality Rate, and Alcohol Consumption in
Hungary against the Background of Gross Domestic Product,
1960–90   59

2.17 Total Fertility Rate and the Difference between Female
and Male Life Expectancies in Countries with a Total
Fertility Rate below Two Children per Woman   66

2.18 Alcohol Consumption per Capita and Average Estimated
Income for Men, 2001   67

3.1 The Dynamics of Russian Foreign Trade, 1995–2004   87

3.2 Exports from Russia's Regions in 2002 to Countries Not
Belonging to the Commonwealth of Independent States   89

3.3 Imports to Russia's Regions in 2002 from Countries Not
Belonging to the Commonwealth of Independent States   90

3.4 The Dynamics of Foreign Direct Investment in Russia,
1994–2005   92

3.5 The Sectoral Structure of Russian Foreign Direct
Investment, 2004   93

3.6 Distribution of Foreign Direct Investment in Russia by
Federal District, 1995–2003   94

3.7 Cumulative Foreign Direct Investment per Capita in
Russia's Regions, 1995–2002   95

3.8 Regional Variations in Gross Regional Product, 1990–2004   97

3.9 Gross Regional Product per Capita in Russia, 2001   103

3.10 Gross Regional Product per Capita in Russia, by Region, 2002   104

Acknowledgments

Having been invited to direct a project on "Russia and the World," I chose the theme of globalization. This is because, it seems to me, globalization is broad enough to furnish a useful vehicle for incorporating diverse analytical approaches and theoretical perspectives, and is at the same time a process of such immense power that it behooves us to grapple with its vast implications. Something is clearly changing at the supra-international, trans-international, and international levels of politics that calls into question the validity of traditional frameworks for parsing the social and political world. This book constitutes an effort to think through some of the more important aspects of this overarching process as it applies to Russia. To be sure, the present volume is far from being comprehensive; the reader will notice that it does not include chapters dedicated specifically to flows of capital, people, or illicit goods, to name just a few of the more obvious lacunae. I ask the reader's indulgence for these omissions. My hope is that the issues and perspectives addressed here will spark further reflection and debate on this critical subject.

On behalf of myself and the other contributors to this volume, I would like to acknowledge the generous support we received from several key sources. This volume is the product of a larger initiative sponsored by the Carnegie Corporation, the Ministry of Education of the Russian Federation, the MacArthur Foundation, and the Open Society Institute, which culminated in the creation of nine Russian Centers for Advanced Study and Education (CASEs) in 2000 at the state universities in Ekaterinburg, Irkutsk, Kaliningrad, Novgorod Velikii, Rostov-on-Don, Saratov, Tomsk, Vladivostok, and Voronezh. The mission of these CASEs is to promote the further development of the humanities and social sciences by providing support for research, travel, and scholarly publications. Subsequently, the Kennan Institute of the Woodrow Wilson International Center for Scholars decided to conduct a series of thematic workshops involving CASE-affiliated scholars as well as other scholars from around the world on three subject areas: (1) Russia and the world (embracing the Far Eastern, Irkutsk, and Kaliningrad CASEs), (2) diverse cultures in contemporary societies (covering the Urals, Voronezh, and Tomsk CASEs), and (3) state and society relations in transitional societies (cosponsored with the Novgorod, Saratov, and Rostov-na-Donu CASEs). The present volume arose from two workshops that addressed the first thematic area, Russia and the world (the working focus was further refined as "identity, globalization, and security in Russia"). The workshops were held in May and November 2005 and were hosted, respectively, by the ISE Center (Information, Scholarship, Education) in Moscow and the Kennan Institute in Washington. A central goal of the CASE program is to expand and enrich the international academic community. I hope that in our own modest way we have advanced this goal.

I wish to express my personal gratitude to those who provided crucial backing for the CASE initiative. In particular, I would like to thank Deana Arsenian of the Carnegie Corporation for her support as well as her friendship over these many years. In addition, I am grateful for the support from another old friend, Andrey Kortunov, now president of the ISE Center.

The road from initial conceptualization to final edits is a long one, and along the way I have benefited greatly from others' help. I would like to specifically acknowledge four staff members of the Kennan Institute who were pivotally responsible for making the project such a success. First and foremost, I am deeply indebted to Blair Ruble, the institute's director, for inviting me to direct the project. His guidance and insight were invaluable in the early stages of conceptualizing and planning the workshops, and his practical suggestions—and good humor—were incredibly helpful throughout. Maggie Paxson, senior associate, was also wonderful to work with. She participated in both workshops with the authors in Moscow and Washington, and we all benefited enormously from her many tactful suggestions and questions. In addition, I will always be indebted to Jennifer Giglio, former program associate, who oversaw the project in its early stages, through the two conferences, and well into the editing process. Jen unfailingly provided prompt and competent administrative support, which was in itself indispensable, but no more so than her unflagging energy and cheerfulness. Finally, Megan Yasenchak, program assistant, did yeoman's work in the final stage of collecting and editing the book's chapters. My heartfelt thanks to all of them. Thanks also to Joseph Brinley, director of the Woodrow Wilson Center Press, for embracing the manuscript, as well as to the staff of the Johns Hopkins University Press for ushering it along to completion.

No list of thanks would be complete without acknowledging my marvelous colleagues in the Program on New Approaches to Russian Security. I have borrowed liberally from many of their works (without, I hope, distorting their views). Having this brain trust available, for both formal and informal discussions, was utterly invaluable in helping me think through the issues addressed in this book.

Finally, I especially wish to express my deep appreciation for the contributors to this volume, who drafted several versions of their chapters, took part in two conferences, and endured what must have seemed like an endless barrage of questions and suggestions from me. I am grateful for their patience but most of all for their creativity and analytical insight. Because of them, it was a pleasure to be involved with this project.

Douglas W. Blum

Russia and Globalization

1

Introduction: Russia and Globalization—
A Historical and Conceptual Framework

Ulf Hedetoft with Douglas W. Blum

Since the fall of the USSR, Russia has been faced with the need to fundamentally rebuild its power and identity—and to do so in the unfamiliar, challenging, and often threatening context of globalization. This volume represents an effort to elucidate interconnections among these issues, as well as the pathways by which Russia seeks to reconcile the tensions between them. We begin with some reflections on the historical and conceptual relationship between Russia and the increasingly important global context. In doing so, we aim to provide a basic framework for conceptualizing the complex dialectic between a Russian Federation both deeply embroiled in as well as affected by globalization, and often at the same time just as actively trying to erect barriers between itself and the world of global dynamics. In the process, Russia pursues (re)centralization while attempting to maintain a clear-cut line of separation between internationalization and globalization. We argue that it is impossible to understand Russian domestic politics (including center-periphery relations) or foreign policy without viewing them as, in part, arenas of response to the challenges of globalization.

It may be useful to start with a brisk, working definition: Globalization is understood broadly here as a process of intensifying transnational flows, leading to changed spatial and social relations, thereby both enabling and constraining states as well as nonstate actors.[1] It thus poses a serious challenge, notably, to borders and territorial demarcations, sovereignty and independence, security and closure, ethnic homogeneity and national identity. For most nation-states and international institutions constructed on principles of egalitarianism and symmetrical interdependence, globalization implies less financial control, more political vulnerability, increased levels of dependence, new supraterritorial processes and transnational networks, more pronounced hierarchies of power, new cleavages, new patterns of adaptation, and new regimes of cooperation. It should be added that globalization is not and certainly no longer can be conceived of as merely the outgrowth of the invisible hand of the marketplace, of economic forces and financial flows, but is actually an increasingly controlled and politically engineered process of neo-imperial design and concomitant power struggles intended to control, constrain, and give direction to ever more intense and multiple transborder dynamics.[2] Consequently, as Michael Cox insists, globalization makes "states into agencies of the globalizing world,"[3] rather than vice versa. A distinguishing feature of this global order is that even reactive forms of anti-globalizing measures need to take account of—and often, despite their outspoken intentions, end up strengthening—globalization.[4]

Although globalization may in the long run tend toward singularity and (more) global homogeneity, it is important to realize that states are positioned differentially in the global context, and globalization therefore has very different consequences and implications for different actors. Among the most significant factors are whether a state is weak or strong, big or small, rich or poor; how it is positioned relative to the global centers of political and economic gravity; and how much weight it is able to pull in pivotal international institutions. Yet states are also positioned relative to one another by virtue of their political institutions, self-Other representations, and internal social cohesion. Alongside material power, these other attributes influence how adequate and innovative state and corporate strategies are for dealing with global challenges. Eduard Ponarin frames Russia's situation in this context: "While European countries associate globalization with good economic prospects, military security, and other advantages that may induce even the French to swallow the burger, Russians associate pro-Western reforms with economic hardship and Russia's loss of global prestige,"[5] in the process equating globalization and Western political strategies while overlooking the fact that Western states are also very differently affected by global forces.

It is true that in one sense these forms of strained relations between (non-European) states and globalization are the rule rather than the exception, and that Russia therefore can be seen as simply embodying more general patterns and tensions in the international system.[6] Conversely, a number of Russian specifics and peculiarities merit a closer look and are rooted both in the former superpower status and aspirations of the USSR and the current ambiguities characterizing relations between a Russia stripped of this status but still a major political and military power, and a West (Europe and the United States in particular) trying hard to influence the political and economic direction and architecture of Russian society. In Ponarin's dramatized interpretation, "Since the end of the Cold War, Russians have encountered a powerful, alien culture that makes them feel powerless, disadvantaged, and inferior. Globalization has nurtured the emergence of a global culture rooted in the North-European Protestant ethic and epitomized by US culture."[7]

More often than not, such normative assessments, strategies of accommodation, and consequent outcomes are deeply embedded in the way they have been determined, shaped, or at least colored by historical developments, (dis)continuities, and relations—both domestic and external, and both regarding the *longue durée* as well as more recent history. This is particularly true in the case of Russia. To see this, we need to frame the global question in more precise terms. The next section addresses the major tensions between nation-states' autonomy and global processes at a general level by means of a model encompassing four thematic nodes as well as their mutual and multiple forms of interaction. This framework, in turn, is applied to the specific Russian case in the ensuing core section of the chapter. Following that, the next section discusses the main historical elements of Russia's relations to global pressures, framing the reasons why Russia today should be seen as both causative of and reactive to globalization,[8] a country "lurching" between "accommodation and confrontation."[9] Finally, the last section extracts several lessons from the analysis and identifies a few pivotal problems and perspectives for the future.

Conceptualizing the Challenges of Globalization

The illustrative model sketched in figure 1.1 rests on the assumption that key aspects of global pressures and reactive forms can be identified by analyzing reflexive relations between globalization and four national "nodes": sovereignty, mass/elite interaction, political history/collective identity, and security and threat scenarios. The four nodes can hardly be disputed as core to national self-perception and independence, though it might be argued that they are not exhaustive. The purpose of this model is to offer an interpretive framework rather than a fully operationalized theory ready for testing. The relations among the elements represented in each node are complex, and the outcomes of globalization are therefore highly contingent. Even so, these elements—and their multiple interlinkages—provide a useful matrix for delineating the major challenges that globalization represents to contemporary statehood.

Starting from the top in figure 1.1, the most immediate victim of globalization is sovereignty, the core feature of modern nation-states. This is because "ultimate control" of the "state of exception"[10] is made increasingly difficult by transnational flows of money, capital, goods, and (to an extent) people; because institutionalized legal or normative regimes of rights and values come into conflict with the exclusive authority of states within their own (no longer so) secure borders; and because the financial, technological, natural, and political resources on which sovereignty is predicated increasingly elude most states, which find themselves embroiled in ever more committal and ineluctable networks of (often regional) collaboration to cushion the blows of global pressures—the European Union being a prime case in point.[11] The levels and depths of what John Tomlinson has termed "complex connectivity" have reached a point where de jure and de facto sovereignty increasingly part ways, and where, in some cases and areas, sovereignty is no longer an operative feature of nation-states. In such cases, states have to look for new avenues of influence, autonomous spaces for maneuvering and collaboration,[12] and novel forms of governance (rather than traditional government) to pursue policy preferences that constantly need to adapt to, constrain, and/or benefit from an ever more present globalizing context.

State strength and state power matter, perhaps especially with respect to the sovereignty node. National interests and national sovereignty tend to become divorced from each other in the process of globalization, most acutely for small, weak, or vulnerable states, or states—like Russia—that are facing serious changes of international standing and recognition. Conversely, more powerful states, notably the United States, are able to proactively have an impact, and even engineer, globalization to match national preferences.[13] Globalization, therefore, is not—at least no longer—an anonymous process

Figure 1.1. Model of the Relations between Globalization and Four National Nodes

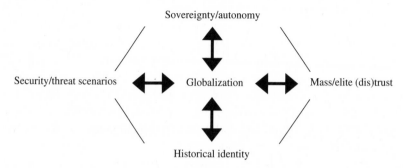

beyond political control but is increasingly an institutionally orchestrated and designed configuration of forces shifting the symmetrical structure of the international order toward asymmetry and hierarchy, distributing benefits and drawbacks unevenly, subdividing the world into weak and strong more clearly than before, and hence reordering the landscape of sovereign authority in fundamental ways. The implication is an important shift that has taken place during the past thirty-odd years, where transnational *economic* forces of capitalist development have, to a significant extent, been *politically* reined in and instrumentalized by powerful nation-states, in the process creating neo-imperial structures of asymmetrical linkages. Hence, forms of dependence for some contrast with degrees of independence for others, and where in most cases states have to seek compensation for the loss of sovereignty in new modes of autonomy, for others globalization tends to reinforce their sovereignty as well as their external capacities for power projection. This does not imply that globalization is necessarily a drawback for small and medium-sized states. They can certainly benefit, but whether they do so or not depends on minutiae of strategic adaptation to global centrifugal forces, over which they have little control.[14] Let us move forward, clockwise, in the model.

Globalization threatens to intervene in the mass/elite nexus by producing increased disaggregation and distrust. Clearly, however, this depends on the forms of globalization that are most relevant to different states; on the modalities of trust or distrust preceding the "intervention" of global pressures; and on the forms of governance chosen by political leaderships to cope with globalization—choices invariably linked to the status of particular states in the international order. These interaction effects need to be carefully teased apart before positing any direct causal relationships, which we do not attempt here. In very general terms, however, the disaggregating effect of globalization pertains to the transformation process of traditional sovereignty discussed above. The more sovereignty and political control at the national level are placed in doubt, the more political preferences and forms of collaboration at the elite level will be oriented toward transnational thinking and practices, and the more the real scope for political choices by democratic national citizenries at the domestic level will be narrowed down. In terms of ontological security, this means that the trust electorates might have placed in elected leaders will be counteracted by the ever more conspicuous dependence of these leaders on global—that is, extraterritorial and supraterritorial—flows and decisionmaking structures in the fields of, for example, trade regulation, international security, migration control, and human rights (as well as leaders' more and more active participation in such transnational processes). Thus, the real or imagined feelings of living within secure, ordered, and separate national universes will tend to dwindle, and popular disenchantment with elites will tend to increase. Conversely, if trust and political confidence were already moderate before the global turn, these novel developments can add extra fuel to such sentiments.

However, the very same developments can give rise to crucial forms of political reaction, reactions that aim either to maintain the compact between government and population or to forge new, global signifiers of loyalty and identity, inter alia, in the form of global (or regional) democratic practices and norms. The possible consequence of both these options is the creation of new horizontal cleavages, at the popular as well as elite levels, and, on aggregate, the uneasy coexistence of new (global), moderate (liberal), and traditional (nationally conservative) politics.

The most significant manifestation of these options is the flourishing of antiglobalizing and anti-immigrant populism—the attempt by political actors to generate sympathy and backing by deploying discourses of national cohesion, negative images of the Other, historical myths of ethnic homogeneity, and cultural interpretations of borders and sovereignty. These political strategies often target disaffected and marginalized sections of populations, or at least sections that do not associate globalization with new opportunities, but rather with a series of threats (to welfare, jobs, security, and/or culture). At the same time, they will attempt to link traditional political leadership with suspect, nonnational motives, or with sheer incompetence, the ostensible effect of both being the neglect of the true interests and desires of the people. The prime object of such nationalist animosity—

and evidence that political leaders have let the people down—is immigrants or refugees from countries in the developing world, who are visible, poor, often dependent on welfare benefits, and culturally very different from "us." The immigration field has become a pivotal point for the symbolic politics of populist antiglobalism attempting to remedy a mass/elite nexus perceived to be falling apart at the seams. However, whether or not such political strategies are successful—or to what degree—significantly depends on the context of political history and collective identity in individual countries. This is the third node.

The dialectics between globalization and collective historical identity are anything but simple (also see the next sections below). If historical identity implies both a confident political as well as cultural sense of homogeneity and solidarity—in other words, if we are talking about a "thick" sense of national identity—the challenges of globalization to sovereignty, territorial integrity, and democratic accountability can be offset or deflected by culturally and historically rooted sentiments of unity and the belief in future cohesion that these may trigger. This will particularly apply if states, even smaller and more vulnerable ones, are used to acting in and adapting to changing international circumstances, and if the continuity of historical identity is complemented by a tradition of accommodating and integrating differences. If, conversely, we are dealing with "thinner" forms of national identity—which have struggled to achieve cohesion and have been subjected to extensive social and political engineering to reach this goal (however temporarily), and where the mass/elite nexus is tenuous—globalization may impinge in much more disruptive ways, opening old wounds and triggering new conflicts.

In these (empirically very different) cases, globalization may be perceived to represent a threat to domestic order, social welfare, or national security (ranging from many African, Middle Eastern, and South American states, through Canada, the Netherlands, and Germany, to Russia, Ukraine, and China). However, the effects of such insecurity scenarios are much less uniform. Globalization may lead to social and cultural cleavages, but, as discussed above, also to a new sense of unity, however short-lived, of either civic purpose (forward-looking—as in China) or ethnic myth (backward-looking—as in Russia). Once more, the complexity and contingency of globalization's effects preclude any easily falsifiable statements about relations between the elements of the model. In addition to the level of societal trust and configuration of sovereignty (the first two nodes in the model), collective identity also interacts with perceptions of national security (the fourth node). Thus even a confident narrative of "thick" national identity may negate itself and produce new divisions, if complacency or paranoid interpretations of global vulnerability hinder a realistic assessment of, and hence successful adjustment to, the threats and opportunities embedded in globalization. This in turn depends heavily on the perceptions of national security and the specific threat scenarios that are pervasive and set the agenda in the public sphere—on the left-hand node of the model.

Globalization is a major challenge to perceptions of national security connected to tight borders, territorial sovereignty, and independent defense capabilities—but also to vaguer notions of societal or human security and its implications of cultural well-being, ontological belonging, and political welfare. In this sense, the fourth node and its interface with global processes engage the other three forms of dialectical tensions illustrated by the model: Security depends on sovereignty, on close mass/elite interaction, and on a perceived sense of historical identity. It straddles high as well as low, foreign as well as domestic politics, while at the same time resting on a foundation of self/other dichotomies, on certain perceptions of threat. This is not because globalization is the wellspring of threats and dichotomization, which are inherent in normal interstate relations. The interesting contribution of globalization is that it produces new threat scenarios by overriding or eroding some of the old interstate dichotomies—the *familiar* structure of uncertainty and threat. Because this kind of security is basically premised on the existence, but also on the political containment of "symmetrical" threats, the perceived new threats of globalization, somewhat perversely perhaps, produce an environment that is seen to be unpredictable, and in that sense uncertain, rather than producing indisputable dangers. It produces "risks," in Beck's and Douglas's terminology,[15] largely because it promises to eliminate old hazards, enemies, boundaries, and battle lines and to replace them with the "asymmetrical" Unknown of ethnic and cultural mixing, transborder economic flows, global communication, civilizational encounters, supranational hegemonies, Islamic extremism, natural disasters, and much more—all of which people more or less indiscriminately associate with globalization.

These new threat and insecurity scenarios are related to the endeavors of states to maintain themselves as discrete political and cultural units in circumstances that in many ways privilege a different mode of interaction than the traditional interstate system. This implies many reactions to globalization—as many as there are states, and as varied as their mutual differences dictate or facilitate. This includes efforts to hem in globalization (new border controls), adapt flexibly to it (welfare strategies combined with liberal economics), redesign its flows (neo-imperial policies), or institutionalize it (managing the flows of people, capital, and commodities). By thus interpreting globalization in terms of threats and risk, globalization itself is affected and given a certain structure and direction.

This interpretation applies to the interaction between globalization and each of the four nodes, as well as to the multiple ways that these four nodes connect with and have an impact on each other. For instance, the transformation of sovereignty is important for the popular distrust of political elites but also for new risk scenarios and security agendas. Historical identity codetermines to a large extent if and how national cohesion may be maintained in the age of global pressures, but it also impinges on new formulations of sovereignty and autonomy. And mass/elite trust or distrust is crucial for possibilities for or obstacles to accommodating more open borders, accepting new risks, and channeling new pressures into new opportunities. The next section applies the model and addresses these questions with direct regard to the salient features of Russia in the global age.

Applying the Model to Russia: Sovereignty

To begin with the first node of the model, the post–Cold War challenges to Russian sovereignty have been considerable. It constitutes not only the most serious problem that the country has had to face but is also linked to the many fluctuations of foreign policy and the uneasy relations with the West characteristic of Russia since 1991. The question subdivides into four separate issues: the shrinking of sovereign space and the border question; relations between military strength and economic weakness; dealing with domestic conflicts within the imperial patchwork of Russia while new norms, questioning the right of states to do what they like within their own borders, have been imposed by the United States or the West and by global institutions; and finally the threats and opportunities of "reinterpreting" sovereignty as autonomy, and thus of adapting to rather than controlling globalization—a point that mainly includes Russia's relations with international and global institutions. The contours of each issue can be drawn briefly.

Space and Borders

The Russian Federation is a direct result of the territorial disintegration of the USSR and hence of the political and military question mark posed to the stability and inviolability of sovereign Russian territory and the borders of

Russia, especially in places like the Caucasus, the Caspian, Kaliningrad, Narva, and the Japanese Islands.[16] As Eduard Solovyev discusses in chapter 11 of this book, the salience of these issues is reflected in the "geopolitical" discourse of foreign policy. Sensitivities about territory arise not only because recent history leaves its imprint on the political mentality of vigilance regarding this issue (hence the "paranoia" of seeing potential encroachments on Russian sovereignty in every enlargement of the European Union and NATO) but also because Russia can still be seen to be an "imperium" comprising ethnicities (some 150 in fact) with low degrees of allegiance to Moscow. This is the core of the difference between *russkie* and *rossiyane*,[17] "ethnic" Russians and citizens of the Russian Federation more broadly. For that reason, the prospect of further disintegration, civil or ethnic unrest, and an outside world trying to capitalize on attendant conflicts is never far away—as particularly the situation in the Caucasus has demonstrated; but Siberia and the Far East are also potential tinderboxes, where ethnonational conflicts are continuously kept aflame by multiple types of cross-border flows, including migration (see chapter 3 of this volume by Michael Bradshaw as well as chapter 4 by Evgeny Vodichev and Vladimir Lamin). The issue of space and borders, then, brings together key aspects represented by each of the four nodes: sovereignty, historical identity, social trust, and national security perceptions.

In this context, the "war on terrorism" following the terrorist attacks of September 11, 2001, came as a godsend to the Kremlin. In dealing with Chechen rebels, President Vladimir Putin has in significant ways been able to cast himself in the role of a politician intent on fighting terrorism on Russian territory and thus to align himself with the American cause in foreign policy. However, though this kind of behavior earned him the endearing label of "my friend Vladimir" from President George W. Bush, it is also fraught with contradictions and new threats, for two reasons. First, it shows the degree to which Russian policies and political rhetoric may be adaptive to the preferences of the world's superpower, if this superpower is willing to frame Russia as a partner and not an adversary.[18] And second, the eventuality always has to be faced that those representing such preferences (including the European Union) might at any time choose to apply the terrorism label to the Russians rather than its domestic opposition, or at the very least require the Russian state to account for its domestic actions as legitimate for a state aspiring to democracy and the rule of law (also see below). In other words, ostensibly accepting the new normative political regime introduced by the West since the early 1990s and seriously limiting the nature of state sovereignty is a double-edged sword for the Russian political establishment. That this is not just a hypothetical scenario is documented by policy statements like the following: "While we acknowledge, for example, the right of Russia to preserve its territorial integrity and its right and responsibility to protect its citizens against terrorism and criminal elements, Russia's use of massive and indiscriminate force against Chechen civilians has raised serious questions about its commitment to international norms and particularly human rights."[19] Putin has repeatedly tried to counter such allegations about the abuse of force by referring to parallel American violations, for instance in Iraq, but with minimal success.

Military Strength, Economic Weakness

The counterargument to this risk scenario would naturally be that Russian sovereignty is secured by the strength of its military and that preemptive strikes are impossible or self-defeating in the case of such a powerful nation. For is it not true that "Russia . . . remains the only country that can destroy the United States in a single large-scale nuclear attack"?[20] Maybe so (though the validity of this statement can legitimately be questioned), but at the very least it would have to accept its own annihilation in the process; and, more important, this is the option that an even more potent USSR found to be unacceptable in the 1980s. In addition, the Soviet legacy is also crippling in another field, as Boris Yeltsin articulated in a speech at the Russian Embassy in Washington in May 1998: "We have inherited from the USSR a situation of a 'one-dimensional state' which possessed considerable military power, but had no solid economic basis"—and in the same speech pointing to the problem that the Commonwealth of Independent States presented to Russian geopolitical aspirations due to "our own indecisiveness, sluggishness, lack of interdepartmental coordination, and formalism."[21] Though Putin has energetically moved to address such deficiencies, many of the same anxieties linger. This is not a country confidently relying on the use of its nuclear arsenal in a major confrontation, but one that would like to be able to (re)build its economic potential and international recognition in other ways, including "equal interaction with the United States."[22]

For the same reason, and in light of its history, Russia is troubled by the expansion of NATO, by the questioning of its territorial sovereignty, and by occasional Chinese saber rattling and border violations in the east, because these processes and events are perceived to undermine the stability, peace, and recognition it needs to consolidate and strengthen its economy. And all this is in addition to the obvious fact that the military still drains this same economy (itself structurally outmoded and insufficiently integrated into the global economy) of vital funds, as long as an external, global threat to Russian sovereignty is perceived to exist. As a result, the institution that was once, in the age of bipolarity, the protection of Russian sovereignty above all else, and in addition at the cutting edge of technological developments, now in many ways works as a barrier to the economic and political adaptation of Russia to global processes (see chapter 6 by Alla Kassianova). This is both because it has in large measure been developed and deployed to deal with domestic and regional conflicts,[23] but also, somewhat perversely, because it has often been opportunistically subordinated to the Kremlin's need to demonstrate a peaceful, collaborative, and multilateral agenda. Thus, "however difficult it might be to accept the role of junior partner to the United States, [Putin and his supporters] argued, it would prove to be of greater benefit to the Russian national interest in the long run."[24] At the same time, as chapter 12 by Alexey Fenenko makes clear, Russia still cherishes its nuclear arsenal. It gives it an international voice and access to international forums (like the UN Security Council). It has a deterrent capability in an age of global insecurity; for that reason, Putin's Security Doctrine of 2000 lowered the threshold for the use of nuclear arms.[25] And it makes, in the final analysis, the use of preemptive *military* strikes against Russia a much riskier option than in most other cases. Conversely, global challenges to Russian sovereignty are not limited to the military arena and generally cannot be addressed by military means.

Here again, the model's nodes, as depicted in figure 1.1, are in play. Military means constitute the classic representation of sovereignty, one that resonates with Russia's historical identity as a great power. Brandishing (or at least discursively reproducing) such might also helps to address traditional threat scenarios confronting national security. And, to the extent that such bids are successful—and if, in the bargain, Russia is granted renewed respect and legitimacy by prominent international actors—the foundation of trust is strengthened in mass/elite relations.

Domestic Conflicts in a New Global Setting

These challenges comprise not just the obvious transborder flows of capital and commodities, but, in a political perspective, the much more serious transformation of global political norms, which increasingly legitimate outside intervention and interference in domestic matters in order to counter human rights abuses, democratize dictatorial polities, disseminate "freedom" and market-based practices, halt nuclear proliferation, and generally hold national leaderships accountable. Russia has repeatedly found itself at the receiving end of this transformation. As Rick Fawn discusses in chapter 10, the United States and the European Union have frequently, and more and more insistently, invoked these new norms and their institutional safeguards. This includes Russian responsibility for the Beslan massacre in August 2004, the killing of Aslan Mashkadov in March 2005, atrocities committed by the Russian army against the civilian population of Chechnya more generally, the Ukrainian political crisis in December 2004 (formally not a domestic issue, but nevertheless one that the Russian leaders saw as belonging within their legitimate sphere of influence), recurrent demands on the Russians to apologize for Stalin's purges and the colonization of the Baltic states, more or less subtle attempts to meddle in the lawsuit against Mikhail Khodorkovsky and Platon Lebedev, and so forth. In each and every instance, not surprisingly, the Kremlin has reacted dismissively, sometimes in an enraged manner to these external encroachments on Russian sovereignty, often scathingly referring to comparable acts and processes in the West (by, e.g., comparing Chechnya with Northern Ireland) while, more in more placatory terms but not very successfully, attempting to lay the groundwork for a shared understanding that "we are all facing similar problems" and trying to mobilize the antiterrorism cause to arrive at consensus.

In spite of all the symbolic sovereign gestures, however, it is difficult to overlook the fact that Russia is deeply bothered by these shifts of normative behavior on the global scene and makes frequent concessions to outside interests. As Fawn argues in chapter 10, this is because it needs to collaborate with the same external agencies and institutions to promote Russian interests and, in a different sense, strengthen its political confidence and identity. After all, in Ukraine, Moscow could do very little to stop the Europeans from interfering and eventually had to accept Viktor Yushchenko as the new president; in the Beslan case, the Dutch presidency did receive an explanation of sorts by diplomatic channels; and as regards the Baltics, Putin, at a meeting with EU leaders in May 2004, did say that he denounced the nonaggression pact between the USSR and Nazi Germany in 1939. Russia's dilemma, in other words, is that it depends on aspects of globalization to modernize and expand but the principal agents of globalization will not allow it to pick and choose as it finds best.[26] Globalization comes as a total package, and to achieve its goals and benefits in some areas, Russia is compelled to give away some of its vital political currency, its sovereignty, in exchange, and adapt to externally determined modalities of global interaction. Yet this also calls into question the same national identities, trust relations, and security arrangements that Russia seeks to consolidate through other endeavors.

Sovereignty as Autonomy and Global Institutions

The most vivid illustration of this dilemma is the often frenetic relationship of Russia with international and global institutions, like the European Union, NATO, the World Trade Organization, the Group of Eight, the World Bank, the Council of Europe, the Organization for Security and Cooperation in Europe, and so forth. The ambition of Russia regarding influence and outcome, based on its self-perception, is to pull a central weight in these forums or at least to be able to contain any negative impact on Russia that they might imply.[27]

The reality is that the Western-based institutionalization of globality is too powerful to resist and thus calls for adaptation, flexible networking, and compromises on sovereign behavior from all but the most powerful if one wants to benefit.[28] The alternative is less than splendid isolation, something that Russia, with its great power ambitions intact but not in possession of matching capabilities, finds difficult to consider. The result, obviously, must be different kinds of attempts to balance between security scenarios and institutions—for example, with the EU but against NATO (as illustrated by different positions regarding the enlargement of the two organizations)—in order to reproduce a desired identity and commensurate role in international affairs. Similarly, we find an attempt to balance with the UN, against U.S. unilateralism (viz. the rifts over the justification of the Iraq intervention); for the World Trade Organization, and against the International Monetary Fund—because the former is seen as a window of global trading possibilities, whereas the latter, due to its restrictive conditionalities, is perceived as a budgetary and financial straitjacket, with all this implies for mass/elite (dis)trust.

Similar ambiguities are also detectable in largely positive Russian relations with the Group of Eight and the Commonwealth of Independent States, but generally skeptical attitudes toward the Organization for Security and Cooperation in Europe and (to a lesser extent) the Council of Europe. Assessed more in terms of outcomes, these institutions, because they represent a dense network of overlapping jurisdictions, actors, and policy fields, collectively exert a gravitational pull that is difficult to avoid. Yet at the same time (partly because they somehow deceptively offer themselves up as a way to contain American neo-imperialism), they increasingly impose adaptive behavior and compromises on formal sovereignty, if Russia is to make headway in globalizing its own political influence and its economic-financial interests.

Applying the Model to Russia: The Other Elements

The sovereignty question is, for historical and political reasons, by far the most significant in this context and has therefore been given ample space. The rest of the model is applied to Russia more cursorily. First, as already discussed, domestic trust and confidence between leaders and citizens are essential for coping adequately with global pressures (cf. the right-hand side of the model in figure 1.1).[29] In Russia, however, the odds militate against this kind of solution due to Russia's historically authoritarian political disposition; the low level of popular expectation vis-à-vis politics; the failure to deliver tangible changes and outputs affecting the average living standard after 1991; the disappearance or weakening of the staples of pride forged in the Soviet period and at least in part dependent on the survival of the USSR (e.g., the authority of Moscow and the heroics of the Great Patriotic War[30]); the multiethnic composition of the population; the difficulties in building consensus based on stereotyping Chechnyans in the two wars of the 1990s;[31] and the lack of representative political parties and movements to embody social and economic demands, disgruntlements, and alternatives. Globalization, on the face of it, will tend to strengthen causes of social disenchantment and distrust—perhaps contributing to rampant alcoholism and other forms of substance abuse (see chapter 2 by Andrey Korotayev and Darya Khaltourina). Social distrust has also materialized in the form of ethnic and populist agitation against oligarchs and outsiders, as well as mass demonstrations against the monetization of welfare benefits, thereby deepening the opposition between ethnohistorical identity perceptions and rational-civic interest formulations of Russianness.

Yet globalization as an independent factor can be—and to some extent has been—used to rebuild trust (albeit often within narrower bounds) by practically all political factions as well as by Yeltsin and Putin. This includes playing the nationalist card; conjuring up foreign threats to Russian identity; staging highly publicized court cases against personal embodiments of global, neoliberal capitalism;[32] and legitimating a Russian version of dem-

ocratic pluralism and the media landscape—while in the process strengthening internal security and "securitizing" policy processes and public debates in the (alleged) interest of protecting the nation-state from terrorist attacks and foreign encroachments.[33]

Here a clear link with the first node: The more perceived sovereignty erosion can be linked to external threats against maintaining a stable and
uniquely Russian civic order, the more securitization policies can be used
to build confidence in the state and the president—who at the same time
tries to project himself as a trusted and indispensable partner of both the EU
and the United States. There is also a link to the fourth node (security/threat
scenarios): Rebuilding trust along these lines implies the advantage for
elites of short-circuiting the democratic option by inflaming social anxieties
and constructing political emergency situations, giving politics a freer hand
to concentrate power in state hands, while at the same time realigning the
exercise of political authority with the totalitarian and statist history of
Russian political culture.

This takes us to the third node: historical identities. Political history in
Russia / the USSR has been riddled with contradictions and unresolved
tensions between continuity and rupture, center and periphery, messianism
and civic/secular orientations, European and Asian orientations.[34] In this
light, global challenges are not all that novel—they have a number of external historical precedents, for example, in the almost constant threat from
and models imposed or offered by the outside world, whether European or
American—but because they coincide with the loss of power status, territorial transformation, and problems of identity vacui, they are necessarily
perceived as extraordinary and also as qualitatively different. Hence the
early post–Cold War attempts by Yeltsin and Andrey Kozyrev to be com-
pliant and follow a Westernizing course was dramatically switched to a Russia First policy line when Yevgeniy Primakov took office in 1996, while an
in-between position, combined with a strong discursive emphasis on the
maintenance of Russian interests, Russian sovereignty, and external Russian representation, has been the preference during Putin's presidency under
the auspices of both Igor Ivanov and Sergey Lavrov. The problem is how to
align past and present with identity and interest, combining Russian excep-
tionalism and international recognition, while at the same time domesticat-
ing global pressures and interests, equipping the country to meet challenges
of the global marketplace, and all in all striking the right median note between projecting and behaving as a great power in military terms and a nor-
malized middling power in economic terms.

To do all this, the handling of the fourth node, security/threat scenarios, is crucial. The political game (and hence the political variants as represented by different parties) is here stretched between great power projections of Russia as militarily strong and independent (cf. military parades, the celebration of past glories and wartime successes and heroism, and the lowering of the nuclear threshold mentioned above), and a different set of images having to do with Russia as continuously under threat and vulnerable to outside (particularly the United States / NATO, but also criminal, corporate, and market-based) interests, pressures, and intentions. In chapter 12, Alexey Fenenko points out that both kinds of projection can be used (independently or together) to underpin and legitimate a discursive politics of securitization and emergency. It is here that the "war on terrorism" enters the fray as a master signifier, allowing Putin and his version of Russian statism simultaneously to play the globally cooperative card (pro-EU and partly pro-American, too), step up internal security measures, agitate and take action against Chechen separatists/terrorists, curtail democratic reform, nationalize energy production and other vital economic sectors, and increase his domestic approval rating—all in the name of protecting the interests of the Russian people, which is being attacked by terrorists, encircled by NATO, and (by means of tax evasion, fraud, capital speculation, and clandestine/unlawful investment and enrichment strategies) undermined by self-serving Russian oligarchs like Roman Abramovich, Boris Berezovsky, Mikhail Khodorkovsky, Sergei Mavrodi, and Artyom Tarasov—not to mention the Russian Mafia. There is little doubt that Putin's popularity derives at least in part from his successful public projection of a determination to maintain the sovereign integrity of Russia (territory, identity, history) in the face of internal and external threats, of standing up to and warding off the negative consequences of globalization.

Much of this is symbolic politics and political discourse, intended to bridge the gap between Russia's economic backwardness and political isolation and its integration into the realities of the global marketplace and a global political order spearheaded by America and entrenched in a complex of global institutions and normative discourses. In chapter 8, Mikhail Troitskiy explains how this is attempted through the language of "justice" in international affairs. Thus, globalizing policies and discourses skeptical about global processes are configured in a specifically Russian way to meet the perplexing challenges of transition and transformation that globalization presents to a state that in terms of cultural history, ethnic heterogeneity, and political core-periphery relations is still a landed empire in the throes of

(further) disintegration and is still grappling with a legacy of global hegemonic ambitions and "peaceful coexistence."[35] This specific Russian configuration is in large measure conditioned by its twentieth-century history,
to which we now turn.

Historical Factors

The two most prominent historical factors for Russia today are the turbulence that it has been facing since its (re)creation in 1991 and the continu-
ities/discontinuities nexus with respect to relations with the USSR, of which
it is the main successor in international legal terms. The specifics of this simultaneous rupture and confluence are key to understanding the implications of Russia's global context.

Russia's history between 1917 and 1991 is characterized by being the
history of *another* political and imperial entity—an entity that it is both distinctly different from, was a part of, in many ways still identifies with, and
whose policies and practices it is frequently asked to take responsibility for.
It was an entity with an international ideology, superpower ambitions, and
a distinct program of global power and influence—a political legacy that
still, both despite the fact that and because it was largely abortive, leaves
significant marks, however ambiguously or tortuously, on the outlook, orientation, identity, and policies of the Russian Federation. Russia is clearly
a separate political construction from the USSR—in Ivanov's words, it is
"a new state functioning in a radically changing system of international relations."[36] But in shared political history, political culture, and political
ambitions, we need to recognize that Russia as the heir of the USSR has
significant degrees of overlap and continuity (great power ambitions, insistence on political sovereignty and territorial borders, and Russia First policies), intertwined with a "Westernizing" desire to be recognized as a "normal" member of the global community of states and to put some distance
between itself and the role of the USSR as a hemispherically dominant
power as well as the primary "constrainer" of neoliberal globalization and
U.S. global power.[37]

Russia, then, "bears the imprint of continuity determined by the country's
geopolitics, history, and culture" but has at the same time "given up the
global messianic ideology that was practiced by the USSR" and "rejects any
'neo-imperial' ambitions,"[38] pragmatically putting national interests and international law before ideological conviction. This is of course official po-

litical rhetoric on the part of the then–Russian foreign minister, diplomatically articulated, while concealing some interesting twists and turns that are
addressed below. What is clearly revealed, however, is the incontestable fact
that important clues to Russia's ambivalent relationship with globalization
can be found by taking a look at the global systemic interface during recent
history seen from the Soviet/Russian angle. Three important, closely inter-
related peculiarities of the Soviet/Russian position vis-à-vis globalization
thus need to be noted here: (1) imperial collapse, (2) decolonization, and (3)
the need to rebuild power and identity in the global context.[39]

Imperial Collapse

Russian / Soviet twentieth-century history is centrally a narrative of unsuccessful empires. The Romanov Empire collapsed during World War I,
due to a combination of external warfare and internal revolution. Its successor, the Soviet Bolshevik state, first attempted to build "socialism in one
country" (even though the "country" was an imperial-type construction),
but after World War II and the tremendous human and material losses incurred during the fight against Nazism, it got embroiled in the geopolitical
confrontation between two warring systems and their underlying ideologies. Thus, during the Cold War, the USSR no doubt harbored global ambitions of its own, actively engaging in the spread of Soviet-style communism while trying to enlist allies and sympathizers, particularly in the
developing world, inter alia by exporting arms, advisers, and financial assistance; by courting the favor and seeking the recognition of the international community in institutions like the United Nations; and not least by
entering into curiously ambivalent relations with the United States, which
simultaneously functioned as the chief competitor and opponent *and* the
primary standard of comparison for the USSR.

   The USSR was a "superpower" all right, following a political trajectory
of maximum global influence and building its status primarily on the
strength of its military in general, and its nuclear arsenal in particular. At
the same time, it did not have a viable economy, partly due to a relatively
dysfunctional political-economic structure, and partly due to the "draining"
effect of the military sector on the civil economy. It was a political-military
giant but an economic dwarf.[40] The West, particularly the Americans, perceived it as a major geopolitical barrier to be overcome and suppressed in
order to create the appropriate conditions for a liberal global hegemony of
the "Washington Consensus" kind.[41]

In the current positioning of Russia vis-à-vis global pressures, these Cold War developments are significant because Russia, unlike many other countries in the international system, did not suddenly, at some point in the 1990s, wake up to the experience of globalization, perceived as an external force and massive challenge to the economic autonomy and political sovereignty of nationhood. The USSR was at the same time an active, albeit rather unwitting and traditionally imperialistic, participant in *and* the political-military object of global politics in the process of engendering global institutions and noninstitutional forms of dominance under U.S./Western control. It is clear that this second Russian imperial implosion of the twentieth century conditioned a set of opposing and conflictual reactions to the Western, neo-imperial structures of dominance that have since tried to harness global flows to their own preferences and that largely owe their new cosmopolitan space for maneuvering to the disappearance of their systemic antagonist.

Decolonization

The history of the USSR/Russia in the twentieth century is furthermore one of belated and piecemeal decolonization. For developed states in the Western world, globalization in its present-day forms represents a set of processes separated from—and logically the extension of—phases characterized by formal (usually overseas) empire structures. In contrast, Russia's landed empire, with its heartland, provinces, cultural plurality, and spatial expansiveness (as described in chapter 3), only underwent a process of decolonization after 1990. Hence it had to face two thoroughgoing transformative experiences at the same time: adjusting to Western-style globalization, and partial and always-imminent territorial disintegration—a different spatial structure and a new structure of sovereignty, both of which are simultaneously being challenged by economic liberalism and the neo-empire of American hegemony.

This temporal overlap of decolonizing and globalizing processes in the Russian case is important for two distinctly different reasons. The first is that most studies indicate that homogeneous, confident, and liberally minded nation-states are better equipped to deal with and adapt to global challenges than heterogeneous, culturally amorphous political entities displaying self-doubt, incomplete cohesion, and a weak sense of collective identity.[42] In the Russian case, this is compounded by the fact that Russia has for very long been split between a "Western" and an "Asian/Slavic" sense of belonging and that the process has not been completed. Russia is formally a federation, but it has kept a number of imperial features and is still a multiethnic empire with potential territorial instability looming round the next corner (see chapter 3).[43]

Furthermore, the belatedness and reluctance of the process engendered a strong desire for separation and independence in formerly dominated areas, notably the Eastern and Central European countries, and a concomitantly high level of distrust and suspicion in interstate relations after the end of the Cold War. The result, across the board—in Poland, Hungary, the Czech Republic, the Baltic States, and many more places—was a political move to combine independence with membership in the "Western club," the EU and NATO above all, to safeguard against the specter of future Russian encroachments. Inversely, this is presented as an object of political demonization of the West in Russia, confirming Russian fears that the Western strategy rested on the encirclement (politically and militarily) of the Russian space—and of Russia in the West, confirming the conviction that Russia was intent on hanging on to its old sphere of influence, had not abandoned its totalitarian and antidemocratic tendencies, and was not ready to be admitted into the club of truly civilized states. Hence Russian political behavior, it has been frequently argued, needs to be monitored closely, particularly Russia's treatment of autonomous provinces (e.g., Chechnya) within the confines of the Russian Federation, proof that Russia is still an empire. On this basis, as discussed in chapter 10, Russia can be taken to task in international institutions like the Council of Europe for violating human rights on its own soil.

Rebuilding Power and Identity in a Global Context

The third point follows directly from the second. As the loser of the Cold War, but also as an actor still in possession of significant power resources and thus suspended between great power and middling power status, the country has had to (re)build its political and cultural identity, its external security, and its domestic as well as international legitimacy in a situation characterized not only by the turbulence of the immediate historical past but also by the pressure exerted by the economic, political, and cultural forces of Western globalization. The difficulties of this transformation process—scaling down power ambitions, finding a new role, and adapting adequately to global pressure—are visible in the marked foreign policy fluctuations and changing security doctrines of the 1990s and early 2000s,[44] but also in the search for a "thicker" sense of Russianness (cf. the problems of deciding on the proper national anthem) and for strong and workable civil institutions (cf. the problems of forging mass media relatively independent of state control).

Such drastic changes and turnabouts are not the hallmarks of a polity at ease with itself and the world but indicate an almost desperate groping for the right dosage of instruments, a workable political identity, as well as political mechanisms linking state and people, center and periphery, around a common project. This situation has been exacerbated by the fact that these shifts of policy and discourse indubitably reflect discontinuity and uncertainty but also replicate some of the touchy features of the Soviet system: the relative weakness of the old center; the lack of a solid, well-defined Russian (as opposed to Soviet, or regional) identity;[45] the ambiguous relationship with the West;[46] the many changes of "doctrinal" policy; and the unsettled question of the link between politics, market, and civil society.

Conclusion: A Strained Relationship

It is clear that, overall, the relationship between Russia and globalization is strained and complicated. This is partly because Russia has been compelled to undergo a transformation process from "hemispheric hegemon" to middling power, and in that sense it must get used to adapting to rather than directing the global environment in which it has to act and prosper. And partly it is because globalization in many ways is perceived to entail threats to the identity and security of the Russian Federation, and to be a double-edged sword consisting of possible benefits but indubitable disadvantages. This in turn is directly related to the bifurcated nature of globalization itself, being a set of operative supraterritorial, neoliberal economic processes linked to the global marketplace *but also* a politically orchestrated process of neo-imperial hegemony on the part of the sole remaining superpower. The Russian reaction to the former of these two constitutive features is discursively accommodating but in policy terms more guardedly regulatory and protectionist, in order to cushion the Russian economy and market against flooding by foreign products and investments and in order to retain maximum political control of economic developments. The reaction to the latter—entailing a significant reduction of sovereign power and a comprehensive adaptation to external conditionalities—is replete with suspicion and anxiety, and even more than the first feature is charged with historical contradictions and choices between a Russian Eurasian "Sonderweg" (isolation from the West) on the one hand, and flexible cooperation and adaptation, on the other. This includes ambivalence and suspicion over the development of civil society—especially insofar as it involves Western or "Western-in-fluenced" nongovernmental organizations—as James Richter highlights in chapter 7. In all these ways, globalization has highlighted and exacerbated old traumas and old cleavages in Russia but has also made clear that old answers will no longer do. Thus, two key questions need to be addressed: Are Russia and globalization compatible? And how does the West—the principal agent of globalization—take an interest in and hence behave toward Russia?

No hard-and-fast answers are possible to either question. As for the first, compatibility is a question of successful economic restructuring, and thus of overcoming the economic dwarf/military giant divide, but also of willingness to adapt to global pressures while still taking advantage of Russian positions of strength in global networks and institutions. What seems settled is that Russia does not have a viable alternative strategy or way out. Neither isolationism nor an alternative regional setup under Russian control (the Commonwealth of Independent States or the like) will do the job, as both Yeltsin and Putin have realized. Willy-nilly, and despite any new security doctrines that the Kremlin may concoct, Russia's future prospects for prosperity and security depend on forging domestic cohesion by, at the very least, building a sense of civic Russianness (including its material foundations in territorial integration and economic redistribution), channeling funds from the military to the civil sector of the economy, and externally on a new type of flexible statecraft, adapting to outside pressures, possibilities, and demands in innovative ways. (As Gennady Konstantinov and Sergey Filanovich explain in chapter 5, these debates are themselves at the heart of the ongoing struggle over the future of Russia's higher educational system.) In other words, Russia's prospects depend on fully modernizing—and thus on "globalizing"—Russian society and politics proactively rather than in a defensive manner and as a last resort. And this requires successfully managing the tensions depicted in the model: between globalization and national identity, social trust, sovereignty, and security.

For this to happen, historical legacies and deep-seated knee-jerk reactions have to be overcome; the current signs are that this is only happening to a limited degree. Another precondition, however, is related to the second question: Western interests in and behavior toward Russia. Globalization can only become a positive process from the Russian perspective if the "globalizers" are willing to let it happen, are interested in aiding the process, and are not motivated by either indifference (China may now seem a more interesting place to trade and invest) or historical vindictiveness. On this front, the jury is still out; the inclusion of Russia in the Group of Eight, the Partnership for Peace, and the cooperation agreement between the EU and Russia (May 2005) are positive signs, as are intermittent political statements by both the European Union and the United States that Russia is an important player to be reckoned with in international affairs, for example, in the "war on terrorism." In chapter 9, Erik Noreen argues that this tendency—as in the case of Russian relations with Estonia, in the context of EU enlargement—reflects a degree of adaptive socialization. But other political actions and statements point in a different direction: the U.S. withdrawal from the Comprehensive Test Ban Treaty in 1999, repeated meddling in Russian politics, criticism of democratic deficits and the human rights situation in Russia, the interference of the EU in the Ukrainian "revolution" of December 2004, George Bush's propaganda trip to Georgia in May 2005, and generally the refusal even to consider why Russia may react to NATO's, and sometimes the EU's, eastward enlargement processes with some trepidation and why the border and security question has high priority in Russian politics.

Thus, many policies pursued by the West vis-à-vis Russia are conducive to retaining high pressure on the Russian security establishment, and thus to draining vital resources that might have been deployed more efficiently in the civil economic sector. Such economic redistribution might not have happened even in the absence of external pressure. In that case, however, it would have been easier to assign Russian policies with direct and sole responsibility for economic neglect or sluggish growth. Now, the situation is more muddied. What seems clear is that Russia cannot successfully come to terms with globalization on its own—it also takes the cooperative efforts of the EU and the United States (and increasingly of China, too), together or separately, to achieve this outcome. The West, like Russia, must divest itself of the negative historical legacy of the Cold War for the old enemy to deal adequately with its strained relationship with the new international order and to become a fully integrated partner in the global community.

Plan of the Book

Having provided a general framework for locating Russia within the context of globalization, the following chapters seek to address a cluster of key empirical and analytical questions. One question concerns the fundamental effects of globalization—particularly on a historically embedded, traditionally powerful, institutionally underdeveloped state actor like Russia. After all, globalization everywhere imposes new constraints on state action, and it thereby requires states to adapt to pursue their desired ends. Though this is true for all states caught up in globalization, the contributors to this volume find a set of specifically Russian conditions and responses. These have to do partly with historical factors—including a cycle of imperial decay, reacquisition, and collapse—the product of which is a lingering imperial mentality as well as an abiding sense of insecurity and unease. In addition, Russia's responses arise from, and seek to address, a number of unstable tendencies in a wide range of areas, including demography, economic development, center-periphery relations, educational policy, civil society formation, foreign affairs, and national security. The result is a cluster of profound tensions: fluidity versus fixity; inclusive versus exclusive identity constructs; hard versus soft forms of power.

The problems associated with managing these tensions are exacerbated by the fact that Russia has been going through an extraordinarily wrenching demographic transition. Though there are many indicators of this transition, here we focus on two in particular: population contraction and redistribution. The former is addressed in chapter 2 by Andrey Korotayev and Darya Khaltourina, who are especially concerned to explain the much-publicized "Russian cross"; that is, the phenomenon that birthrates are falling while death rates are rising. Sifting through the literature on this remarkable development, Korotayev and Khaltourina are at pains to show that none of the many explanations to date—including per capita alcohol consumption—are fully convincing. Instead, marshaling an impressive body of cross-national data along the way, they argue that only the *particularly* rapid ingestion of hard liquor, in conjunction with escalating drug abuse, can account for the observed trends in the data (including predominantly male mortality). This phenomenon seems likely to be at least partly linked to the cultural and institutional dislocation caused by globalization.

In chapter 3, Michael Bradshaw explores the globalization of the Russian economy, asking how it affects development and wealth distribution across regions. He finds, first, that Russia is only weakly integrated into global production chains, except in the sense of providing raw materials. However, globalization clearly does matter in reverse, in the influx of foreign goods and services; he points out that Russian producers are facing increasing competitive pressure from world economy. In addition, he high-

lights the role of foreign direct investment in influencing Russian economic
and political development. Though Russia's share of total foreign direct investment is still quite small relative to China, India, and Eastern Europe, its
impact within the Russian context is nevertheless quite significant, and it
has produced winners and losers on a regional level. He draws the inevitable
conclusion: "Globalization promotes increased inequality and it has serious
implications for Russia's territorial cohesion."

The connection between globalization and center-periphery relations is
also explored by Evgeny Vodichev and Vladimir Lamin in chapter 4. As
they suggest, the problems of center-periphery relations are associated with
the intertwined problems of national economic development and collective
identity formation. In particular, they underscore the difficulties facing
many regions in generating capital and conducting their own successful
economic policies, in light of the recentralizing reforms introduced under
Putin. Regional identities are also very much in flux, because a range of different identity projects are still evolving in Russia, including pan-ethnic,
civic, and regional-level identities. As Vodichev and Lamin argue, the link
between these processes of globalization and regional identity formation is
vividly apparent in Siberia today, and much hinges on the outcome. In their
view, one regional identity narrative centers around a pan-Siberian (nonethnic) construct. Though conceivably it could also be productive in consolidating the region's institutional integrity, and thereby facilitating its entry
into globalized processes, they warn that it could also lead to splintered
identity constructs among the peoples of the region, and thus the fragmentation of Russian political space.

Although the identity implications of globalization are often complex
and cross-cutting, their institutional implications are more straightforward,
especially in areas relevant to technical and economic performance. These
issues are highlighted by Gennady Konstantinov and Sergey Filonovich in
chapter 5 on Russian higher educational reform. While Konstantinov and
Filonovich note the existence of sharp disagreements between those who
wish to conserve the traditional system and those who seek to introduce
changes in line with Western practices, they emphasize the emergence of a
clear trend toward competitive, self-financing universities with broadly
standardized degree programs. In particular, this includes participation in
the EU's Bologna Process. They suggest that Russia's involvement in this
project not only symbolizes but also provides a practical mechanism for
closer integration into European cultural and institutional space. In their
view, this tendency reflects the pressures of globalization, including the

emergence of a knowledge-based, postindustrial society. The educational reform process is thus part and parcel of a larger effort to boost the competitiveness of Russian business in a global economy.

Some of these same issues of globalization and political stability are taken up by Alla Kassianova in chapter 6. As she shows, the military-industrial complex (MIC) illustrates both the potential for, and obstacles to, regional and national development in the context of globalization. Though it might conceivably serve as an engine driving Russian economic integration and technological dynamism, and thereby alleviating some of the tensions to which Vodichev and Lamin point, Kassianova argues that this has not yet happened. More troubling, she contends that it seems unlikely to happen in the foreseeable future, for reasons that pose a stark counterpoint to higher education reform. This is partly a problem of the parochial mentalities of many managers, who have remained insulated from and suspicious of the global economy. However, the same mentality is not entirely alien even to the policymaking elite, including some who champion integration and entrepreneurship. As Kassianova suggests, one of the core ambivalences that characterizes Russia today has to do with the simultaneous tendency to encourage private initiative—including independent arrangements with foreign actors—and to limit the extent of foreign penetration into security-sensitive sectors. In other words, it has to do with the tendency both to control and to relinquish control.

In chapter 7, on developments in civil society, James Richter sheds light on one of the central foci of this ambivalence. According to his analysis, international actors, associated with a global neoliberal agenda, sought to export a model of democratic development to Russia. This involved creating a vanguard of civic activists, who would jump-start the process while acting in accordance with rational individualism. He argues that this effort failed, due to a number of obstacles: (1) the activists themselves, including their inherent aloofness and wish to reproduce their own special status; (2) the incentive structure presented by foreign donors, which encouraged conformity with ideas and approaches that lacked resonance in Russian discourse; (3) state resistance under Putin; and (4) broad social resistance. This last factor—much like the state's resistance—expressed suspicion of outside involvement, as well as a recognition that nongovernmental organization activists essentially represented a Soviet-era elite. It is precisely the disjunctures between outside and inside, embedded in social assumptions and carried in both elite and popular discourse, that highlight the thematic linkage between globalization, identity, and security in Russia.

One of the most vivid expressions of Russia's encounter with globalization has to do with its simultaneous acceptance and contestation of key international norms. This theme is taken up in the chapters by Mikhail Troitskiy, Erik Noreen, and Rick Fawn. As Troitskiy contends in chapter 8, this is evident in the nature of Russian demands for "justice," or reciprocity in foreign affairs, in return for compliance with international institutions and normative standards. Troitskiy observes that such demands followed a particular course, from being prominent in the 1990s, to declining in the first several years of Putin's tenure in office, and rising again after 2003. He suggests that this pattern has followed a learning curve, yet one inflected by traditional notions of power and place. Thus despite the collapse of the Soviet Union, Russia continued to feel that it was owed treatment befitting high status, even while it was reduced to requesting fairness in rather plaintive terms. Under Putin, an initial shift away from this approach reflected the emergence of a new (but contested) identity as a "midrange power." Though being a midrange power represented a reduction in international status, it was nevertheless accompanied by more assertive actions—but now intended to achieve relatively limited goals, within a regional sphere of influence. However, because Russia was no longer empowered to demand such a high measure of respect, and also because its foreign policy goals often involved a departure from international norms, Moscow became willing to compromise on matters of justice. Troitskiy argues that his changed yet again after the "colored revolutions" (e.g., the Orange Revolution in Ukraine). The earlier, more strident discourse resurfaced—but now buttressed by greater self-confidence, as Russia insisted on certain "rules of the game" within its own borders and throughout Eurasia.

Notwithstanding the vicissitudes of identity formation, in chapter 9, Noreen contends that a fairly consistent socialization process has been under way, and as a product of this, both Estonian and Russian policymakers increasingly feel an affinity for constructs sanctioned by the EU. In particular, he argues that the process of working toward EU integration by the late 1990s marked the advent of a new trend in Estonian and Russian identity discourses. Like the other Baltic states, Estonia sought to demonstrate its "Europeanness" with regard to a range of relevant practices, including its treatment of the Russian minority. This in itself was consequential in helping to change Russian understandings of the Estonian Other and in recasting Russian attitudes toward security cooperation throughout the region. Meanwhile, one important tendency in Russian discourse has been to articulate a European identity and to seek closer political and economic relations with the EU. Furthermore, despite strains in relations with NATO and the

United States, Russian (and Estonian) policymakers have increasingly focused on terrorism and other shared, nonconventional threats, rather than traditional hard power sources of insecurity. The combined result is that both Russian and Estonian threat assessments are changing. Estonian policymakers are less worried about Russia, and, in turn, Russian policymakers are less distraught about Estonian discrimination against co-ethnics and are more willing to think in terms of a security community.

Yet, as Fawn demonstrates in chapter 10, this cooperative tendency has been, and continues to be, anything but steady and smooth. As he carefully traces the contours of Russia's engagement with the Council of Europe, he shows how membership—and criticisms of membership—have been closely linked to post-Soviet identity formation. On the one hand, being a member allowed pro-Western figures to convincingly articulate a set of values for domestic and foreign policy. From this perspective, the attractiveness of such ideas, as well as the status of membership, were more important than the potential benefits of trade, aid, and investment resulting from closer integration with Europe. For others, however, the required trade-offs between unilateral security and identity were always of questionable worth, and they became still more dubious as the prospect of tangible benefits waned. Despite some apparent (and relatively minor) concessions on Chechnya, then, over time the Russian position hardened. Nevertheless, Fawn suggests that some degree of socialization did occur, as evidenced in changing patterns of language, and that this may well have a lasting, albeit subtle effect. He also argues that the council might be well served to follow a more nuanced policy, of standing firm against human rights abuses while also emphasizing clear successes as well as the advantages gained from membership.

The overarching conceptual and identity-based issues related to Russian foreign policy are addressed by Eduard Solovyev in chapter 11. He traces the broad contours of what he terms "geopolitical" discourse within several schools: liberalism, neo-Eurasianism, geopolitical populism, and communist geopolitics. In doing so, he suggests that the widespread tendency toward such geopolitical thought is rooted in Russian political culture, that is, the persistent notion that the power of the state is tied closely to the size and the location of its territory. Solovyev also suggests that such ideas play a crucial role in current Russian identity discourse, as both a language of opposition and as material for the construction of a new Russian national identity. On the one hand, it helps to mobilize various alternative—yet equally grandiose—visions of Russia's future in the world. On the other hand, objectively, it also represents a diminution of the prevailing Soviet identity, in which Russia functioned as the pivotal force behind a truly global messianic project. In this sense, Solovyev argues, geopolitical thinking today represents a symptom of Russia's transformation from a supranational empire to a nation-state.

Globalization has also had a wide range of other effects on Russian foreign and security policy, as Alexey Fenenko argues in chapter 12. On the one hand, it has brought about a wide-ranging reconceptualization of security, along the lines of the "soft security" perspectives articulated in the West. As a result, nontraditional actors and other sources of threats are recognized today, and a more variegated set of policy responses has been developed to meet them. Nevertheless, Fenenko observes that this shift in orientation has only augmented, but has not replaced, the traditional approach. Military approaches continue to prevail among much of the policymaking elite, and this is reflected in procurement patterns as well. The result is that globalization introduces far greater complexity rather than clarity. That is, it compounds an already cluttered agenda with new ideas and concerns, but without allowing policymakers to differentiate among levels of threat, or to easily determine which modality to employ in response.

In the conclusion, chapter 13, Douglas Blum combines the above insights, returning once more to the tensions that are inevitably bound up in the state's attempt to control borders—including all aspects of the sprawling interface between the national and the global—while also engaging in beneficial forms of cross-border exchange. As the preceding chapters illustrate, alongside Putin's recentralization one also finds significant trends in the direction of decentralization and international integration—potentially moving beyond the state's ability to manage effectively. Yet allowing these latter trends to deepen will have important consequences for all areas of social, economic, and political organization, as well as collective identity formation. The result is a series of profound ambivalences about the nature of the state and society, as well as relations between them. Blum explores these ambivalences, while seeking to tease out some of their more intriguing implications for thinking about Russia's place in the world—and the world's place in Russia—as the two become ever more closely entwined.

Notes

1. For further discussion, see chapter 3 in this volume by Bradshaw; see also David Held et al., "Introduction," in *Global Transformations: Politics, Economics and Culture,*

ed. David Held, Anthony McGrew, David Goldblatt, and Jonathan Perraton (Cambridge: Polity, 1999).

2. Ulf Hedetoft, "Globalization and US Empire: Moments in the Forging of the Global Turn," in *Globalization and Autonomy,* ed. Will Coleman et al. (Vancouver: University of British Columbia Press, forthcoming).

3. Michael Cox, "Rethinking the End of the Cold War," *Review of International Studies* 20 (1994): 187–200.

4. Ulf Hedetoft, *The Global Turn: National Encounters with the World* (Aalborg: Aalborg University Press, 2003); and Ulf Hedetoft, "The Forces Driving Globalization: Modalities, Actors and Processes," in *Jorden runt igen: Nya bidrag till en gammal globalhistoria,* ed. Arne Jarrick and Alf Johansson (Stockholm: Almqvist & Wiksell, 2004), 124–46.

5. Eduard Ponarin, "Security Implications of the Russian Identity Crisis," Policy Memo 64, Program on New Approaches to Russian Security, 1999, 3.

6. E.g., see John Baylis and Steve Smith, eds., *The Globalization of World Politics* (Oxford: Oxford University Press, 1997); Ulrich Beck, *What Is Globalization?* (Cambridge: Polity, 2000); Paul Hirst and Grahame Thompson, *Globalization in Question* (Cambridge: Cambridge University Press, 1996); A. G. Hopkins, ed., *Globalization in World History* (London: Pimlico, 2002); Frank J. Lechner and John Boli, eds., *The Globalization Reader,* 2nd ed. (Oxford: Blackwell, 2004); James Mittelman, *The Globalization Syndrome* (Princeton, N.J.: Princeton University Press, 2000); and Jan Aart Scholte, *What Is Globalization? The Definition Issue—Again,* Working Paper GHC 03/4, Institute on Globalization and the Human Condition (Hamilton, Ont.: McMaster University, 2003).

7. Ponarin, "Security Implications," 3.

8. Hedetoft, *Global Turn,* chap. 1.

9. Angela E. Stent, "Russia: Farewell to Empire?" *World Policy Journal,* Fall 2002, 85.

10. Carl Schmitt, *The Concept of the Political* (Chicago: University of Chicago Press, 1996; orig. pub. 1932). One can argue with Schmitt's definition of sovereignty as regards his "state of exception" thesis, but he is clearly right that the ideal convergence of formal and real sovereignty lies in the power of final authority and decisionmaking competence, basing itself on exclusive jurisdiction from within and corresponding recognition from without. Thus the source of state sovereignty is both domestic and external.

11. Edgar Grande and Louis W. Pauly, eds., *Complex Sovereignty: Reconstituting Political Authority in the 21st Century* (Toronto: University of Toronto Press, 2005); Ulf Hedetoft, "Sovereignty Revisited: European Reconfigurations, Global Challenges, and Implications for Small States," in *Globalization and Autonomy,* ed. Coleman et al.

12. "Autonomy" is used here to mean the freedom and space to govern and act, but in conditions ultimately determined by (an) extraneous agency (or agencies) or set of forces. It is thus to be distinguished from legal and political sovereignty proper. In fact, it is quite possible for autonomy to increase while sovereignty is eroded.

13. Robert Hunter Wade, *The Invisible Hand of the American Empire* (London: OpenDemocracy, 2004), available at http://www.opendemocracy.net.

14. Hedetoft, "Globalization and US Empire."

15. Beck, *What Is Globalization?;* Mary Douglas, *Risk & Blame: Essays in Cultural Theory* (London: Routledge, 1994).

16. Dmitri Trenin, *The End of Eurasia: Russia on the Border Between Geopolitics and Globalization* (Washington, D.C.: Carnegie Endowment for International Peace, 2002).

17. Bo Petersson and Charlotte Wagnsson, "A State of War: Russian Leaders and Citizens Interpret the Chechen Conflict," *Statsvetenskaplig Tidskrift* 101 (1998): 167–81; Valery Tishkov, *Ethnicity, Nationalism and Conflict in and after the Soviet Union: The Mind Aflame* (Beverly Hills, Calif.: Sage, 1997).

18. James M. Goldgeier and Michael McFaul, *Power and Purpose: U.S. Policy toward Russia After the Cold War* (Washington, D.C.: Brookings Institution Press, 2003).

19. U.S. Department of Defense, *Strengthening Transatlantic Security: A U.S. Strategy for the 21st Century* (Washington D.C.: U.S. Government Printing Office, 2000), http://www.bits.de/NRANEU/EuropeanSecurity/TransatlSec21stCent.htm.

20. Celeste A. Wallander, "Wary of the West: Russian Security Policy at the Millennium, in Arms Control Association," *Arms Control Today,* March 2000, http://www.armscontrol.org/act/2000_03/cwmr00.asp?print.

21. Boris Yeltsin, "Russia's Place and Role in the Period of Multipolar World Formation," speech delivered at the Russian Foreign Ministry, Washington, May 12, 1998, http://www.bits.de/NRANEU/EuropeanSecurity/Yeltsin_12May1998.htm. It is worth remembering that 1998 was the year when the Russian economic situation was close to disastrous and state finances were teetering on the brink of collapse, partly due to domestic mismanagement (state assets in oil and minerals had been sold off at bargain prices three years earlier), and partly as a consequence of the crisis of the Asian "tiger economies."

22. Ibid.

23. Wallander, "Wary of the West."

24. Stent, "Russia," 83–84.

25. Wallander, "Wary of the West."

26. The situation regarding the pricing of gas deliveries to the Ukraine in December 2005 and January 2006 provides a good example. When Russia, for political reasons, raised the price to world market levels, probably in the belief that this would be acceptable to the West in the context of economic globalization, the reaction was hostile, both on the part of the United States, because Ukraine is a major political defector from the old Soviet camp and should not be penalized for its Western orientation, and the European Union, because it was indirectly affected in economic terms. Gazprom's retreat—to return to the old extent of deliveries in order to accommodate the west, while keeping negotiations with the Ukraine alive—was prompt. What Russia regarded as a major economic-political weapon (a kind of substitution for the nuclear threat)—creating global dependencies on Russia rather than vice versa—in this way rapidly demonstrated its shortcomings and relative lack of efficacy. Or, to put it differently, Russia found that globalization is a Western invention and that its political reality is different from its normative (economic) ideal.

27. See, e.g., Vladimir Baranovsky, ed., *Russia and Europe: The Emerging Security Agenda* (Oxford: Oxford University Press, 1997); Jakob Hedenskog et al., *Russia as a Great Power: Dimensions of Security under Putin* (London: Routledge, 2005); Igor S. Ivanov, *The New Russian Diplomacy* (Washington, D.C.: Nixon Center and Brookings Institution Press, 2002); Dmitri Trenin, "A Russia-within-Europe: Working toward a New Security Arrangement," paper prepared for International Institute for Strategic Studies / Centre for Economic Policy Research European Security Forum, Brussels, January 14, 2002, http://www.eusec.org/trenin.htm.

28. Rosemary Foot et al., eds., *US Hegemony and International Organizations* (Cambridge: Cambridge University Press, 2003).

29. The application of the binary of masses and elites, rather than that between society and state, is in itself a reflection of Russia's transformation and the added context of globalization as compared with Soviet times. In the latter, the state and its *nomenklatura* were practically identical with the ruling elites, cultivating a relationship of domination to society as a catchall category embracing a variety of economic and social groups. In the current era, powerful elites also constitute private actors and civic institutions, and the mass/elite binary hence is now applicable to Russia also, even though the autocratic Russian state still represents the overwhelming hub of power.

30. Nina Tumarkin, *The Living & the Dead: The Rise and Fall of the Cult of World War II in Russia* (New York: Basic Books, 1994).

31. Bo Petersson, *National Self-Images and Regional Identities in Russia* (Aldershot, U.K.: Ashgate, 2001). However, Putin was slightly more successful in the second war than Yeltsin had been in the first.

32. See Hugh Fraser, "Russia's Oligarchs: Their Risky Routes to Riches," BBC News, July 27, 2004, http://news.bbc.co.uk/1/hi/business/3927523.stm.

33. Charlotte Wagnsson, *Russian Political Language and Public Opinion on the West, NATO and Chechnya: Securitization Theory Reconsidered* (Stockholm: Stockholm University and Department for Strategic Studies, Swedish National Defense College, 2000).

34. Nicolai Berdyaev, *The Origins of Russian Communism* (Ann Arbor: University of Michigan Press, 1960; orig. pub. 1937); James Billington, *The Icon and the Axe* (New York: Vintage Press, 1970); James Cracraft and Daniel Rowland, eds., *Architectures of Russian Identity: 1500 to the Present* (Ithaca, N.Y.: Cornell University Press, 2003); Ulf Hedetoft and Antje Herrberg, "Russia and the European Other: Searching for a Post-Soviet Identity," in *Which Identity for Which Europe?* ed. Antje Herrberg (Aalborg: Aalborg University Press, 1999); Assen Ignatov, *Die "russische Idee" in der gegenwärtigen Diskussion: Die russische Identität und die "neuen Ideologien"* (Cologne: Bundesinstituts für ostwissenschaftlichen und internationale Studien, 1992); Neil Malcolm, *Russians beyond Russia: The Politics of National Identity* (London: Royal Institute of International Affairs, 1995).

35. See Ivanov, *New Russian Diplomacy.*

36. Igor Ivanov, "The New Russian Identity: Innovation and Continuity in Russian Foreign Policy," *Washington Quarterly* 24, no. 3 (Summer 2001): 7.

37. Hedetoft, "Globalization and US Empire."

38. Ivanov, "The New Russian Identity," 11.

39. The first two points, imperial collapse and decolonization, are clearly two sides of the same coin, but it pays off to treat them separately. "Imperial collapse" deals with the external and domestic causes of political, social, and economic implosion and the weakening of center-periphery relations. "Decolonization" constitutes one specific—political, ethnic, and territorial—consequence of this process (one out of many) and the continuation of pressures and asymmetries that carry the seeds of further territorial fragmentation.

40. Brian D. Taylor, *Politics and the Russian Army: Civic-Military Relations 1689–2000* (Cambridge: Cambridge University Press, 2003).

41. John Williamson, "What Washington Means by Policy Reform," in *Latin American Adjustment,* ed. John Williamson (Washington, D.C.: Institute for International Economics, 1990).

42. John Campbell et al., eds., *National Identity and the Varieties of Capitalism: The*

Danish Experience (Montreal: McGill University Press, 2006); Peter Katzenstein, *Small States in World Markets* (Ithaca, N.Y.: Cornell University Press, 1985); Mary McAuley, *Russia's Politics of Uncertainty* (Cambridge: Cambridge University Press, 1997).

43. Trenin, "A Russia-within-Europe." See also chapter 4 in this volume by Vodichev and Lamin.

44. This is as discussed above. Also see Stent, "Russia"; Trenin, "Russia-within-Europe"; and Wallander, "Wary of the West"; as well as Vladimir Frolov, "A New Post-Soviet Doctrine," *Moscow Times,* May 20, 2005.

45. Petersson, *National Self-Images.*

46. E.g., Iver B. Neumann, *Russia and the Idea of Europe* (London: Routledge, 1996).

Part I

Globalization and Domestic Processes

2

The Russian Demographic Crisis in Cross-National Perspective

Andrey Korotayev and Darya Khaltourina

Globalization has radically changed demographic processes in all parts of the world, including Russia. However, we argue that it is important to consider globalization in long-term perspective. Before the start of the modern phase of the globalization (i.e., most of history) humankind remained at the first phase of demographic transition, characterized by very high fertility and mortality rates, very low life expectancies (for both males and females), and very low levels of per capita gross domestic product (GDP).[1] At present, only a few least-developed countries (mostly in tropical Africa) remain close to this situation. Here (in the range of $400–$3,000 per capita GDP), even a very small growth in per capita GDP leads to considerable growth in life expectancy for both males and females (from the age of fewer than

The authors acknowledge support provided for the writing of this chapter by the Russian Humanitarian Scientific Foundation (Grant 06-06-020-72, for the project "Demographic Processes as Factors of the Image of Russia in the Modern World") and by the Russian Foundation for the Support of National Science.

thirty to almost seventy years). This is achieved through the elimination of famine, introduction of cheap medicines, improvements in sanitation, and so on. From this perspective, globalization has positively affected demographic and social dynamics nearly all over the world.

However, in the range between $3,000 and $10,000 per capita GDP, the correlation between growth and increases in life expectancy drops almost to zero. Indeed, the average life expectancy in countries with per capita GDP between $3,000 and $4,000 is about 69 years, whereas in countries with per capita GDP between $8,000 and $11,000 the average life expectancy for males is around 70 years (i.e., higher by just a year). Of course, in the richest countries of the world (i.e., those with per capita GDP of more than $25,000), the average life expectancy for males is significantly higher still: 75.6 years. However, this increase is achieved through the investment of billions of dollars in modern health care.[2]

What is striking is that life expectancy in Russia (and the other culturally similar countries of the former Soviet Union) is anomalously low for the level of economic development achieved by these countries. Indeed, dozens of countries with a much lower per capita GDP have much higher life expectancies.[3] This is attributable to anomalously high mortality rates, which powerfully affect the demographic situation in Russia. Moreover, it has occurred at a time of rapidly increasing globalization. In the following sections, we argue that this pattern is explainable largely due to widespread, rapid alcohol consumption among men (in addition to other, secondary factors).

Comparative Demographic Dynamics in the Former USSR

The collapse of the Soviet Union was accompanied by a demographic crisis, the so-called Russian cross (see figure 2.1). In this period, the birthrate dropped from 17.2 to 9.4 live births per 1,000 people, whereas the total fertility rate fell from 2.0 to 1.3 children per woman. The mortality rate grew from 10.4 deaths per 1,000 people in 1986 to 15.7 in 1994, a catastrophic and abnormal level. In the period 1991–92, the mortality rate equaled the birthrate and soon substantially exceeded it. This resulted in a rapid population decline.

Russia is not the only country that has faced such problems. In addition to the Russian "cross," one can point to the early Hungarian "cross" and also to the Bulgarian, Belarusian, Estonian, Latvian, and Ukrainian "crosses." Almost all these countries shifted to a quite adverse demographic pattern in the early 1990s, which still persists. Consequently, it is necessary to con-

Figure 2.1. Dynamics of Birthrate and Mortality Rate (per 1,000 people) in Russia, 1978–2003 ("Russian Cross")

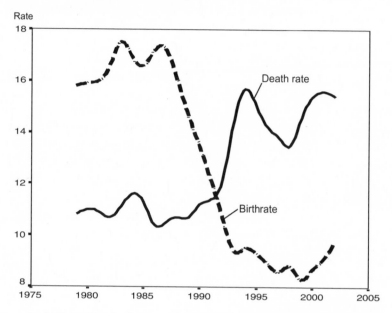

Source: World Bank, *World Development Indicators 2004* (Washington, D.C.: World Bank, 2004).

centrate on this transition period in order to explain both the nature of the shift and the contemporary demographic realities in the region.

Several hypothetical causes of the abnormally high mortality rates in Russia have been suggested. One of the most frequent explanations is the economic and social crisis, which has resulted, among other things, in social depression and high levels of stress.[4] Vishnevskiy and Shkolnikov point out that the long-term death crisis in Russia could be at least partially caused by the unfinished second phase of epidemiological transition, or in other words the transition from passive struggle with causes of mortality to active struggle for high levels of health care. According to them, this situation was caused by the low efficiency of the Soviet administrative system, which had no serious motivation to develop effective health care for citizens.[5] Additionally, medical research shows that the consumption of alcohol, drugs, and tobacco has had a significant impact on high morality rates in Russia.[6] In fact, most researchers consider alcohol to be the major factor behind the country's abnormal mortality rate.[7]

Our study aims to determine the differential impact of the above-mentioned factors on the demographic crisis in Russia, through extensive statistical analysis. Cross-national research is important as well, because similar factors ought to have similar influences on human populations in different countries.

Psychological Stress

A comparison of polling data and demographic indicators shows quite clearly that sociopsychological factors are not the key determinant of mortality in Russia. A nationwide monitor of public opinion in Russia reflects considerable improvement in the estimation of quality of life by Russian citizens from 1998 to 2001 (figure 2.2). Yet at the same time, the mortality rate increased greatly, from 13.5 percent in 1998 to 15.6 percent in 2001.[8]

Economic Collapse

Moreover, even preliminary observations show that economic explanations for the abnormal mortality rate in post-Soviet countries are insufficient (figures 2.3 and 2.4). For example, the economic crises in Armenia and Geor-

Figure 2.2. Answers to the Question "Generally speaking, was this year better, worse, or the same as the previous one?" for the Period 1996–2004

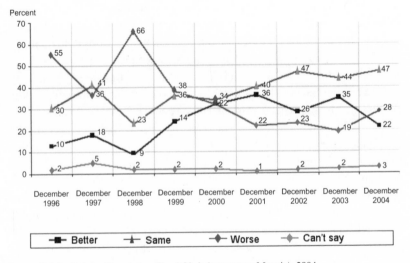

Source: Public Opinion Foundation (Fond Obshchestvennoe Mnenie), 2004.

Figure 2.3. Per Capita Gross Domestic Product in Estonia, Russia, Georgia, Armenia, and Uzbekistan, 1990–94 (index: 1990 per capita gross domestic product = 100)

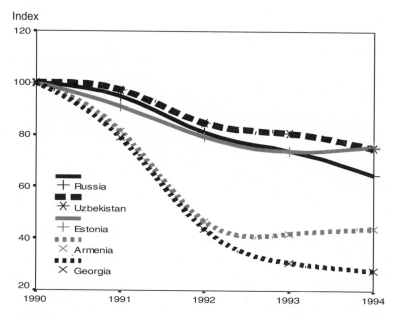

Source: Angus Maddison, *Monitoring the World Economy: A Millennial Perspective* (Paris: Organization for Economic Cooperation and Development, 2001), 341.

gia were far more serious than that in Russia. Between 1990 and 1994 (when the "Russian cross" began), Russian GDP per capita declined from $7,762 (in 1990 international dollars, at purchasing power parity) to $5,024, whereas in Armenia it fell from $6,142 to $2,701; in Georgia, the drop was even more catastrophic—from $7,569 to $2,100.[9]

As mentioned above, in this period the mortality rate in Russia increased by more than 40 percent (and reached 15.7 percent); at the same time, in 1990–93, mortality in Armenia—which experienced a much more catastrophic economic decline—increased by less than 20 percent (reaching 7.4 percent). What is more, already in 1994 the mortality rate in Armenia decreased to 6.6 percent, just 107 percent of the 1990 level, whereas by 1998 it fell to 6.1 percent, even though by that year Armenian per capita GDP had only recovered to half of the 1990 level and constituted less than 75 percent of Russian per capita GDP.

Figure 2.4. Dynamics of Mortality Rates (per 1,000 people) in Estonia, Russia, Georgia, Armenia, and Uzbekistan, 1990–94

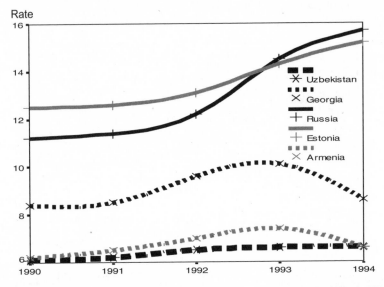

Source: World Bank, *World Development Indicators 2004* (Washington, D.C.: World Bank, 2004).

The post-Soviet economic crisis was especially catastrophic in Georgia, where in 1990–93 per capita GDP dropped more than three times as compared with the 25 percent decline in Russia (even though the per capita GDP in Russia in 1993 was more than twice as large as Georgia's). However, at the same time the Georgian mortality rate increased just 20 percent (from 8.4 to 10.1 percent), as compared with a 30 percent increase (from 11.2 to 14.5 percent) in the same years in Russia. Already by 1994, despite continuing economic decline, the mortality rate in Georgia dropped almost to the precrisis level (to 8.6 percent), whereas by 1996 it had decreased well below the precrisis level (7.1 percent in 1996, as compared with 8.4 percent in 1990).[10]

The magnitude of economic decline in post-Soviet Estonia and Uzbekistan was approximately the same; between 1990 and 1994, in both countries per capita GDP decreased about 25 percent. Note, however, that in 1994 per capita GDP in Estonia (in absolute terms) was more than 150 percent higher than in Uzbekistan ($8,123, as compared with $3,199).[11] Because a per capita GDP decline leads to higher mortality rates in low-income than in middle-income countries,[12] one has grounds to expect that if the post-Soviet mortality increase was caused mainly by economic crisis, in 1990–1994 the mortality rate in Uzbekistan should have increased much more than in Estonia. In reality, we observe just the opposite. In Uzbekistan in 1990–94, the mortality rate grew just 8 percent (from 6.1 to 6.6 percent). At the same time, in much more prosperous Estonia, the mortality rate grew more than 20 percent, and by 1994 it reached a catastrophic 15.2 percent. By 1998, the Estonian economy had more or less recovered to the precrisis level, whereas in Uzbekistan the per capita GDP was still at only 77 percent.[13] Yet in the meantime, the mortality rate in Uzbekistan fell below the precrisis level (to 5.9 percent), whereas in Estonia it remained well above (at 14 percent).

Of course, one might suspect that the above-mentioned differences between the former Soviet countries might be accounted for by a difference in age structure. Hence, it makes sense to study the mortality rate dynamics for different age groups separately. Figure 2.5 gives the mortality rate

Figure 2.5. Mortality Rates for Children under Five Years Old (per 1,000 live births) in Estonia, Russia, Georgia, Armenia, and Uzbekistan, 1990–94

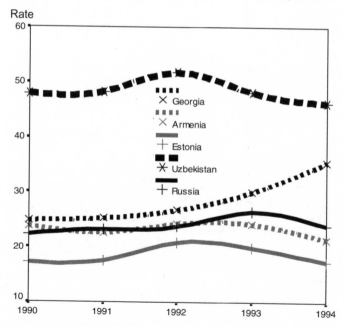

Source: UNICEF, *Innocenti Social Monitor 2004* (Florence: UNICEF Innocenti Research Centre, 2004), 68.

dynamics for children below five years of age for Estonia, Russia, Armenia, Georgia, and Uzbekistan in 1990–94. Thus, in 1991–93 a rise of child mortality was observed in all the countries in question (in fact, it was observed in all countries of the former Soviet Union without exception. To a considerable extent, this was connected with a rise of infant mortality rates (figure 2.6).

In sum, there does not seem to be any serious doubt that the rise in child and infant mortality in the former Soviet countries in the early 1990s was caused mainly by the post-Soviet economic crisis, whereby a sharp decline in per capita GDP led to serious underfunding of the health care system, a shortage of medicines in maternity hospitals, and so on. Similarly, a rise in mortality rates in Uzbekistan (and other former Soviet Central Asian countries) in the early 1990s appears to have been caused to a considerable extent by a rise in infant and early child mortality rates. The influence of this factor also seems to be rather important for Georgia (which was struck by

Figure 2.6. Infant Mortality Rates (per 1,000 live births) in Estonia, Russia, Georgia, Armenia, and Uzbekistan, 1990–94

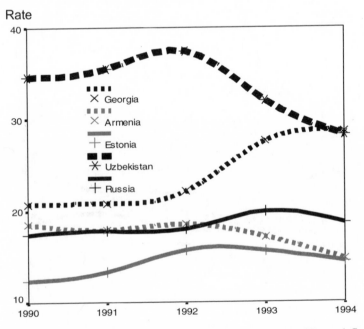

Source: UNICEF, *Innocenti Social Monitor 2004* (Florence: UNICEF Innocenti Research Centre, 2004), 68.

the post-Soviet economic crisis in the most serious way). This explanation, however, does not appear to be applicable to Russia, Estonia, and the other countries in the European part of the former USSR. No doubt, the rise of the infant and early child mortality contributed to the increase in the mortality rate in Russia in the early 1990s; however, this contribution appears to account for a very small fraction of the increase. Suffice it to mention that between 1990 and 1994, the child mortality rate in Russia grew 7.2 percent, whereas the overall mortality rate increased 40.2 percent.[14]

Organized Violence

To explain the causes of the catastrophic rise in mortality in Russia, as well as in the former Soviet countries of Europe and Transcaucasia, it seems relevant to consider mortality rates for older age groups (especially males). Let us start with males in the age groups twenty to twenty-four years, twenty-five to thirty-nine years, and forty to fifty-nine years (see figures 2.7, 2.8, and 2.9).[15]

As one can see, the sex-age specific mortality rate dynamic is characterized by strikingly different patterns in different parts of the former Soviet Union. In Uzbekistan in 1990–94, we do not observe any significant growth of male mortality for any of the age groups analyzed above. We do observe some growth in Armenia and Georgia, but it is very different from the pattern in Estonia and Russia. In Armenia, we find a very significant growth of mortality rates among males of age twenty to twenty-four years during the period 1990–94. However, already by 1995 it had fallen almost to the pre-crisis level, which coincides with the Karabakh 1994 cease-fire. It is also remarkable that the sharp rise in mortality rates among males age twenty to twenty-four during the period 1990–94 was accompanied by only a moderate increase in mortality among Armenian males age twenty-five to thirty-nine, and no increase at all among males age forty to fifty-nine (as we shall see below, the same can be also said about Armenian females). Thus, the mortality rate increase in Armenia was restricted entirely to "fighting-age" males, and thus was probably connected to the Karabakh war.

In Georgia in 1990–93, we observe a mortality rate increase among all analyzed age groups of males. However, it was sharpest among those age twenty to twenty-four, less pronounced among those age twenty-five to thirty-nine, and weakest among those age forty to fifty-nine. As we shall see below, a relatively weak but significant growth of mortality rates is also observed during these years among Georgian females. However, after 1993,

Figure 2.7. Mortality Rates (per 1,000) for Males Age Twenty to Twenty-Four Years in Estonia, Russia, Georgia, Armenia, and Uzbekistan, 1990–94

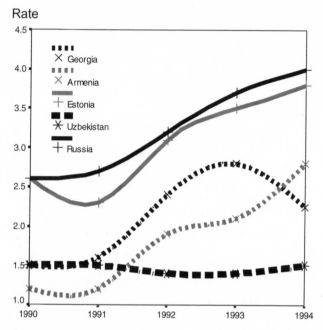

Source: UNICEF, *Innocenti Social Monitor 2004* (Florence: UNICEF Innocenti Research Centre, 2004), 72.

mortality rates drop sharply to precrisis (or almost precrisis) levels among all analyzed sex-age groups. This suggests that the rise in mortality rates in Georgia during the period 1990–93 was connected almost exclusively with the rise of violent conflict (especially the Abkhazia war). In Georgia this conflict was internal (unlike the Karabakh war for Armenia), and it there-fore involved a considerable death toll not only on the part of fighters but also on the part of the civilian population (both male and female). However, casualties among the "fighting-sex and -age" groups were significantly higher, and this appears to account for the characteristic sex-age mortality rate we find in Georgia for the period 1990–94.

The pattern in Russia and Estonia (and in fact for all the other European countries of the former Soviet Union)[16] is the precise opposite of that for Georgia and Armenia; that is, we observe a sharp growth of mortality rates

Figure 2.8. Mortality Rates (per 1,000) for Males Age Twenty-Five to Thirty-Nine Years in Estonia, Russia, Georgia, Armenia, and Uzbekistan, 1990–94

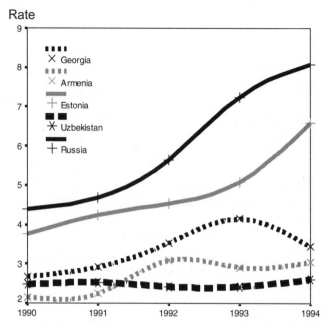

Source: UNICEF, *Innocenti Social Monitor 2004* (Florence: UNICEF Innocenti Research Centre, 2004), 73.

among all the age groups of males; however, among older age groups, it was stronger than among those age twenty to twenty-four. Obviously, this pattern cannot be accounted for by either political-military or economic factors. It also seems relevant to consider age-specific female mortality (figures 2.10, 2.11, and 2.12).[17]

Let us start with the observation that for Uzbekistan in 1990–94, we find a significant (though weak, relative to the other former Soviet countries) increase in mortality rates, which stands in remarkable contrast to the mortality rate dynamics for Uzbek males, for whom no such growth in mortality is observed. It seems plausible to connect this mortality increase with the post-Soviet economic crisis, which suggests that the burden of the crisis fell on Uzbek females to a higher extent than on Uzbek males (which in turn may be connected to the emphatically dominant position of males in

Figure 2.9. Mortality Rates (per 1,000) for Males Age Forty to Fifty-Nine Years in Estonia, Russia, Georgia, Armenia, and Uzbekistan, 1990–94

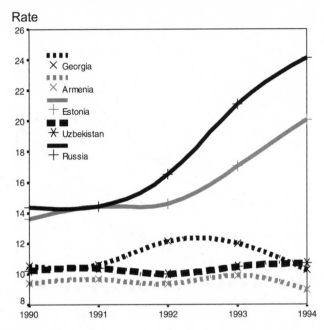

Source: UNICEF, *Innocenti Social Monitor 2004* (Florence: UNICEF Innocenti Research Centre, 2004), 74.

Central Asian countries). Neither this economically generated mortality increase nor even the warfare-produced mortality increase observed in the countries of Transcaucasia, can be compared with the enormous increase in Russia, Estonia, and the other European countries of the former USSR.

In contrast, the absence of any significant mortality increase among all analyzed age groups of Armenian females confirms the conclusion that the overall mortality increase found in Armenia during these years is almost exclusively accounted for by an increase in mortality rate among fighting-age Armenian males, due to warfare in Karabakh.

Mortality rate dynamics among all analyzed age groups of Georgian females follows quite closely the pattern for non-fighting-age Georgian males; that is, it increased during the period of intense internal warfare (especially in connection with the war in Abkhazia); however, this increase was dramatically smaller than that observed among fighting-age Georgian

Figure 2.10. Mortality Rates (per 1,000) for Females Age Twenty to Twenty-Four Years in Estonia, Russia, Georgia, Armenia, and Uzbekistan, 1990–94

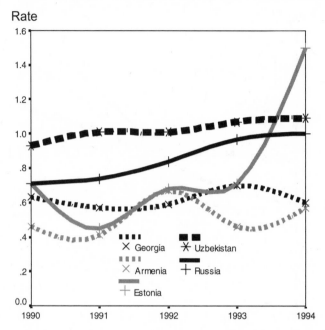

Source: UNICEF, *Innocenti Social Monitor 2004* (Florence: UNICEF Innocenti Research Centre, 2004), 71.

males. The end of intensive internal warfare led to an immediate drop in mortality rates among all analyzed sex-age groups, although naturally this drop was especially strong among fighting-age Georgian males. The difference between the Armenian and Georgian mortality rate dynamics is accounted for by the difference between external and internal warfare patterns. That is, external warfare in Karabakh led to a rise in the mortality rates among fighting-age Armenian male citizens only, whereas the rise in the mortality rate in Georgia was caused by internal warfare, from which all sex-age groups suffered, although fighting-age males suffered most.

With regard to the difference between male and female mortality rate dynamics, Russia and Estonia stand in sharp contrast to Armenia and Georgia, on the one hand, and Uzbekistan (as well as the other former Soviet Central Asian states),[18] on the other. In Russia and Estonia, in all analyzed age groups during the period 1990–94, female mortality increased rather substantially

Figure 2.11. Mortality Rates (per 1,000) for Females Age Twenty-Five to Thirty-Nine Years in Estonia, Russia, Georgia, Armenia, and Uzbekistan, 1990–94

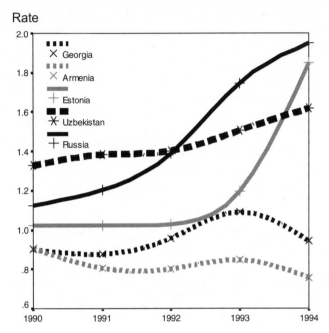

Source: UNICEF, *Innocenti Social Monitor 2004* (Florence: UNICEF Innocenti Research Centre, 2004), 72.

(and much more than in Central Asia or Transcaucasia). However, male mortality in all analyzed age groups increased much more than female mortality.

Yet there are no rational grounds for assuming that the economic crisis should increase male mortality far more than female mortality (in fact, the case of Uzbekistan suggests that females might suffer from economic crisis significantly more than males). Against this background, the fact that male mortality in Russia and Estonia during the period 1990–94 increased to a qualitatively higher level than female mortality provides additional evidence that economic crisis was not the main cause of the sharp increase in overall mortality rates.[19]

Logically, this pattern of mortality dynamics should have led to a situation in which female life expectancies in Russia, Estonia, and the other European countries of the former Soviet Union (but not Central Asia and

Figure 2.12. Mortality Rates (per 1,000) for Females Age Forty to Fifty-Nine Years in Estonia, Russia, Georgia, Armenia, and Uzbekistan, 1990–94

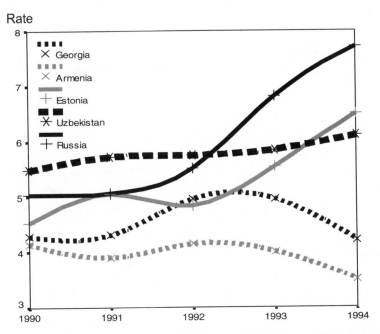

Source: UNICEF, *Innocenti Social Monitor 2004* (Florence: UNICEF Innocenti Research Centre, 2004), 73.

Transcaucasia) should have decreased significantly; however, male life expectancies should have decreased far more, which in turn should have led to a dramatic gap between male and female life expectancies. And indeed this was the case.

First, in figure 2.13 we compare the life expectancy dynamics in Russia, Georgia, and Uzbekistan. As we see, in Uzbekistan in the years 1991–94, both male and female life expectancies experienced a certain decline (in fact, it was rather small in comparison with the countries of the former Soviet "North"). However, the decline in male life expectancy was smaller than that for females. As a result, during these years in Uzbekistan, we observe a certain decrease in the gap between male and female life expectancies.

As one would expect from the data on sex-age specific mortality dynamics in Georgia, during the period 1990–93 the internal warfare in this

Figure 2.13. Life Expectancy at Birth in Russia, Georgia, and Uzbekistan, 1990–94

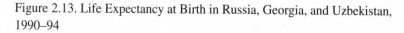

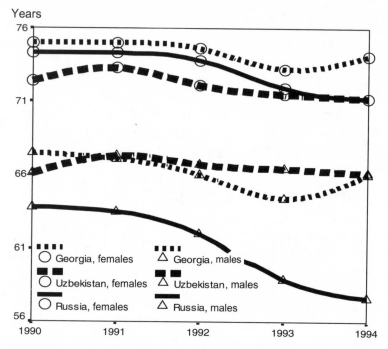

Source: UNICEF, *Innocenti Social Monitor 2004* (Florence: UNICEF Innocenti Research Centre, 2004), 70–71.

country led to a sizable decline in both male and female life expectancies. Predictably, however, the decline of male life expectancies during these years was somewhat more pronounced, and this did lead to a certain widening of the gap between the male and female life expectancies. Yet the end of intense internal warfare immediately narrowed this gap.

In Russia, we observe a dramatically different pattern. In the period 1990–94, female life expectancies in Russia declined more than in either Georgia or Uzbekistan. However, even this tragic decrease pales in comparison with the truly catastrophic drop in male life expectancies, as a result of which the largest increase in the gap between male and female life expectancies occurred in Russia. As we shall see below, to a considerable extent this also accounts for the dramatic drop in fertility rates in Russia during these years.

The Deterioration of Health Care

A number of researchers have explored the possibility that a deterioration of the medical care system was the major cause of the mortality crisis. However, as Shkol'nikov and Cherviakov argue, "In spite of what looks obvious, Russia avoided a sharp decline in health care expenses during 1992–1995. According to two independent estimates, the decline (taking into account inflation) was about 10 percent. The number of hospital beds per thousand people remained almost the same. Thus, the collapse did not take place."[20]

A number of other facts also indicate that the degradation of the Russian medical care system was not catastrophic. For example, a study of stroke rates in Novosibirsk covering the period 1987–94 shows that stroke mortality increased because of an increase in the number of strokes but that the fatality rate for those who suffered a stroke did not change.[21] Moreover, the recent decline in maternal and infant mortality, as well as in mortality among children suffering from leukemia, indicate positive dynamics in Russian medial care that must be connected with the economic growth.[22]

Moreover, Andreev and his colleagues calculated morality from treatable causes in Russia and Great Britain. Their calculations suggest that if the Russian health care system were to improve to the British level, the difference in life expectancy between the two countries would only decrease by 1.7 years for men and 1.5 years for women. However, the actual difference is currently 12 years for women and 16 years for men.[23] Finally, Breinerd and Cutler performed a cross-national statistical analysis of factors affecting male mortality in postsocialist countries, including private and public medical spending. According to their analysis, increased medical spending is *positively* related to increased mortality.[24] This could be explained by the fact that the poorest countries, such as the Transcaucasian and Central Asian states, experienced the lowest increase in mortality among postsocialist countries during the 1990s.[25]

The key point is that the major share of excess deaths (in comparison with Western countries) in Russia (as well as in Belarus, Ukraine, and the Baltic states) is concentrated among working-age males.[26] This distribution implies the importance of alcohol as a factor, because the East Slavic and Baltic states, unlike the Central Asian or Transcaucasian countries, have severe problems with alcoholism.

Annual alcohol consumption per adult varies from a few milliliters of pure alcohol in the poorest and Islamic nations to 15 to 20 liters in some European, Caribbean, and tourist-oriented countries (in the latter cases, data on alcohol consumption often seem exaggerated).[27] According to the World Health Organization, alcohol consumption in Russia was 10.7 liters of pure alcohol per adult per year in 2001.[28] However, in fact alcohol consumption in Russia is higher than this, because of the illegal industrial and domestic production of spirits. According to experts, real alcohol consumption is Russia is about 14.5 liters of pure alcohol per adult per year, which corresponds to approximately 180 bottles of vodka per adult male per year.[29]

According to careful calculations made by Aleksandr Nemtsov, about one-third of all deaths in Russia are directly or indirectly due to alcohol.[30] He also suggests that 72.2 percent of murders, 42.1 percent of suicides, 52.6 percent of other deaths from external causes, 67.6 percent of deaths from kidney cirrhosis, 60.1 percent of deaths from pancreatic disease, 23.2 percent of deaths from cardiovascular disease, and 25.0 percent of all other deaths are alcohol related.[31] These findings are more or less supported by other researchers as well. For example, autopsies in Izhevsk showed significant levels of blood alcohol in 61.8 percent of males age twenty to fifty-five years.[32] In most cases, alcohol is not a direct cause of death (as in the case of alcoholic poisoning) but is rather a stimulator of cardiovascular and other crises. In such cases, alcohol is not recorded as a cause of death in official death reports, which leads to a great underestimation of the impact of alcohol on mortality rate in official statistics.

A study of the impact of an antialcohol campaign (1985–87) on mortality rates in the Soviet Union also reveals the significance of the alcohol factor. During this campaign, a 25 percent decrease in alcohol consumption led to a decline in the mortality rate of 12 percent for males and 7 percent for females. Mortality due to alcohol poisoning declined by 56 percent.[33] The male mortality rate from accidents and traumas declined by 36 percent, from pneumonia by 40 percent, from other ventricular diseases by 20 percent, from infectious diseases by 20 percent, and from cardiovascular diseases by 9 percent. Yet after the end of the antialcohol campaign, mortality rates—especially male mortality rates—increased sharply due to a growth in alcohol consumption and other negative social tendencies.[34]

A comparison of various regions of the Russian Federation also supports the alcohol hypothesis. First, it should be noted that life expectancy is highest in Ingushetia and Dagestan, which are the poorest (except for Chechnya) but are deeply Islamic, and thus have the lowest rates of drinking in Russia. In Russia, average life expectancy was fifty-nine years for men and seventy-two years for women in 2002. The corresponding numbers were seventy and seventy-nine for Ingushetia and sixty-seven and seventy-six for Dagestan. A cross-regional statistical analysis performed by Nemtsov confirmed that about one-third of Russian mortality is caused by alcohol. He also showed that alcohol-related problems in Russia increase from South to North and from West to East (just as in Europe).[35]

It is important to recognize that in some countries, an equally high level of alcohol consumption is not accompanied by abnormally high mortality rates. Among these countries we find Portugal, Ireland, the Czech Republic, France, Germany, and Austria. We would argue that this is related to the *structure* of alcohol consumption, that is, the main type(s) of alcoholic beverages consumed. Of course, life expectancy is influenced by a number of factors, such as income levels, the quality of health care, environmental situation, psychological factors, and so on. These factors ought to affect men and women in more or less similar ways. However, men consume significantly more alcohol than women. Consequently, the effect of various types of alcoholic drinks should be reflected not only in overall life expectancy indicators but also especially in the difference between female and male life expectancy. The distribution of this factor among industrially developed countries in the "beer," "wine," and "vodka" belts (based on the alcoholic drink type that represents the largest amount of pure alcohol consumed in the country) is displayed in figure 2.14.

This shows distinctively the divergence between beer, wine, and vodka belts in terms of the difference between female and male life expectancy. Note that in abstemious Islamic countries with developed health care systems, the difference between female and male life expectancy is only three to five years. In beer-drinking countries, this difference equals, on average, six years. It is a little higher in Finland and the Czech Republic, where beer is predominant but hard liquor is also quite popular.[36] The difference between female and male life expectancy is eight years in wine-consuming, industrially developed countries.[37] The greatest gap between female and male life expectancy among the wine belt countries is in Hungary, where hard liquor is only a bit less popular than wine.[38]

However, the gap between female and male life expectancy is largest in the vodka belt, where the average value of this parameter exceeds 10 years. The only exceptions are Slovakia and Moldova. In Slovakia, the hard liquor component is comparable to the beer component in total alcohol consumption. The other exception is Moldova, which is traditionally a wine-producing and wine-consuming country; indeed, data from the Global Alcohol Database that represent Moldova as the world leader in the consumption of

Figure 2.14. Difference between Female and Male Life Expectancy (years) in Industrially Developed Countries with Alcohol Consumption of More Than 9 Liters of Pure Alcohol per Adult per Year

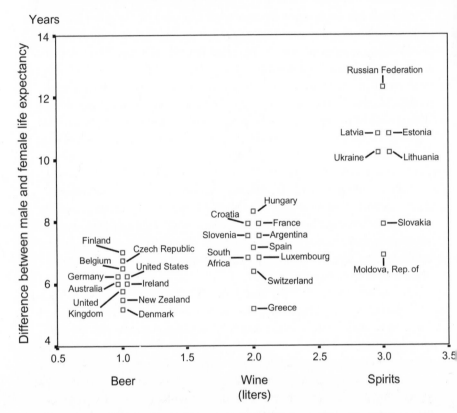

Note: Rho = +0.79; *p* = .000000001. Note that we selected only countries with alcohol consumption of more than 9 liters of pure alcohol per adult per year.

Sources: The data on life expectancy are from United Nations Development Program, *Human Development Report 2001* (New York: Oxford University Press, 2001). The data on alcohol consumption are from World Health Organization, "Global Alcohol Database." The structure of alcohol consumption in Latvia, which is not specified in the World Health Organization database, was taken from A. Brunovskis and T. Ugland, *Alcohol Consumption in the Baltic States,* Fafo Paper 4 (Oslo: Fafo, 2003), http://www.fafo.no/pub/rapp/702/702.pdf, 14. The data on Ukraine were corrected according to data from A. I. Minko, "Alkogolizm: Mezhdistsiplinarnaya problema (vyyavleniye, lecheniye, reabilitatsiya, profilaktika)," *Ukrains'kiy v³snik psikhonevrolog³i* 9 (2001): 6–7. Brunovskis and Ugland convincingly argue that alcohol consumption in Estonia is underestimated in the World Health Organization database. Estonia is therefore classified as a country with alcohol consumption exceeding 8 liters of pure alcohol per adult per year.

hard liquor seem suspect.[39] In any case, the unfortunate position of leadership in the difference between female and male life expectancy belongs to Russia, where in 2002 this indicator was 13.5 years.[40]

In sum, based on the above-mentioned data, we may conclude that alcohol consumption is a major predictor of male mortality in industrially developed countries, and that the type of alcoholic beverages consumed is of major importance.[41] Wine, being a stronger alcoholic beverage, seems to have a more harmful effect on a drinker's health than beer, and hard liquor is the most threatening factor for health and longevity.

Hungary provides another case study showing why abnormal mortality rates in countries with "demographic crosses" cannot be explained by economic troubles alone. The demographic cross took place in Hungary well before perestroika, against the background of impressive economic growth in the period 1970–80. As can be seen in figure 2.15, the increase in mortality rates in Hungary was accompanied by a sharp growth in alcohol consumption.

Successful economic reforms introduced by the János Kádár regime during the 1960s and 1970s resulted in the liberalization of the Hungarian economy, which led to fairly rapid economic growth. Conversely, the growth of the agricultural sector resulted in an increased production of cheap wines and spirits. Between 1965 and 1985, alcohol consumption in Hungary tripled. As figure 2.16 demonstrates, this resulted in a significant rise in mortality rates, which was accompanied by a sharp decline in fertility after 1976.

The Russian demographic crisis took place against a background of economic decline (the GDP of the Russian Federation decreased 1.79 times from 1989 to 1998). In contrast, the Hungarian cross occurred during the 1970s, a rather successful period of Hungarian economic history, when GDP rose by 58 percent—an exceptional achievement for socialist economies at that time. Yet what was common to Kádár's Hungary and Boris Yeltsin's Russia was that in both cases, the radical liberalization of the economy (including alcohol production and marketing) led to an unprecedented availability of alcoholic beverages in general and hard liquor in particular. It is also crucial that both Russia in the 1990s and Hungary in the 1970s experienced a decline in alcohol costs relative to income.[42]

Drugs

Drug consumption is another significant factor behind the mortality crisis in Russia, resulting from an abrupt increase in addictive drug use during the 1990s.[43] According to the Russian drug control agency Gosnarkokontrol,

Figure 2.15. Birthrate, Mortality Rate (per 1,000 people), and Alcohol
Consumption (liters per adult per year) in Hungary, 1960–95

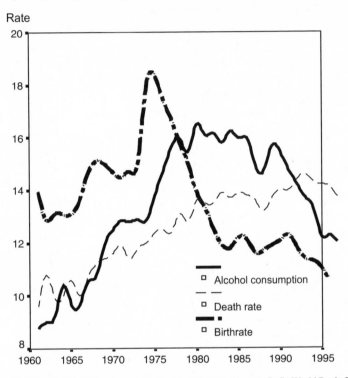

Sources: World Bank, *World Development Indicators 2004* (Washington, D.C.: World Bank, 2004);
World Health Organization, "Global Alcohol Database."

the number of drug addicts in Russia is close to 4 million, whereas sociological surveys indicate that 13.9 percent of Russians age eleven to twenty-
four years use addictive drugs of various kinds, of which 4.2 percent use
opiates.[44] Heroin is a particularly lethal drug because addiction emerges after only three to five injections, and the majority of heroin addicts die at an
early age (average life expectancy is only seven to ten years after starting
to take drugs regularly). The chances of curing this addiction are extremely
low, as leading clinics can only guarantee that about 10 percent of their pa-
tients will not start taking drugs again within one year after therapy (and obviously even some of that 10 percent will start taking heroin again later).[45]
It follows that perhaps 4 percent of Russia's youth will not survive to reproduce because of heroin and other injected opiates.

Figure 2.16. Birthrate, Mortality Rate (per 1,000 people), and Alcohol Consumption (liters per adult per year) in Hungary against the Background of Gross Domestic Product (index: gross domestic product of 1961 = 10), 1960–90

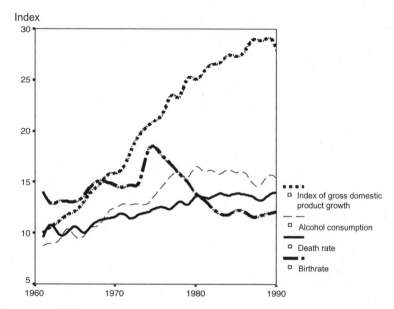

Sources: World Bank, *World Development Indicators 2004* (Washington, D.C.: World Bank, 2004); World Health Organization, "Global Alcohol Database."

Of course, opiates are not the only lethal drugs in Russia. Another group includes amphetamine-based injective drugs. Addiction to these drugs is even stronger than for heroin, and life expectancy for addicts is approximately ten years. According to one survey, 0.8 percent of Russian young people consume amphetamine-based injective drugs.[46] In short, straightforward calculations suggest that Russia will loose at least 5 percent of its young population due to drugs.

The Relative Impact of Factors: Statistical Analysis

Having identified a set of factors affecting Russian life expectancy, we performed multiple regression tests using cross-national data.[47] To avoid the effect of demographic and first epidemiological transitions, we selected a sample of countries with total fertility rates of fewer than two children per woman (table 2.1).

The R^2 value in the above data implies that this regression model explains more than 87 percent of the overall data dispersion. This model shows that the most significant factor affecting male life expectancy is per capita GDP. This is in no way surprising; the value of GDP per capita affects the quality

Table 2.1. Regression Model of Male Life Expectancy Factors for Countries with Total Fertility Rate below Two Children per Woman

Element of Model	Unstandardized Coefficients		Standardized Coefficients: Beta	t-value	Significance
	Beta	Standard Error			
Constant	70.728	1.312		53.896	$<10^{-17}$
Gross domestic product per capita (2001 dollars at purchasing power parity)	0.00027	0.00005	0.536	5.769	0.000004
Spirits consumption (liters per adult per year)	–0.531	0.152	–0.348	–3.498	0.002
Opiates (percentage of population age fifteen to sixty-four years consuming)	–2.964	0.992	–0.244	–3.213	0.003
Cocaine (percentage of population age fifteen to sixty-four years consuming)			1.127	0.270	
Cannabis (percentage of population age fifteen to sixty-four years consuming)			1.764	0.090	
Beer consumption (liters per adult per year)			–1.543	0.135	
Wine consumption (liters per adult per year)			0.364	0.719	
Cigarette consumption per adult per year, 1992–2000			–0.664	0.512	
Dependent variable: life expectancy at birth, male					

Note: $R = .936$; $R^2 = .876$; $p = .000000002$. We use a stepwise method of multiple regression.
Sources: United Nations Development Program, *Human Development Report 2001* (New York: Oxford University Press, 2001); United Nations, *World Drugs Report 2004* (New York: United Nations, 2001); World Health Organization, "Global Alcohol Database."

of life, average health expenditures, caloric consumption, nutritional quality, crime and stress levels, and so on. The data show that each dollar of GDP per capita adds about 0.00027 year of life for men. Thus, to increase life expectancy in a given country by one year, GDP per capita must increase by about $3,700.[48]

However, the second strongest factor affecting male life expectancy is the hard liquor consumption level. According to this model, each liter of hard liquor consumed by adults per year in a given country costs men a half year of longevity, on average.[49] Consequently, the average Russian man looses 5.5 years of life by consuming 11 liters of hard liquor in the form of vodka, *samogon,* and so on.[50]

This result is consistent with the calculations of other scholars based on different methodological foundations. According to Nemtsov, each liter of alcohol consumption above 8 liters of pure alcohol per adult per year (the maximum recommended by the World Health Organization) deprives men of eleven months and women of four months of their lives, on average. According to these studies, alcohol decreases male life expectancy in Russia by 5.5 years.[51]

The above regression model interprets wine and beer as insignificant factors for life expectancy (the significance value for these variables exceeds the 0.05 level). Of course, excessive beer and wine consumption undoubtedly affects health and life expectancy negatively (as was discussed above). However, the relative impact of hard liquor is so dramatic that, by comparison, beer and wine appear insignificant in the multiple regression analysis. The same could be observed for the consumption of cigarettes, cocaine, and cannabis.[52]

Our analysis shows that the third most powerful factor affecting male life expectancy is opiate consumption. According to our model, each percent of the population consuming opiates corresponds to a decrease of three years in average male life expectancy at birth. This is a huge value, and it requires some additional comments.

Theoretically, a 1 percent level of injective opiate drug addicts in a given society should decrease average life expectancy at birth by less than half a year. However, it should affect male life expectancy almost twice as much, because the majority of addicts are men. Moreover, it should be noted that injective drugs increase mortality rates even among people who are not taking these drugs, by promoting the spread of HIV, syphilis, hepatitis, and so on. Mortality might be also somewhat increased via the general criminalization accompanying widespread illegal drug use. In sum, increased opiate usage since the mid-1990s in Russia (and throughout the former socialist countries) is a powerful factor affecting young male mortality.[53]

Table 2.2 presents a regression model of the factors affecting life expectancy for women. This model explains 77.8 percent of the data dispersion. According to the model, GDP per capita is also the main factor for life expectancy for women, with each dollar of GDP per capita adding 0.0002

Table 2.2. Regression Model of Factors of Female Life Expectancy in Countries with Total Fertility Rate below Two Children per Woman

Element of Model	Unstandardized Coefficients		Standardized Coefficients: Beta	t-value	Significance
	Beta	Standard Error			
Constant	73.828	0.698		105.779	$<10^{-15}$
Gross domestic product per capita (2001 dollars at purchasing power parity)	0.0002	0.00004	0.602	4.940	0.00003
Spirits consumption (liters per adult per year)	–0.369	0.127	–0.354	–2.903	0.007
Opiates (percentage of population age fifteen to sixty-four years consuming)				–1.241	0.225
Cocaine (percentage of population age fifteen to sixty-four years consuming)				–1.241	–1.241
Cannabis (percentage of population age fifteen to sixty-four years consuming)				0.046	0.964
Beer consumption (liters per adult per year)				1.515	0.141
Wine consumption (liters per adult per year)				–1.210	0.237
Cigarette consumption per adult per year, 1992–2000				0.981	0.335
Dependent variable: life expectancy at birth, female					

Note: $R = .882$; $R^2 = .778$; $p = .0000000007$.

Sources: United Nations Development Program, *Human Development Report 2001* (New York: Oxford University Press, 2001); United Nations, *World Drugs Report 2004* (New York: United Nations, 2001); World Health Organization, "Global Alcohol Database."

year to average female life expectancy. The second most important factor is hard liquor consumption. Each liter of spirits consumed per adult per year corresponds to a 0.4 year decrease in female life expectancy. All other factors appear insignificant based on our model.

We also analyzed the effect of a country's economic situation—together with the consumption of beer, wine, hard liquor, cannabis, cocaine, opiates, and cigarettes—on the difference between male and female life expectancy (table 2.3). The only significant factors explaining the difference between male and female life expectancy are the consumption of hard liquor and opiates. All other factors—such as GDP per capita and the consumption of beer, wine, cigarettes, cocaine, and cannabis—were considered as insignificant within the scale of research. According to the model, each liter of hard liquor consumption per capita per year increases the gap between female and male life expectancy by 3.5 years, and each percent of the population taking opiates accounts for 1.9 years of this gap.

There is also reason to expect that excessive male mortality is an independent factor contributing to low fertility. High mortality among males of reproductive age automatically increases the percentage of small families, and it also should result in a growing percentage of single women who have no (or few) children.[54] Moreover, one might speculate that sharply rising male mortality leads women to doubt whether their husbands will be able to support them through the critical period before and after childbirth (especially if their husbands are heavy drinkers or drug addicts). In such situations, women may be unlikely to risk giving birth to a third, second, or even first child.

Table 2.4 presents a multiple regression test of the hypothesis that excessive male mortality contributes to low fertility, as well as the suppositions that fertility rates are influenced by GDP per capita, total employment, female employment, higher education among women, and level of urbanization. This multiple regression test identifies the difference between male and female life expectancy as the only significant factor negatively affecting fertility for the countries in question. According to the model, each year of difference between female and male life expectancy corresponds to a decline in the total fertility rate of 0.08 children per woman. All other factors—such as GDP per capita, employment, female employment, higher education among women, and urbanization level—are insignificant. This implies that economic growth will be insufficient to meet the low fertility challenge in Russia unless the problems of alcohol and injective drugs are resolved.[55]

Table 2.3. *Regression Model of Factors Affecting the Difference between Male and Female Life Expectancy, for Countries with a Total Fertility Rate below Two Children per Woman*

Element of Model	Unstandardized Coefficients		Standardized Coefficients: Beta	t-value	Significance
	Beta	Standard Error			
Constant	4.656	0.400		11.639	$<10^{-11}$
Spirits consumption (liters per adult per year)	0.350	0.086	0.539	4.068	0.0003
Opiates (percentage of population age fifteen to sixty-four years consuming)	1.913	0.684	0.371	2.796	0.009
Gross domestic product per capita (2001 dollars at purchasing power parity)				−1.549	0.133
Cocaine (percentage of population age fifteen to sixty-four years consuming)				−1.976	0.058
Cannabis (percentage of population age fifteen to sixty-four years consuming)				−0.625	0.537
Beer consumption (liters per adult per year)				−0.117	0.908
Wine consumption (liters per adult per year)				1.164	0.255
Cigarette consumption per adult per year, 1992-2000				0.927	0.362

Dependent variable: difference between female and male life expectancy at birth, years

Note: $R = .780$; $R^2 = .609$; $p = .000002$.
Sources: United Nations Development Program, *Human Development Report 2001* (New York: Oxford University Press, 2001); United Nations, *World Drugs Report 2004* (New York: United Nations, 2001); World Health Organization, "Global Alcohol Database."

The relationship between the two parameters can be identified with correlation analysis as well (figure 2.17). We conclude that excessive male mortality (resulting in a large gap between female and male life expectancies) is a major independent factor affecting fertility decline. Furthermore, high alcohol consumption—especially in the form of hard liquor—as well as injective drug use cause excessive male mortality in Russia (and other

Table 2.4. Regression Model of Factors Affecting the Total Fertility Rate in Countries with a Total Fertility Rate below Two Children per Woman

Element of Model	Unstandardized Coefficients		Standardized Coefficients: Beta	t-value	Significance
	Beta	Standard Error			
Constant	1.996	0.128		15.620	$<10^{-15}$
Difference between female and male life expectancy (years)	−0.075	0.018	−0.544	−4.256	0.0001
Gross domestic product per capita (2001 dollars at purchasing power parity)				0.883	0.382
Female employment (percent), 2001				−0.522	0.605
Female tertiary school enrollment (percent gross), 2000–2				−0.840	0.406
Unemployment, total (percentage of total labor force), 2000–2				−0.435	0.666
Urbanization (percent)				−0.680	0.500
Dependent variable: total fertility rate					

Note: $R = .549$; $R^2 = .301$; $p = .0001$.

Sources: For female tertiary school enrollment and unemployment, World Bank, *World Development Indicators 2004* (Washington, D.C.: World Bank, 2004). For other elements of the model, United Nations Development Program, *Human Development Report 2001* (New York: Oxford University Press, 2001); United Nations, *World Drugs Report 2004* (New York: United Nations, 2001); and World Health Organization, "Global Alcohol Database."

countries), and thus negatively affect fertility levels. At the same time, because lethal drugs and excessive vodka drinking also kill young women, they affect fertility directly as well.

There is no reason to believe that a high level of alcohol consumption is caused by economic crisis; the cross-national data do not support such a hypothesis. In Hungary, alcohol consumption rose to a dangerous level in the context of economic growth. Figure 2.18 presents the distribution of alcohol consumption by GDP per capita levels in 2001 (Islamic countries are excluded). As one can see, alcohol consumption is insignificant in the poorest countries because the population in these countries simply has no possibility to spend a lot of resources on purchasing or producing alcohol.

Andrey Korotayev and Darya Khaltourina

Figure 2.17. Total Fertility Rate and the Difference between Female and Male Life Expectancies in Countries with a Total Fertility Rate below Two Children per Woman

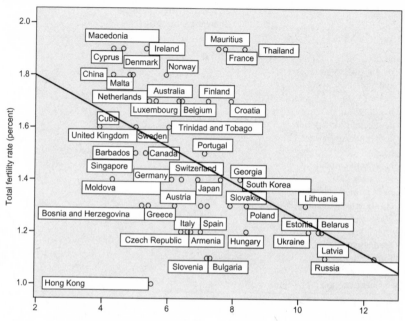

Difference between female and male life expectancy at birth (years)

Note: r = – .48; p = .0002.
Sources: United Nations Development Program, *Human Development Report 2001* (New York: Oxford University Press, 2001); World Health Organization, "Global Alcohol Database."

As we see, in general, a growing economic surplus leads to rising alcohol consumption.[56] However, after a country reaches a certain level of GDP per capita, alcohol consumption increases to what might wryly be called its saturation level. In fact, some decline in alcohol consumption can be observed among developed countries.

The "alcoholization" of Russia followed the same scenario as in the rest of the world. The main specifics of Eastern Europe is that the most popular type of alcohol happens to be hard liquor. Moreover, the largest growth in alcohol consumption in Russia took place in the 1960s and 1980s, when Soviet per capita income increased substantially. The greater economic availability of alcohol was the leading factor behind this growth in consumption.

Figure 2.18. Alcohol Consumption per Capita and Average Estimated Income for Men (in dollars at purchasing power parity), 2001

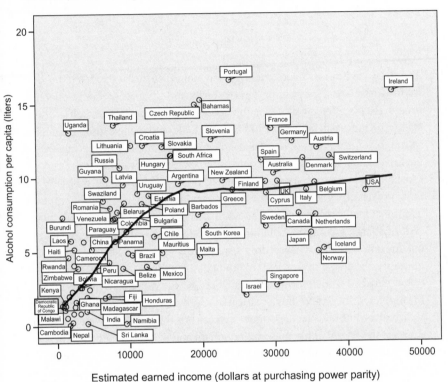

Sources: United Nations Development Program, *Human Development Report 2001* (New York: Oxford University Press, 2001); World Health Organization, "Global Alcohol Database."

Much the same might be said about drug use. In the early 1990s, countries around the "Golden Triangle" in South East Asia (where large opium poppy plantations were located) had the most serious problems with heroin abuse in the world. Since the early 1990s, opiate production has been growing in Afghanistan, where yields are three times higher than in the Golden Triangle.[57] As a result, the number of heroin-related deaths has decreased in Southeast Asia and catastrophically increased in the Commonwealth of Independent States, the region directly adjacent to Afghanistan.[58] Consequently, the narcotic epidemic in Russia has been caused not simply by economic crisis but also (primarily) by a rapid increase in the availability of drugs since the collapse of the Soviet Union, which itself was partly a function of the weakness of state institutions.

Conclusions

To briefly review our major findings, the main factors for excessive mortality in Russia are the consumption of spirits and drugs (especially injective drugs); the post-perestroika economic crisis affected mortality much less substantially. In Russia between 1990 and 2001, alcohol alone caused the deaths of roughly 7 million people, which exceeds the number of deaths caused by terrorist attacks (outside of Chechnya) by several thousand times. This was especially due to the consumption of hard liquor, which affects mortality far more powerfully than wine and beer consumption. Drug use was a significant additional factor responsible for these ravages, and at this point at least 5 percent of Russia's young population are doomed to die at an early age due to opiate- and ephedrine-based drug use. Finally, by causing excessive male mortality, the consumption of hard liquor and injective drugs also contributes to low fertility. The notorious "Russian cross" is explained by these factors. In sum, hard liquor and drugs constitute real threats to national security.

We also find that the economic crisis is not the only (or even the main) cause of the recent epidemics of alcoholism and narcotics addiction in Russia. Rather, these epidemics occurred against the background of the growing availability of alcohol and drugs, as well as the weakness of government policies regarding substance control. Thus, although economic growth might conceivably lead to some decline in mortality and growth in fertility, economic growth alone will be insufficient to solve Russia's demographic crisis. On the contrary, it is impossible to solve the demographic crisis without reducing the consumption of high-alcohol beverages and opiate- and ephedrine-based drugs.

Of course, the ultimate solution of demographic crisis in Russia lies in the sphere of family policy. Western countries achieved limited success in stimulating fertility by increasing financial support for families (especially poor families), with third child subsidies, and so on.[59] However, these and other expensive measures will have little effect until the major "black holes" of Russian mortality—vodka-type alcohol consumption and injective drug use—are eliminated. This suggests the importance of introducing measures to radically reduce the consumption of these substances.[60]

Our analysis leads us to expect that a significant reduction in hard liquor and drug consumption would not only lead to a radical decline in mortality but would also have the following positive social consequences: a decline in the rate of murders, rapes, robberies, car hijackings and other crimes, as well as in the rates of suicides, accidents, divorces, and abortions. It would also help decrease expenditures on subsidies to single mothers, orphans, and invalids. The introduction of more moderate forms of alcohol consumption would probably also lead to the alleviation of homelessness. Moreover, the Russian economy would experience a net benefit from a reduction in hard liquor production, sales, and consumption, because this would probably lead to a decline in absenteeism and work-related accidents (some of the loss of tax revenue would presumably be offset by an increase in tax revenues from beer and wine production). However, the most significant effect would be a dramatic growth in returns from human capital investment, because (as argued by Konstantinov and Filonovich in chapter 5 of this volume) human capital is the major factor behind modern economic growth.[61]

In keeping with the main themes addressed in this volume, it is worth concluding by considering the role of identity and globalization in Russia's ongoing security problem. First, it should be noted that vodka was not always an integral part of Russian identity and everyday culture. It was only introduced in the sixteenth century. At that time, vodka was largely a source of state tax revenue; under Ivan the Terrible, a network of drinking houses (*kabaks*) was created for this purpose. Still, before the 1917 Revolution, alcohol consumption per adult was three times lower than today, and frequent cases of excessive drinking were balanced by a popular temperance movement.[62]

The increase in vodka production was a goal set by Joseph Stalin:

Two words about . . . vodka. There are people who think that it is possible to build socialism in white gloves. It is the rudest mistake, comrades. Since we do not have loans, since we are poor with capitals, and besides, we cannot go into debt servitude to West European capitalists, we cannot accept those . . . conditions which they offer us, and which we have denied. The only thing to do is to look for other sources. . . . Here we have to choose between debt servitude and vodka, and people who think that it is possible to build socialism with white gloves make a serious mistake.[63]

In a conversation with foreign laborers in 1927, Stalin declared that state vodka production was a temporary measure that would be stopped as soon as possible.[64] However, in a private letter to Vyacheslav Molotov in 1930, he called for maximally increasing vodka production.[65] Even beyond revenue generation, the drink came to be seen as a necessary social support in times of duress. A decree issued by the State Defense Committee in August 1941 prescribed 100 grams of vodka for every Soviet soldier on the front lines. Vodka subsequently became a symbol of Soviet fortitude during the war, and in the process it penetrated deeply into Russian identity. Indeed, in a study conducted among Russian students in 1999, we found that vodka placed second (after Pushkin) on a list of most frequent associations with "Russian culture."[66] At this point, vodka has at least a partly positive connotation in Russian culture; for example, masculine movie heroes drink together to express their respect for each other.

Against this background, globalization could potentially play a constructive role with respect to Russia's demographic crisis. As was mentioned above, vodka has come to be regarded by an alarmingly high percentage of Russians as an integral part of national identity. In this respect, some "dilution" of this aspect of Russian identity due to globalization and Westernization might have a positive impact on Russian demography, especially if it takes the form of a shift away from vodka to wine and beer. According to some sources, beer consumption has become much more popular among younger Russians in recent years, squeezing out vodka from this market share; not surprisingly, the mortality rate for young Russians has declined modestly since 2000.[67] Conversely, globalization could also have—indeed, has already had—a negative impact. Perestroika, with its openness to the West, led to the diffusion of teen subcultures and countercultures, including the tolerance and even propagation of drug use. Such drug use became widespread among Russian youth after the fall of the Iron Curtain. Since then, Russia's inclusion in global drug trafficking networks has further exposed the Trojan Horse of globalization.

Appendix Table 2A. Summary of Mortality Rate Dynamics, 1990–94

	Russia		Estonia	
Females, 20–24 years old	Mortality rate in 1990	0.71	Mortality rate in 1990	0.71
	Mortality rate in 1994	1.00	Mortality rate in 1994	1.50
	Mortality rate change between 1990 and 1994	+0.29	Mortality rate change between 1990 and 1994	+0.79
Males, 20–24 years old	Mortality rate in 1990	2.60	Mortality rate in 1990	2.60
	Mortality rate in 1994	4.00	Mortality rate in 1994	3.80
	Mortality rate change between 1990 and 1994	+1.40	Mortality rate change between 1990 and 1994	+1.60
Females, 25–39 years old	Mortality rate in 1990	1.13	Mortality rate in 1990	1.02
	Mortality rate in 1994	1.95	Mortality rate in 1994	1.85
	Mortality rate change between 1990 and 1994	+0.82	Mortality rate change between 1990 and 1994	+0.83
Males, 25–39 years old	Mortality rate in 1990	4.38	Mortality rate in 1990	3.76
	Mortality rate in 1994	8.08	Mortality rate in 1994	6.58
	Mortality rate change between 1990 and 1994	+3.70	Mortality rate change between 1990 and 1994	+2.82
Females, 40–59 years old	Mortality rate in 1990	5.04	Mortality rate in 1990	4.52
	Mortality rate in 1994	7.71	Mortality rate in 1994	6.50
	Mortality rate change between 1990 and 1994	+2.67	Mortality rate change between 1990 and 1994	+1.98
Males, 40–59 years old	Mortality rate in 1990	14.35	Mortality rate in 1990	13.58
	Mortality rate in 1994	24.11	Mortality rate in 1994	20.07
	Mortality rate change between 1990 and 1994	+9.76	Mortality rate change between 1990 and 1994	+6.49

(continued)

Appendix Table 2A. Continued

		Georgia	Armenia
Females, 20–24 years old	Mortality rate in 1990	0.63	0.46
	Mortality rate in 1994	0.59	0.57
	Mortality rate change between 1990 and 1994	−0.04	+0.11
Males, 20–24 years old	Mortality rate in 1990	1.50	1.17
	Mortality rate in 1994	2.25	2.84
	Mortality rate change between 1990 and 1994	+0.75	+1.67
Females, 25–39 years old	Mortality rate in 1990	0.90	0.91
	Mortality rate in 1994	0.94	0.76
	Mortality rate change between 1990 and 1994	+0.04	−0.15
Males, 25–39 years old	Mortality rate in 1990	2.68	2.15
	Mortality rate in 1994	3.44	3.05
	Mortality rate change between 1990 and 1994	+0.76	+0.90
Females, 40–59 years old	Mortality rate in 1990	4.28	4.14
	Mortality rate in 1994	4.22	3.51
	Mortality rate change between 1990 and 1994	−0.06	−0.63
Males, 40–59 years old	Mortality rate in 1990	10.52	9.38
	Mortality rate in 1994	10.24	8.95
	Mortality rate change between 1990 and 1994	−0.28	−0.43

	Uzbekistan		Ukraine	
Females, 20–24 years old	Mortality rate in 1990	0.93	Mortality rate in 1990	0.61
	Mortality rate in 1994	1.09	Mortality rate in 1994	0.77
	Mortality rate change between 1990 and 1994	+0.16	Mortality rate change between 1990 and 1994	+0.16
Males, 20–24 years old	Mortality rate in 1990	1.47	Mortality rate in 1990	2.60
	Mortality rate in 1994	1.48	Mortality rate in 1994	4.01
	Mortality rate change between 1990 and 1994	+0.01	Mortality rate change between 1990 and 1994	+1.41
Females, 25–39 years old	Mortality rate in 1990	1.33	Mortality rate in 1990	1.04
	Mortality rate in 1994	1.62	Mortality rate in 1994	1.39
	Mortality rate change between 1990 and 1994	+0.29	Mortality rate change between 1990 and 1994	+0.35
Males, 25–39 years old	Mortality rate in 1990	2.47	Mortality rate in 1990	3.57
	Mortality rate in 1994	2.61	Mortality rate in 1994	5.11
	Mortality rate change between 1990 and 1994	+0.14	Mortality rate change between 1990 and 1994	+1.54
Females, 40–59 years old	Mortality rate in 1990	5.48	Mortality rate in 1990	4.84
	Mortality rate in 1994	6.11	Mortality rate in 1994	6.14
	Mortality rate change between 1990 and 1994	+0.63	Mortality rate change between 1990 and 1994	+1.30
Males, 40–59 years old	Mortality rate in 1990	10.22	Mortality rate in 1990	13.10
	Mortality rate in 1994	10.67	Mortality rate in 1994	17.38
	Mortality rate change between 1990 and 1994	+0.45	Mortality rate change between 1990 and 1994	+4.28

Source: UNICEF, *Innocenti Social Monitor 2004* (Florence: UNICEF Innocenti Research Centre, 2004).

Notes

1. For more detail, see Andrey Korotayev, A. Malkov, and Darya Khaltourina, *Introduction to Social Macrodynamics: Compact Macromodels of the World System Growth* (Moscow: KomKniga/URSS, 2006).

2. Ibid.

3. Ibid.

4. See, e.g., N. Rimashevskaya, "Russkiy krest," *Priroda* 6 (1999): 3–10; V. Shkol'nikov and V. V. Chervyakov, eds., *Politika po kontrolyu krizisnoy smertnosti v Rossii v perekhodnyy periode* (Moscow: Programma razvitiya OON, Rossiya, 2000); J. DaVanzo and G. Grammich, *Dire Demographics: Population Trends in the Russian Federation* (Santa Monica, Calif.: RAND, 2001); I. A. Gundarov, "Dukhovnoye neblagopoluchiye i demograficheskaya katastrofa," *Obshchestvennye nauki i sovremennost'* 5 (2001): 58–65; B. B. Prokhorov, "Zdorov'ye rossiyan za 100 let," *Chelovek* 2 (2002): 54–65; and E. Brainerd and D. Cutler, "Autopsy of the Empire: Understanding Mortality in Russia and the Former Soviet Union," unpublished paper, 2005, http://www.wcfia.harvard.edu/conferences/demography/papers/Brainerd.pdf.

5. A. G. Vishnevskiy and V. Shkol'nikov, *Smertnost' v Rossii: Glavnyye gruppy riska i prioritety deystviy* (Moscow: Moskovskiy Tsentr Karnegi, 1997).

6. J. L. Bobadilla, Ch. Costello, and F. Mitchell, eds., *Premature Death in New Independent States* (Washington, D.C.: National Academy Press, 1997); E. Shcherbakova, "Narkomaniya ugrozhayet bezopasnosti strany," *Naseleniye i obshchestvo* 60 (December 2001), http://www.demoscope.ru/ acrobat/ps60.pdf.

7. O. J. Skog, "Public Health Consequences of J-Curve Hypothesis of Alcohol Problems," *Addiction* 91 (1996): 325–36; D. A. Leon et al., "Huge Variation in Russian Federation Mortality Rates 1984–1994: Artifact, Alcohol or What?" *Lancet* 350 (1997): 383–88; L. Chenet et al., "Alcohol and Cardiovascular Mortality in Moscow: New Evidence of a Causal Association," *Journal of Epidemiology and Community Health* 52 (1998): 772–74; Martin McKee and A. Britton, "The Positive Relationship between Alcohol and Heart Diseases in Eastern Europe: Potential Physiological Mechanism," *Journal of the Royal Society of Medicine* 91 (1998): 402–7; Shkol'nikov and Chervyakov, *Politika po kontrolyu krizisnoy smertnosti v Rossii v perekhodnyy periode;* DaVanzo and Grammich, *Dire Demographics;* A. V. Nemtsov, *Alkogol'naya smertnost' v Rossii 1980–90-e gg.* (Moscow: NALEX, 2001); A. V. Nemtsov, "Alkogol'naya smertnost' v Rossii," *Naselenie i obshchestvo* 78 (2003), http://www. demoscope.ru/acrobat/ps78.pdf; A. V. Nemtsov, *Alkogol'nyi uron regionov Rossii* (Moscow: NALEX, 2003); Prokhorov, "Zdorov'ye rossiyan za 100 let"; Brainerd and Cutler, "Autopsy of the Empire"; World Health Organization, *Global Status Report on Alcohol* (Geneva: World Health Organization, 2004), 2; Yegor T. Gaydar, *Dolgoye vremya. Rossiya v mire—Ocherki ekonomicheskoy istorii* (Moscow: Delo, 2005).

8. World Bank, *World Development Indicators 2004* (Washington, D.C.: World Bank, 2004).

9. A. Maddison, *Monitoring the World Economy: A Millennial Perspective* (Paris: Organization for Economic Cooperation and Development, 2001), 341.

10. Ibid.

11. Ibid.

12. Andrey Korotayev and Darya Khaltourina, *Introduction to Social Macrodynamics: Secular Cycles and Millennial Trends in Africa* (Moscow: KomKniga/URSS, 2006).

13. Maddison, *Monitoring the World Economy,* 341.

14. In fact, the relative contribution of the growing child mortality was even much smaller than 17 percent (7.2 divided by 40.2, multiplied by 100), because, due to a very low birthrate, children under five years of age constituted a very small fraction of the total population. In addition, its proportion decreased very significantly during the period 1990–94 due to a dramatic decline in birthrates. See UNICEF, *Innocenti Social Monitor 2004* (Florence: UNICEF Innocenti Research Centre, 2004), 115.

15. The source for the following three figures is ibid., 68.

16. Ibid., 74–76.

17. The source for the following three figures is ibid., 73–75.

18. Quite predictably, Kazakhstan in this respect occupies an intermediate position between the European and Central Asian parts of the former USSR, whereas Tajikistan combines features of Central Asian and Transcaucasian patterns, as the mortality crisis in this country in the early 1990s is accounted for primarily by internal warfare dynamics. Ibid., 73–76.

19. Conversely, the fact that unlike in Armenia, Georgia, Azerbaijan, and Tajikistan male mortality in the first cluster countries increased much more in the nonfighting age groups than in fighting age ones indicates that military-political instability was not a major cause of the male mortality increase either.

20. Shkol'nikov and Chervyakov, *Politika po kontrolyu krizisnoy smertnosti v Rossii v perekhodnyy periode,* 18, citing C. Davis, "Economic Transition, Health Production and Medical System Effectiveness in the Former Soviet Union and Easter Europe," paper presented at the Project Meeting on Economic Shocks, Social Stress and the Demographic Impact, Helsinki, April 17–19, 1997, ??. See also J. Shapiro, "Russian Health Care Policy and Russian Health," *Russian Political Development* (London: Macmillan, 1997); and United Nations Development Program, *Human Development Report 1995* (New York: Oxford University Press, 1995).

21. Note that alcohol consumption increases the probability of hemorrhagic stroke. See, e.g., P. Anderson, "Alcohol and Risk of Physical Harm," in *Alcohol and Public Policy: Evidence and Issues,* ed. H. D. Holder and G. Edwards (Oxford: Oxford University Press, 1995), 93–97.

22. World Health Organization, table titled "Number of Registered Deaths: The Russian Federation," in "World Mortality Database," available at: http://www.who.int/healthinfo/morttables/en/index.html.

23. E. Andreev et al., "The Evolving Pattern of Avoidable Mortality in Russia," *International Journal of Epidemiology* 32 (2003): 437–46; World Bank, *World Development Indicators 2004.*

24. Breinerd and Cutler, "Autopsy of the Empire," 12. The two major factors in Breinerd and Cutler's model are alcohol consumption and the male suicide rate. We argue that it is incorrect to include male suicide rates in the analysis as an independent variable, because the suicide rate is significantly influenced by alcohol consumption. On this point, see, e.g., S. Andreésson, P. Allebeck, and A. Rosmelsjö, "Alcohol and Mortality among Young Men: Longitudinal Study of Swedish Conscripts," *British Medical Journal* 296 (1988): 1021–25; O. J. Skog, "Alcohol and Suicide: Durkheim Revised," *Acta Sociologica* 34 (1991): 193–206; D. R. English et al., *Quantification of Drug Cause Morbidity and Mortality in Australia, 1992* (Canberra: Commonwealth Development of Human Services and Health, 1995); A. Romelsjö, "Alcohol Consumption and Unintentional Injury, Suicide, Violence, Work Performance and Intergenerational Effect," in *Al-*

cohol and Public Policy, ed. Holder and Edwards, 126–28; I. Rossow, K. Pernanen, and J. Rehm, "Accidents, Suicides and Violence," in *Mapping the Social Consequences of Alcohol Consumption,* ed. I. Klingemann and G. Gmel (Dordreht: Kluwer Academic Publishers, 2001), 93–112; World Health Organization, "World Mortality Database," 39–42. Social depression is an additional factor; however, when Breinerd and Cutler included a direct measure of social pessimism in their analysis, it turned out to be insignificant.

25. Also see A. Korotayev, A. Malkov, and D. Khaltourina, *Zakony istorii: Kompaktnye makromodeli evolyutsii Mir-sistemy—Demografiya, ekonomika, voyny* (Moscow: URSS, 2005), 291–323.

26. A. G. Vishnevskiy and V. Shkol'nikov, *Smertnost' v Rossii: Glavnyye gruppy riska i prioritety deystviy* (Moscow: Moskovskiy Tsentr Karnegi, 1997); Shkol'nikov and Chervyakov, *Politika po kontrolyu krizisnoy smertnosti v Rossii v perekhodnyy periode.* As is clear from figures 2.7 through 2.9 (and appendix table 2A), in the period 1990–94, the mortality rate among Russian working age males increased far more than child mortality. Conversely, in 1990–94 the mortality rate among Russians sixty or more years of age grew by 22 percent as compared with 84 percent growth among Russian males twenty-five to thirty-nine years of age. UNICEF, *Innocenti Social Monitor 2004,* 76. Note that these were Russian pensioners whose incomes declined catastrophically during this period, whereas the incomes of working-age males decreased much less. This in itself indicates that rising poverty was not the main cause of the Russian mortality crisis.

27. World Health Organization, "Global Alcohol Database," http://www3.who.int/whosis/menu.cfm?path=whosis,alcohol&language=english. These data indicate the volume of pure alcohol in drinks. One liter of pure alcohol corresponds to five half-liter bottles of vodka, twenty-six bottles of 10 percent wine, and fifty bottles of 4 percent beer.

28. Ibid.

29. A. K. Demin and I. A. Demina, "Zdorov'ye naseleniya i alkogol'naya epidemiya v Rossii: lekarstvo ot zhizni?" in *Alkogol' i zdorov'e naseleniya Rossii 1900–2000,* ed. A. K. Demin (Moscow: Rossiyskaya Assotsiatsiya obshchestvennogo zdorov'ya, 1998), 15; Nemtsov, *Alkogol'naya smertnost',* 7.

30. Nemtsov, *Alkogol'naya smertnost';* Nemtsov, "Alkogol'naya smertnost' "; Nemtsov, *Alkogol'nyi uron.*

31. Nemtsov, "Alkogol'naya smertnost' "; Nemtsov, *Alkogol'nyi uron.*

32. Dead men who died from infectious diseases, neoplasm, and unclear causes were not taken into account. Shkol'nikov and Chervyakov, *Politika po kontrolyu krizisnoy smertnosti v Rossii v perekhodnyy periode,* 117.

33. Leon, "Huge Variation in Russian Federation Mortality Rates 1984–1994."

34. D. Wasserman and A. Varnik, "Reliability of Statistics on Violent Death and Suicide in the Former USSR, 1970–1990," *Acta Psychiatry-Scand Supplement* 394 (1998): 34–41.

35. Nemtsov, "Alkogol'naya smertnost' "; Nemtsov, *Alkogol'nyi uron.*

36. I.e., with per adult consumption of 3 liters of pure alcohol per year in the form of spirits. World Health Organization, "Global Alcohol Database."

37. The value of this parameter is the smallest in Greece and Cyprus. However, it is possible that the data on alcohol consumption in these countries is exaggerated because a substantial part of alcoholic drinks sold in Greece and Cyprus is consumed by tourists, and these countries might best be excluded from the analysis.

38. World Health Organization, "Global Alcohol Database."

39. Ibid. At the same time, demographic data on Moldova show a sharp rise in the mortality rate in 2004, which might be partly related to increasing consumption of spirits. World Bank, *World Development Indicators 2004.*

40. UNICEF, *Innocenti Social Monitor 2004,* 72–73.

41. Spearman's coefficient for the correlation between the prevailing type of alcoholic beverages (ordinally arranged), on the one hand, and the difference between female and male life expectancy, on the other, is +0.79.

42. Nemtsov, *Alkogol'naya smertnost'.*

43. According to the UN Drugs and Crime Office, 2.1 percent of the Russian population used opiates in 2001, 3.9 percent used cannabis, and about 0.1 percent used amphetamines, cocaine, and ecstasy. United Nations, *World Drugs Report 2004,* vol. 2, http://www.unodc.org/unodc/en/world_drug_report.html, 195–208.

44. F. E. Sheregi and A. L. Aref'ev, *Otsenka narkosituatsii v srede detey, podrostkov i molodezhi* (Moscow: Optim Grupp, 2003).

45. I. N. Pyatnitskaya, *Klinicheskaya narkologiya* (Moscow: Meditsina, 1975).

46. Sheregi and Aref'ev, *Otsenka narkosituatsii v srede detey.*

47. It should be acknowledged, following Bongaarts and Feeney, that the traditional formula used to calculate life expectancy at birth has certain flaws: it tends to exaggerate life expectancy when it increases and to understate it when it declines. As a result, life expectancy is overestimated a year and a half for the US and Sweden, and 2.4 years for France. J. Bongaarts and G. Feeney, "Estimating Mean Lifetime," *Proceedings of the National Academy of Sciences* 100 (2003): 13127–33.

48. This is as measured by purchasing power parity, using 2001 dollars.

49. The value of this coefficient and its significance survive replication of the test with a sample of Western countries only.

50. A. V. Nemtsov, *Alkogol'naya situatsiya v Rossii* (Moscow: NALEX, 1995).

51. Ibid.

52. There is no doubt that smoking is one of the most serious negative health factors and has a significant impact on excessive mortality in Russia and globally. See C. J. Murray and A. Lopez, *The Global Burden of Disease* (London: Oxford University Press, 1996). The absence of a significant relationship in our analysis can probably be attributed to the lagged effect of tobacco on mortality. Besides, Brainerd and Cutler, "Autopsy of the Empire," point out that the smoking rate has increased only slightly in Russia since the Soviet collapse. Therefore, smoking per se cannot be considered a major factor in the catastrophic Russian mortality crisis of the 1990s. One should keep in mind the possibility of an interaction between greatly increased hard liquor consumption and high (but not much increased) tobacco consumption. However, this issue requires additional research.

53. E.g., the number of registered HIV cases in the former Soviet Union and the number of registered drugs addicts per 100,000 people grew until 2001. United Nations, *World Drug Report* (New York: United Nations, 2004), vol. 1, 86. This suggests that the rate of drug-related deaths will grow for another decade, even were stabilization to occur.

54. Excessive alcohol use is also known to cause reproductive health problems for men. Nemtsov, *Alkogol'naya situatsiya.*

55. Of course, there are other factors affecting the fertility rate after demographic transition that were not included in our analysis, e.g., demographic waves, housing availability, labor migrations, sociopsychological attitudes.

56. See also R. Weeden, "Alcohol Studies from an Economic Perspective," in *Economics and Alcohol* , ed. G. Marcus and A. Plant (New York: Gardner Press, 1983), 37.

57. Afghanistan is now the world leader in the heroin production. The production of opiates in the Golden Triangle considerably declined due to competition with Afghan producers and the antidrug policies of South East Asian states. United Nations, *World Drug Report,* vol. 1, 87.

58. Ibid., 61.

59. A. H. Gauthier, *The State and the Family* (Oxford: Clarendon Press, 1996).

60. Shkol'nikov and Chervyakov, *Politika po kontrolyu krizisnoy smertnosti v Rossii v perekhodnyy periode,* 129.

61. See also V. A. Mel'yantsev, *Vostok i Zapad vo vtorom tysyacheletii* (Moscow: MGU, 1996); V. A. Mel'yantsev, "Tri veka rossiyskogo ekonomicheskogo rosta," *Obshchestvennye nauki i sovremennost'* 5 (2003): 84–95; V. A. Mel'yantsev, *Genezis sovremennogo (intensivnogo) ekonomicheskogo rosta* (Moscow: Gumanitariy, 2004).

62. Nemtsov, *Alkogol'nyi uron.*

63. I. V. Stalin, "Politicheskiy otchet tsentral'nogo komiteta. 18 dekabrya 1925 g.," in *Sochineniya,* vol. 7 (Moscow: Politizdat, 1952), 43.

64. I. V. Stalin, "Beseda s inostrannymi rabochimi delegatsiyami. 5 noyabrya 1927 g." in *Sochineniya,* vol. 10 (Moscow: Politizdat, 1952), 121.

65. I. V. Stalin, *Pis'ma I. V. Stalina V. Molotovu. 1925–1936 gg.* (Moscow: Rossiya molodaya, 1995).

66. Darya Khaltourina and Andrey Korotayev, "Concepts of Culture in Cross-National and Cross-Cultural Perspectives, or 'Cognitive World Maps' of American and Russian Students," *World Cultures* 12 (2001): 25–74.

67. For consumption trends see, e.g., Mikhail Dymshits, "Pobeda PR nad razumom," paper delivered at the conference "New Electoral Technology," Moscow, July 8–9, 2004 (based on the TNS/Gallup "Marketing Index" for 1997–2003). For mortality rates among young Russians, see UNICEF, *Innocenti Social Monitor 2004,* 73–74.

3

Globalization, Regional Change, and the Territorial Cohesion of the Russian Federation

Michael Bradshaw

This chapter examines the interrelationships between economic-geographical globalization and the changing territorial configuration of Russia's economy and settlement. Globalization is conceived of both as the wider context for current geographical change in Russia and as a particular phase in the development of global society that is the consequence of a set of processes that operate unevenly across space and time to shape global geographies and in so doing constantly rework the relative positions of peoples, places, and states. Thus, globalization is not an outcome; nor is it a single trajectory or an explanatory variable that can be used to explain societal change. However, it is particularly significant that Russia's current

The author thanks Blair Ruble and the Kennan Institute for inviting him to participate in the workshop series where this chapter originated, Douglas Blum for being such an effective chair and editor, and his fellow participants for their fascinating insights and sense of humor. He also thanks the reviewers for the comments on this chapter; any errors remain his responsibility.

systematic transformation is taking place in an era of heightened "globalization," and many would argue that it was the Soviet Union's failure to respond to the competitive forces that heralded the current era that resulted in its collapse.

As others in this volume have suggested, it would seem that Russia wishes to erect barriers to protect its economy and polity against globalization, which it sees as a Western neoliberal project; but Russia cannot remain immune from globalization and seemingly has no choice but to play the global game—even if the rules are not of its making—to sustain its economy, to gain recognition, and to curry influence. For example, to gain economic and political legitimacy, Russia is now relying heavily on its role as a major supplier of oil and gas that does not belong to the Organization of the Petroleum Exporting Countries; but at the same time, it is seeking to recover state control over its energy economy and wishes to determine the basis upon which foreign capital can gain access to its hydrocarbon reserves.

Thus, Russia's current economic recovery is in large part sustained by the export of energy and other raw materials to the global economy, but Russia wishes to set its own terms when it comes to integration into that global economy. Put another way, Russia wants to have it both ways: it wants to profit from trading in the global economy, but it also wants to isolate its own economy from the competitive pressures of that same global economy. Neoliberals argue that such a position is ultimately unsustainable, because such protectionism will nurture an uncompetitive economy—after all, is that not why the Soviet Union collapsed in the first place? Thus, the only tenable policy prescription for the likes of the International Monetary Fund and the World Bank (the architects of the so-called Washington Consensus) is for Russia to liberalize its economy and open itself fully to international competition, a process that may well be forced upon it by membership of the World Trade Organization. The problem here is that Russia's inherited economy remains uncompetitive beyond the resource sector, and such liberalization would undoubtedly result in widespread social hardship. Which brings us to the purpose of this chapter: to consider the interrelationship between globalization and the territorial cohesion of the Russian Federation.

In relative terms, Russia today is a far more open and liberal economy than it was during the late Soviet period; even then, patterns of regional development were influenced by the nature of the Soviet Union's interaction with the global economy. During the 1990s, there was an opening up of the Russian economy to inward investment; the country now plays a more active role in international trade, and foreign investment and trade activity are increasingly important to its economic performance. At the same time, Russia's emergent "New Economy" is linked to the development of the telecommunications network, such that the country is literally being plugged into the global economy. The purpose of the current analysis is to determine how these processes are contributing to contemporary patterns of regional development in Russia and if, in turn, they are reinforcing existing patterns of inequality or generating new geographies of growth that promote convergence between Russia's cities and regions. Is globalization a force for cohesion, or is it contributing to the territorial fragmentation of Russia? The following discussion is divided into four sections. The first discusses how geographers theorize and conceptualize globalization, the aim being to tease out a set of ideas and concepts that can be employed in our study of the territorial consequences of globalization for Russia. The second section then turns to analyze the key dimensions of Russia's interaction with the global economy; the emphasis here is on the emergence of a new market-driven economic geography. The third section examines the patterns and dynamics of regional inequality in Russia. The fourth and concluding section considers the interrelations between globalization processes and spatial inequality in Russia and the implications of this analysis for understanding Russia's place in the world.

Geography and Globalization

It is not the purpose of this section to present a comprehensive review of globalization; such an endeavor is likely beyond any individual. Nor is it my intention to review all the work of human geographers on this issue; this may be a more plausible exercise, but it has been done by others and is beyond the requirements of the current analysis.[1] Rather, I want to present a brief review of some of the more important writers and works that seek to present a set of "concepts" that might be employed to explore the "geographical dimensions" of globalization. Before doing that, it is useful to present a definition of globalization that can help to shape our discussion. Discussion of globalization is often framed in terms of debate between the "skeptics" on the one hand and the "hyperglobalizers" on the other.[2] The focus of this debate is less on the nature of globalization and more on the issue of whether it is anything new and whether it is all-pervasive. This is a rather pointless argument, and I would prefer to see globalization as shorthand for the times in which we live—the challenge, then, being to seek to explain the essential characteristics of "contemporary globalization." The following definition by David Held and colleagues provides a useful starting point. Globalization can be thought of as

> a process (or set of processes) which embodies a transformation in the spatial organization of social relations and transactions—assessed in terms of their extensity, intensity, velocity and impact—generating transcontinental or interregional flows and networks of activity, interaction and the exercise of power.[3]

Accordingly, what makes the contemporary situation different from the past is a quantitative and qualitative difference in the *extensity* of global networks, the *intensity* of global interconnectedness, the *velocity* of global flows, and the *impact* of global interconnectedness. Undoubtedly, many would take issue with this definition; it is recognized that globalization is itself a social construction, and thus there are many different versions of globalization (though most of the literature seems to focus on globalization as a neoliberal project)—but one has to start somewhere. For the purposes of the current analysis, this definition is particularly useful because its starting point is that globalization is "a transformation in the spatial organization of social relations and transaction." Human geography, as a social science, is concerned with the spatiality of social processes; thus, it follows that globalization, as defined above, is inherently geographical. That said, geographers have had a limited impact on the geographical debate.[4] This is not because of a lack of research by geographers; rather, the other social sciences have been blind to the contributions made by human geography. This is unfortunate, because human geography has much to contribute to a study of contemporary globalization by providing explicitly geographical ways of thinking about some of the essential ingredients that characterize our global world.

David Harvey is probably the most-often-quoted human geographer writing on globalization. In his 1989 volume, *The Condition of Postmodernity,* he developed the concept of "time-space compression" to explain the changing relationship between space and time.[5] He suggested that since the beginning of the 1970s, the world has been experiencing "an intense phase of time-space compression that has had a disorientating and disruptive impact upon political-economic practices, the balance of class power, as well as upon cultural and social life."[6] Advances in telecommunications and transportation are central to this process, which is synonymous with post-

Fordism. Thus, there is a fundamental shift in the relation between distance (space) and time; the global information highway renders the friction of distance redundant. But this is a far-from-universal process, it does not have an impact on all aspects of economic activity (there are large parts of the contemporary economy that are far from weightless), and it benefits some and not others, generating new rounds of uneven development. Rather than precipitating the end of geography, contemporary globalization adds new complexities. In many ways, geography is even more important as an individual agent's, region's, or state's place is defined by its relationships and relative position in a set of global networks. Even without knowing, contemporary consumers are entwined in global production networks when they visit the supermarket and go about their weekly shopping.

Geographers are particularly interested in the importance of *place* as a source of individual and collective identity—what Doreen Massey calls a "global sense of place."[7] Globalization is not a homogenizing force that renders everywhere the same; individuals and regions resist threats to their identity and rework external influences, producing hybrid identities. Notions of *scale* are central to geographical research on globalization, but there is no consensus on how one should theorize scale.[8] Clearly, contemporary globalization tends to favor the global as a scale of analysis, but little empirical work on globalization is truly global in scope. Instead, the focus tends to be upon the impact of globalization on the functioning of the state (this book is a case in point); here, globalization is most often portrayed as threatening the legitimacy and/or effectiveness of a state; thus, a state may have been "hollowed out." The response, then, is to look at regionalism, both as a form of cooperation between states (e.g., the European Union) and as a substate scale as a means by which it is possible to counteract globalization. Thus, economic integration is seen as a means for member states to protect their own interests and values against global competition. At the regional scale, "new regionalism" represents an attempt by regions to negotiate their own place in the global economy independent of the national state.[9] Here, regions seek to market themselves to attract global capital and thus benefit materially.[10]

Rather than theorize scale in terms of a simple global/local dichotomy, geographers see the reworking of scale as a central component of contemporary globalization. Scale is itself a social construction, and it serves the neoliberal globalization project to privilege the global over the local and thus to see the force of globalization as inevitable and irresistible. However, this is not the case; contemporary globalization is highly contested. Massey

84 Michael Bradshaw

has developed the idea of "power geometry" to examine how different social groups and individuals are placed in relation to the shifting flows and interconnections that characterize contemporary globalization. Erik Swyngedouw has offered the notion of *glocalization* to explain the complex reworking of scale synonymous with contemporary globalization.[11] Thus, we get a sense of globalization as a complex network of actors (e.g., these actors could be states, transnational corporations, international agencies, regional governments, nongovernmental organizations and other coalitions, and even individuals) with differing degrees of influence and power. The boundaries of the networks are fluid, and these networks are not fixed in space or time but are in constant flux, making and then remaking relations between institutions, people, and places. The very nature of a place is thus defined by its place in the network, which is a product of its relationship with other places.

To return to Held and his colleagues' definition of globalization, what is qualitatively different about contemporary globalization are the extensity, intensity, and impact of this global interconnectedness. In a useful review of geographer's work on globalization, Eric Sheppard introduces the notion of "positionality" to the conceptual armory. Borrowing on feminist and postcolonial writings, as well as network theory, Sheppard proposes the term "positionality" "to describe how different entities are positioned with respect to one another in space/time."[12] Another term might be "geographic situatedness," which relates to an agent's position relative to others and the power relations that flow from that position and thus the ability of the agent to bring about change.[13] It is not just that individuals are positioned differently in the power geometry of contemporary globalization; different places are as well. For example, the observation that Africa has fallen off the map is a reflection of the fact that some places are "better" situated than others. This reflects the geographically uneven nature of contemporary globalization, which reinforces the need to pay attention to the spatial consequences of the globalization processes.

To summarize our discussion so far, for geographers contemporary globalization is characterized by a qualitative change in the relationship between space and time. But far from heralding the end of geography, globalization creates conditions whereby geography matters more than ever. Contemporary globalization is characterized by a complex reworking of scales and networks; scale in not reduced to a simple global/local dichotomy, with the global dictating local outcomes; rather, places are a product of complex power geometries that are contested and generate multiple outcomes. How else can one explain the persistence of local identity? Contemporary globalization is characterized by spatially uneven processes that privilege certain actors and places, often at the expense of others, and that generate uneven patterns of material development and political power. Furthermore, the ability of agents to influence their situation is related to their position relative to other agents; thus, not all agents and places are equal in the global network. In fact, contemporary globalization is seen by some as a particular geographical imagination that is the product of a powerful elite representing U.S. political and economic interests. But this does not mean resistance is futile. It is possible for institutions and agents to bring about change. As Massey observes, if that were not the case, what would be the point of politics?[14]

When it comes to globalization, it is all too easy to engage in "informed commentary," as I just have. But the real challenge is to ground globalization in a theoretically informed, empirically rigorous analysis of outcomes.[15] In the current context, the key question is: How has economic-geographical globalization affected patterns of regional change in Russia? According to Peter Dicken: "Today, we live in a world in which *deep integration,* organized primarily between geographically extensive and complex transnational production networks and through a diversity of mechanisms, is becoming increasingly pervasive." Furthermore, for Dicken, "globalization is a syndrome of processes and outcomes that are manifested very unevenly in both time and space."[16] Thus, we are homing in on an empirical project that seeks to examine Russia's post-Soviet incorporation into those transnational production systems via its involvement in international trade and its success in attracting inward investment. As a project in economic-geographical analysis, we are interested in how Russia's increasing connectedness with the global economy benefits particular regions and excludes others, thus, contributing to patterns of uneven development.

Russia's Interaction with the Global Economy

This section address two sets of questions. First, what is Russia's involvement in foreign trade, and which regions are most engaged in foreign trade activity? And second, what is the nature of foreign investment in Russia, and which regions are the major beneficiaries of foreign direct investment?[17]

In considering Russia's interaction with the global economy, it is important to note that even during the late Soviet period, foreign economic activity was vitally important to the Soviet economy.[18] First, this was because trade with Eastern Europe, principally the supply of cheap energy and raw materials, was an essential means by which Moscow ensured the loyalty of its client states. Second, this was because trade with the "West" was an important source of imports of food and technology, both of which compensated for major failings in the domestic economy. It is widely accepted that the windfall profits that accrued to the Soviet Union in the mid-1970s played a major role in propping up a failing economy and that the decline in energy revenues in the mid-1980s revealed the underlying weaknesses of the Soviet economy that played a major part in the collapse of the Soviet system. Thus, it was not the case that the Soviet Union (and its constituent republics) was totally isolated from the global economy. However, it is the case that foreign economic relations were carefully managed by the central planning system via the state monopoly on foreign trade. This served to isolate enterprises and regions from the competitive pressures of the global economy.

In the late Soviet period, there were attempts to partially liberalize the domestic economy, and Soviet enterprises were permitted to create joint ventures with foreign companies. However, the collapse of the Soviet system and the subsequent liberalization of the Russian economy have dramatically changed the scale of engagement between economic actors in Russia and the global economy. Now the stocks of some Russian companies are traded on foreign stock markets, Russian companies regularly seek finance from international capital markets, and foreign companies can set up 100 percent foreign-owned subsidiaries in Russia. But, as we shall see, liberalization has not resulted in a substantial change in the structure Russia's trade with the global economy. Nor has the geographical impact of Russia's trade changed that much. Thus, there is both continuity and change.

The Geography of Russian Foreign Trade Participation

Since the mid-1990s, there has been a steady growth in the value of Russia's foreign trade. Figure 3.1 shows a dramatic growth in export earnings and a corresponding increase in imports following the 1998 financial crisis. The initial impact of the crisis was to depress the level of imports as the fourfold devaluation of the ruble made imported goods prohibitively expensive. But as exports recovered and then grew rapidly as a result of increased revenue from energy (and the increased volume of oil exports) and other resource exports. So imports recovered, but at a slower rate, resulting in a substantial positive trade balance. The commodity structure of Russia's exports reveals

Figure 3.1. The Dynamics of Russian Foreign Trade, 1995–2004

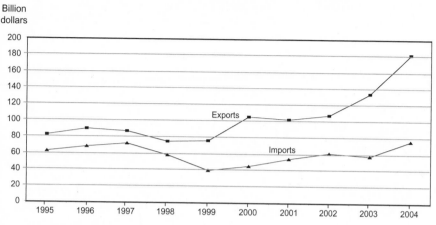

Source: Rosstat.

a very strong resource orientation; in 2004, according to UN data, exports of mineral fuels and products accounted for 50.2 percent of Russian exports (Russian statistics suggest that 41.2 percent was mineral products).[19]

In addition, iron and steel accounted for a further 8.8 percent, aluminum for 2.7 percent, and wood and wood products for 2.5 percent. Together, these commodities accounted for 64.2 percent of Russia's exports, and there is now a great deal of debate about its reliance on the resource sector and the significance of high oil and gas prices to its recent economic recovery.[20] The commodity structure of Russian imports is very different; according to Rosstat, in 2004 machinery and equipment accounted for 41.2 percent of imports and consumer goods accounted for 18.3 percent. Items such as cars and mobile telephones figure heavily in machinery imports, and thus the growth of imports seems more related to growing consumer demand than increased investment by industry. In the late Soviet period, export earning were used to import Western technology to compensate for the failings of the domestic innovation system in key industries, but this does not now appear to be the case, and there is growing concern about the lack of investment in Russia's industrial economy. As things stand at present, Russia's international comparative advantage is as a supplier of natural resources and little else. This does not bode well for the country's sustainable economic recovery.[21]

Given the rather narrow nature of Russia's foreign trade activity, one might think it would be relatively straightforward to determine the geography of foreign trade participation. Table 3.1 lists the country's top ten exporting and importing regions, and figures 3.2 and 3.3 map the geographical distribution of exports and imports. In both instances, the data are for trade with countries that are not members of the Commonwealth of Independent States. These data must be treated with caution. On the export side, there are problems as a result of "transfer pricing," a practice whereby the resource extraction companies do not record the value of the trading associated with their production, which is passed on to a subsidiary "trading company" that is often located in Moscow rather than in the resource-producing region.

Furthermore, that trading activity is recorded as a service activity. The impact of transfer pricing is quite clear in table 3.1, where Moscow accounts for just over 25 percent of Russia's exports but the major oil and gas regions are located in Tyumen Oblast in West Siberia. In fact, with the exception of Moscow and Leningrad, all the other top ten regions have some degree of resource specialization. The problem with the import data is more general, in that they do not identify the final region where imported goods are utilized.

Thus, the top ten regions contain all of Russia's major port regions, plus the Moscow region and one or two major industrial centers. Consequently, the geographic patterns of exports and imports are different. The exporting regions are predominantly in the Volga-Urals region and Siberia, and the

Table 3.1. Top Ten Exporting and Importing Regions in Russia, 2002

	Exports			Imports	
Region	Value (million dollars)	Percentage of Total	Region	Value (million dollars)	Percentage of Total
Moscow	22,946.8	25.12	Moscow	14,732.6	41.06
Khanty-Mansi	14,528.3	15.61	Saint Petersburg	4,731.7	13.19
Irkutsk	3,631.9	3.98	Moscow Oblast	2,803.5	7.81
Samara	3,166.3	3.47	Kaliningrad	1,544.2	4.30
Sverdlovsk	2,763.0	3.02	Leningrad	967.7	2.70
Tatarstan	2,595.6	2.84	Krasnodar	872.7	2.43
Yamal-Nenets	2,227.0	2.49	Primorskiy	754.7	2.10
Bashkortostan	2,202.7	2.41	Samara	659.6	1.84
Leningrad	2,111.8	2.31	Yekaterinburg	487.9	1.36
Perm	1,930.2	2.11	Nizhniy Novgorod	441.9	1.23
Total	58,103.6	63.36	Total	27,996.5	78.02

Source: Goskomstat Rossii, *Regioni Rossii 2003* (Moscow: Goskomstat, 2003).

importing regions are the port regions in the northwest south and east, plus the major urban agglomerations in European Russia and some resource-rich regions in Siberia. However, viewed across the country's entire eighty-nine regions, there is actually a close coincidence between importing and exporting regions.

The correlation between the two data sets mapped in figures 3.2 and 3.3 is actually 0.8; this is likely because the greatest number of regions have a low level of involvement in both imports and exports. As table 3.1 shows, the top ten regions account for 63.4 percent of exports and 78 percent of imports, but only three regions appear on both lists. So we can conclude that Russia's exports are predominately generated by the natural resources from regions in the Volga-Urals and Siberia and that its imports are principally aimed at satisfying consumer demand in the major urban agglomerations and some resource-rich regions.

Figure 3.2. Exports from Russia's Regions in 2002 to Countries Not Belonging to the Commonwealth of Independent States

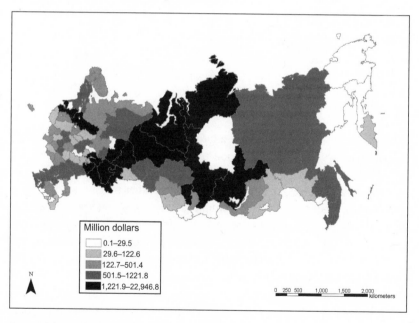

Source: Goskomstat Rossii.

Figure 3.3. Imports to Russia's Regions in 2002 from Countries Not Belonging to the Commonwealth of Independent States

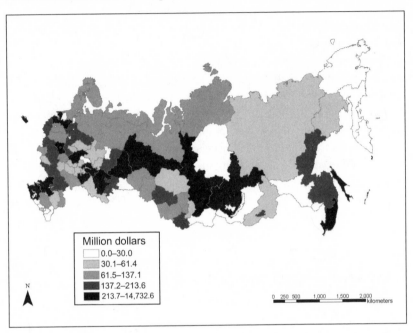

Source: Goskomstat Rossii.

The Geography of Foreign Investment in Russia

With a population of 146 million, a large industrial economy, and substantial resource wealth, there are good reasons to expect that Russia would have emerged as a major attractor of foreign direct investment (FDI). However, this has not been the case; relative both to other transition economies and to other emerging market economies; Russia has underperformed. As Ögütçü observes: "The cumulative figure for FDI in Russia from 1991 through the end of 2001 represents $18.2 billion, or only 5 percent of domestic fixed capital formation. This performance may be compared with FDI in China of $46 billion on 2000 alone, and more than $2,000 billion in the United States in 2001, and a global total of $1,270 billion in 2000."[22] In absolute terms, Russia's level of FDI compared well with the other transition economies, coming third in 2000 behind Poland and the Czech Republic; but on a per capita basis, Russia is well down the list. The reasons for this relative underperformance are well understood and are related to the unstable nature of the investment environment and the high level of country risk resulting from political instability. Though the Vladimir Putin era has brought relative stability, the actions against the oil company Yukos and other events have undermined confidence in the security of property rights in Russia. A final indicator of a lack of confidence, this time on the part of Russian investors, is that the level of capital outflow, or capital flight, continues to be high relative to the level of capital inflow. However, some of the capital flight is now returning in the form of FDI, and that accounts for the much of the growth in 2005.

The dynamics of FDI in Russia between 1994 and 2005 are shown in figure 3.4; during this period, the total amount of FDI was nearly $60 billion and the average was just over about $4.5 billion. Total foreign investment in Russia is much higher because the statistics include portfolio investments and a category called "other," which is primarily credits from international financial organizations, such as the European Bank for Reconstruction and Development. On average, between 1995 and 2003 annual total foreign investment was in the region of $13 billion, and FDI accounted for 36.7 percent of total capital inflow.[23] Recent data from the United Nations show that in 2004 total inward FDI stock was valued at $98.4 billion and accounted for 16.9 percent of gross domestic product (GDP) (and outward FDI accounted for 14.0 percent). This compares with China in 2004, where inward FDI stock was $245.5 billion, which accounted for 15.9 percent of GDP (outward FDI stock was only 2.4 percent of GDP).[24] Thus, in both a relative and absolute sense, FDI in Russia is of limited significance to the national economy. However, if it is concentrated in certain sectors and regions of the economy, then it can have a more significant impact, both in terms of its contribution to the national economy and its impact on regional development.

There is a considerable body of literature on the regional distribution of FDI in Russia.[25] For the purposes of our analysis, discussions focuses on three aspects of FDI inflows: the sectoral structure of FDI (see figure 3.5), its geographical origins, and its regional distribution The theories on the motives for FDI suggest a number of reasons why a foreign company might invest in a host country. In addition, the context of the post-Soviet economic transition provides a host of new opportunities as new sectors of activity, such as the service economy, need to be developed and the antiquated industrial base requires modernization if it is to remain internationally competitive. Furthermore, the labor force in most transition economies is well educated and labor costs are relatively low by international standards. Con-

Figure 3.4. The Dynamics of Foreign Direct Investment in Russia, 1994–2005

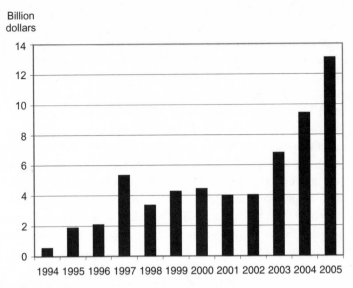

Source: Goskomstat Rossii.

sequently, in East Central Europe in particular, investors have set up production facilities to export to third markets; the automotive industry is a case in point. The sectoral structure of FDI in Russia suggests two motives: market access and resource development. Producing manufacturing goods for exports to third markets is not a factor in Russian FDI at present. Thus, Russia is not fully incorporated into global production chains beyond the supply of basic energy resources and raw materials. Before the 1998 financial crisis, the service sector was the major recipient of FDI, and since 1998, industry has come to predominate, with the oil and gas and retail industries receiving the most investment.

An analysis of the geographical origins of Russia's FDI reveals some surprising results; Cyprus ($5.1 billion) is the single largest investor, followed by the United States ($4.3 billion), the United Kingdom ($2.8 billion), the Netherlands ($2.8 billion), and Germany ($2.5 billion). Luxembourg and the Virgin Islands also figure in the top ten investors. Japan, a major source of FDI for the global economy, ranks ninth, with an accumulated investment $1.3 billion. Obviously, the appearance of Cyprus, Luxembourg, and the Virgin Islands in the top ten reflects the return of Russian "flight capital," and in a sense it is not "foreign" investment. However, it does suggest that Russian entrepreneurs are increasingly optimistic about the prospects for the Russian economy because they are willing to invest funds offshore in the domestic economy. In addition, as "insiders," these investors are better placed to know where the best investment opportunities are compared with their foreign competitors. Data on investment by sector and by geographical origin suggest that returning flight capital is aimed at the retail and service sectors of the economy, rather than industry. If one strips away the flight capital elements of Russian FDI, then the United States and the core economies of the European Union are the major investors and the current dynamics suggest an increasing role for the EU relative to the United States. This is certainly the case when one looks at the Russian oil and gas industry, where companies such as BP, Royal-Dutch Shell, Total, and ConocoPhillips are substantially increasing their investment activity in Russia.

Figure 3.5. The Sectoral Structure of Russian Foreign Direct Investment, 2004

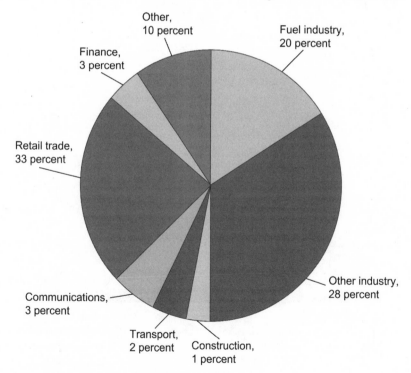

Source: Rosstat Web site (http://www.gks.ru).

The final category of this analysis is the geographical distribution of FDI in Russia. Figure 3.6 shows the distribution of FDI by Russia's seven federal districts, while figure 3.7 maps cumulative FDI per capita at the oblast level. Figure 3.6 reveals the major roles played by the Central and Far Eastern districts, but this prominence is due to a small number of regions.

Table 3.2 shows the top ten recipient regions in the period 2000–2, plus accumulated FDI for the period 1995–2002. Because the total volume of FDI is relatively small in any given year, it is possible for one or two projects to change the regional pattern of FDI. There has been one constant, the dominance of the Moscow region (defined as Moscow City and the surrounding Moscow Oblast); however, in recent years the extent of that dominance of has dwindled. In the mid-1990s, when the service sector was the major recipient of FDI, well over half of FDI was destined for Moscow City. Since the 1998 financial crisis, industry has attracted the majority of FDI,

Figure 3.6. Distribution of Foreign Direct Investment in Russia by Federal District, 1995–2003

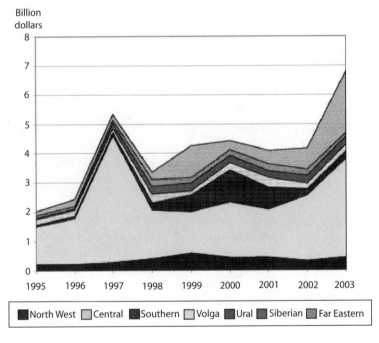

Source: Goskomstat Rossii, various years.

Figure 3.7. Cumulative Foreign Direct Investment per Capita in Russia's Regions, 1995–2002

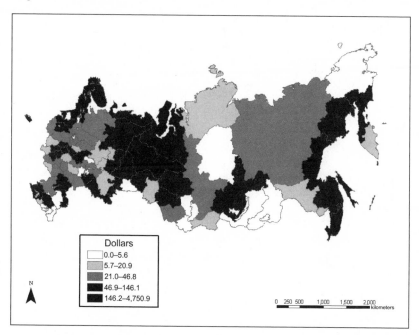

Source: Goskomstat Rossii.

and the share of the capital city has declined relative to the surrounding oblast, and since 1998 the majority of FDI in Russia has been located outside the Moscow region, although in 2002 the region did reclaim its dominant position.

At the federal district level, the changing fortunes of the Central District are entirely due to Moscow region. Saint Petersburg and Leningrad Oblast explain the relative significance of the Northwest. In the case of the Southern District, FDI has been significant in the food industry, and there has been a construction boom related to the construction of an oil pipeline from Tengiz in Kazakhstan to Novorossiysk in Krasnodar Kray. The position of the Far Eastern District is largely explained by the multi-billion-dollar oil and gas projects offshore of Sakhalin Island. In 2005, the total expenditure on the Sakhalin projects was $4.7 billion.[26] Figure 3.8 illustrates that FDI in Russia is actually concentrated in a relatively small number of regions. On aver-age, the top ten regions account for well over 75 percent of total FDI

Table 3.2. Top Ten Recipients of Foreign Direct Investment in Russia, 2000–2 and 1995–2002

Recipient, 2000	Percentage of Investment, 2000	Recipient, 2001	Percentage of Investment, 2001	Recipient, 2002	Percentage of Investment, 2002	Recipient, 1995–2002	Percentage of Investment, 1995–2002
Moscow City	33.25	Moscow	29.01	Moscow	37.7	Moscow	39.62
Krasnodar	21.65	Krasnodar	17.24	Sakhalin	16.99	Moscow Oblast	9.40
Sakhalin	5.56	Sakhalin	9.41	Moscow Oblast	14.72	Sakhalin	8.64
Leningrad	4.64	Moscow Oblast	7.86	Tyumen	4.22	Krasnodar	8.12
Moscow Oblast	4.63	Leningrad	5.98	Leningrad	2.88	Saint Petersburg	4.28
Novosibirsk	3.43	Samara	2.96	Sverdlovsk	2.49	Leningrad	3.41
Tyumen	3.34	Saint Petersburg	2.87	Samara	2.44	Tyumen	2.51
Saint Petersburg	3.31	Tyumen	2.77	Arkhangelsk	2.41	Samara	2.26
Volgograd	1.74	Sverdlovsk	2.55	Krasnodar	2.25	Novosibirsk	2.04
Kaluga	1.68	Novosibirsk	2.24	Saint Petersburg	2.10	Sverdlovsk	1.85
Top 10 percent	83.23	Top 10 percent	82.89	Top 10 percent	88.2	Top 10 percent	82.13

Source: Goskomstat, Regioni Rossii 2003 (Moscow: Goskomstat, 2003).

Figure 3.8. Regional Variations in Gross Regional Product, 1990–2004 (coefficients of variation)

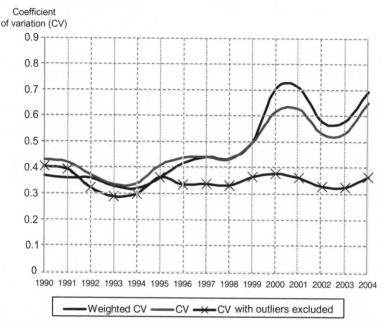

Coefficient
of variation (CV)

——Weighted CV ━━CV ─✕─CV with outliers excluded

Sources: The data used in this analysis were obtained from Nadezhda Mikheeva, "Analysis of In-terregional Inequality in Russia," *Studies on Russian Economic Development* 10 (1999): 514–21; Goskomstat Rossii, *Regioni Rossii 2002* (Moscow: Goskomstat, 2002); Goskomstat Rossii, *Regioni Rossii 2003;* Goskomstat, *Regioni Rossii 2005* (Goskomstat, Moscow, 2005); and Goskomstat, *Regioni Rossii 2006* (Goskomstat, Moscow, 2006). The statistical analysis was conducted by Karen Vartapetov. Data for 1990–93 gross regional product per capita were obtained from Mikheeva, "Analysis of Interregional Inequality in Russia"; on the 2000–4 employed from Goskomstat, *Regioni Rossii 2006*. For 1992–93 and 2000–3, interregional price levels were meas-ured on the basis of a "food basket" with nineteen to twenty-one items; for 1994–99, data on regional "subsistence minimum" were used. These data were not available for all regions for 1992–94. Due to this, the number of regions varies over the period (seventy-six in 1992–94, sev-enty-eight in 1995–2004). Data for 1990–91 were not adjusted for regional price levels, because the Soviet statistics did not provide these figures.

in Russia. Furthermore, the list of regions appearing in the top ten is rela-tively stable. Data for 2003 are now available, but the pattern has changed little. Given that there are eighty-nine federal subjects or regions within the Russian Federation, the majority of Russian regions are untouched by foreign investors.

On the basis of previous research, it is possible to identify a number of different types of regions among the major recipients of Russia's FDI:[27]

- The Moscow region (Moscow City and Moscow Oblast) serves as the premier entrepôt and the control center for the national economy. Moscow is also a major market in its own right.

- A number of regional industrial/financial centers serve a regional market: Saint Petersburg and Leningrad Oblast in the northwest, Krasnodar in the south, Samara on the Volga, Sverdlovsk in the Urals, and Novosibirsk in Siberia.

- Some regions have a major port or gateway function: Saint Petersburg and Leningrad Oblast act as Russia's gateway to the Baltic Sea and northern Europe; Krasnodar provides access to the Black Sea and also acts as a transit route to Central Asia; and Primorye in the Far East acts as the gateway to northeast Asia and the Pacific.

- Some regions benefit from substantial mineral wealth and have attracted foreign investments, for example, Tyumen (the most important oil- and gas-producing region in Russia) and Sakhalin (the location of the two largest foreign oil and gas projects in Russia).

- Some regions benefit from the post-1998 growth of import substituting activity. This activity, which is diminishing as the ruble continues to appreciate, serves to reinforce the dominance of the regional/industrial centers located in the European regions of the country.

A more quantitative analysis using econometric analysis to empirically "unbundle" the determinants of the regional distribution of FDI within Russia suggests that market size, infrastructure development, and policy framework factors explain most of the observed variation in FDI across Russia's regions.[28] However, it also clear that natural resource endowment and relative economic-geographic position also play an important part. The question now remains, How do the geographies of foreign economic activity map onto to the geographies and economic growth and inequality in Russia? Is Russia's increased involvement in the global economy contributing to growth in regional inequality?

Regional Economic Performance and Inequality in Russia

This section addresses three questions. First, what factors have influenced regional development in Russia since the collapse of the Soviet Union in 1991? Second, what impact has regional performance had on levels of interregional inequality? And third, what has been the policy response of the federal government in Moscow?[29]

Regional Economic Performance

It is now generally recognized that the Soviet central planning system promoted a geographical distribution of economy and settlement that was different from that that might have been developed in a market-driven economic system. There is a tendency to describe the economic geography of the Soviet Union as illogical and inefficient, resulting in people doing the wrong things in the wrong places. This misses the point; the spatial logic of the Soviet system, such as there was one, was not driven by market economics but by the primacy of ideological and strategic concerns. Thus, Soviet locational decisions should be understood within the wider framework of the political-economic system of the time and not the logic of the market economy. Russia's resultant economic geography becomes a problematic inheritance when systemic transformation changes the logic of the system to one based on market principles. It is only then that one can talk of an economic geography ill suited to the needs of Russia's contemporary market economy, where quite literally people are doing the wrong things in the wrong places. Hill and Gaddy's *The Siberian Curse* is the most persuasive and eloquent analysis of this problem.[30] Using a measure of "temperature per capita," they demonstrate how the Soviet system promoted settlement and economic development in regions far more remote and northerly than made economic sense in market terms. They conclude that Russia must now "warm up" by relocating its economy to the more hospitable climes of European Russia. But, as this analysis is demonstrating, this is no easy matter because Russia is reliant upon a resource economy that is predominantly in those northern and eastern regions.[31] However, that does not means that there have not been changes to Russia's economic geography since the collapse of the Soviet Union.

The immediate consequence of the collapse of the Soviet system and the liberalization of the economy was the so-called transitional recession, a substantial decline in the level of economic activity. This shock to the economic system was felt differently across the sectors and regions of the Russian economy. There has now been a good deal of academic research examining the patterns of regional economic change during the 1990s.[32] For the period 1991–98, the consensus appears to be that the key factor influencing regional economic performance was inherited economic structure. Urban agglomeration effects were also important, but there is little evidence that either a region's attitude toward economic reform or its political complexion had much influence on its actual economic performance.[33] To summarize, the regions that performed the best, or suffered the least, were those dominated by economic activities that declined the least during the transitional recession. Those economic activities were predominantly in the resource sector, and the sectors that suffered the most included machinery manufacturing and light industry.[34]

The geographical consequences of this situation were that the northern and eastern regions suffered the least, while the European regions, where the bulk of the population resides, suffered the most. The 1998 Russian financial crisis marks both continuity and change. The devaluation of the ruble reduced the relative cost for domestic producers and increased the cost of imported goods. This was good for exporters, for it increased their profit margins. It was also good for the food industry, which now finds itself able to compete against imported goods on price and still make a profit. The decline in production related to the transitional recession and import competition meant that domestic producers had idle capacity and where able to increase production, albeit using antiquated equipment, without having to make substantial new investments. The geography of the import-substituting recovery favored the European regions of the country, while the resource exporters remained strong. Thus, the post-1998 geography of economic performance appears more balanced. Russia's recent economic performance has had the result of further bolstering the status of the resource regions and has also lead to a strengthening of the ruble such that the real exchange rate has now past pre-1998 levels. A recent report by the World Bank suggests that this is changing the nature of regional economic performance:

> The factors that supported broad-based growth in the post-crisis period have now been practically exhausted. The ruble has appreciated back to its pre-crisis level, capacity constraints are increasingly binding, and Russian labor is now relatively expensive compared to most countries in the region. Under these conditions, Russian producers have come under increasingly competitive pressure, and only those sectors and firms that achieved the most rapid growth since the late 1990s are proving themselves equipped to meet these pressures.[35]

Thus, we may be moving into a new phase in the relationship between regional economic performance and regional equality, a phase that could have worrying implications for territorial cohesion.

Regional Inequality

The literature on post-Soviet regional equality in Russia is in agreement on a number matters. First, Russia displays high levels of interregional inequality, with very substantial gaps between the richest and poorest regions (a characteristic that is amplified by the two rich outliers of Moscow City and Tyumen Oblast). Second, in the first part of the 1990s, those levels of inequality increased. Third, although there is less research on the matter, there also seems to be a growing consensus that after 1998 the level of inequality stabilized and then declined.[36] This suggests a process of relative convergence brought about by the import-substituting benefits of the ruble's devaluation in 1998, which prompted a recovery in light manufacturing and food processing in the European regions of Russia. However, although inequality is calculated on a per capita basis, this measure only tells us about the degree of variation between the richest and poorest regions; it tells us nothing about the share of the total population living in the poorer regions, an issue that is discussed below. Furthermore, the ruble has now appreciated past its pre-1998 levels, and there are now renewed competitive pressures on domestic manufacturing, suggesting a potential reverse in the fortunes of the European regions of the country. Fourth and finally, there is less agreement on the relationship between the levels of inequality between regions (interregional) and within regions (intraregional).[37] The analysis of inequality within regions is based on household surveys, whereas the analysis between regions uses the standard statistical indictors published by the State Statistical Service, Rosstat.

Furthermore, the results from such research vary widely, depending on the variable used. A recent World Bank study concludes that within-region differences are more important than interregional differences as a driver of national-level inequality. The study concludes that most of Russia's poor people live in "average regions" in terms of socioeconomic development.[38] An earlier study concluded that "the share of inequality in Russia coming from the between-regions component is large (close to a third of total inequality), growing, and accounts for most of the increase in national inequality over 1994–2000."[39] The two conclusions are not necessarily contradictory. The World Bank study was for the 1999–2002 period, when we know that interregional inequality was declining, whereas the earlier study was for the earlier period, when it was increasing. It may be that within-region inequality has always been the dominant source and it is the relative share of interregional inequality that has changed. By international standards, the level of interregional equality is high, but not as high as China, for example. For our current purposes, it is interregional inequality that is of interest: first, because we wish to examine the relationship between globalization, regional change, and regional inequality; and second, because there is every indication that the level of interregional inequality will increase in the future.

The information in figures 3.8, 3.9, and 3.10 helps to illustrate our discussion so far. Figure 3.8 shows the results of an ongoing analysis of level of interregional variation in gross regional product (GRP). The measures charted are standard techniques for measuring regional inequality, known as the coefficient of variation (CV); the weighted CV accounts for variation in the population regions, and the CV (outliers excluded) measure excludes the very rich regions of Moscow City and Tyumen Oblast and the poorest region of Ingushetia. The analysis suggests that the levels of inequality have increased since 2002, but the removal of the outliers makes clear the distorting impact of Moscow and Tyumen. For present purposes, it is the dynamic that matters and the realization that this is a measure of variance around the mean and not an absolute measure of inequality against a constant benchmark. An increase in the value simply means that there is a greater degree of variance.[40] The analysis, minus Moscow and Tyumen, suggests a limited amount of variance in relative inequality, but it tells us nothing of the absolute levels. Figures 3.9 and 3.10 are a less technical portrayal of the situation in 2001–2.

The information presented in figures 3.9 and 3.10 is the value of production in a region on the basis of domestic prices. Therefore, this is not a measure of income or living standard. There is a reasonable relationship between living standards and GRP per capita, but here we are more interested in the relationship between GRP per capita and foreign trade and investment activity. Figure 3.8 shows a dynamic that matches the discussions above of regional economic performance, with regional inequality increasing during the early 1990s when the transitional recession resulted in an economic crisis; the post-1998 import-substituting economic recovery is then mirrored in reductions in levels of inequality. Figure 3.9 shows the clear northerly and easterly impact of resource specialization. Of course, the relatively

Figure 3.9. Gross Regional Product per Capita in Russia, 2001

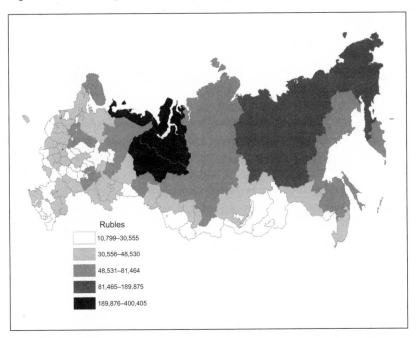

Source: Goskomstat Rossii.

small population in those regions exaggerates this; but in absolute terms, they do make a major contribution to both GRP and GDP. Figure 3.10 dramatically illustrates the fact that there is a relatively small number of regions with higher than average GRP, twenty-two in 2002. In 2001, the top ten regions accounted for 50.7 percent of GRP. Outside Moscow and Saint Petersburg, all the others, with the possible exception of Krasnodar on the Black Sea, have a strong resource orientation. Furthermore, the twenty regions where the resource sector makes up more than 40 percent of industrial output together accounted for 33.3 percent of total Russian GRP in 2001.[41] It seems reasonable to conclude that Russia's resource orientation and the relative success of this sector have been factor factors shaping regional economic performance and levels of interregional inequality since the early 1990s.

It is beyond the scope of this analysis to dwell on the complexities of fiscal federalism,[42] but the actual level of living standards in a given region is not just a product of the value of production. In a large country such as Rus-

Figure 3.10. Gross Regional Product per Capita in Russia, by Region, 2002

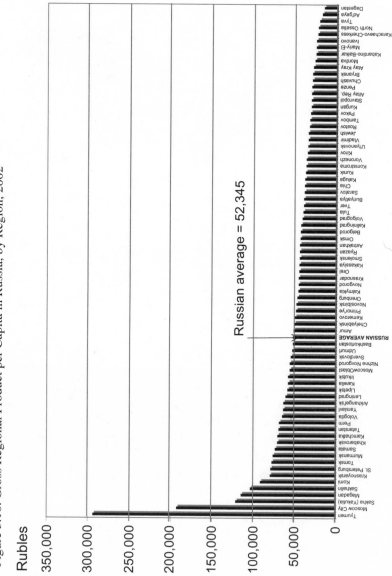

Russian average = 52,345

Source: Goskomstat Rossii.

sia, with wide variations in the level of economic development and relative performance, the federal government plays a role in equalizing living standards by orchestrating transfer payments from rich (donor) regions to poor (recipient) regions. Because of the situation presented in figure 3.10, there are relatively few donor regions and a large number of net recipients. An analysis by Hanson shows that about thirty of the poorest regions in Russia regularly depend on transfers from the federal budget for half or more of their own budgetary revenue.[43] These regions contain about 30 percent of the country's population and geographically they are concentrated in the southern regions. Hanson's study also reveals that in comparative terms the amount of national income (i.e., GDP) redistributed among the regions by the fiscal federal system is relatively modest. Furthermore, as many studies have revealed, it is far from transparent and open to political manipulation.

Unfortunately, the tax reforms introduced by President Putin have increased the degree of central control over the tax system, though the levels of funds dispersed to the regions has not declined as a result. Until recently, despite its obvious regional problems, Russia did not have a regional policy nor a ministry responsible for regional development. This changed in late 2004, when a new Ministry for Regional Development was created, and in June 2005 the ministry issued a concept for a strategy for the socioeconomic development of the country's regions. This concept suggests a change of tack; instead of trying to promote growth across all Russia's regions, it proposes focusing on ten or so propulsive regions. The exact status of the strategy document is unclear, and as of early 2006 no further progress had been made. What those propulsive regions will be is unclear; however, it is suggested that they will not be resource regions. Instead, those regions will provide the tax revenue to promote a set of internationally competitive growth regions. Clearly, this is a major departure and is recognition that the current geography of Russia's engagement with the global economy is not going to generate a sustainable economic recovery that benefits the majority of the population. Until there are more details, it is too early to assess the prospects for success.

Conclusions

Four main conclusions can be reached on the interrelationship between Russia's contemporary engagement with the global economy and the affects of that activity on processes of regional development and territorial cohesion.

First, Russia's engagement with the global economic system is primarily as a supplier of energy and natural resources. Recent price trends have delivered sizable windfall profits, but this is not likely to be sustainable in the long run and is already distorting the economy. Furthermore, as was the case in the late Soviet period, there is a substantial transfer of "resource rent" from the resource-producing regions in Siberia and the major consuming regions, primarily in the European regions of Russia. The dramatic rejuvenation of Moscow and the current high living standards enjoyed by its growing elite and middle class are likely paid for by oil and gas exports from Tyumen as well as the output of other resource regions.

Second, as hinted at above, the sectoral and regional consequences of Russia's trade relations and pattern of foreign investment are clearly serving to aggravate regional inequality. The resource sector has proven resilient, but the economic fortunes of the regions where most of the population reside have been less positive. It is not so much the outliers at the top and the bottom that are the problem as the large number of average regions that are totally isolated from the global economy and where the majority of Russia's poor reside. This is a clear case of how globalization promotes increased inequality, and it has serious implications for Russia's territorial cohesion. On the one hand, the successful regions will want to keep what they have and will be resentful of funds being siphoned off to support other regions; one the other hand, the social pressures felt in the poorer regions may challenge the integrity of both the regional and federal governments.[44]

Third, the nature of Russia's engagement with the global economy is serving to promote imbalance and inequality, which require serious attention. Though there are signs of improvement, the current fiscal federal structure does not seem up to the task, and a new regional development strategy emphasizing selective growth will likely put even more stress on the federal transfer and welfare system to support those average regions that will not benefit from priority investment. Clearly, the hope is that people will move from poor to rich regions, but the population is not that mobile. Furthermore, many of Russia's most disadvantaged groups do not want to leave the social networks they have created to survive in the harsh realities of the market economy. If the propulsive regions grow and the resource regions continue to thrive, there is a real danger that the rest of the regions will be left behind and that this will create real social tensions, particularly if that poverty maps onto Russia's potentially explosive ethnic map.

Fourth and finally, there is an obvious gap between the theoretical elegance of geographical writing on globalization and the more traditional empirically based analysis of regional patterns of foreign trade and development. An empirical analysis clearly illustrates how the increased internationalization of the Russian economy, an obvious component of globalization, is linked to processes of uneven economic recovery and interregional inequality. However, to explain the processes generating these changes requires a case study approach to particular regions and projects, which is beyond the scope of this chapter.[45]

Nevertheless, there is much research that should be done on the asymmetrical impact of globalization upon the regions, places, and people that constitute contemporary Russia. Yet one should not overestimate the significance of such external factors; their significance is that they serve to amplify underlying and long-established patterns of regional development and inequality. The point is that the current nature of Russia's engagement with the global economy contributes to regional inequality, which could threaten the internal cohesion of the state. This does not mean that Russia is going to collapse. Rather, regional inequality presents challenges that the current patterns of recentralization seem ill-equipped to deal with, and the Russian government may have to reassess center-regional relations to address these issues.

Notes

1. For a review of geographical theorizing on globalization, see Eric Sheppard, "The Spaces and Times of Globalization: Place, Scale, Networks, and Positionality," *Economic Geography* 78 (2002): 307–10.

2. Paul Hirst and Grahame Thompson, *Globalization in Question: The International Economy and the Possibilities of Governance,* 2nd ed. (Cambridge: Policy Press, 1999) is a key text representing the skeptical position. Kenichi Ohmae, *The Borderless World* (London: Collins, 1990) is seen as typical of the hypergloblist camp.

3. David Held et al., "Introduction," in *Global Transformations: Politics, Economics and Culture,* by David Held, Anthony McGrew, David Goldblatt, and Jonathan Perraton (Cambridge: Polity Press, 1999), 16–17.

4. Peter Dicken, "Geographers and 'Globalization': (Yet) Another Missed Boat?" *Transactions of the Institute of British Geographers* 29 (2004): 5–26.

5. David Harvey, *The Condition of Postmodernity* (Oxford: Blackwell, 1989).

6. Ibid., 229.

7. The concept of a "global sense of place" is discussed by Doreen Massey, *Space, Place and Gender* (Cambridge: Polity).

8. For discussions of this issue, see Eric Sheppard and Robert B McMaster, eds., *Scale in Geographic Inquiry: Nature, Society and Method* (Oxford: Blackwell, 2004); and Neil Brenner, *New State Spaces: Urban Governance and the Rescaling of Statehood* (Oxford: Oxford University Press).

9. See Kevin R Cox, ed., *Spaces of Globalization: Reasserting the Power of the Local* (New York: Guildford Press, 1997).

10. Ash Amin and Nigel Thrift, "Holding Down the Global" in *Globalization, Institutions and Regional Development in Europe,* ed. Ash Amin and Nigel Thrift (Oxford: Oxford University Press, 1994), 1–13.

11. Erik Swyngedouw, "Neither Global nor Local: 'Glocalization' and the Politics of Scale," in *Spaces of Globalization,* ed. Cox, 137–66.

12. Sheppard, "Spaces and Times of Globalization," 318–19.

13. This is a point made by Hedetoft in chapter 1 of this volume: "Globalization therefore has very different consequences and implications for different actors."

14. Doreen Massey, *For Space* (London: Sage, 2005), 11.

15. For a discussion of the importance of studying outcomes, see Gavin Bridge, "Grounding Globalization: The Prospects and Perils of Linking Economic Processes of Globalization to Environmental Outcomes," *Economic Geography* 78 (2002): 361–86.

16. Dicken, "Geographers and 'Globalization,' " 8.

17. This section is based in part on "Foreign Economic Relations and Regional Development in Russia: Continuity and Change," by Michael Bradshaw, *Geographica Polonica* 78 (2005): 9–31.

18. A recent paper by Gaddy and Ickes makes clear the size of the windfall gain accrued during the late Soviet period from the exporting of oil and gas to the West. Cliff Gaddy and Barry Ickes, "Resource Rents and the Russian Economy," *Eurasian Geography and Economics* 46 (2005): 559–83.

19. The UN data were obtained from the Commodity Trade Statistics Database (COMTRADE) and the Russian statistics from the Rosstat Web site (http://www.gks.ru).

20. See Organization for Economic Cooperation and Development, *OCED Survey of the Russian Federation* (Paris: Organization for Economic Cooperation and Development, 2004); World Bank, *Russia: Transition Meets Development—Country Economic Memorandum for the Russian Federation* (Moscow: World Bank, 2004); Rudiger Ahrend, "Russia's Post-Crisis Growth: Its Source and Prospects for Continuation," *Europe-Asia Studies* 46 (2005): 1–24; and Shinichiro Tabata, "Observations on the Influence of High Oil Prices on Russia's GDP Growth," *Eurasian Geography and Economics* 47 (2006): 95–111.

21. See Rudiger Ahrend, "Can Russia Break the 'Resource Curse'?" *Eurasian Geography and Economics* 46 (2005): 584–609.

22. Mehmet Öğütçü, "Attracting Foreign Direct Investment for Russia's Modernization," paper presented at Organization for Economic Cooperation and Development–Russia Investment Roundtable, Saint Petersburg, June 19, 2000, 3.

23. B. I. Safronov and B. L. Mek'nikov, *Inostrannyyee investitsii v Rossiyskoye Federatsii (1995–2003gg.)* (Moscow: Prime-Tass, 2004), available at http://www.prime-tass.ru.

24. There are numerous inconsistencies in the statistics relating to foreign investment in Russia. In this chapter, official Russian government statistics published by Goskomstat, available in the statistical yearbook and on the Goskomstat Web site (http://www.gks.ru) are used for internal measures and year on year comparisons. However, data from international organizations, e.g., the United Nations Conference on Trade and Development and the Organization for Economic Cooperation and Development, are used for international comparisons. The data from Goskomstat and United Nations Conference on Trade and Development are not compatible, hence the different levels of FDI reported in this section. The comparative data used here were obtained from

United Nations Conference on Trade and Development, *World Investment Report 2005, Country Fact Sheet: Russian Federation* (New York: United Nations Conference on Trade and Development, 2005), available at http://www.unctad.org.

25. For review of this literature, see Ichiron Iwasaki and Keiko Suganuma, "Regional Distribution of Foreign Direct Investment in Russia," *Post-Communist Economics* 17 (2005): 153–72.

26. The Sakhalin-1 project, operated by ExxonMobil, invested $1.719 billion; and the Sakhalin-2 project, operated by Shell, invested $2.943 billion. Source: *Commercial Update: Sakhalin Region, February 2006,* http://bisnis.doc.gov/bisnis/bisdoc/0602 Sakhalinnews.htm.

27. Michael Bradshaw, "The Changing Geography of Foreign Investment in the Russian Federation," *Russian Economic Trends* 11 (2002): 33–41.

28. See Daniil Manaenkov, *What Determines the Region of Location of an FDI Project? An Empirical Assessment,* Working Paper BSP/00/036E (Moscow: New Economic School, 2000); Harry Broadman and Francesca Recanatini, *Where Has All the Foreign Investment Gone in Russia?* Working Paper 2640 (Washington D.C.: World Bank, 2001); and Iwasaki and Suganuma, "Regional Distribution of Foreign Direct Investment in Russia."

29. This section builds on the research presented in "A New Perspective on Regional Inequalities in Russia," by Michael Bradshaw and Karen Vartapetov, *Eurasian Geography and Economics* 44 (2003): 403–29; and "The Russian Heartland Revisited: An Assessment of Russia's Transformation," by Michael Bradshaw and Jessica Prendergrast, *Eurasian Geography and Economics* 46 (2005): 83–122.

30. Fiona Hill and Clifford Gaddy, *The Siberian Curse: How Communist Planners Left Russia Out in the Cold* (Washington, D.C.: Brooking Institution Press, 2003).

31. Fiona Hill, "Siberia: Russia's Economic Heartland and Daunting Dilemma," *Current History* (October 2004): 324–31.

32. See Philip Hanson and Michael Bradshaw, eds., *Regional Economic Change in Russia* (Cheltenham, U.K.: Edward Elgar, 2000).

33. For early work on this issue, see Douglas Sutherland and Philip Hanson, "Structural Change in the Economies of Russia's Regions," *Europe-Asia Studies* 48 (1996): 367–92; and Bert van Selm, "Economic Performance in Russia's Regions," *Europe-Asia Studies* 50 (1998): 603–18. For a more recent analysis, see Rudiger Ahrend, "Speed of Reform, Initial Conditions or Political Orientation? Explaining Russian Regions' Economic Performance," *Post-Communist Economies* 17 (2005): 289–317.

34. For a comparative analysis of the restructuring of the Russian economy, see Paul Gregory and Valery Lazarev, *Structural Change in Russian Transition,* Discussion Paper 896 (New Haven: Economic Growth Center, Yale University, 2004).

35. World Bank, *Russian Economic Report, November 2005* (Moscow: Moscow Office, World Bank, 2005), 13; available at http://www.worldbank.org.ru.

36. Peter Westin and Alexei Vorobiev, *A Guide to Russia's Regions* (Moscow: Aton Capital, 2004).

37. See Nadezhda Mikheeva, "Analysis of Interregional Inequality in Russia," *Studies on Russian Economic Development* 10 (1999): 514–21; Irina Dolinskaya, *Transition and Regional Inequality in Russia: Reorganization or Procrastination?*" IMF Working Paper WP/02/169 (Washington, D.C.: International Monetary Fund, 2002); Leonid Fedorov, "Regional Inequality and Regional Polarization in Russia, 1990–99," *World Development* 30 (2002): 443–56; and Bradshaw and Vartapetov, "New Perspective on Regional Inequalities in Russia."

38. World Bank, *Russian Federation Reducing Poverty through Growth and Social Policy Reform,* Report 28923-RU (Washington, D.C.: World Bank, 2005), 37–40.

39. Ruslan Yemstov, *Quo Vadis? Inequality and Poverty Dynamics across Russian Regions,* Discussion Paper 2003/67 (Helsinki: United Nations University and World Institute for Development Economics Research, 2003), 1.

40. For a discussion of the technical aspects of these measures and other techniques and variables, see Bradshaw and Vartapetov, "New Perspective on Regional Inequalities in Russia."

41. This analysis is presented in Bradshaw and Prendergrast, "Russian Heartland Revisited."

42. For an early discussion of how Russia's fiscal federal system was manipulated to political ends, see Daniel Triesman, "The Politics of Intergovernmental Transfers in Post-Soviet Russia," *British Journal of Political Science* 26 (1996): 299–335. For an up-to-date analysis of the relationship between fiscal federalism and regional inequality in Russia, see Karen Vartapetov, "Territorial Justice and Fiscal Equity: The Case of Post-Communist Russia," D.Phil. thesis, University of Oxford, 2007.

43. Philip Hanson, "Federalism with a Russian Face: Regional Inequality, Administrative Capacity and Regional Budgets in Russia," unpublished paper, Centre for Russian and East European Studies, University of Birmingham.

44. See Henry E. Hale and Rein Taagepera, "Russia: Consolidation or Collapse? *Europe-Asia Studies* 54 (2002): 1001–1125, for a wide-ranging discussion of the triggers that might threaten Russia's cohesion in the future.

45. I am carrying out such research in the context of the Sakhalin oil and gas projects in the Russian Far East. This research is an ongoing project, and further details can be obtained from my Web site (http://www.leicester.ac.uk/geography/people/mjb41.html).

4

Russian Identity and Siberia's Self-Identification: Historical Traditions in a Global World

Evgeny Vodichev and Vladimir Lamin

There are two notable trends in the formation of civic identity in Russia today. On the one hand, attempts are continuing to find or artificially formulate a hypostasis capable of creating cohesion in Russian society and replacing what was known in the USSR as the "Soviet people." On the other hand, the processes of self-identification are developing rapidly in Russia, not only within ethnic and religious communities but also across large territorial communities. However, attempts to formulate a new Russian identity together with the search for the new "national idea" are still rather vague at the moment and are not well harmonized with the objective processes of developing ethnic and regional self-identifications. Contrary to some expectations, therefore, Russia's engagement with globalization has not contributed to smoothing out the discrepancies between "the whole" and "the parts" of this large country.

The research for this chapter was supported by the Russian Foundation for the Humanities (Project 07-01-00420a).

These divergent processes of national identity harmonization and fragmentation will likely play a defining role in the future of the Russian Federation, not only for the foreseeable future but in the long term as well. Issues of self-identification will be especially important for Siberia, the region
that stretches from the Urals to the Pacific Ocean and gives Russia not only
its unique geopolitical significance but also its economic independence.

Modernization and the Territorial Expansion of Russia to the East

Over the course of centuries, both the role and significance of Russia's policy toward Asia have increased. The Russian Empire expanded to the west
and the south, but primarily to the east and northeast: first to the Urals, and
then to Siberia and the Far East, which became Russia's internal colonies.
Territorial expansion into Asia was the result of objective factors. The strategy of creating a continental empire required that the borders be moved as
far as possible from the central area of the country to ensure security. But
this led to a historical paradox. In many cases, though Russia was attempting to position itself as a European power, the geopolitical, strategic, and
economic justification for its place on the world political stage came from
the east, from Asia.

This was due to the fact that, for all its particular characteristics, beginning in the eighteenth century Russia attempted to use, albeit in "prepared"
form, European models of socioeconomic development. The modernization
of the country, which involved increasingly rapid industrial development
and the urbanization and bureaucratization of society, required a constantly
expanding resource base. The country possessed such resources on a seemingly unlimited scale in the east. Moreover, in contrast to some other newly
acquired areas, the eastern regions were not burdened by the traditional
forms of Russian economy, which hindered the process of modernization.

At the end of the nineteenth and beginning of the twentieth century, the
logic of modernization made it necessary to shift production further and further to the east. The implementation of the imperatives for this new stage
of modernization occurred after the Soviet period had begun. The eastern
regions—Siberia first and foremost—became the resource center of the
USSR and the primary justification for the country's position on the geopolitical stage. Since World War II, the eastern areas of Russia have played the
additional role of strategically vital rear areas.

Thus, at various stages of Russia's historical development, the "eastern vector" in the modernization process was not only predetermined by economic, political, and geopolitical imperatives but, in contrast to many other strategies, could actually be implemented. Resources were mined in the east. Various scenarios for socioeconomic, demographic, and sociocultural policies were developed in the east. As a Russian geopolitical and strategic resource and as the location of a significant portion of the country's military capacity, for most of the twentieth century its eastern territories had a stabilizing effect as it pursued its global and international policies.

The experience of the development of the eastern regions and Siberia in particular teaches many lessons that are important both for current political reality and for the formulation of long-term economic and geopolitical strategies. The main lesson is that the relationship between European Russia and Asian Russia in the past always took the form of a "home country—colony" dichotomy. Paradoxically, the symbol of Russia's colonial strategy in the eastern part of the country was expressed by the great Russian scientist Mikhail Lomonosov: "Russia's power will grow based on the strength of Siberia," which was a source of pride in the region until recently. The principle of strictly construed national expediency allowed no significant deviations in favor of a development vector based on the dominant or even adequate consideration of regional expediency; any regionalism was viewed as a potential threat to the foundation of the country and its methods of governance. Such were the laws of empire.

In its basic components, this strategy was largely passed on to the Soviet period in Russian history. As at the end of the previous century, the moving of industry to the eastern regions was dictated by modernization.[1] In the second half of the nineteenth century and the first part of the twentieth century, Russia achieved clear success in the process of capitalist modernization, but this process was nonetheless far from complete in 1917. As a result, the new regime faced the same challenges of economic and social transformation into an industrial society.

To a great extent, the immutable nature of these challenges also gave rise to the methods and mechanisms that had been tried previously to promote modernization. Under the Soviet regime, the eastern regions of the country were given an even more prominent role in meeting the challenges of modernization. For the new Soviet state, which positioned itself as "surrounded by enemies," "the intra-continental vector of industrial expansion became the decisive factor in the survival of the Soviet regime."[2] Expansion into Asia in order to develop production capacity was the obvious choice. Thus, despite the layers of ideology, in the technological sense the country maintained its old nineteenth-century model of modernization, which established the "colonial" approach to relations with the eastern regions.

Alternative scenarios did arise occasionally. For example, in the late 1920s and early 1930s, there was discussion of developing the Ural region as a self-contained complex, a "region for itself." However, the projects that were implemented in the east in the prewar period were clearly based on a different modernization paradigm: the "region for the country."[3]

After the end of World War II, when Russia faced challenges of getting involved in the postindustrial era, no serious changes were made. The opportunity to replace the semicolonial vector of Siberian development with a policy of balanced and comprehensive growth was lost. During the entire second half of the twentieth century, the economy remained a function of geopolitics, the aim of which was to achieve and then maintain the country's status as superpower. In these conditions, despite the fact that the resources of the eastern regions were broadly integrated into the Soviet Union's economic strategies, the plan to shift industrial production to the east was entirely subservient to the concept of the "region for the country." The "Eastern Shift" was seen during this period not only (and, in our view, not mainly) as an opportunity to improve the geographic allocation of industry; it also reflected the growing demand for natural and energy resources by the developed western areas of the country."[4] This situation remained until the collapse of the USSR in 1991 without much change.

Siberian Regionalism during Empire Building in the Nineteenth and Twentieth Centuries

The processes by which both the Russian and the Siberian identities were formed reflect the scenarios of socioeconomic development in Russia's eastern territories. The development of Russian identity is a common trait throughout the history of Russian empire building. But the critical need to establish this identity in reality was revealed for the first time by the territorial expansion to the east, into Siberia.

The colonization of Siberia was mostly peaceful, for two reasons. The reasons for this are obvious. First, Siberia never suffered from a lack of land. There was more than enough space in the new territories. Second, it did not make economic sense to eradicate the native population. For many years the native inhabitants of Siberia had enriched the coffers of Russia by hunting and supplying valuable furs. Third, there was no need to drive the native population from the land in order to use it for agriculture. The Siberian lands were not considered arable or of interest agriculturally until the second half of the nineteenth century. The native population east of the Urals, which was numerically small and ethnically diverse, could not resist the expansion of the more technologically advanced culture, although the methods of settling the new lands changed with time.

This does not mean that there were no conflicts and clashes with the native population. Local conflicts with aboriginal people were regular and numerous. However, from a formal standpoint, there were no wars with native feudal governors of Siberia in the process of colonization. Both in West and East Siberia, Russian army detachments were always accompanied by a huge number of peasants and people engaged in different industries. All of this lead to a softer form of colonization and a tolerant manner of spreading into Siberia a Russian national identity based on the principles of autocracy and Orthodoxy. "This became the essence of colonization as a multi-dimensional, contradictory historical process."[5]

It took more than three hundred years to lay the demographic foundation for a Russian identity in Siberia. However, this construct turned out to be much less durable in Siberia than in the center of the country, although even there the sense of identity was not particularly deep. In Siberia, the spread of Russian Orthodoxy, a key element of Russian identity, was met with passive yet unyielding Buddhism and Islam. In many cases, the native ethnic groups accepted Orthodoxy only superficially. In addition, even among the historically Orthodox population, the process was highly contradictory, because the population of Siberia has never been particularly religious.[6]

Siberia began forming its own regional identity against the backdrop of a fragile, developing Russian identity that had not completely penetrated the eastern territories. Currently, there is a debate in philosophical and cultural circles about whether this phenomenon is typical of Russian society. It has been proposed that Russia has always been culturally uniform and did not display any pronounced variations. The current manifestation of these ideas is the theory of an "aspatial" Russian culture, which leads some philosophers to conclude that there is no regional identity in Russia.[7] However, there is insufficient historical evidence for this view, and the results of sociological research show that it does not hold up under experimental scrutiny in the historic nucleus of European Russia, much less in the peripheral regions.[8]

The Siberian region possesses many objective geographical prerequisites for the formation of an individual regional identity. Experts analyzing phenomena such as the identity of large territories usually look at several criteria—including ethnoreligious, linguistic, political, and historical factors—while recognizing the significance of socioeconomic distinctions.[9] It appears that in the case of Siberia, the role and influence of political, historical, and socioeconomic factors were determinative. In accordance with contemporary historiography, one could easily agree that "Siberian regionalism was usually economically motivated."[10]

It is likely that the formation of a Siberian identity first began at the end of the eighteenth century, although this process was not manifested very clearly until the middle of the following century. We should not think that the development of a Siberian identity went unnoticed in the Russian capital or that it was not a cause for concern for Moscow. On the contrary, there was a great deal of talk in the country about the "the case for Siberian secession from Russia" in the late 1860s. Certain young people were suspected of the "malicious and ridiculous intent" of breaking Siberia away from the European part of the country. Despite the fact that the conversations and correspondence of these people were dismissed as "ridiculous," they all received harsh criminal sentences. This demonstrates that the central authorities were in shock after being blindsided by their political investigation of "bandits."[11]

Somewhat later, practical steps were taken to reinforce Russian identity in the east. They were ascribed to Piotr Stolypin and his policies and experience with Siberian peasant settlement. It is believed that the massive migration to Siberia at this time was caused not only by increasing social tensions in the European part of the country and the need to protect Russia's eastern flank from foreign threats but also by the need to reinforce ideological bonds in the country and prevent the loss of a loyal Russian identity among the Siberian populace and by the increasing popularity of regional ideologies.

In reality, the mass colonization of Siberia, like the mass exile, did not lead to an increase in pro-Russian sentiment but rather polarized the population and radicalized both the "old timers" and the more creative, intellectual segment of the population. At the turn of the century, these processes were manifested in an ideology of Siberian provincial consciousness, attributed primarily to N. Yadrintsev and G. Potanin. Contemporary historians and sociologists are once again in agreement with the proponents of provincial consciousness, seeing such factors as Siberia's insularity and isolation from the rest of the country, the history of tolerance between natives and settlers, and the greater freedom of action and democratic attitudes in the social order as the starting point in the formation of a Siberian culture.

However, for the first time the situation had gone much farther than the identification of sociocultural differences between the inhabitants of European Russia and Siberia. The formulas posited by the "provincialists" assumed the characteristics of a sociopolitical ideology. There was, in the words of A. Boronoyev, a Russia-Siberia "binary pair,"[12] and a contradistinction emerged between the whole (Russia) and one of its parts (Siberia). Thus, by the beginning of the twentieth century, Siberia had become a typical example of a region where "the territory creates a collective consciousness that epitomizes the concept of a 'homeland.'"[13]

The proponents of provincial identity advocated an end to the mass sending of exiles into the region; increased industrial development; educational development, including the creation of a Siberian university; the resolution of "alien" issues; and the regulation of migration based on regional interests. Obviously, this platform was anticolonial, a logical reaction to the central government's economic policies toward Siberia. Accordingly, the Siberian regional identity conceptualized by the proponents of provincial identity was to a certain extent "anticolonial." Ultimately, Moscow's one-sided Siberian policy and the obvious fracture along "home country" and "colonial" lines served as the historical basis for Siberian regionalism. Changing this situation would require a radical improvement in relations between the central government and the eastern region. However, as noted above, this did not happen either during the tsarist period or after the radical change in the political regime.

Soviet Identity and the Archetype of Siberian Self-Identification

The turbulent events of the early twentieth century brought a natural halt to the transfer of the previous Russian national identity to Siberia. These events also demonstrated that the Russian national identity was incapable of acting as a stabilizing factor in Russian society in the eastern areas of the empire. This is evidenced by, if nothing else, this fact: Settlers who arrived in Siberia relatively recently, primarily during the Stolypin reforms, tended to be more involved in the revolution than the Siberian old-timers. At the beginning of the twentieth century, mutiny and unrest regularly erupted in southern Siberia, specifically in the territories that had been settled by migrants from the European part of the country. Indeed, in historical studies these regions are sometimes referred to as an "arc of instability."[14]

The new regime recognized the extreme danger that the ideological and sociocultural vacuum posed to the new government. For this reason, during the Soviet period the problem of identity was always a top priority for the Communist Party and the government elite. Orthodoxy was rejected as an ideological platform for the formation of a Soviet identity, and on the institutional level Orthodoxy was targeted for total destruction. However, its methodology for building a new identity was preserved. Orthodoxy was replaced by other "articles of faith," in the form of Communist ideals. The only significant departure from the previous views in the area of identity was the principle of nation building during the Soviet regime, which allowed—albeit formally—for ethnic autonomy and which promoted the emergence of a multitude of ethnic and national identities that, as a temporary compromise, were allowed to coexist with the general Soviet identity. This planted a ticking time bomb in the national and social order that went off seven decades later.

The building of the new Soviet identity culminated in the 1960s and 1970s. The quintessence of this process was the declaration of the formation of a "Soviet people" as a "new historical community." This implied the conclusion that a national and social "melting pot" had managed by this time to transform the enormous polyethnic area with distinct territorial variations into a uniform demographic mass, the binding element of which was the single national identity. However, this conclusion was premature.

Despite the fact that certain characteristics of a national civic identity were actually formed in the country and a portion of the population began to identify as "Soviet," certain fundamentally important contrary circumstances came to light less than two decades later. The seeds of ethnic and national autonomy and the corresponding ethnic and national identities, which had been originally planted in the early stages of nation building in the USSR, not only came to the surface but began to prevail over the common national identity. Moreover, the preservation of the traditional relationship between the central government and the periphery, which had existed even in imperial Russia, led to a natural growth in previously suppressed regional identities. After having weakened somewhat in the Leonid Brezhnev era, therefore, the diverse palette of regional identities acquired new colors and hues by the 1980s, as the country was reeling from systemic crisis.

With respect to Siberian self-identification, during the Soviet period the region's cultural identity was recognized, but it was never seen as a potential threat to national stability. But in the later 1970s and 1980s, Siberian self-identification and the concept of Siberian identity began to change gradually. The economic, social, and political component, which goes beyond the sociocultural characteristics of the "Siberian character" and personality type—and is therefore potentially dangerous for national unity and national identity—began to intensify. There were several reasons for this. First, as most of the large economic projects were completed, Siberia ceased to receive regular, large-scale demographic injections from other regions of the country. The migration patterns changed, the population of Siberia stabilized, and previous migrants began to thoroughly adapt to their new place of settlement. Second, as the process of drawing administrative borders in the eastern part of the country was completed, the economic insularity of the region increased, and this also stimulated regionalism. These processes were typical of the entire country, but in Siberia many of them were expressed more distinctly than in other regions. Third, a group of leaders appeared in the republics, regions, and provinces of Siberia, who had been in power for many years or even decades. And a group of stable regional elites, with a good understanding that their interests were tied to the region, began to form around these leaders.

This process culminated in 1990 with the formation of large interregional associations throughout the country, including Greater Urals, Greater Volga, Far East, and, of course, Siberian Compact, the most prominent and powerful of all such associations with a membership including nineteen republics, regions, and provinces within Siberia. These associations reflected the functional interests of local elites, who accumulated power rapidly and exploited the power vacuum that had formed in the country. However, the leaders of these associations, along with other regional leaders, began to actively appeal to the regional specifics and interests, relying on the seeds of regional identity that had begun to germinate earlier. Thus, the loop was completed: The functional interests of the regional elites promoted the emergence of regional identities, and the regional identities served as the justification for promoting regional interests. This phenomenon was manifested most clearly in the early 1990s, after the Soviet Union had already collapsed.

In 1991, the Soviet Union disappeared from the political map of the world. Its centralized power, represented by the party and government apparatus, was incapable of governing a huge country facing larger and more complex challenges in a globalizing world. The more the country came under the influence of globalization, the more opportunities opened for regional leaders. Moreover, economic factors had a major effect, and this was also the result of Russia's growing dependence on the world economy. It is true that the Soviet Union was never fully isolated from the global economy. However, due to the existence of the planned economy, Russia's regions and individual enterprises were cut off from participating directly in the world economy and from the competitive effects of globalization. With the collapse of the Soviet Union and the economic liberalization that followed, this shield fell away, and the nature of the relationship between Russian and the global economy changed fundamentally (see chapter 3 in this volume by Bradshaw). In this context, the formation of interregional associations, mentioned above, became a way for regions to protect themselves from the impact of the global economy by integrating regional interests as the previous management system and the old economic model collapsed. Globalization contributed to the situation, in which "the political paralysis at the center pushed the regional elites into the foreground."[15]

An equally significant role in the collapse of the Soviet Union was played by the crisis in Soviet identity, which could not withstand the pressure of ethnic and regional challenges that drastically intensified under the influence of globalization. The fact that the Soviet state disintegrated so rapidly demonstrates that the Soviet identity, which took most of the twentieth century to create, collapsed in what was, on a historical scale, a single moment. It seems that the inability to create a national identity that could stand up to external pressures and internal turmoil, along with the vulnerability of the identity that was actually created, became one of the key factors in the fall of the erstwhile superpower. The single common civic identity was replaced by a multitude of ethnic, national, denominational, and religious identities, leaving very little room for the preservation of any unifying identity markers in the USSR.

In the first years following the Soviet collapse, the Russian elite failed to mobilize around a common identity narrative. The first half of the 1990s became known as the "parade of sovereignties"; that is, the political situation in the country continued to develop largely according to the same scenario that was put in place at the time of Mikhail Gorbachev. Admittedly, the country had very limited room to maneuver. By the early 1990s, the processes of ethnic self-identification had gone too far, and any attempt to level them off in favor of a common identity could have been disastrous for the country.[16] This fact explains the desire of the Boris Yeltsin administration to "play to" the ethnic elites by giving them "as much sovereignty as they can handle" to ensure the loyalty of ethnic leaders and preserve the country's territorial integrity, now within the borders of Russia. The application of these policies to entities like the republics of Tatarstan, Bashkotorstan, and the Northern Caucasus, and in Siberia to Sakha-Yakutia and Buryatia, has been thoroughly described in the literature. In places where this process did not involve ethnic and religious components, regional self-identification was not seen at that time as an equally significant threat to the integrity of the country. Therefore, the interests of the "nonethnic" territories were sacrificed to ethnic interests. As a result, an enormous socioeconomic, political, and legal asymmetry arose in Russia that has not been resolved even today, and that remains an obstacle to the formation of a common Russian identity.[17]

Globalization, Russia's Positioning in Europe, and Siberian Eurasianism

Russia has had to deal with the issue of its geopolitical and strategic development since the earliest days of its existence as a full-fledged subject of international law. With the democratization of its society and the liberalization of its economy, and in light of geographical factors, Russia was primarily interested in Europe as in economic partner. It was a united Europe, rather than the United States—the USSR's foremost adversary in the Cold War—that was seen as both an example to imitate and a key geopolitical and strategic ally. Attempts to set up a stable instrumental framework for cooperation with the European Union, resulting in the Partnership and Cooperation Agreement in June 1994, provide significant evidence of this.[18] Moreover, despite the fact that these kinds of geopolitical strategies seem far removed from the issues of Siberian identity, they have had a significant effect on the development of various scenarios for Siberian self-identification.

Russian geopolitical hopes were tied to Europe for most of the 1990s. Russia declared itself a European country with European roots, and its plans to integrate into a unified European space were a priority in its foreign policy. These plans coincided with an increasing trend toward the "Westernization" of the principles upon which the government and society operated. This process, which was apparently based on a European model, included a restructuring of the system of national government, municipal administration, and business organization as well as attempts to transform the country's scientific and educational systems. Metaphorically speaking, in the 1990s the authorities clearly intended to quickly and effectively break through not just a "window" but a "door" into Europe in order to remain there forever. Yet attempts to tie the country's future to an exclusively European perspective were not entirely successful. These failures were caused by numerous internal and external circumstances. Among the most important, in our view, was the fact that the new geopolitical strategies were contrary to the objective qualities inherited from a prior, but still not fully formed, Russian identity. It is useful to discuss this in more detail.

For more than a decade and a half, Russia has searched for way to cooperate with the European Union and to find the best ways to pursue this strategy. However, despite expectations, this process has been far from easy. There have been many obvious reasons for these difficulties. It is widely believed that they were due to Russia's natural and geographic circumstances (i.e., its size and location on two continents), economic factors (an economy that is unstable and structurally inconsistent with European standards), and politics (the limited nature of liberal reforms and an inclination toward the political ambitions characteristic of a former "superpower"). This is why views on the likelihood of Russia moving closer to the EU vary so widely, depending on whether the country's socioeconomic situation and political landscape improve or deteriorate. In the early 1990s, it seemed possible that these processes could lead to a very high level of integration with the countries of the European Union, with Russia perhaps even joining the EU in the foreseeable future. Today the prevailing viewpoint is far less optimistic.

To explain these events, one overriding fact must be emphasized. The current stage of European integration and Russia's involvement in this process are occurring against the backdrop of a radical acceleration in the globalization of the world economy. Globalization has been the topic of numerous debates and arguments. But most experts define globalization as the process of creating a single economic space based on modern information technology. Key to this concept is the notion of a worldwide market with no national boundaries and where goods and services can circulate freely.[19]

In economic terms, globalization is an entirely objective process. But as with any other large-scale economic phenomenon, there are noneconomic criteria for it as well. It would be a major mistake to reduce globalization to merely economic phenomena. From a social science perspective, globalization entails "the creation and affirmation of the unity, interconnectedness, interdependence, and integration of the world and the acceptance of these phenomena in the social consciousness. . . . Globalization embraces all aspects of society. But at its core are a sociocultural nexus and all the fundamental characteristics of [an integrated] world."[20]

Experts in economic geography use an approach to globalization that is useful in interpreting the complex, systemic process of integration. The dominant paradigm in this field defines globalization as a set of qualitative changes in the relationship between space and time. These changes certainly do not signify the end of geography and cannot be reduced to a simple dichotomy between the global and the local, where the global criterion plays the defining role. We believe this approach explains the stability of a construct, where local identity is maintaining and even enhancing its role in a global environment.

From this perspective, the combined processes of globalization and European integration create an interesting multidimensional construct. In economic terms, European integration may be interpreted as a phenomenon as significant as globalization. The economic integration of the European countries was prompted by the same factors that triggered globalization and is part of the universal processes taking place throughout the world, including in Europe. In political terms, European integration and Russia's involvement in that process are to a certain extent a response to the challenges of globalization and an attempt to combine the economic potential of the European countries into a huge megaregion. In chapter 3 of this volume, Michael Bradshaw rightly notes that "Russia cannot remain immune from globalization and seemingly has no choice but to play the global game, even if the rules are not of its making, to sustain its economy, to gain recognition, and to curry influence."

We should view the convergence of the EU and Russia in this context. In many ways, it will depend on the extent to which Russia and the EU are capable of sharing a common value system.[21] Sociocultural factors must be considered when assessing the prospects for Russia's attempt to position itself in Europe or integrate into the EU. Depending on the strategy chosen and the viability of the end result, sociocultural factors including identity could be viewed either as an incentive for integration or a barrier to it. In any case, clearly understanding and reducing the effect of the sociocultural barriers to the integration of Russia and the leading European countries are some of the most important challenges of our time. They could determine the long-term prospects for development in Eurasia and, to a certain extent, the future of Europe. However, the opportunities to control these barriers are themselves limited.

Theoretically, there are three main possibilities for cooperation between the Russian Federation and the EU. The first is for Russia to exist outside the European family in economic isolation. The second is the complete integration of Russia into a unified Europe. And third is for Russia to cooperate with the European Union while preserving a significant degree of freedom and maintaining its balance of interests with the nations of the Asian-Pacific region. Having embraced the market economy and democratic social development, the first option appears unlikely for obvious reasons. The other two strategies both have large numbers of proponents and opponents. The debate usually focuses on either economic or political factors. Much less frequently, there is an analysis of the sociocultural aspects of the possible integration of Russia into a unified Europe, that is, an analysis that takes identity into account.

This is exactly where the issues become complicated. Both for economic reasons and to ensure geopolitical stability on the continent, Europe needs Russia as much as Russia needs Europe. But as noted above, the process of convergence between the European Union and Russia is not moving as fast as some optimists would like. It appears that this is largely the result of sociocultural factors. One question is key: To what extent do the fundamental principles of European cultural identity apply to Russia, and does the country—both the elite and the "average Joe"—identify itself with European civilization? Finding a consensus about this is extremely difficult, as evidenced by the polarized opinions of numerous experts and commentators. Here, we mean a consensus on both what these European values are and whether they apply to Russia.

In chapter 10 of this book, Rick Fawn notes the differences in the European and Russian interpretations of human rights, which often make it difficult for Russia to work with Europe's institutional structures, particularly the Council of Europe. In his opinion, this is explained to a great extent by persistent differences in European and Russian identity narratives, notwithstanding the substantial degree of socialization that has occurred. In Europe, the formation of a common identity—or rather, a codification of norms and practices based on common European approaches in which human rights is an absolute value—is seen as a key factor in ensuring security throughout Europe. Russia, by contrast, still has its own values, which are not fully consistent with the principles of the EU. Erik Noreen takes a similar position in chapter 9, arguing that despite the considerable convergence between Russian and Estonian positions, having to do with a shared interest in demonstrating "Europeanness," it is extremely difficult to claim that all the principles of European identity are accepted in Russia.

Recent studies conducted in various regions of Russia confirm the doubts of these European experts. Despite the fact that, according to sociologists, more than 40 percent of Russian citizens surveyed believe that Russia is part of Europe and its future is tied to Europe, 35.5 percent said they supported concept of "Eurasia." Interestingly, more than 60 percent of Russians surveyed consider their culture to be generally European. However, the respondents' concept of what it means to be "European" is fundamentally different from the values of Western Europe residents. This is especially evident in views on such topics as the role of the government and democracy, law and order, legal principles, the connection between political rights and liberties, and so on. As a result, the meanings of the terms "Western Europe" and "Russia" have almost nothing in common in the answers of the Russians surveyed.[22]

Still, it appears that the situation is not so dramatic, if we choose to leave our illusions behind. Russia's prospects for European integration depend to a great extent on the point of reference. Europe is striving for unity not only for economic and political reasons. One of the most important motives, which has yet to be fully recognized, is the goal of avoiding an external threat to European cultural identity—sometimes called the "fall of civilization."[23] It does not matter where this threat originates, but the feeling that it exists has recently become ubiquitous in Europe. In this regard, Russia is potentially interesting to Europe. A refusal to converge with Europe would increase the significance of the Asian origins of Russia's cultural and political traditions, which could have dramatic consequences for both Europe and Russia.

Therefore, the convergence of Russia and the European Union seems unavoidable and predetermined by a series of economic and political factors. This process is accelerating under the pressure of globalization. However, existing sociocultural limitations—significant differences between European and Russian cultural identities, along with Russia's geographic position in Eurasia—make us doubt that Russia will integrate fully with the European Union even in the rather distant future. This issue will continue even in the most favorable economic and political scenario. Basing a strategy for integration on economic and political priorities alone, while ignoring sociocultural factors, may lead to significant problems for both Russia and the European Union. This already occurred in the late 1990s, when Russia's initial illusions of convergence with the EU led to disappointment due to domestic political problems and differing interpretations of the events in Chechnya and the former Yugoslavia. At the same time, doubts arose in Europe about whether Russia would ever liberalize its economy and democratize its sociopolitical system enough to meet European standards of quality. As a result, Russia's first experience with its European positioning was not entirely successful.

Of course, this does not make it unnecessary or impossible for Russia to cooperate closely with a unified Europe. However, Russia will not benefit by ignoring its historic, geographic, and sociocultural traits and advantages. An attempt to position the country exclusively as a European nation will almost certainly preserve its colonial approach to the exploitation of its eastern territories, and will pose a real threat of losing them in the more or less distant future.

Conversely, the basic elements of Russian civilization are as far removed from Asia (in the cultural sense) as they are from Europe. For this reason, it would also be impossible for Russia to integrate with the Asian countries on their terms. Therefore, Russia appears doomed to a balancing act and dialogue with both the East and the West, in languages that are mutually understandable and yet different. In this way Russia can preserve, develop, and capitalize on its own transcontinental identity. Both Russia and the European Union should understand and recognize this. If they do, they can replace false and unattainable goals with a constructive strategy.

Similarly, cooperating with Europe while not integrating into the EU will allow Russia to develop close relationships with countries to the east and southeast. Here we mean the geographical Eurasian Russia, without the ideological meaning with which the term is usually loaded. Like Russia's links with Europe, this process is driven by globalization and based on the fact that the economic systems of Russia, with its expansive Eurasian territory, and of the Asian countries are strategically compatible. Conceived and translated into a political strategy, the process is expressed as a movement toward the East in contemporary Russian foreign policy that has clearly intensified in recent years. And from an economic and geopolitical perspective, it would be a major mistake to remain on the sidelines in the Asia-Pacific region. This is even more true because, in the opinion of many experts, the new level of cooperation within Asia today demonstrates a strategic realignment of world economic centers toward the region.

Russian Regional Strategies and Siberian Self-Identification in the Post-Soviet Period

The formation of a conscious Asian vector in Russian foreign policy is not only geopolitically important. It also has great conceptual significance for the Russian and Siberian identities. As noted above, when Russia decided in the 1990s to orient its policy of integration with other countries predominantly toward Europe, it essentially determined that globalization would influence the evolution of its economic and sociopolitical institutions only from the West. However, the Russian political elite are paying more attention now to Asia and the Asian experience of coping with globalization. They believe the lesson of the Asian experience is to reject radical Westernization and emphasize a gradual process of globalization while preserving a higher degree of autonomy in the country's political and economic doctrines. The most recent demonstration of Russia's interests in this area was President Vladimir Putin's visit to Kuala-Lumpur in December 2005 and the negotiations with the members of the Association of Southeast Asian Nations, as well as his visits to China in 2006 and India in January 2007, all of which confirmed the new vector in Russia's geopolitical doctrines.

One would think the new emphasis on Asia in Russia's foreign policy would immediately result in new strategies toward the country's regions to the east and northeast of Moscow. Siberia is the quintessence of Russia's Eurasian status and a natural bridge between Europe and Asia. Russia's "Asian facade" could become a showcase of the country's economy, attractiveness as an investment, and willingness to integrate into the world economy, not only as a source of raw materials (the traditional role of a colony) but also as an outpost for the development of the "new economy." Siberia, broadly construed to include the Far East, could become a testing ground for the placement of promising new business technologies developed in the countries of the Asia-Pacific region. This could have a profound effect on Siberian identity, which could preserve the region's uniqueness while serving as Russia's conduit to the global world and the "knowledge economy."

For this reason alone, Siberia deserves an entirely different place in the system of national priorities. But the old stereotypes have not changed. Notably, China—Russia's closest neighbor in the east and a rapidly developing center of power—has taken a very different course by radically changing its plans for the development of its peripheral yet strategically vital areas. In recent years, China has dramatically increased investment in the economic revitalization of Inner Mongolia, to which China's new strategy allocates the role of the country's link to the outside world. As a result, according to the available data, in 2004 the gross regional product of the Autonomous District of Inner Mongolia grew at a rate twice the national average.[24] This has become a stable trend.

However, there is little evidence in Russia that the central government's relationship with the eastern territories has changed significantly in the post-Soviet era. Despite the economic growth in Russia during the past several years, which has been based almost entirely on fuel, energy, and raw materials from Siberia, the socioeconomic development of the Siberian region continues, with a few exceptions, to lag behind development in the northwest and central parts of the country. The vast majority of so-called vertically integrated companies operating on Siberia's raw materials markets are registered in Moscow or, to a much lesser extent, Saint Petersburg. This makes it possible to divert away from the region not only the profits of these companies, in the form of natural resource rent payments, but also tax revenues to the local governments. The situation continues to develop in this direction. The most recent controversial Russian business deal was the acquisition of Sibneft by Gazprom. Plans have been announced to move the company's headquarters from Omsk to Saint Petersburg and to reregister it there. According to experts, this will reduce the budget of Omsk Province by half.[25] And although the Russian Ministry of Finance says it is willing to adjust the federal budget to compensate for these losses, such promises are difficult to believe. A mere comparison of the "looks" of Moscow and the majority of Siberian cities shows how the country distributes the revenues that it derives primarily from the continuing exploitation of Siberia's resources. This situation, though logical in the context of the imperial scenario of development that prevailed until 1991, is clearly inconsistent with the economic and political values that are now espoused.

Moreover, in the 1990s the situation in Russia's East worsened significantly as a result of the radical structural reforms that began after the fall of the USSR. This is demonstrated by the increasingly rapid outflow of population from east to west. This process is unique, as this is the first population exodus since Russia began to settle the eastern areas beyond the Ural Mountains. As a result, experts estimate that by 2020 the population of Siberia may decrease to 17 million (for further discussion, see chapter 3 in this volume by Bradshaw). It is clear that, on the one hand, the increasing economic problems pose a threat of political and social instability in many regions of eastern Russia and could stimulate the debate over the advantages of regionalism. On the other hand, these processes are the basis for the view that Russia has no future as a Eurasian country, a view that has become quite popular among a portion of the intellectual elite both in Russia and abroad.[26] This view leads to the conclusion that Russia should position itself as a European nation, the Asian part of which is merely a source of natural resources to support the country. This conclusion attempts to provide new ideological justifications for the old colonial practices.

The consequences of the past policy toward the peripheral regions were readily predictable. The preservation of the old regional strategies had an important effect on Siberian self-identification. In a sense, the rise of self-identification in Siberia and other regions was a natural reaction to the chaos and economic dislocation of the early 1990s. As noted above, the impact of the structural changes in the economy was felt more strongly in the country's eastern territories than in many central and southern areas. Accordingly, empirical studies conducted in the mid-1990s indicate that the notion of Siberian identity reflected the desire of the region's population to return to a better and more stable past, a sort of reminiscence of historical traditions.[27]

Sociological observations made on the basis of a representative sample of one city in Eastern Siberia, which is fairly typical of the region—Shelekhov, in Irkutsk Province—indicate that 87.2 percent of those polled consider themselves Siberians, including about 95 percent of those who were born in Siberia and more than 68 percent of those who moved to Siberia from elsewhere. This suggests that the residents of Siberia feel a very strong connection to the region. This feeling varies by age (almost 90 percent of those under thirty years of age and 95 percent of those over fifty consider themselves Siberians) and ethnicity (almost 92 percent of Russians polled consider themselves Siberians, as do 85.7 percent of Ukrainians, 63.6 percent of Tatars, and 71.3 percent of persons belonging to other ethnic groups).[28] A large majority (84.4 percent) of the population of Shelekhov believes there is a "Siberian character" and see themselves as part of it. Of those surveyed, 66.5 percent believe the concept of "Siberian character" applies to half or more of the population of Siberia.[29] These data indicate that sociocultural self-identification among the population of Siberia, which has always carried significant weight in the Siberian identity, did not decrease during the 1990s.

According to other data, even among ethnic groups that are problematic from the perspective of Russian and Siberian self-identification, such as the Tuvins, more than 20 percent of the population consider themselves Siberians and therefore share certain values and attitudes that are common to the region as a whole.[30] It may be said that one-fifth is not a large number. But it should be remembered that this is a native ethnic group. Moreover, the Republic of Tyva, which did not become part of the USSR until 1944, later than all other national entities within Russia, has had the most nonconformist attitude toward the central authorities of any entity in the eastern part of the Russian Federation.

The territorial component of self-identification is particularly strong. This creates a favorable environment for the formation of various political concepts related to the promotion of the region's interests. As noted above, for a long time these concepts were not prominent in Siberian self-identification, and Siberian identity was seen primarily as a cultural phenomenon. But in the final years of the USSR, regional interests started to rise to the surface, and the era of the "triumph of regionalism" began after the Soviet Union collapsed. There are many reasons for this: the crisis of power and the economic chaos, the federalization of the country, the increasing influence of regional elites, the ethnic revival in the Russian provinces, the growth of economic independence in the regions, the worsening economic relations with the central authorities, and so on.[31] This was the time when the driving forces of regionalism, for which the foundations had been laid several decades earlier, first appeared openly. Naturally, the regional elites understood these processes and quickly added them to the political arguments they use in relations with the central authorities.

By the end of the twentieth century, the Siberian sociocultural identity, which had continued to exist throughout the Soviet period, began to take on anticolonial elements and become economically, socially, and politically partisan. Especially prominent was the economic and political conceptualization of the place and role of Siberia in Russia and the world, along with certain political practices that arose as the Siberian identity was internalized. This began to occur after the collapse of the Soviet Union. This tendency was not uniform and had its ups and downs, but the general trend is clear. It has fairly been said that the Siberian identity "could take on an expressly political form that could instill fear of Siberian separatism, especially if the population and the elite move to the West and the central authorities are unable to offer solutions to Siberia's socioeconomic problems while continuing to profit from its resources."[32]

Moreover, the currently developing Siberian identity clearly relies on much earlier antecedents and historical traditions. According to the well-known sociologist V. Yadov, "the past . . . is a direct determinant of social identification in the present."[33] It should be clearly understood that regional identities do not arise by themselves. Rather, they are outlined by the societal elite and "formed on the basis of previously existing markers."[34] The key factor, as in the past, is the dichotomy between Siberia and European Russia, which has existed for two hundred years but was not so pronounced in the Soviet era. During the economic chaos of the early 1990s, there were attempts by regional elites to exploit and exacerbate this contrast in order to promote regional consolidation and to serve their own political interests, which may or may not have been consistent with the interests of the region as a whole. Persuasive evidence for this is the activity of the Siberian Compact association in the early 1990s.

The growth of Siberian self-identification was not uniform or linear, however. The current strengthening of Siberian regional self-identification is linked with another equally important phenomenon. Despite the hypothetical predictions, globalization has not erased existing national borders. Rather, it has stimulated the ethnic, religious, and cultural components of social consciousness. This trend has been manifested in many regions of the world, including the countries of the European Union. In Siberia and in Russia as a whole, the social turbulence of the 1990s released a colossal amount of ethnic and national energy. It was catalyzed by the country's increasing participation in the global economy based on the existing development strategies, which were still ineffective from the perspective of Siberian and regional considerations.

A review of current trends in the development of social consciousness among the native populations of Siberia living in their titular areas demonstrates the prevalence of highly developed ethnic components. The process of ethnic self-identification among the native peoples of Siberia has had a leveling effect on the ruins of the Orthodox identity that could not be created in the region and the Soviet identity that could not be sustained there. In this sense, the basic way in which ethnic self-identification occurs in Siberia is not significantly different from the way it occurs in the western and southern regions of the former USSR. The process of self-identification in the ethnic regions of Siberia is somewhat inconsistent with the development of a regional self-consciousness. These processes, although they have been identified by researchers, have not been completely understood or studied. Despite the fact that the native population of Siberia represents a relatively small percentage of the region's total population, and that the level of attachment to identity tropes varies among different groups, it is clear that the process of ethnic and religious self-identification among a portion of the population could have a significant effect on the future development of a common Siberian identity.

Finally, as the region has been drawn into the process of globalization, one other interesting fact has been observed: In certain subregions of Siberia, a transnational identity based on ethnicity or religion has begun to form and to extend beyond the borders of Siberia and Russia.[35] Moreover, this type of self-identification has begun to dominate and define the hierarchy of identities. It is typical primarily among ethnic groups that are separated by national borders and is manifested in various cross-national identities, for example, the Greater Altai.

However, it does not only occur in this context. In the context of globalization and centrifugal economic policies, this type of identity can arise within a single large region, reflecting the region's role in the development of international business. Events in the Primorye region appear to be developing along these lines; this region is isolated from Central Russia by an enormous distance, many time zones, and different living conditions and historical traditions. This region long ago began to orient its economic interests toward the countries of the Asia-Pacific region, and Moscow and Central Russia are seen as merely an annoying hindrance.[36]

Siberia has a frontier feel today. The social and ethnic situation in the region, which seemed so stable a few decades ago, is fragile.[37] In this environment, the factor of Siberian (i.e., common Siberian) identity as a specific expression of territorial identity could be seen not as a threat but as a means to preserve the balance of power in a huge megaregion, which could otherwise radically destabilize the situation in the country. In this sense, Siberian self-identification could perform two key functions. First, given the transitory state of Russian society, it could promote the process of making the region a livable place and helping its marginal population survive.[38] During an international conference on identity issues held in 2003, participants agreed on the urgent need to find and establish a unifying "Siberian idea" built on the concept of tolerance in interethnic relations.[39] From a historical perspective, Siberia represents a good example of tolerant coexistence and solidarity among various ethnic groups and also among old-timers and new arrivals.

As many experts have correctly noted, the relationship between the center and the periphery in Russia remain deeply troubled. Turovskiy sums up this situation well, arguing that it

> has always been complicated and marked by conflict, but now the economic, political, and cultural conflicts between Moscow and rest of the country are becoming systemic in nature. . . . Anti-Moscow feeling is

growing in the country as provincial areas are more frequently trying to acquire their own identity and demonstrate it to themselves and everyone else. . . . The schism between Moscow and the provinces has become more profound in recent years, and many researchers have identified a "Muscovite subethnos" resulting from the cultural transformation that has caused Muscovites to lose their connection with the rest of Russia. This worsening schism is a precursor for the development of regionalism and autonomy in Russia's regions.[40]

Indeed, this situation is applicable to Siberia today. Experts agree that the primary basis for Siberian self-identification is not so much the territorial and cultural characteristics that Siberians share as their opposition to Moscow, which is far removed from Siberian interests and inhabitants. Siberians today define "we" as the opposite to the "they" in Moscow. This is obvious to any outside observer. For example, the well-known researcher and commentator Marshall Goldman notes with some regret: "People who live outside the capital do not see Moscow as the engine of development. They see it as a vacuum cleaner that sucks up just about everything it can from the Russian provinces. . . . Businesspeople and officials in cities like Novosibirsk view Moscow as an enemy and speak of it in words that are unsuitable in polite company."[41] This quotation may be somewhat emotional, but it accurately reflects the situation. Moscow is an antithesis around which the Russian provinces (and not only in Siberia) are building their regional identities.[42]

Thus, having developed a habit of using Siberia's natural resources, Moscow has been unable to capitalize on a resource that is just as vital: the positive impact of Siberian self-identification. Russia has not taken advantage of the aspects of Siberian identity that are defined by the region's geopolitical role and that create opportunities for Russia to extend its influence further to the east, into neighboring countries and regions. Continuing with the previous unbalanced economic strategies and treating Siberia as an unequal partner of Moscow creates the danger that Siberia will be tempted to integrate all its diverse ethnic and religious identities into a single megaregional identity. This process would not be easy or without conflicts, but it is theoretically possible.

The most regrettable outcome would be if Moscow is replaced by Russia itself (or its European part) in the Siberian system of values "destructive to Siberian identity," while the current negative attitudes maintain same intensity. This has already occurred in certain ethnic communities and therefore among some ethnic identities. If events continue to develop according to this scenario, the disintegration of the Russian Federation, the danger of which seemed to have been eliminated about ten years ago, could again become an objective possibility. We need to remember that in the late 1990s, the idea of the predominantly Russian regions, to say nothing of the ethnic regions, seceding from Russia was supported by the majority of the population and had a potential of becoming ever more popular. According to information published in the scientific press, proposals to secede from Russia were supported by 20 percent of the population in the Far East, over 15 percent of the population in Eastern and Western Siberia, and 13 percent of the population in the Urals.[43] These data indicate that, while a critical mass is still far off, all the eastern regions of Russia are a "risk area."

The changes in the vertical power structure implemented by President Putin indicate that Moscow understands the danger of regionalism in Siberia and elsewhere. Putin's reforms included three basic components: (1) the creation of seven federal districts, each led by a representative of the president; (2) a change in the status of the Council of the Federation and removing regional leaders from that body; (3) and an end to the popular election of regional governors, replaced them with the selection of regional leaders by legislative assemblies at the recommendation of the president. Even earlier, the plans of interregional associations like the Siberian Compact to formulate an independent regional policy had been scuttled. But all these actions, which have come to symbolize the current trend toward the new centralization of power, will certainly not halt the growth of ethnic and regional self-consciousness in Russia's regions. In fact, according to some experts, they may even stimulate the formation of a macroregional identity.[44]

Conclusion

Like Soviet history, the history of the Russian Empire left a varied and often inscrutable imprint on the contemporary economic, political, and sociocultural landscape of the Russian Federation. The historical experience provides persuasive evidence of an interesting phenomenon: The more problems the central government had in settling and developing the peripheral territories and keeping them within its influence, the more intensively the processes of self-identification and the formation of a regional identity occurred in these areas. These processes were especially evident in Siberia.

Regional identities always include two distinct aspects: the historical-cultural and the territorial. But in both cases, self-identification is not an objective phenomenon. It is the result of reflex, consciousness, and self-determination by the local population in a given historical environment. This interpretation of regional identity is similar to the currently popular concept of "imagined economies." Yoshiko Herrera, the American researcher who originated this concept, argues that regional economic and political interests are determined by the set of prevailing beliefs about the economic situation and the region's economic needs, as well as the ability of regional players to formulate and advocate these needs in specific institutional circumstances. Accordingly, the various manifestations of Russian regionalism arise not so much from economic variations among the regions as from how a region's economic interests are conceived.[45] By analogy to the imagined economy, we might say that regional identities are the result of images of self-identification determined by the prevailing markers of identity in the region and the skill of key players in exploiting them in various economic, political, and sociocultural conditions. As demonstrated in this chapter, beginning in the nineteenth century, the set of markers in Siberia included an anticolonial reflex. In various historical periods, the changing institutional conditions either allowed or did not allow these arguments to be used as instruments of political influence.

Since the beginning of the systemic crisis in the USSR and even more so in the 1990s, the process of creating regional self-identification in Siberia has accelerated. The institutional conditions have changed, and trends that were latent for many years have risen to the surface. Is the process of creating a Siberian regional identity complete, or can it ever be completed? Surely the answer to both these questions cannot be yes. At the present time, the Siberian regional identity (the set of formal and informal rules belonging to this group; the formulation of common goals for development; the formulation of rules to distinguish "us" from "them"; and the creation of a common worldview)[46] does not yet have significant subregional, ethnic, religious, and other variations. But clearly, a platform already exists for the further integration of common values and their transformation into a system of economic and political interests. Much will now depend on the development of the institutional context.

In the search for a new model of social development, the factor of a common Siberian identity may play a constructive and stabilizing role for the country. However, this will be possible only if the general concept for Siberian development within Russia is positive. As long as the colonial model for the development of Siberia remains in place, the unifying principles of Siberian self-identification will probably take the form of opposition to Moscow.

Notes

1. V. V. Alexeyev, ed., *Opyt rossiyskikh modernizatsiy XVIII–XX veka* (Moscow: Nauka, 2000), 15.

2. V. V. Alekseyev, Ye. V. Alekseyeva, K. I. Zubkov, and I. V. Poberezhnikov, *Aziatskaia Rossiia v geopoliticheskoy i tsivilizatsionnoy dinamike: XVI–XX veka* (Moscow: Nauka, 2004), 79.

3. V. V. Alexeyev, M. K. Bandman, and V. V. Kuleshov, eds., *Problemnye regiony resursnogo tipa: Ekonomicheskaia intergatsiiae evropeiskogo severo-vostoka, Urala i Sibiri* (Novosibirsk: Rossiyskaia akademiia nauk, Sibirskoe otdelenie, Institut ekonomiki i organizatsii promyshlennogo proizvodstva, 2002), 44.

4. V. V. Alekseyev et al., *Aziatskaia Rossiia v geopoliticheskoy i tsivilizatsionnoy dinamike,* 144.

5. D. Ya. Rezun and M. V. Shilovskiy, *Sibir', konets XVI–nachalo XX vekov: Frontir v kontekste etnosotsial'nykh i etnokul'turnykh protsessov* (Novosibirsk: Sova, 2005), 130.

6. This was commented on by one of the key officials of the Imperial administration, manager of the Trans-Siberian Railways Committee A. N. Kulomzin. See A. N. Kulomzin, *Vsepoddaneyshiy otchet po poezdke v Sibir' dlia oznakomleniia s polozheniem pereselencheskogo dela* (Saint Petersburg: N.p., 1896), 123–24.

7. L. V. Smirnyagin, "Territorial'naia mifologiia rossiyskogo obshchestva kak otrazhenie regional'nogo chuvstva v russkoy kul'ture," in *Regional'noe samosoznanie kak faktor formirovaniia politicheskoy kul'tury v Rossii,* ed. M. V. Il'in and I. M. Bousygina (Moscow: MONF, 1999), 108–15.

8. M. P. Krylov, *Regional'naia identichnost' v istoricheskom iadre Rossii,* http://SocIs.isras.ru/SocIsArticles/2005_03/krylovmp.doc.

9. R. F. Turovskiy, "Regional'naia identichnost' v sovremennoy Rossii," in *Rossiyskoe obshchestvo: Stanovlenie demokraticheskikh tsennostey?* ed. Michael McFaul and A. V. Riabov (Moscow: Gendalf, 1999), 91.

10. Manuel Castells and Emma Kiselyova, "Russian Federalism and Siberian Regionalism, 1900–2000," *City: Analysis of Urban Trends, Culture, Theory, Policy, Action* 4, no. 2 (July 1, 2000): 193.

11. N. V. Serebrov, *Delo ob otdelenii Sibiri ot Rossii: Sbornik dokumentov iz fondov GARF* (Tomsk: Tomskiy gosudarstvennyi universitet, 2004), 350.

12. A. O. Boronoyev, " 'Sibirstvo' kak forma territorial'noy identichnosti," *Materialy gorodskogo seminara "Sibir i sibirskiy mentalitet,"* Saint Petersburg, April 25, 2002, http://sibident.narod.ru/text/boronoev.doc.

13. Bo Petersson, *National Self-Images and Regional Identities in Russia* (Aldershot, U.K.: Ashgate, 2001), 28.

14. M. V. Shilovskiy, *Politicheskie processy v Sibiri v period sotsyal'nykh kataklizmov 1917–1920-kh* (Novosibirsk: Sibirskiy Khronograf, 2003), 22.

15. Dmitri Trenin, *The End of Eurasia: Russia between Geopolitics and Globalization* (Washington, D.C.: Carnegie Endowment for International Peace, 2002), 22.

16. Jessica Griffith Prendergrast, *Regional Identity and Territorial Integrity in Contemporary Russia: A New Russian Heartland?* http://www.le.ac.uk/geography/research/RussianHeartland/index.html.

17. D. Yuill and V. Ye. Seliverstov, eds., *Regional'naia politika, napravlennaia na sokrashchenie sotsial'no-ekonomicheskoy i pravovoy asimmetrii* (Novosibirsk: EKOR i Sibirskoe Soglashenie, 2000).

18. "Soglashenie o partnetrstve i sotrudnichestve mezhdu Rossiiskoy Federatsiey s odnoy storony, i Evropeyskimi soobshchestvami i ikh gosudarstvami-chlenami s drugoy storony," in *Dokumenty, kasaushchiesia sotrudnichestva ES i Rossii,* ed. Yury Bortko (Moscow: Rossiyskaia akademiia nauk, Institut Evropy, 1996), 84–210; Evgeny G. Vodichev, *Evropeiskiy Souz i Sibir': Opyt realizatsii programm tekhnicheskogo sodeistviia v Sibirskom regione* (Novosibirsk: SibAGS, 2004). 33–58.

19. See, e.g., "Globalizatsia: eto kolonizatsia? Diskussiia v Mezhdunarodnom evraziyskom institute s uchastiem akademika N. Shmeleva, N. Gonchara, M. Deliagina i S. Kaspe," *Russkiy Zhurnal,* February 12, 2002, http://www. oldruss.ru/politics/20020212–stol.html.

20. M. O. Mnatsakian, "Globalizatsia i natsional'noe gosudarstvo: tri mifa," *Sociologicheskie issledovaniia* 5 (May 2004), http://SocIs.isras.ru/SocIsArticles/2004_05/mnatsakanyan.doc.

21. Tatiana Samsonova, "Rossiia v sotsiokul'turnom prostranstve Zapada," in *Rossiia i Evropeyskiy Souz,* ed. Ye. Alexeyeva (Moscow: ROO Sodeystvie sotrudnichestvu Instituta im. Dzh. Kennana s uchenymi v oblasti sotsial'nykh i gumanitarnykh nauk, 2004), 79.

22. Grigoriy Klucharev, "Evropa i Rossiia glazami rossiian," in *Rossiia i Evropeyskiy Souz,* ed. Alexeyeva, 30–58.

23. Samuel Huntington, "Stolknovenie tsivilizatsiy?" *Polis* 1 (February 1994): 35.

24. Boris V. Bazarov, "Vnutrenniaia Mongoliia v geopoliticheskom vzaimodeistvii regionov Rossii i Kitaia," in *Rossiia i Kitayn Na dal'nevostochnykh rubezhakh: Most cherez Amur, Vypusk 7,* ed. A. P. Zabiiako (Blagoveshchensk: Amurskiy gosudarstvennyy universitet, 2006), 44–61.

25. "Sibneft' prinimaut v bol'shuu sem'u Gazproma," *Izvestia,* October 19, 2005.

26. These debates have been inflamed recently by the book by Fionna Hill and Clifford Gaddy, *The Siberian Curse: How Communist Planners Left Russia Out in the Cold* (Washington, D.C.: Brookings Institution Press, 2003).

27. N. V. Sverkunova, "Fenomen sibiriaka," *Sociologicheskiy zhurnal* 8 (August 1996): 90–94.

28. Ibid.

29. Ibid.

30. V. S. Dongak, "Sibir' i sibirskiy mentalitet," in *Materialy gorodskogo seminara "Sibir' i sibirskiy mentalitet,"* Saint Petersburg, April 25, 2002, http://sibident.narod.ru/text/dongak.doc.

31. R. F. Turovskiy, "Regional'naia identichnost' v sovremennoy Rossii," in *Rossiyskoe obshchestvo,* ed. McFall and Riabov, 99.

32. Michael Bradshaw and Jessica Prendergrast, "The Russian Heartland Revisited: An Assessment of Russia's Transformation," *Eurasian Geography and Economics* 46, no. 2 (March 2005): 104.

138   *Evgeny Vodichev and Vladimir Lamin*

33. V. A. Yadov, "Simvolicheskie i primordial'nye solidarnosti v usloviiakh bystrykh sotisal'nykh peremen," in *Problemy teoreticheskoy sotsiologii,* ed. A. O. Boronoyev (Saint Petersburg: Petropolis, 1994), 171.

34. Prendergrast, *Regional Identity and Territorial Integrity,* 15.

35. Ibid., 13.

36. Tamara Troyakova, "A Primorsky Republic: Myth or Reality?" *Communist Economies & Economic Transformation* 10, no. 3 (September 1998): 402.

37. See S. I. Bakhtin, Yu. V. Popkov, and Ye. A. Tugashev, *Terror–antiterror: Sibirskoe izmerenie* (Novosibirsk: Sibirskoe naychnoe izdatelstvo, 2006).

38. A. O. Boronoyev, " 'Sibirstvo' kak forma territorial'noy identichnosti," in *Materialy gorodskogo seminara "Sibir' i sibirskiy mentalitet."*

39. V. V. Simonova, " 'Sibir': Mezhdistsiplinarnyy vzgliad," *Sotciologicheskie issledovaniia* 5 (May 2004), http://SocIs.isras.ru/SocIsArticles/2004_05.

40. Turovskiy, "Regional'naia identichnost' v sovremennoy Rossii," 88.

41. Marshall Goldman, "Russia's Bleeding Heartland," *Central European Economic Review,* September 1997, 6.

42. Petersson, *National Self-Images and Regional Identities,* 178–79.

43. Based on data in Turovskiy, "Regional'naia identichnost' v sovremennoy Rossii," 102.

44. Henry E. Hale and Rein Taagepera, "Russia: Consolidation or Collapse?" *Europe-Asia Studies* 54, no. 7 (November 2002): 1115; Bradshaw and Prendergrast, "Russian Heartland Revisited," 104.

45. Yoshiko Herrera, *Imagined Economies: The Sources of Russian Regionalism* (Cambridge: Cambridge University Press, 2005).

46. An interesting methodology for analyzing identity as a social category is presented in "Identity as a Variable," by Rawi Abdelal, Yoshiko Herrera, and Alastair Iain Johnston, http://www.ncd.ie/euiteniba/pdf/Identity%20as%20a%20Variable.pdf.

5

The Transformation of the Russian System of Higher Education

Gennady N. Konstantinov and Sergey R. Filonovich

The transformation of the Russian educational system since the 1990s has occurred under the influence of the overall reforms that took place in Russia during this time. In particular, the modern reform of Russia's system of higher education has evolved under the influence of three major drivers of change: the overall social, political, and economic transformation of Russia; globalization; and the development of the knowledge economy. As this chapter argues, the central thrust of this transformation has been to embrace the reforms represented by the Bologna Process—including the notion of universities as autonomous institutions of free intellectual exchange, as well as the adoption of Western standards for degrees and certification.

We begin with a brief background overview of Russian educational reform. Second, we present the key aspects of the Bologna Process and indicate the main lines of debate associated with its adoption in Russia. The third section analyzes the connection between the Bologna Process and the larger problem of economic change and globalization. We conclude with the thoughts about current tendencies in educational reform in Russia today.

Background: Russian Educational Reform

The modern Russian higher education system was developed in Soviet times and consists of three basic levels. The first is the equivalent of the undergraduate degree in the West. Thus, after completing their program, students at universities or other higher education institutions receive a bachelor's (*bakalavr*) diploma. At that point, the student can pursue higher education as a researcher. Known as the *aspirantura* level, this requires completing several years of additional study, qualifying exams, and a dissertation, and it culminates in the award of a *kandidatskaya* degree. Finally, those wishing to continue working as a researcher are eligible to receive the highest (*doktorskaya*) degree upon completion and defense of an additional, major body of published work.

Pressure to reform the traditional system originated in the early 1990s. Democratic tendencies and a desire for rapprochement with the West shaped a process that involved transforming the educational system "from the bottom-up," that is, at the level of the leading universities. The latter, on their own initiative, began to move toward a two-tier system of higher education and to develop joint programs with European and U.S. universities. First and foremost, this process affected the area of business education and management. In 1991, the Department of Economics of Moscow State University was the first in Russia to switch over to a multitiered system of training economists by introducing master's and bachelor's programs.[1] In the same year, Irkutsk University and Vladivostok State University opened schools of management as joint undertakings with the University of Maryland University College.

At this stage, a bachelor's degree from a Russian university was not officially accepted by the government. Rather, it was offered and accepted only at the university level. The first official step by Russian authorities directed at the transformation of the higher educational system was associated with a decree of the Committee on Higher Education, "On the Introduction of a Multitiered Structure of Higher Education in the Russian Federation."[2] In reality, this decree legalized the bachelor's and master's degrees in Russia while retaining the traditional diploma that had existed during the time of the Soviet Union. In 1992, the federal law "On Education" went into effect, confirming the principles of academic and economic independence for educational institutions and of freedom of choice in education for teachers and students, and creating a legal foundation for educational reform.

In implementing this reform, Russia's first minister of education, E. D. Dneprov, removed Communist Party committees from the schools and began to implement measures to democratize education. However, because of disagreement with the social policy then being conducted, Dneprov resigned his post as minister at the end of 1992. Partly as a result, the democratic steps taken in the early 1990s bogged down. Not until 1997 was another attempt made to implement the next phase of educational reform, but this only served to confirm the deficiencies of state policy in this area. As Dneprov has noted, the major reasons for the collapse of educational reform in the 1990s were the radicalism of its initiators and the desire to save money on education and transfer the costs of supporting it to the entire population.[3]

At the same time, by the end of the 1990s, a critical mass of reform proponents had emerged within Russia's evolving civil society. The first group of reformers came together within the Graduate School of Economics under the leadership of its rector, Ya. I. Kuzminov, and it operated within the framework of German Gref's Center for Strategic Developments. The second group formed around the Russian School forum. As a result of their efforts, in May 2000, a document titled *A Strategy for Russia: Education* was circulated. One important breakthrough in this document was the adoption of a basic thesis on modernization, according to which the modernization of education—including the reinvention of its content and structure—was central to the modernization of the nation in general. During public discussion of the new document, it became clear that there were two main opposing forces, supporting opposite trends: the reform forces accepted the modernization of education and of the nation; but the conservative forces wanted to retain the old system of education without tying this process to the process of modernizing the country and creating a modern civil society in Russia.[4]

The reformers' initial theses relating to the existing educational system rested on three key points. First, the existing educational system does not provide equal access to a high-quality education. Second, serious conflicts of interest exist between the tendencies of the current educational system and needs for social development, between the market for educational services and the labor market, and between the government and private educational sector. Third, the entire system of education rests on an outmoded system of economic relationships.

As a consequence of this critique, the reformers put forward an alternative proposal. This envisioned a shift to a single state examination, which would eliminate the archaic system of dual educational standards (i.e., graduation exams confirming the high school diploma and a university entrance examination, which virtually ignored the results of high school exams). In addition, it called for a change in the system for financing higher education, by means of vouchers provided to individual students. This part of the reform was intended to create an effective basis for competition among government-supported universities. In both ways, the reformers' plan reflected an interest in bringing Russia into the Bologna Process. The following section provides an overview of this framework and Russia's proposed place within it.

The Bologna Process and Russia

The processes of integration into Europe that has evolved in connection with the Maastricht and Amsterdam treaties naturally include the integration of European education. The basic principles for harmonizing the architecture of the European higher education system were confirmed in the Sorbonne Declaration, which was signed by the ministers of education of France, Germany, Italy, and the United Kingdom in 1998 at the celebration of the Sorbonne's 800th anniversary. The Sorbonne Declaration clearly stresses the active participation of universities in implementing the integration process, proclaiming, "We must build and strengthen the intellectual, cultural, social, and technical base of our continent. To a great extent, this means the universities, which continue to play a breakthrough role in this development."[5]

The four basic principles of the integration processes were expressed earlier (1988) in the "Magna Carta of the University,"[6] signed in Bologna by the rectors of European universities, who had gathered to commemorate the 900th anniversary of the university. The first principle affirms institutional autonomy and the moral and scientific independence of the university from political and economic powers. The second affirms the inseparability of research and teaching in universities. The third defines the university as a space for dialog and the free exchange of knowledge among instructors and students. And the fourth recognizes that universities strive to attain universal knowledge, overcome political and geographical boundaries, and foster interaction among different cultures.

Several other developments accentuated the movement in this direction. In June 1999, in Bologna, the ministers of education of the European countries signed a declaration defining the basic principles for harmonizing educational systems. "A Europe of Knowledge is now widely recognized as an irreplaceable factor of social and human growth and as an indispensable component to consolidate and enrich the European citizenship, capable of giving its citizens the necessary competencies to face the challenges of the new millennium," the Declaration notes.[7] In March 2001, in Salamanca, the Association of European Universities was founded and stated in its own declaration the goal of forming a unified space for European higher education.[8] And in a declaration adopted in 2003, the members of the European Association of Universities confirmed their commitment to the Bologna Process. This last declaration noted that, in the previous phase, the Bologna Process remained within the framework of political interests and had developed "from the top down."[9]

Accordingly, the moment had come to acknowledge that the goals espoused could be realized only if the Bologna principles were deeply integrated into the activities of universities, and thus constituted the foundation for constructing a stable university system. As Pursiainen and Medvedev note, "The Bologna Process should be viewed not only as an internal and isolated phenomenon relevant to the institutions of higher education and academic circles of Europe, but also as a part of vastly more wide-ranging efforts to meet the challenges facing European nations in the context of globalization."[10]

In September 2003, Russia accepted the Bologna Declaration and, in May 2004, it signed a protocol on collaboration with the European Commission on major developmental directions, including those related to general political rapprochement with the European Union. Also in 2003, the EU and Russia agreed to develop a strategic partnership by forming four common areas: economics, internal security and justice, external security, and science and education. On a practical level, these agreements were directed at increasing the ties between the economies of Russia and the EU. The stated goals with regard to forming a common space for science and education reiterated the main goals of the Bologna Process. This suggests that the Bologna Process is becoming not only an example of the rapprochement of Russia and the EU but also an example of effective measures to form all four common spaces.

During this phase, the Russian government served as a conduit for the ideas of the Bologna Process. The deeper principles underlying the understanding of the role of education in rapprochement processes are reminiscent of Edgar Morin's well-known thesis concerning the democracy of reason, and it is these principles that are endorsed by the supporters of the Bologna

Process in Russia. As the rector of Nizhegorod State Linguistic University, Gennadiy Ryabov, writes in his article, "Integration of Knowledge":

> It is precisely the university that has the role of the main partner in international relations, enabling exchanges of instructors and students and, as a result of educational curricula with international orientation, the dissemination of the most advanced methods of instruction and knowledge. Thus, the university again is acquiring its original intellectual and social mission in society in the form of a guarantor of universal values and cultural heritage.[11]

Likewise, the chairman of the Federation Council, Sergey Mironov, stated that "education is the load-bearing structure of modern society. If we want to be worthy participants in the civilization of the third millennium, then a national doctrine of education must become an integral part of the national idea."[12]

The reactions of the professional community to adopting the Bologna Process have varied. There are essentially two dominant viewpoints on this issue. A large and influential group within the educational community supports the persistent propagandistic point of view that the Soviet system of education is the best in the world, and that the main objective should be to retain it as long as possible. For example, consider the argument advanced by the rector of Moscow State University, Viktor Sadovnichiy:

> Let us take, for example, the fifth year of mechanics and mathematics at [the university] and compare the curricula, workloads, subjects, the sequence in which subjects are taught, and the ultimate competence conferred to the competence of a graduate majoring in any discipline from a foreign university. The comparison will come out in favor of our student. Why then do we need a four year course in mathematics when we are number one in the world in the competence of our graduates?! The conclusion is as follows: We must integrate, accept each other's degrees, but we should not decrease the level of Russian education for the sake of allowing students to obtain a bachelor's degree according to a foreign model.[13]

In contrast, the second group believes that Russian higher education was "constructed to be the base of the pyramid of the command economy," is therefore "archaic," "fails to correspond to the new profile of society," and requires total reinvention.[14] The main points of discussion are presented in table 5.1. Evidence of differences in the views of Russians regarding the prospect of Russia's adopting the Bologna Process is based on the results of a survey conducted on the MGIMO Web site.[15] Respondents were asked to answer the question, "What consequence of Russia's adopting the Bologna Process do you fear most?" The answers to this question are included in table 5.1 (the total number of respondents was 1,641).

Those who favor the integration of Russian regional universities and colleges into the European educational space suggest taking the "easy road" to entering the Bologna Process.[16] They propose to concentrate on the pragmatic task of harmonizing the architecture of European higher education, undertaking only the transformations necessary for this goal, while keeping them separate from radical reforms in education.

The European Union supports the transformation of the Russian system of education. A significant role here is played by the tempus Program. The interim results of this program were discussed at a working meeting of the Netherlands Economic Institute on April 15, 2003.[17] Participants in the working meeting noted a general positive trend in the transformation of the Russian system of higher education. Access to higher education had been broadened. The number of university and college students per 10,000 population increased from 176 in the 1993–94 academic year to 327 in 2000–1, while the number of universities increased from 514 in 1990–91 to 965 in 2000–1. The number of non-government-supported universities rose from 78 (14 percent of the total) to 358 (37 percent) during the same period. Curricula were revised; distance education evolved; international contacts were actively created; and the process of integration into the global educational community continued. At the same time, participants in the working meeting identified acute problems, including a huge gap in the quality of education at different Russian universities and colleges, a failure of the educational system to correspond to the needs of the labor market, the excessive rigidity of the educational system, inefficient budgeting at the macro as well as micro levels, a low level of financing for universities and colleges, unequal access to educational services resulting from the combination of free and tuition-based universities, and impeded student mobility.

In late 2003, the EU approved a new program, Erasmus Mundus, which is directed at increasing the quality of European higher education and creating a favorable environment for intercultural understanding, resulting from collaboration with non-EU countries.[18] The program first provides financial support for university consortia, which will jointly develop new

Table 5.1. Answers to the Question "What consequence of Russia's adopting the Bologna Process do you fear most?"

Advocates of the Bologna Process	Advocates of the Unique Advantages of Russia's System of Higher Education
Level playing field for graduates of Russian colleges and universities on the global labor market	*Brain drain*
Russia's educational system must create a level playing field for its graduates on both the Russian and the European labor markets. The Bologna process provides the environment needed for achieving this goal. The desire of talented high school graduates for this advantage would allow them to obtain their education in Russia. Currently the incompatibility among educational systems motivates many secondary school graduates to seek higher education outside of Russia. The system of international grants creates conditions enabling efficient screening of talents immediately after secondary school, during study in a university or college, and, most important, during the process of obtaining master's level education.	The creation of a unified education space creates additional opportunities for a "brain drain." The "brain drain" is a real scourge of Russian science. According to various estimates, the size of this exodus is 200,000 people. The most talented emigrate to the West, contributing to the foreign science and to the flourishing of the nations who entice our scholars."[a] A total of 24.5 percent of survey respondents believe that adopting the Bologna process will lead to brain drain.
An educational space with a single structure	*A threat to fundamental science*
Shift to a three-tier system of "bachelor-master-doctor" would make our educational system internationally "understandable." This could attract students from other countries to the Russian educational system. This system is more "democratic" and allows students more flexibility in the design of their own educational process. The well-being of Russian scholarship would improve as a result of enhancement of the research potential at colleges and universities and their cooperation with European universities.	The three-tier system will decrease the general level of education in our country. The bachelor's degree is excessively general and is more similar to the level of secondary technical education. Elimination of the degrees of "candidate in science" and "doctor of science" will also decrease the value of scientific degrees. This will make the higher level of graduate degrees more accessible. The three-tier system is a serious threat to the entire system of credentialing scientific (scholarly) workforces.
Transparency of the educational space	*Subordination of the Russian educational system to other social requirements*
The Bologna process will help to define the role and place of the Ministry of Education in the system of higher education in a new way and to adopt the experience of European universities, which interact with their ministries of education and retain university	The Bologna process dictates measures to transform the system of education. "All reforms in education must not be reduced to the Bologna process. Russia must have its own educational policy and, in parallel

Table 5.1. *Continued*

Advocates of the Bologna Process	Advocates of the Unique Advantages of Russia's System of Higher Education
autonomy while still being accountable to a reasonable extent to the state. This will facilitate adoption of new forms of institutional accreditation: In addition to the frequently formal government accreditation, accreditation by professional associations will also begin to be used and is vastly more demanding, involving acknowledgment by the professional community of the quality of work of a university or college.[b] "We are talking about a system of education that is more open. But it must be opened not by an administrative 'skeleton key,' but through the creation of normal social institutions,"[c] notes the minister of education and science, Andrey Fursenko.	to its participation in the Bologna process, develop its own specific system of education, based on its internal needs and oriented toward global tendencies," argues S. Smirnov, an adviser to the Russian Ministry of Education.[d] The role of the government will decrease in this area. A total of 15.42 percent of survey respondents believe that, as a result of participating in the Bologna process, government control over higher education will be weakened.
Improvement of educational financing Participation in the Bologna process will stimulate the transition to Western standards for financing higher education.	*Decrease in government spending on education* The government supports the Bologna process, because free education will be provided only at the bachelor's level. Higher levels will require payment. A total of 4.45 percent of respondents consider that adopting the Bologna process will lead to decreases in funding for universities and colleges.
Student mobility and the system of academic credits A unified system of credits and a mobility program will create more differentiated educational programs and give students the opportunity to plan their education independently and to individually tailor a configuration of knowledge.	*Decrease in the significance of degrees issued by the leading colleges and universities* The system of academic credits will lead to a decrease in the overall quality of higher education in our nation's universities and colleges. A student may matriculate in one of the leading Russian institutions of higher education and then "accumulate" a large number of credits in weaker institutions, nevertheless claiming a degree from the leading one.

a. Sergey Leskov, "Utechka umov stanovitsya molozhe," http://www.inauka.ru/science/article 32675.html.

b. For further discussion, see Andrey Yu. Mel'vil', ed., *"Myagkiy put" vkhozhdeniya rossiyskikh vuzov v Bolonskiy protsess* (Moscow: Olma Press, 2005).

c. Andrey Fursenko, "Kriterii uspekha," *Ekonomika i obrazovaniye segodnya,* June 2005.

d. S. Smirnov, "Bolonskiy protsess: Perspektivy razvitiya v Rossii," *Vysshee obrazovanie v Rossii* 1 (2004), http://www.informika.ru/text/magaz/higher/archiv.html#04.

master's programs. The second direction of the program involves grants to Russian students for study in European master's programs, to Russian instructors for teaching in Europe and conducting scholarly research, and to instructors in the EU for teaching in other countries. Finally, the program's third direction is in support of mutual recognition of degrees awarded in higher education.

This transformation of the system of higher education in the first half of the 2000s occurred under the dominant influence of globalization and concomitant integrative processes. Public discussion was significantly tied to the Bologna Process, and it covered issues such as the number and structure of educational levels, the transformation of standards and control systems, the introduction of a credit system, and the allocation of time for the study of various disciplines. Nonetheless, this transformation failed to reflect the broader social changes in the world associated with the formation of a knowledge economy.

The Knowledge Economy and Incipient Trends

It has become almost a truism that we live in a knowledge economy. A comparison of the economic successes of various countries shows that supplies of natural resources are no longer the primary basis for the creation of economic wealth and national prosperity. Rather, the key resource determining a country's prosperity is the human mind. Knowledge has become an economic category, and the capitalization of knowledge is one of the most important economic processes.[19] This in no way means that natural resources are insignificant; the precipitous increase in oil prices is clear evidence of the continuing importance of traditional resources. However, the technologies for using these resources have a completely different basis, and they now rely on scientific knowledge. The same may be said of methods of conducting business. The new instrumentation that information technology has brought about makes those who have mastered it more efficient, influential, dynamic, and successful. Obviously, in connection with all this, the significance of education is changing, as are the areas in which knowledge is generated and the ways in which new generations are prepared for life under new social and economic conditions.

An economy based on knowledge is generally understood to mean one in which the traditional economic factors—labor, capital, and land—have been joined by a new factor—knowledge. Here the role of knowledge has become crucial to the creation of competitive advantages and the formation of economic value. In essence, knowledge acts not as a resource but as capital, which is subject to reproduction in economic cycles. In a 2003 report, the European Commission notes that the core of an economy based on knowledge and of a knowledge society is found in a combination of four independent elements: the production of knowledge, the transmission of knowledge through education, the dissemination of knowledge through the mass media and communications technologies, and the use of knowledge in technological innovations.[20] If we understand knowledge not as disembodied information but as the result of thinking, which may take place formally or informally, then the role of the individual in business, as in society, must change significantly. One of the consequences of such changes is individual competition.

Another consequence of these changes is the substantial growth in the importance of trust in society and the transformation of social capital into the basic source of economic growth. Coleman first introduced the concept of social capital as the capacity of individuals to work together to realize a joint goal.[21] Fukuyama, however, further refined social capital to include the potential of a society (or its components) to develop as a result of trust among its members.[22] By trust, Fukuyama has in mind the shared expectation that arises in the members of a community that other members will conduct themselves in a predictable way, with integrity and consideration of the needs of those around them, and in accordance with certain common standards. Indeed, social capital and the mechanisms for increasing it have always played a role in economic development, but today we can anticipate a significant transformation of the mechanisms for increasing social capital and a sharp increase in its significance in economic development. Fukuyama has noted that in societies with low levels of trust, the network form of organization may lead to paralysis and idleness. At the same time, it is clear that in a knowledge economy, a significant shift toward network organizations in business may be anticipated. The issue of new mechanisms for creating trust arises in this context, and it is not impossible that the central element in the new mechanisms will be the university. Under these conditions, the role of universities in society must change substantially.

From the time when the first universities appeared in Europe (in the thirteenth century), the idea of the role that university education should play was substantially reformulated a number of times. During the initial phase, this role consisted of creating a secular and religious elite capable of running the government and also retaining and transmitting the knowledge that had been accumulated by that time. The limitation and danger for society of this understanding of the university's role was clearly demonstrated by the French philosophers of the Enlightenment, and their ideas influenced the shift to the second phase.

The second phase was associated with the adoption of Enlightenment ideas in the form proposed by Wilhelm von Humboldt in Germany and the theorists of the French Revolution. Humboldt developed a model of the university as an institution for the independent generation and translation of knowledge. The Frenchmen who developed l'École Supérieure created a model of effective instruction, which solved the problem of combining fundamental scientific and practical training (particularly for engineering). The English lagged behind in the transition to the second phase and were able to overcome this only in the mid–nineteenth century.

The third phase, which could be called the transition to mass higher education, is associated with the creation of the U.S. two-tier university system, the basic features of which evolved in the late nineteenth and early twentieth centuries. During this period, it was considered almost self-evident that increasing the proportion of the able-bodied population that had received higher education was virtually perfectly correlated with an increase in the economic prosperity of the corresponding country.

At the present time, there is weighty evidence for concluding that the third phase in the existence of universities has come to an end. A very well-grounded study by the British scholar Alison Wolf, showing that there is virtually no direct relationship between the proportion of a population with higher education and the economic prosperity of its society, is one of the clear demonstrations of this.[23] In addition, Steve Fuller has noted that the transformation of a university education into a mass phenomenon, on the one hand, diminishes the role of secondary education, resulting in an inevitable decrease in its quality and, on the other hand, leads to the need for elite forms of higher education.[24] In all fairness, however, these arguments are clearly insufficient to guide a constructive revision of the role of the university in a knowledge society.

The Current Phase of Reform of Higher Education in Russia

Thus, today's universities are confronting extremely serious challenges whose means of resolution have only been vaguely sketched. This is true globally. For Russia, the selection of a specific method for forming unique competitive advantages on a national scale by means of transforming the university system may have a significant effect on national identity. "In Russia we must form a competitive system for generating, disseminating, and utilizing knowledge. Only such a system can become the basis for stable rates and high quality of economic growth in our nation," remarked Russian president Vladimir Putin in a speech delivered at a session of the Council on Science, Technology, and Education in October 2004.[25]

The new change vector for higher education is virtually fixed, and it is associated with the competitiveness of nations in a knowledge economy. "We must create the foundation for breakthrough innovative development of our country for enhancing its competitiveness. It is obvious that this requires special measures of government support for universities and schools that actively adopt innovative curricula," President Putin stated at a meeting with administration members, the directors of the Federal Assembly, and members of the Presidium of the State Council in September 2005.

In 2006, the National Education Policy Project was announced, which is directly associated with the modernization of Russian education. It is intended to support "growth points" of new high-quality education and the incorporation of new management mechanisms and approaches to stimulate centers for crystallizing institutional changes in education. This project directly targets support of innovative programs in universities and colleges. Thus, a new vector for the transformation of higher education has emerged, and a new stage of reform has begun. What is remarkable about this stage is the active participation of business and the state in the search for alternative ways of developing education, with a critical accent on its globalization. As stated by Aleksandr Shokhin, the president of the Russian Union of Industrialists and Entrepreneurs, "The fact that, today, education is a crucial project for business, as well as for government, is self-evident."[26]

Notes

1. A.Sh. Khodzhayev, "Podgotovka bakalavrov na ekonomicheskom fakultete MGU: Desyatiletnii opyt transformatsii obrazovaniya," http://www.econ.msu.ru/cd/153/; I. G. Teleshova, "Magistratura kak novaya forma podgotovki kadrov v oblasti ekonomiki i upravleniya," http://www.econ.msu.ru/cd/154/.

2. "O vvedenii mnogourovnevoy struktury vysshego obrazovaniya v Rossiyskoy Federatsii," Decree of Committee on Higher Education, no. 13, March 14, 1992.

3. E. D. Dneprov, "Modernizatsiya rossiyskogo obrazovaniya: Impretiv obrazo-

152   *Gennady N. Konstantinov and Sergey R. Filonovich*

vatelnoy politiki," in *Modernizatsiya rossiyskogo obrazovaniya: Dokumenty i materialy* (Moscow: Graduate School of Economics, Moscow State University, 2002).

4. Ibid. The main conservative forces proved to be within the educational environment—the Russian Academy of Sciences and the university rectors.

5. "Sorbonne Joint Declaration," joint declaration on harmonization of the architecture of the European higher education system, signed by the ministers of education of France, Germany, Italy, and the United Kingdom, Paris, May 25, 1998.

6. "Magna Carta of the University," Bologna, September 18, 1988.

7. "Bologna Declaration of 19 June 1999," joint declaration of the European ministers of education.

8. "Shaping the European Higher Education Area," message from the Salamanca Convention on European Higher Education Institutions, Salamanca, March 29–30, 2001.

9. "Graz Declaration," Leuven, July 4, 2003.

10. Christer Pursiainen and Sergey Medvedev, *The Bologna Process and Its Implications for Russia* (Moscow: RECEP, 2005).

11. G. Ryabov, "Integratsiya znaniy," *Ekonomika i obrazovaniye segodnya,* June 2005, 20.

12. Sergey Mironov, "Obrazovaniye i nauka na puti k demokratii razuma," *Ekonomika i obrazovaniye segodnya,* January 2005, http://www.eed.ru/opinions/o_41.html.

13. Viktor Sadovnichiy, "Uspekh reformy v mnogovariantnosti," *Ekonomika i obrazovanie segodnya,* April 2005, 8.

14. See Andrey Yu. Mel'vil', ed., *"Myagkiy put" vkhozhdeniya rossiyskikh vuzov v Bolonskiy protsess* (Moscow: Olma Press, 2005).

15. See http://bologna.mgimo.ru/votes.php?vote_id=1.

16. E.g., a project for this purpose was initiated by the National Fund for Training of Scholars jointly with the nongovernmental organization INO Center, within the program for Interregional Studies in Social Sciences (MION).

17. See http://www.nei.ru/rus/pdf/higher%20Education.doc.

18. "Erasmus Mundus Programme Decision," http://europa.eu.int/comm/education/programmes/mundus/index_en.html.

19. Valeriy Makarov, "The Knowledge Economy: Lessons for Russia," *Social Sciences* 35 (2004): 19–29.

20. European Commission, "Education and Training 2010," 11 November, 2003.

21. James Coleman, "Social Capital in the Creation of Human Capital," *American Journal of Sociology* 94 (1988): 95–120.

22. Francis Fukuyama, *Trust: The Social Virtues and the Creation of Prosperity* (New York: Free Press, 1995).

23. Alison Wolf, *Does Education Matter? Myths about Education and Economic Growth* (London: Penguin Press, 2002).

24. Steve Fuller, *The Intellectual* (London: Icon Press, 2005).

25. See http:///www.kremlin.ru/text/appears/2004/1078524.html.

26. Shokhin's comments were made on the NTV program *Mir,* October 10, 2005.

6

The Russian Defense Industry in the Age of Globalization

Alla Kassianova

In the modern world, the domestic capability to produce weapons is an essential element of the power and security of the state. Both extant and aspiring great powers strive to develop and maintain an indigenous defense industrial base that can guarantee their defense and war-fighting effectiveness. To the extent that weapons production always relies on a nation's natural, human, technological, and manufacturing resources, the defense industry is embedded in the wider domestic economy and is ruled by the same laws that apply to other sectors of productive activity. Conversely, products of the defense industry are of special significance for the state, because they are perceived to provide for the state's security. Thus, the defense industrial sector, even in the market economies, is accorded a special status of extra support and protection from the free sway of market forces. Weapons that are developed and produced will be dependably purchased by the government or allowed to be sold abroad with generous export subsidies and massive diplomatic backing of the deal. More than any other commercial exchange, trade in arms is an "illiberal trade,"[1] with a protected domestic market, subsidized exports, government control over foreign purchases and sales, and political conditionality attached to arms deals.

Yet with the pervasive force of economic globalization, the classical pattern of a nationally bounded defense industrial base, operating on a noncommercial basis, is becoming less tenable than it used to be. The defense industries of the Western world are increasingly acceding to market rules and engaging in cross-border activities, much in line with processes in the world economy as a whole. Changes in the conditions of production for advanced weapons systems are leading to shifts in the character of the state-industry relationship domestically and also provide an adjusted perspective on the meaning of autonomy and interdependence in the quest for security on the world stage.

It is in this context that the defense industrial transformation in Russia becomes part of the larger process of defining Russia's economic and security course in the globalizing world. Russia is facing the pressures of globalization while locked into a vulnerable systemic position of global resource supplier and simultaneously striving to construct a post-Soviet identity that would provide a direction and sense of purpose in this challenging environment (see chapter 3 by Bradshaw and chapter 4 by Vodichev and Lamin). Because the Soviet military industrial complex was at the heart of the Soviet state identity, the current trajectory of the Russian defense industry—its direct descendant—tells a great deal about the evolving nature of the Russian state. Although the major stake in the nation's integration into the world economy appears to be in the area of energy supply, it is also acknowledged that energy export capacity should be complemented by an equally strong high-technology potential. Currently, the imbalance between the two is glaring: High-tech industrial exports constitute a fraction of the nation's overall export sales.[2] Because defense industrial production makes up at least half the volume of high-tech exports, the industry anchors much of Russia's hope for a more prominent profile in the world technological sphere. It is with this prospect in view that, at the turn of the century, the Russian state attempted to consolidate its control over the defense industrial sector and streamline the industry's transformation according to broader national objectives in both the economic and security spheres. However, so far the government has failed to establish either a consistent set of priorities or a working implementation process for defense industrial reform.

Throughout the 1990s, a certain part of the Russian defense industry was engaged in spontaneous cross-border activities that effectively placed some of the companies within the globalized space of international cooperation, mostly outside military production. Other companies specialized in weapons production oriented exclusively toward export, so that the range of their products was determined by the needs of foreign customers rather than of the national army. However anomalous from the point of view of the "normal" role of a national defense industry, the experience of survival during the 1990s delineated the possible ways industry could adjust to the progressively globalizing environment.

Initially, this process occurred in the absence of any conscious state strategy. At present, with the turn to the concept of a "strong power," the current political regime is set to implement a set of reforms designed to optimize defense industrial capacity as a political and strategic resource. However, the policy that has taken shape over the course of the last several years apparently fails to heed the implications of the increasingly global and market-based environment of defense production. The ideological foundations of defense industrial policy, centered on extended state control and the "sovereign" quality of the defense industrial base, undercut the prospects for technological revival and new approaches to security.

This chapter looks into relations between the two protagonists of the defense industrial development: the Russian state and the industry itself, with a stress on the dysfunctional nature of this relationship. It starts with a condensed analysis of relevant policies adopted by the governments of the major arms-producing nations, as the latter have sought to adapt their defense industrial bases to the challenges of the emerging epoch. Next, it characterizes the shape and trends of the transformation of the defense industrial sector in Russia. Specifically, the analysis emphasizes the forms and conditions of international involvement on the part of defense companies. This is followed by a discussion of the ends and means of state policy toward defense industrial reform. On the basis of this comparative overview, the chapter argues that the Western model—that is, breaking out of the national scale of defense production—sets the criteria for a viable development strategy for the defense industry under the pressures of technological innovation and globalization.

The Defense Industry Sector in the Zone of Globalization: U.S. and European Models

Even though analyses of the changes within the defense industry in leading weapons-producing nations often take the end of the Cold War as their starting point, there are grounds to look for the first signs as far back as the mid-1970s. It was then that the expanded application of dual-use technologies in the defense industry "led to fundamental changes in the nature of weapons development" and, specifically, to the "explosion in significance of both interfirm alliances [including cross-border ones] and international sourcing in key dual-use technologies."[3]

Technological progress emerges as a paramount agent of this change. It precipitated the ever-increasing sophistication of weapons and the complexity, cost, and scope of their development, well before the end of the Cold War. Already in the 1980s, U.S. firms in the information technology industry, one of the key dual-use sectors for weapons production, maintained at least 39 percent of their interfirm alliances outside national borders, with companies from Western Europe and Japan.[4] Teaming, including those across borders, allowed companies to share the risks and costs, and stimulated innovation.

From the side of the state, strategic calculations also had an impact on overcoming the national framework of defense production. Interests such as the interoperability of NATO forces and alliance cohesion compelled the United States to admit the expediency of the principle of reciprocity in arms trading and offset arms sales to European allies with licensing and coproduction arrangements, which increased cross-national ties between the American and European industries. In the late 1970s, the U.S. government started signing bilateral memorandums of understanding on reciprocal procurement with its NATO allies, and it continued the practice with an extended group of countries through the 2000s.[5]

Yet it was the end of the Cold War that set off a sea change in defense production. In 1994, the year that proved to be the lowest post–Cold War point in defense expenses, world military spending dropped 35 percent from the level of 1986. U.S. defense spending declined in the same period by 21 percent.[6] In Europe, restrictive military spending was also necessitated by fiscal obligations under the Maastricht Treaty. With reduced military budgets, governments were no longer able to support high levels of weapons production. Companies sought to compensate for the fall of domestic orders with sales on the international market, thereby stumbling on a strategy that pushed them toward commercialization. As the share of arms imports in total imports in the world fell from 1986 to 1996 by more than three times,[7] while all Western arms-producing industries were resorting to exports to level out falling sales, the international weapons market turned intensely competitive.

It is well known that the answer to these suddenly adverse conditions, on the part of the state and the weapons producers, was a concerted effort of defense industrial restructuring. The 2002 *Yearbook* of the Stockholm International Peace Research Institute identifies these elements as "concentration, internationalization, and privatization."[8] Most visibly, the *consolidation* of the industry occurred at the level of major prime contractors, through a series of mergers and acquisitions. The result was the emergence of a handful of U.S. defense giants, whose annual defense revenues run from $10 billion to $30 billion, and a few comparable entities in Europe with defense revenues in the range of $7 billion to $20 billion (e.g., BAE Systems).[9] The concentration of the defense industry proceeded unevenly across different sectors and has lately slowed down, but it remains a continuous trend, now occurring at the second- and third-tier supplier level. *Privatization* and *internationalization* are interwoven processes, because the privatization of formerly public defense enterprises was undertaken with a view toward attracting private investment, a considerable portion of which comes in the form of cross-national shareholdings. Another source of privatization is the growing outsourcing of services to private companies, which further commercializes the defense industrial sector.[10]

A broad view of internationalization extends the notion to all forms of cross-border activities: international trade, foreign investment, subcontracting, licenses, mergers and acquisitions, joint ventures with looser forms of agreements including coproduction, management consortia, and teaming arrangements.[11] Alternatively, a number of approaches attempt to capture the essence of the process with the notion of *globalization* or *transnationalization.* This approach emphasizes such key aspects as subcontracting to a transnational supplier base and building interfirm alliances primarily targeted at technological development.[12] Or, more narrowly, it includes the consolidation strategies pursued by firms seeking to become viable global players.[13] To the extent that the current restructuring of defense industries is geared toward a market- rather than state-regulated domain, the term "internationalization," which reinforces the idea of state agency, appears less preferable than the term "transnationalization," which underscores a less statecentric view. Despite the continued critical role of the state in defense industrial transformation, which will be discussed further, the choice of terms should acknowledge the shifting balance between the respective agencies of the state and the industry, a trend that makes the current process so remarkable.

Transnationalization emerges as a striking feature of the restructuring of the defense industry. A certain part of the consolidation mentioned above occurred across national borders.[14] Apart from full acquisitions, cross-shareholdings with a complicated structure of transnational ownership are now a characteristic feature of some defense sectors in Europe.[15] This emerging situation does not easily fit with the old view of a "national" defense base. BAE Systems, which is still often referred to as a "British national champion," at several points in 2003 and 2004 had up to 54 percent of its stock owned by foreign shareholders.[16] Many of the key European players are using the purchase of shareholdings in the wider world "to reach into other markets," buying across the Atlantic and within Europe, as well as in South Africa, Australia, South Korea, and other countries.[17] Cross-shareholding relations are complemented (as well as complicated) by joint ventures and teamings that spring up around weapons development programs. All contemporary weapons programs involve international collaboration, as a way to share the development costs and ensure longer production runs by committing the partners to procure the system. Finally, as suggested by Brooks, defense production is increasing its transnational "dispersal" by virtue of running enormously long supplier chains, which inevitably spread beyond the national borders. This also occurs as a result of companies' reliance on commercial technologies that have long acquired a global scope.[18] Assessments of defense industrial capability and technology performed by the U.S. Bureau for Industry and Security generally reveal that varying degrees of import dependency exist across most industrial sectors selling to the Department of Defense.[19]

As a result of these changes, the notion of a "national defense industrial base" in the experience of the Western weapons-producing nations is being revised in at least two respects. The idea of "national" is losing its connotation of "autonomous," and "national" is no longer the only possible framework for conceptualizing defense production. In the same way, the assumption of "defense industry" existing as a distinctive domain within a national economy is rendered increasingly incongruous, because weapons production is being gradually blended into the globalized, market-ruled economic context. It is true that the major prime-contractor tier of weapons production preserves a recognizable defense industrial front, because either whole companies or their subdivisions are predominantly oriented toward developing and manufacturing weapon systems. At the same time, they have all the appearances of standard multinational corporations engaging in commercial activity on a global scale, ready to clash in competition and fully in their element among other market players. As for the thousands of smaller prime contractors selling directly to defense departments, or the still more thousands of subcontractor companies further down the production chain of major weapons systems, these are completely normal market players subject to the same market laws as any other company for which the defense market is unattractive, irrelevant, or hard to enter.

The Role of State Regulation

Yet even with all this globalized blending, the products delivered by the top defense contractors at the end of the multitiered and sometimes transnationally dispersed production chains are different from the other products on the market, because the state depends on them to provide for its conventional security. Traditionally, the relationship between the national government and national defense producers rested on the exercise of government regulation and intervention. The fact that today's defense industries have restructured to fit the standards of today's economy—which is globalized in scope and neoliberal in character—is a necessary condition for preserving companies' efficiency but insufficient for their full market emancipation. As was suggested above, defense markets are inherently illiberal, insofar as governments are both exclusive buyers and regulators. To quote Skons and Baumann, "Defense budgets determine domestic demand for military equipment and provide the bulk of R&D [research and development] funding, while procurement policy determines the degree of competition faced by the domestic companies. Governments formulate policies on foreign ownership in the arms industry and exert influence through intergovernmental cooperation."[20]

The new conditions of weapons production, and especially the astronomical cost of advanced technologies, require flawlessly calculated policies on the part of governments. On the one hand, to cope with the rocketing costs of weapons development, they have to endorse the transnationalization and commercialization of defense production. On the other hand, a number of traditional national security considerations, deeply embedded in policymaking structures and process, run squarely against these trends. The three principal concerns are

- the fear of losing an effective domestic defense industrial base;
- the risk of compromising the lead in advanced weapons technologies; and
- the threat of escalating arms proliferation.

As a result of such concerns, what on a general level can be called government policy is actually highly differentiated, with key divisions among the relevant actors. In the United States, interests clash around enhancing versus weakening the "buy American" provisions in defense procurement, and tightening versus loosening arms export controls. The House of Representatives in Congress traditionally is strongly in favor of restrictive domestic procurement, whereas the Senate may show more flexibility.[21] Within the government, the Defense Department is seen to be increasingly siding with defense companies in pressing to slacken arms export controls, in the hopes of spreading "development costs of a weapon system more broadly through exports," whereas the State Department is less willing to subordinate security concerns to commercial aspirations.[22]

In Europe, defense industrial policy has lately come to be aggregated on the EU level, which may be recognized as one of the most impressive manifestations of European integration. The introductory remarks on the European Defense Agency Web site read like a manifesto: "No national defense budget in Europe is any longer large enough to sustain a full spectrum of defense technological and industrial capabilities on a national basis. Greater pooling of efforts and resources, and greater reciprocal dependence, is inevitable if Europe is to retain world leading capabilities."[23]

The notion of a defense and technological industrial base thus makes new sense as a system of crossing over from the national to the "truly continental" level. The new scale of the European defense and technological industrial base, however, only reinforces the idea of an efficient "domestic" defense industrial base as a key condition of collective military capability. The language clearly states that the changes "aim to foster intra-European rather than international competition" and seek to minimize "the competitive advantages currently enjoyed by non-European industries."[24]

Defense industrial regulation by the Western leaders of weapons production—though complex, multiform, and grappling with many sets of divisive interests—nevertheless betrays some general similarities that evidently contribute to its apparent competence. First, governments take a proactive attitude toward the problem and base their policy on close interaction with the actors involved. In the United States, the Pentagon set the direction for consolidation of the defense industry in the early 1990s. In the United Kingdom, the government has both offered the concept of "value for money" and provided energetic leadership in its implementation, placing emphasis on "developing regular dialogue."[25] In France, the government has exercised large-scale intervention through technological support programs, and it is indeed closely integrated (in spite of recently opting for greater privatization) with industry through market and nonmarket relationships.[26] On the EU level, from the late 1990s to the present, governments have been realizing "continental-scale demand and market," step-by-step setting up mechanisms and procedures for joint capability assessment, coordination of acquisition, collaborative development projects, and European-wide competition in national defense procurement. Both in the United States and Europe, the appropriate agencies keep track of the state of the industry through regular surveys or assessments, and they maintain a "culture of transparency" beneficial to prospective contractors in matters of acquisition and procurement.

Second, arising from this close interaction, and clearly visible in government language, is an appreciation by the state of the specifics of the commercial domain as well as a respect for the commercial concerns of industrial actors. From the governments' perspective, "market forces" are there to help achieve cost efficiency and competitiveness. Governments are conscious of the superior effectiveness of market regulations, and they are also aware of the fact that companies in the most numerous category of defense contractors—that supplying components and subsystems—have an option to exit the field if the costs imposed by the complexity of procurement procedures and bureaucratic constraints bear too heavily on profit margins.[27] The imperative, therefore, is to fine-tune regulation, based on the perceived interests of the state as well as the sensitivities of the commercial players. The state, however, firmly stands by its own sensitivities in the matter of arms export controls.

Transnationalization presents a tough test for government defense industrial regulation, and it remains an area of conflicting pressures. At least two effects can be singled out as important. First, the transnationalized zone developed historically on the basis of allied relations. Strategic alliance considerations (as well as the culture of accumulated trust) continue to weigh heavily in policy debates against the traditionalists' aspirations of autonomy and protectionism. Second, as weapons producers are turning into "normal" market players, and the defense production chain cannot realistically be controlled or even monitored beyond the first two tiers of participating companies, the trade-off between autarchic defense industrial capability and technologically advanced, cost-effective defense industrial capability is bound to become increasingly difficult. Within Europe, the states have accepted the idea that "greater reciprocal dependence is inevitable if Europe is to retain world leading capabilities." In contrast, U.S. defense industrial policy is still strongly influenced by a belief on the part of the political establishment that an effective state defense industrial base, ideally not dependent on foreign sources of supply, is indispensable for national security.[28]

The Russian Defense Industry:
Structural Characteristics and Trends

What is the shape of the Russian defense industrial sector as measured against the demands of the globalizing trend in weapons production? Are Russian defense companies fit to be successful market players?

From a historical perspective, the institutional legacy—much of which was accumulated during the Soviet period—is hardly amenable to market culture. The relationship between the state and the defense industry during Soviet times went beyond the total dependence of the industry on the state for guaranteed access to resources, priority of supply, and secure sales; in fact, it extended to a full symbiosis, or merger, between the two.[29] For all its brutal effect, the decade of the 1990s—during which the former military-industrial complex (MIC, or VPK) ceased to exist as an economic entity and the defense companies had to start faring on their own—failed to break from the old identity. By the 2000s, the old concept of the MIC was still around in the language (changing the attribute "Military" to "Defense," but still presuming a "complex") and in the organizational approach. Among several possible criteria for identifying a defense enterprise, the choice went to the formal attribute: The enterprise was considered as belonging to the Defense Industrial Complex (OPK) if it fell under the administration of a dedicated federal authority—no matter what its share of military output. The state's policy is firmly based on the idea of a distinct place occupied by the sector within the Russian economy, with all its enterprises listed in the government registry, so that in any given year an exact number of companies can be produced to describe its size.[30] The defense industry is thus presumed to be a closed-circuit system, as opposed to being integrated with the rest of the economy. The special status of the defense industry is also supported by another registry, which lists "strategic" enterprises subject to special bankruptcy and ownership regulations. This registry lists enterprises providing for "strategic interests, defense capability and security of the state, protection of morale, health, rights and lawful interests of Russian Federation nationals," and it includes most of the Russian defense companies.[31]

The ownership pattern of the defense industry remains ambiguous. The ownership structure is usually presented as being broken into three groups:

fully state-owned "unitary" enterprises (roughly 36 percent in 2003); "stock companies with state participation" (33 percent); and "stock companies without state participation" (31 percent).[32] Over the years, the first group has tended to hollow out, for many unitary enterprises are slated to be transformed into stock companies. During the 2000s, several hundreds of formerly public enterprises went through this transformation, which in most cases signified a change more in form than in substance, as the newly created stock companies normally become 100 percent state owned. Given this trend, the three-tier breakdown disguises an actual prevalence of state-controlled forms of ownership. In most of the second-tier companies, the state enjoys a controlling position through "the golden share" (or controlling share) scheme, whereas in the third, formally "private" category, some collective shareholders are merely a front for state interests.[33]

Another part of the ownership issue is the nominal status of companies that are formally characterized as stock companies. In 2003, out of some 900 formal stock companies in the defense sector, only 87 had their stock listed on the Russian stock market, and only 24 had their stock actually traded that year.[34] Out of all Russian private defense firms, only the aircraft builder Irkut Corporation has been listed on the London Stock Exchange since 2005; Irkut's stock is also the absolute leader, in turnover, of Russian aviation and defense industry stocks. According to experts, crucial factors discouraging investors include low liquidity, strategic uncertainty, nontransparent management, and the fractionated character of the industry. It is generally believed that the emerging integrated defense entities (so-called holdings) will be more attractive for stock market players. At the same time, analysts are wary of the still-unclear intent of state policy in relation to private stockholders in the defense industry.[35]

These ownership issues are indeed central, as the state unrolls a program of consolidation of the Russian defense industrial base, which is to occur through the creation of several dozen integrated "holdings" specializing in specific armaments sectors. The process is administered in a top-down fashion and is firmly embedded in a statist doctrine of expanding control over "strategic" areas of the economy. From this standpoint, the presence of a private segment within the defense industry cannot but complicate the process. The existing solution edges toward renationalizing private defense companies by offering to transfer a part of their stock to government agencies or state-control entities. Various ideas for deprivatizing schemes have included claiming state ownership of intellectual property created during Soviet times, or of the land occupied by a company's facilities, and converting these ownership rights to a share in the company's stock.[36] For example, in setting up a helicopter "holding" during 2005–6, privately owned Rosvertol was expected to issue new shares and transfer them to the state in exchange for capital investment; it was then to have an additional issue bought by a state-owned head enterprise, so that the state-controlled stock amounted to a blocking share.[37] The increased state defense order (Gosoboronzakaz, or GOZ) has provided leverage to make defense companies accept the benefits of state participation in their stock, because procurement orders preferentially go to enterprises under the state's control.

Given the preexisting condition of weak state regulation and broad differentiation within the industry, complications associated with private ownership are only part of the maze of property and control conflicts inherent in the consolidation process. As against the original plan of setting up several dozen holdings by 2004, as of 2006 the tally was hardly half a dozen, with several in different stages of organization. Moreover, the entire process remains remarkably opaque with regard to interfirm cooperation and integration.[38]

The low attractiveness of investment in defense companies negatively affects the financial well-being of the sector. Data from a defense managers survey collected over six years indicate that "outdated equipment" was seen as a relentlessly growing factor standing in the way of successful performance. In 2002, only 2 percent of respondents considered the equipment base at their enterprises sufficient to meet international standards, while 64 percent characterized it as outdated. "Shortage of capital" was pointed to as the second most important factor inhibiting adaptation to market conditions.[39] It is interesting that during an eight-year spell (1995–2002), the "outdated equipment" factor showed a clear progressive trend, while the "shortage of capital" factor moved in the opposite direction. This may suggest that whereas overall investment in the defense industry was growing, capital investment was being made in increasingly insufficient quantities.

Since 2000, the defense sector has been receiving increased allocations from the federal budget, both for capital investment through federal target programs and for "state defense orders" (i.e., GOZ) which cover defense R&D, procurement, modernization, and repair of military equipment. Still, for Russian industry in general, the share of investment in fixed capital from of the companies' own funds is much larger than the share provided by the federal budget.[40] And borrowed funds, including bank loans and external investment, appear to be the weakest link. On balance, the effect of the increased federal budget funds that have been channeled into the industry is mixed. Given the nontransparent process through which funds are distributed, the politics of the enlarged GOZ and federal programs appear to be designed to empower the bureaucracy and cultivate the industry's dependency on the state.

Defense industrial companies do perform comparatively well on the domestic civil market. Between 1998 and 2001, the number of the companies with a predominantly (more than 50 percent) civil production was twice the share of companies with predominantly military output.[41] The defense industrial sector provides a greater share (from 75 to 100 percent in different economic sectors) of high-technology civil production, and in recent years it has strongly contributed to national economic growth.[42] Still, the domestic market remains narrow. According to the directors' survey data, at no time from 1997 to 2002 were defense enterprises able to realize more than 57 percent of their productive capacity.[43] Furthermore, though civil production in the overall defense industry output amounts to 43 percent, 85 percent of the industry's export sales come from military items.[44] This suggests that the supposedly hi-tech civilian goods manufactured by Russian defense companies are not competitive enough outside the domestic market. One of the latest trends in advancing the diversification of defense companies is attracting investment and orders from the energy sector. Only 10 percent of the funds allocated by a federal program to develop high-tech equipment for fuel and energy industries comes from the federal budget.[45]

The irony of post-Soviet defense industry development is that military output throughout the period overwhelmingly went to foreign armies. It is a broadly admitted fact that the technological core of the Russian defense industry survived by producing for export. On the surface, the international performance of Russian defense producers looks good. Exports sales kept growing each year until they hit a high point of $5.8 billion in 2004.[46] Russian companies are present in the annual rankings of world's top defense firms compiled by the Stockholm International Peace Research Institute and *Defense News,* even though they occupy places closer to the bottom of the list. The best performer, the aircraft builder Sukhoi, was in the thirty-fourth position in 2005.[47] Yet these firms' success in the international market, though no doubt hard earned, cannot be a direct indicator of the market maturity of the Russian defense industry as a whole and even of the individual exporting companies. Literally a handful of companies hold licenses to independently sell their end-products in the international market; about twenty others hold licenses for direct sales of spare parts. Between most companies and the market stands the so-called state intermediary Rosoboronexport, which is authorized to perform the entire range of export-related activities on behalf of defense producers. Since 2000, when Rosoboronexport was established under its present name, this "state corporation" has hardened its claim on monopolist status in military exports and extended its influence in the defense industry by planting representatives on the boards of directors of major defense companies, buying stock and investing in R&D for export-designed systems. The creed behind this strategy falls squarely in line with strengthening the "presidential *vertical* of running the system of military and technical cooperation."[48] However efficiently this system may appear to run from the state's viewpoint, it constraints international exposure—and the general faculty of independent agency—on the part of individual companies.

The ranking lens on the industry helps reveal a deep structural problem. As repeatedly pointed out by the Moscow-based Center for the Analysis of Strategies and Technologies (CAST), which pioneered monitoring the performance of defense enterprises, companies make their way to top sales ranking positions exclusively by selling for export.[49] This ranking shows that, so far, the dramatic nominal growth of the state defense order (i.e., GOZ) has not started to balance the export bias among the factors driving defense production. With the amount of the GOZ in 2004 and 2005 comparable to the amount of export sales, the sales figures of the top-selling companies have not registered the supposed growth of the domestic market. A whole range of different factors are relevant to explain this situation. It is known that a large but unspecified share of the GOZ goes to the nuclear strategic sector, whose figures have never yet been made public; another significant share is allocated to R&D and therefore has a longer-term effect; and yet another share is spent to overhaul and repair.[50] More important, the seemingly traceless dispersal of the $5 billion procurement funds in 2004 and $6 billion in 2005 indicate a problem—on the one hand, with the system of state regulation, which is not able to efficiently administer procurement; and, on the other, with the disintegrated and weak state of the industry, which easily absorbs federal money but lacks its own resources to generate a noticeable return. A serious downside of this continuing export reliance is the contingent character of financing for R&D, which mostly comes as self-financing from export revenues. This makes even the more successful exporting Russian defense companies incapable of strategic technological innovation, because their R&D priorities may be shaped by the needs of their foreign customers while their funding tends to depend on the dynamics of the market.

The International/Transnational Dimension

An in-depth look at the international dimension of the Russian defense sector must go far beyond arms export statistics. In addition to the arms trade, the international activities of defense industries include arms trade with reciprocal purchases, licensed production, coproduction, and codevelopment (i.e., cooperative R&D).[51] In view of the globalization of defense production, which is extending the production chains of complex weapon systems deep into dual-use and civil sectors and widely across the globe, the transnational inclusion (defined as participation in transnationally dispersed production) of Russian defense companies should be examined as well.

Starting with the basic forms of international activity, arms sales for export remain the most visible part of Russia's international presence in defense industries. According to official data, Russia is engaged in "military-technical cooperation" with more than eighty countries, and in the past three years it has annually sold more than $5 billion worth of weapons. In spite of the rising volumes of export sales, experts have expressed caution about maintaining this dynamic. They have pointed out that the export structure is poorly diversified in terms of both customer countries (in 1994–2004, China and India together bought 57 percent of the Russian armaments exported[52]) and products (combat aircraft long were the absolute leader in sales). Even more threatening has been the looming exhaustion of the bank of technologies that had been developed as far back as the 1970s and 1980s, with no developments of comparable scope currently under way. In fact, the results of recent years have shown that export policy has been directed toward the diversification of products and customers, because the leading export categories include not only aircraft but also naval equipment and air defense systems; exporters have made inroads into the Middle East, North Africa, Latin America, and Southeast Asia. Steps have been taken to complement these arms sales with the provision of maintenance; Rosoboronexport and individual companies are setting up service and training centers in customer countries; and exporting spare parts is the only kind of independent international activity for individual companies that is favored by the state. Though these developments fall within the global pattern of the commercialization of the arms trade, the central trend in the Russian case gravitates toward the extension of state control and putting more weight on the political instrumentality of weapons exports. The state has reintroduced the export support credit system, which had been absent in the 1990s, and has continued to pursue arms-export-for-debt schemes, including some as ambitious as the expected $4 billion deal with Algeria.[53]

Throwing the Russian state's weight behind securing arms deals may not necessarily be beneficial for the industry. Some of the markets "inherited" from the Soviet Union—China, Iran, and Syria—for political reasons lie outside the activity area for Western arms producers, and thus sales in these markets cannot be accurate indicators of the competitiveness of Russian weapons. Similarly, producing for these markets may not offer the strongest stimulus for innovation; nor can it provide optimal conditions for collaborative technological development. And from a political standpoint, strong military ties with some of the internationally marginalized states may constrict Russia's range of policy options.

In this respect, the institutional framework supporting international defense cooperation is of special importance. In the case of transatlantic defense industrial ties, the culture and structures of security cooperation within NATO have been cultivated for decades; and in the trans-European case, security ties have been part of a powerful momentum for European integration. With Russia, the only comparable existing framework is the Collective Security Treaty Organization (CSTO) of the Commonwealth of Independent States (CIS). Unlike the transatlantic and European security communities, where the common strategic and political project was historically primary and fed the momentum for cross-border defense industrial integration, in the CSTO the defense industrial layer of cooperation actually appears to sustain the political part of the process. It may be argued that the basis for this lies in the cross-border enterprise-to-enterprise ties surviving from the Soviet period. In this sense, even though the agency of the state is a prerequisite for authorizing cross-border cooperation in the production of weapons, the impulse for cooperation comes from economic agents and bears a transnational (as opposed to state-mediated, international) quality. According to a state official, in 2005 some 500 defense companies in Russia maintained "cooperative ties" with more than 1,200 enterprises from the CIS.[54] Even with all the negative bilateral dynamics on the political level, in late 2005 some 400 Russian defense firms still used Ukrainian supply components. Conversely, Russian companies supplied about 75 percent of components for the Ukrainian-built space carrier *Zenith*.[55]

The Russian defense industry has a significant interest in the CIS markets, with a view to upgrading the older Soviet-made weapons and securing new procurement contracts as well as maintaining a cost-efficient supply base. For its part, the Russian state has its own political and strategic priorities in the region that can be served by military-technical cooperation. The case of international defense cooperation in the CIS gives a good demonstration of the interplay of the political and economic: With a roughly even spread of Soviet weapon production chains across today's Russia, Belarus, Ukraine, and Kazakhstan, most state support on the Russian side goes to dynamic defense integration with Belarus, whereas many former ties with Ukrainian firms have been cut, some joint production systems have been discontinued, and others have been reoriented to alternative (sometimes Western) supply bases for predominantly political reasons. All in all, the CIS (or CSTO) framework can offer the Russian defense industry neither the necessary scale of activity nor the stimulating partnerships or incentives to innovate. With regard to non-CIS large customers, the high figures for arms sales do not entail the development of a "security community" type of relationship. This holds true for other forms of cooperation as well (with certain reservations for India, as discussed below).

In the context of globalization, coproduction and codevelopment partnerships become the crucial forms of defense industrial cooperation. Coproduction often springs from offset arrangements in the arms trade and involves manufacturing components or eventually whole systems under license. Because this process includes technology transfer, it is a state-mediated activity normally based on interstate agreement. In the Russian arms trade, licensed production and assembly continue to display a distinctly Soviet pattern: In the early 1990s, Russia sold licenses—including for the production of tanks, antitank missiles, and portable SAM missiles—to honor Soviet contracts with Poland, Romania, Bulgaria, Yugoslavia, North Korea, Iran, and India. The second round of licensed production deals, notably for aircraft, came in the middle to late 1990s with China and India.[56]

With respect to codevelopment, the Russian record has not stood up to the challenge of the times. The Western practice of collaboratively developing major weapon systems, concentrating public and private resources, lies outside the international experience of Russian defense companies. Collaborative codevelopment projects on a major scale involving shared risks and investment are virtually nonexistent. One major exception is the Indian-Russian Brahmos joint venture, which was started between NPO Mashinostroyenia on the Russian side and the Defense Research and Development Organization of the Indian Ministry of Defense in1998 to develop and produce a supersonic cruise missile for the Indian Navy. Investment in the project amounted to $240 million, with the stakes in the joint venture being 61 percent for India and 39 percent for Russia. By 2004, the missile was tested and was ready for serial production, by both the Russian and Indian industries. Other joint ventures of comparable scale are hard to name: The Russian-Ukrainian project to develop and coproduce the AN-70 transport aircraft was crippled by ineffective management and political vendettas, increasingly turning out to be an embarrassment instead of a binding venture. International Launch Services between Lockheed Martin, Khrunichev, and Energia has worked successfully since 1993, but it can hardly be counted as a codevelopment project because its launchers had been essentially developed autonomously in the United States and the Soviet Union / Russia.[57] Russian officials have brought up the prospect of developing a fifth-generation fighter aircraft in partnership with India, but practical steps, if any, have been unintelligible so far. Russian defense firms are, however, teaming with the Indian HAL Corporation in developing a transport aircraft.

However archaic the overall makeup of the Russian defense industrial sector, some of its entities do in fact lie within the transnational space of cross-border production chains. The air and space industries offer a generic example of both civil-military integration and cross-border supplier ties. Some of the cases have been well publicized: The private Irkut Corporation partnered with EADS to market and sell Be-200 amphibious aircraft, which have avionics developed by a U.S.-Russian joint venture, an airborne observation system designed by an Israeli company, a cabin interior provided by a U.S. firm, and (prospectively) an engine produced by Rolls-Royce.[58] Conversely, Irkut and another private aircraft group, Kaskol, have signed an agreement to manufacture parts for the European Airbus. Kaskol's president, Sergei Nedoroslev, was an outspoken advocate of the "niche" integration of Russian aircraft builders into global production chains, even at the expense of surrendering system integrator status.[59] Individual cases of Russian firms becoming part of transnational production chains include the Vyborg vessel-building plant constructing a sea platform for U.S. sea-based radar deployed as part of the U.S. missile defense system in 2002[60] and a 2005 contract by the state-owned Omsk company Polyot to build, as a subcontractor for a German-Italian joint venture, a satellite platform for a satellite ordered by the U.S. Coast Guard. Polyot also subcontracts to the German company OHB-System AG to build launchers for five German military satellites.[61] Dozens of other examples might be mentioned, all of which reveal that individual Russian defense companies are in fact more effectively integrated into the global than the national economic space.

The Handicap of the President's "Power Vertical"

The basic problem for the Russian defense industrial sector is that the national space, which is supposed to be the primary arena for companies producing for defense, provides neither the direction nor regulation necessary for meaningful development. The structural weaknesses and disparities within the sector make it especially important for the government to conceive an intelligent strategy for restructuring the defense industry in the context of globalizing trends. However, both in its conceptual foundation and (especially) its implementation process, Russian defense industrial policy does not stand up to this challenge.

With regard to conceptual development, the years 1999–2000 were a turning point that revealed the political will needed to reverse the apparent decline of the defense industrial sector, optimize regulation, and ensure a strong defense industrial base. Yet the ideology behind this determination remains ambiguous. On the one hand, some key officials in charge of the economy as a whole (German Gref, minister of economic development and trade) and the defense industry in particular (Boris Alyoshin, head of the Federal Industry Agency) have consistently emphasized expanding the use of market instruments in the defense industry. On the other hand, the constituency for the Soviet-like model of direct state administration of the sector is wider, and it includes officials across most relevant ministries and institutions. The resulting official line is inconclusive. In 2001, Russia's president insisted that "the breakthrough development of defense industrial complex, qualitative increase of its efficiency and competitiveness are only possible today on the basis of a consistent and conscious introduction of market instruments. There is no other way."[62] In 2005, Defense Minister Sergei Ivanov, having just been appointed vice prime minister specifically in charge of the defense industry, observed while visiting the tank manufacturer Uralvagonzavod that its possible privatization could only be imagined by "feverish minds of not quite sensible people."[63] Several concepts and programs adopted in 2001–5 include equal reference to both market transformation and state control.[64]

The policies that transpired over the same period, however, are less ambiguous, and they point to the steady expansion of state control. Manifestations of this intent are numerous:

In both legislation and real life, there has been a noticeable preference for increasing the share of state-controlled ownership of defense companies. Procurement contract awards are biased toward state-owned firms, and the state secures a controlling stake in the "integrated structures" (holdings) that are created as part of industry restructuring. Only companies with 51 percent of stock controlled by the state (and none by foreign shareholders) are allowed by current law to have an independent presence in the international market.

The state monopoly on international sales has concentrated much authority in Rosobornexport, which is turning into a metaholding with powers to regulate access to the world market and manage financial flows. It is also becoming a state proxy in the area of ownership, acquiring shares in attractive companies and newly created holdings as well as investing in projects with guaranteed prospects for exports.

A craving for control may offer a plausible explanation for the creeping multiplication of institutions and officials in charge of overseeing this sector. Merely compiling a list of committees, federal agencies, ministry departments, and other institutions regulating the defense industry is a daunting task; understanding how their respective competencies interrelate is simply not possible. One of the last developments, which placed ultimate "coordinating" authority in the person of the defense minister, has further complicated rather than simplified the regulatory system.

However, any monochromatic or aggregate view might be misleading. The enormity of resources needed to modernize the defense industrial sector pushes officials to recognize the necessity of attracting nonstate investment. Characteristically, most defense-related federal target programs envisage the share of "nonbudget" funds to exceed the funds allocated from the federal budget. State policy visibly places value on the international success of Russian defense companies; state officials use their international contacts to invite partners for collaborative ventures. The latest program of national social and economic development through 2015 (adopted at the beginning of 2006) envisages civil diversification up to 70 percent of the defense industry's output, as well as cooperation with "leading foreign firms" in advanced civil aerospace projects. The same program, however, also emphasizes the protection of a comprehensive, autonomous defense production base.[65]

It is obvious that this lack of conceptual clarity results from the struggle of interests within the bureaucracies connected to the defense sector. In the words of the defense analyst Ruslan Pukhov, "about half a dozen economic and politico-bureaucratic groups . . . even as they are hoisting up the banner of state control in the 'strategically key industry' are actually pursuing quite pecuniary interests."[66] In the last several years, a firmly established trend reflects the prevalence of group interests—especially associated with individuals from security service backgrounds—in gaining control of strategically significant (and, by coincidence, highly profitable) sectors or companies. Weapons production for export brings billions of dollars in annual sales to one of the most nontransparent sectors of activity, still shrouded in the tradition of "state secrets." Likewise, in the absence of legislative and public control, the progressively growing state defense order (i.e., GOZ) and military budget in general raises the bureaucratic stakes of controlling financial flows. In this context, the weakness of state policy means an inability to set up procedures and mechanisms for evaluating the validity of interests as well as the impact of competing groups. Defense industrial policy is of course no different from the general pattern of the decisionmaking process, which itself is embedded in the feeble culture of public control and accountability.

On the implementation side, the elaborate top-down system of defense industrial policy that was set up in recent years has so far been spectacularly inefficient. Administrative reorganizations happened almost on a rolling basis; adopted programs were invariably left unrealized. With the defense budget increased to impressive numbers, the actual disbursements of funds occur with delays that in 2002–3 generated about 55 billion rubles of arrears in state payments to companies.[67] Even more surprising, given the stated objective of increasing effectiveness through the state regulation system, has been the chronic mismatch between the volume of state defense orders and the benchmarks established in the foundational State Armaments Program. The 2001–6 program (whose detailed content is classified) is believed to have failed, with the new program for 2007–15 reportedly again relying on unrealistic assumptions. Official comments have not been offered, but observers cannot but point to the gap between the billions spent on state defense orders during the past several years and the literal handful of new weapon systems acquired by the armed forces. Because independent audits and external assessments are extraneous to the Russian political system, it is only through random media comments that many aspects of long-term armaments planning are problematized, with no discernible effect on policy.

Conclusion

At this point, Russian defense industrial policy has not yet developed a strategy adequate to the challenges posed by the technological revolution and globalization of production. In assessing the new conditions, Russian strategic thinking is trapped within a time-honored school of thought that posits military force, and its embodiment in weapons, as essential for national security and international standing. The technological and industrial base for weapons production is thus supported as an "instrument of foreign policy designed to reinforce the state's positions in specific regions."[68] Such an approach is embraced by most nations with weapons-producing capacity. However, both the United States and Europe now have recognized the impossibility of containing this base within a national format and have devised conscious strategies to address the situation.

Russian defense industrial policy lacks a reflective quality that could define the problem and set requirements for such a strategy. And yet this policy unquestionably reflects an awareness of the state of the industry across the world. It implicitly accepts the superiority of the Western model as incarnated by the few powerful defense giants that define the cutting edge of technological sophistication. In analyzing their performance, Russian thinking selectively picks a certain set of characteristics related to the size and scope of these firms, their close relationship with government, the scale of their budget support, and the apparent efficiency of the system regulating the sector. However, another set of properties of the Western defense industrial model is left out of consideration. This includes the essentially commercial nature of firms, the liberalized economic environment, and the global scale of production, as well as the culture of civic accountability permeating the regulatory structures. None of the latter have received any sustained attention in the Russian discussion. On the contrary, the fundamental problem of the impossibility of remaining at the technological cutting edge single-handedly as a nation has not been posed at the conceptual level, and neither of course has a noncontradictory solution been offered.

This does not mean that the problem is not raised in the industry or by experts, or that on a practical level it is not addressed in the strategies employed by individual companies and the international projects supported by the state. At present, Russian defense enterprises maintain ties in a whole range of directions: the CIS, India, Israel, Europe, and the United States. Each partnership combination entails requirements with respect to the conditions of collaboration and bears different potential for the nature and scope of defense industrial integration. Yet despite the many attractions lying in the European direction, Russian state policy—true to its underlying paradigm—reserves caution about the ownership and regulatory issues of joint ventures. At the most basic level, the European integrationist model rooted in the principle of security interdependence remains alien to Russian strategic thinking.

India, with its dynamic and deeply statist approach to defense policy as well as its prominent strategic status, continues to gain in attractiveness as a defense cooperation partner for a wide array of Russian defense interests. Yet, simultaneously, India is increasingly receptive to a variety of international cooperation initiatives from Europe and the United States. Even as they are growing, collaborative ties with an ideologically compatible Indian defense industry will be increasingly challenged by such exposure to more liberalized Western models. For a nation determined to maintain an advanced technological level, the transnational reality of technological development cannot be held at bay by selective partnering but instead must be engaged with all resources available for strategic decisionmaking.

To be viable, any model of policy aiming to retain the edge in globalizing defense production needs to incorporate flexibility, because state regulation constantly has to adjust for the productive interplay of market and administrative stimuli. The fundamental weakness of Russian defense industrial policy in the globalized environment is not its apparent "dirigiste" bent. There is nothing inherently flawed in state regulation as such. Rather, the problem lies in the impotent quality of state regulation, which has failed to meet the challenges of new conditions. This problem is not confined to defense industrial policy but is determined by complex social and political conditions, which allow for an uncontested, uncontrolled policymaking process that is disconnected from the inputs of concerned groups in society. This quality of policymaking, rather than any structural characteristic of the Russian economy, inhibits the opportunity to ride the wave of globalization instead of being swept away by it.

Notes

1. This term is used by Ann Markusen, "Arms Trade as Illiberal Trade," in *Arms Trade and Economic Development : Theory, Policy, and Cases in Arms Trade Offsets,* ed. Jurgen Brauer and J. Paul Dunne (London: Routledge, 2004), 66–88.

2. In 2004, total Russian exports amounted to $181.5 billion. The share for machines and equipment was 7.8 percent, or $14.1 billion. See "Osnovnye pokazateli statistiki vnesheekonomicheskoi deyatel'nosti," available at http://www.gks.ru/. The armaments export in 2004 was $5.8 billion.

3. Stephen Brooks, *Producing Security. Multinational Corporations, Globalization, and the Changing Calculus of Conflict* (Princeton, N.J.: Princeton University Press, 2005), 84.

4. Ibid., 86.

5. The U.S. Department of Defense site for Defense Procurement and Acquisition Policy provides the texts of twenty-one agreements, most of which are with European countries; see http://www.acq.osd.mil/dpap/paic/mou.htm.

6. Carl Conetta and Charles Knight, "Post–Cold War US Military Expenditure in the Context of World Spending Trends," http://www.comw.org/pda/bmemo10.htm#1.

7. The share fell from 2.5 to 0.8 percent in 1996; "Arms Transfer Deliveries and Total Trade, 1986–1996, by Region, Organization, and Country," http://www.fas.org/man/docs/wmeat98/w98tbl2.pdf.

8. Elisabeth Skons and Reinhilde Weidacher, "Arms Production," in *SIPRI Yearbook, 2002: Armaments, Disarmament and International Security* (Oxford: Oxford University Press, 2002), 325.

9. The best known of these are Lockheed Martin, Boeing, Northrop Grumman, Raytheon (United States), BAE Systems (United Kingdom), Thales (France), EADS (Europe), and Finmeccanica (Italy); "The Defense News Top 100," http://www.defense news.com/content/features/2005chart3.html.

10. Skons and Weidacher, "Arms Production," 344.

11. Ibid., 331.

12. Brooks, *Producing Security,* 85.

13. See Derrick J.Neal and Trevor Tailor, "Globalization in the Defense Industry: An Exploration of the Paradigm for US and European Defense Firms and the Implication for Being Global Players," *Defense and Peace Economics* 12 (2001): 337–60.

14. SIPRI data on "major transatlantic and West European acquisitions of arms producing companies" for the four years between 2001 and 2004 list about fifty deals across the Atlantic and some thirty inside Europe. In spite of formidable bureaucratic regulations, European-based BAE Systems, EADS, Airbus, Smiths, Thales, and Rolls-Royce are all known to have bought U.S. defense industrial assets. The British BAE Systems established a North American subsidiary with annual U.S. sales of $10 billion in 2005, and it presents itself as "a truly transatlantic company with a balance of employees, shareholders and business portfolio in both the U.S. and U.K." BAE Systems, "Corporate Overview," http://www.na.baesystems.com/PressKit/North_America _Overview.pdf.

15. An unofficial reference tool is provided under the title "Western European Industry Ownership Jigsaw," http://defence-data.com/ripley/pagerip1.htm.

16. As of January 2006, foreign shareholding went down to 43 percent. Updates are available on a biweekly basis at http://ir.baesystems.com/bae/shareholder_info/foreign/. However, the situation of previous years prompted U.K. defense secretary Geoff Hoon remark that "BAE Systems could no longer be regarded as a British company because more than 50% of its shares were foreign-owned"; http://news.bbc.co.uk/2/low/business/2679213.stm.

17. Neal and Tailor, "Globalization," 352.

18. Brooks, *Producing Security,* 80–128.

19. E.g., a 1998 assessment of the optoelectronics industry, for which sales to the Defense Department in that year represented 15 percent of the total market, reported that "the diverse group of survey respondents listed dependencies on a wide variety of foreign sources for materials, components and equipment used in the manufacturing process. . . . Of the firms responding, 43.2 percent indicated that they need foreign sources to maintain their current levels of quality and/or price. And 54 percent said that

they will continue to be dependent on foreign sources, as use of domestic suppliers will not allow them to remain competitive." "Executive Summary," in *Optoelectronics 1998: Critical Technology Assessment of the U.S. Optoelectronics Industry,* http://www.bis.doc .gov/DefenseIndustrialBasePrograms/OSIES/D\efMarketResearchRpts/optoelectronics 1998.html.

20. Elizabeth Skons and Hannes Baumann, "Arms Production," in *SIPRI Yearbook 2003* (Oxford: Oxford University Press, 2003), 388.

21. Amy Klamper, "Senate Prepares to battle 'Buy American' Defense provisions," June 1, 2004, http://www.govexec.com/dailyfed/0604/060104cdpm1.htm.

22. Markusen, "Arms Trade as Illiberal Trade.".

23. European Defense Agency, "Industry and Market," http://www.eda.eu.int/ iandm/iandm.htm#European_Defence_Technological_and_Industrial_Base.

24. European Commission, European Union, "Frequently Asked Questions: New Commission Initiatives on More Open and Efficient Defence Procurement," http://europa .eu.int/rapid/pressReleasesAction.do?reference=MEMO/05/467&format=HTML&aged =0&language=EN&guiLanguage=fr.

25. "First Review of the Implementation of Defence Industrial Policy, November 13, 2003," http://www.dti.gov.uk/aerospace/pdfs/1st_review-defence_industrial_policy.pdf.

26. To stress the bond between defense governmental organizations and industrial companies, Serfati has used the term "meso-system." Claude Serfati, "The Adaptability of the French Armaments Industry in the Era of Globalization," *Industry and Innovation* 8, no. 2 (2001): 221–39.

27. See, e.g., "Assessment of Industry Attitudes on Collaborating with the US Department of Defense in Research and Development and Technology Sharing: A Report for the Department of the Air Force Prepared by the U.S. Department of Commerce Bureau of Industry and Security Office of Strategic Industries and Economic Security," January 2004, http://www.bis.doc.gov/defenseindustrialbaseprograms/OSIES/DefMarket ResearchRpts/Research_and_Development_Study.pdf.

28. The U.S. Congress persistently presses for proactive measures to protect the domestic armaments production base. See, e.g., "National Defense Authorization Act for Fiscal Year 2004, H.R.1588," http://thomas.loc.gov/cgi-bin/query/D?c108:7:/temp/ ~c108Z5wzkb.

29. Cited by Tarja Cronberg, *Transforming Russia: From Military to a Peace Economy* (London: I. B.Tauris, 2003), 22. For thorough overview of the role of the defense industry in the Soviet Union, see Julian Cooper, *The Soviet Defense Industry: Conversion and Reform* (London: Royal Institute of International Affairs, 1991); Clifford Gaddy, *The Price of the Past: Russia's Struggle with the Legacy of a Militarized Economy* (Washington, D.C.: Brookings Institution Press, 1996); and Vlad.Genin, ed., *The Anatomy of Russian Defense Conversion* (Walnut Creek, Calif.: Vegapress, 2000).

30. In this way, according to the lists maintained by the government, in 2000 the Russian OPK officially numbered 1631 enterprises; in 2003, the revised registry included 1,279 companies.

31. The list, as approved August 4, 2004, is available at the official presidential site, http://www.kremlin.ru/text/docs/2004/08/75174.shtml.

32. The exact numbers differ by years but the proportion holds on. These data are taken from "Struktura sobstvennosti VPK," http://ia.vpk.ru/localfonds/ca_demo/cd_ struct/2003/page_9_1.html.

33. E.g., the state-owned export monopolist Rosoboronexport increasingly buys

stock in defense companies that, in their turn, then become shareholders in private enterprises the state is interested to control. E.g., see "Vchera stalo izvestno o smene sobstvennikov OAO Motovilikhinskie Zavody," *Kommersant,* May 26, 2005.

34. During the year, 351 deals were concluded with the defense stock to the amount of $6,428,997. See "Ekonomika VPK Rossii (October–December 2003)," http://ia.vpk.ru/localfonds/ca_demo/regmat/5_fin/5_1_2003_4.htm#5.

35. Oleg Maltzev, " 'Letatel'nye' aktzii," *Finance,* January 16–22, 2006, 30–33.

36. For analysts, this trend was already clearly discernible as early as 2000; see Ksenia Gonchar, *Russia's Defense Industry at the Turn of the Century,* Brief 17 (Bonn: International Center for Conversion, 2000), 31–32.

37. Alexander Khlebnikov, "Vertoletnyi holding: Vremya aktivnyh deistvii" (Interview with Dennis Manturov, director of *Oboronprom*), *Vertolet* 3 (2005), http://www.oboronprom.com/cgi-bin/cms/mnews.cgi?news =00000000591.

38. The highest-profile one of the already existing "integrated" structures, *Concern PVO "Almaz-Antei,"* was officially established in April 2002. However, four years later, the "History" section of the Web site "almaz-antey.ru" recounted the history of the *NPO Antei,* the base enterprise of the new entity, without any reference to any of the other forty-six companies "integrated" into the holding. In the same way, the separate Web site of *NPO Almaz,* the company lending the other component of the holding name, provided no narrative indication of the fact that *NPO Almaz* was now a part of a larger entity. (See http://www.almaz-antey.ru/hystory.php; http://www.raspletin.ru/about/activities.php.) In December 2005, the chief executive of *Almaz-Antei* was still talking about the necessity of "setting up cooperation between the enterprises, forming collegial management bodies, and building a decision-making system." "Concern PVO Almaz-Antei sozdaet edinoye konstruktorskoe byuro," *Interfax-AVN,* December 9, 2005, http://www.almaz-antey.ru/news.php?id=72.

39. V. Ya. Vitebski, O. A. Kolesnikova, L. Ya. Kosals, M. I. Kuznetzov, P. V. Ryvkina, Yu. A. Simagin, and Yu. S. Uvitskaya, *Oboronnye predpriyatiya Rossii: 1995–2001* (Moscow: Institute for Social and Economic Problems of the Russian Academy of Sciences, 2002), 123.

40. See table 22, "Structure of Investment in Fixed Capital," in *The Russian Economy in 2004: Trends and Outlooks* (Moscow: Institute for the Economy in Transition, 2005), 212, http://www.iet.ru/files/text/trends/2004eng/2004eng.pdf.

41. A. V. Sokolov, *Oboronnaya promyshlennost Rossii: Sostoyaniye i tendentzii razvitiya* (Novosibirsk: Institute for Economy and Management of Industrial Production, 2003), 65.

42. Ekaterina Samarova, "Marsh-brosok," October 25, 2005, http://www.minprom.gov.ru/activity/defence/pub/0.

43. Vitebski et al., *Oboronnye predpriyatiya,* 150.

44. Samarova, *Marsh-brosok.*

45. Federal capital investment programs operate within a range of amounts of funds. The federal program "National Technological Base" for 2002–6 envisaged spending 17.5 billion rubles, 10 billion of which would have been from the federal budget; the "Reform and Development of the Defense Industrial Complex," for 2002–6, 35.7 billion rubles, 14.7 billion of which would have been from the federal budget; and the Federal Targeted Investment Program in 2004, 64 billion rubles, 3.4 percent of which went to the defense industry. See "Federal'nyi budget i VPK: Gosudarstvennyi oboronnyi zakaz [July–December 2003]," http://ia.vpk.ru/localfonds/ca_demo/regmat/index.htm?economy.

46. Conflicting reports have appeared about the amount of export sales in 2005. Different state agencies' assessments varied from $5.1 billion to $6.1 billion. "Objom proshlogodnego voennogo eksporta uvelichilsya v tretii raz," February 9, 2006, http://lenta.ru/news/2006/02/09/export.

47. Defense News Top 2005, http://www.defensenews.com/content/features/2005 chart3.html. In the SIPRI list, Sukhoi takes the twenty-ninth position in 2003 and thirty-fifth in 2002; http://www.sipri.org/contents/milap/milex/aprod/sipridata.html.

48. See the interview of the Rosobornexport director Sergei Chemezov: Anatoli Antipov, "Sdelano v Rossii!" *Krasnaya Zvezda,* November 3, 2005, http://dlib.eastview .com/sources/article.jsp?id=8516639.

49. See some of CAST comments: Ruslan Pukhov, "Korabli potesnili samolety," June 29, 2004, http://www.cast.ru/comments/?id=13; and Lyuba Pronina, "Aviation Tops '04 Arms Revenues," http://www.cast.ru/eng/?id=181, 7.

50. Dmitry Vasiliev, "V poiskah nevidimki," June 28, 2004, http://www.cast.ru/ comments/?id=138; Aleksei Nikolskii, "VPK na golodnom paike," June 9, 2005, http:// www.cast.ru/comments/?id=180.

51. CSIS Atlantic Partnership Project, *Making Transatlantic Cooperation Work: Findings and Recommendations of the CSIS Atlantic Partnership Project* (Washington, D.C.: Center for Strategic and International Studies, 1996), 8.

52. SIPRI Arms Transfer Database, http://www.sipri.org/contents/armstrad/atrus _data.html.

53. Lyuba Pronina, "Russia, Algeria to Strike $4Bln Arms Sale Deal," January 26, 2006, http://www.cast.ru/eng/?id=218.

54. E.g., the production of the air defense system S-300 relies on inputs from 103 companies from Armenia, Belarus, and Ukraine; the MiG-29 fighter includes components produced by 568 companies across the CIS. "Rosoboronexport predlagaet novye podkhody v oblasti torgovli oruzhiem," http://www.idelf.ru/site.xp/05105712404905 6053124.html.

55. Valentin Badrak, "Sotrudnichestvo s Rossiei v voenno-promyshlennoi sfere mozhet obespechit' ukrainskii proryv na mirovom oruzheinom rynke," *Voenno-promyshlennyi kur'er,* November 23, 2005.

56. SIPRI Arms Transfer Database, "Transfers and Licensed Production of Major Conventional Weapons: Exports Sorted by Supplier—Deals with Deliveries or Orders Made 1994–2004," http://www.sipri.org/contents/armstrad/atrus_data.html.

57. In September 2006, Lockheed Martin announced the sale of its ownership interest to Space Transportation Inc.; "Lockheed Martin Announces Sale of Its Interest in International Launch Services and LKEI," September 7, 2006, http://www.ilslaunch .com/zmedia/newsarchives/newsreleases/rec347/.

58. See http://www.beriev.com/eng/core_e.html.

59. For Nedoroslev's position, see his spirited contribution at a round table discussion: "Reforma armii i buducshee OPK," *Otechestvennye Zapiski,* November 5, 2002, http://www.strana-oz.ru/?numid=11&article =494.

60. Pavel Podvig, "Rossiiskoye uchastiye v sozdanii RLS morskogo bazirovaniya sistemy PRO SShA," June 26, 2004, http://russianforces.org/podvig/rus/publications/ 20040626web.shtml.

61. Oksana Snitzar', "Poyot" zapustit sputnik dlya SShA," *Kontinent Sibir,* August 26, 2005, http://com.sibpress.ru/26.08.2005/companies/68936/.

62. "Introductory Word by President Putin at the Joint Session of the Security Coun-

cil and State Council of the Russian Federation," October 30, 2001, http://www.ln
.mid.ru/bl.nsf/0/b47db1a9dd59664343256af6002c8d8e?OpenDocument.

63. Gennadi Pulin, "Pervaya poezdka v novom kachestve," *Voenno-Promyshlennyi Kurier* 45 (2005), http://www.vpk-news.ru/article.asp?pr_sign=archive.2005.112.articles .army_03.

64. Among the principal ones are "Foundations of Russian Federation's Policy in the Area of Defense Industrial Complex Development until 2010 and Further" (signed by the president on November 10, 2001); Federal Goal-Oriented Program, "Reform and Development of the Defense Industrial Complex (2002–2006) (adopted on October 11, 2001); "Concept of Russian Federation State Policy in the Area of Military and Technical Cooperation with Foreign Countries until 2010"; "Concept of Russia's Military and Technical Cooperation with Member States of Collective Security Treaty" (both signed July 2, 2001); and "State Program for Development of Armaments, Special-Purpose and Military Equipment for 2001–2010" (signed January 23, 2002).

65. Alexander Babakin, "Tret' produktzii voennym, ostal'noe- grazhdanskim," *Nezavisimoye Voennoe Obozreniye,* February 10, 2006, http://nvo.ng.ru/forces/2006-02-10/1_opk.html.

66. Ruslan Pukhov, "Vyzhivaet sil'neishii: Gosudarstvennoi politiki v oboronke bol'she net," June 29, 2004, http://www.cast.ru/comments/?form=print&id=135.

67. See Vladimir Tyemnyi," Oboronnui syuzhet dlya ugolovnogo kodeksa," April 13, 2004, http://grani.ru/Politics/Russia/President/p.66999.html.

68. This quotation is from Mikhail Dmitriev, head of the Federal Service of Military and Technical Cooperation, in "Interesy Rosii - prevyshe vsego," ed. Anatolii Antipov, *Krasnaya Zvezda,* December 1, 2005, http://www.redstar.ru/2005/12/01_12/1_01.html.

7

Integration from Below?
The Disappointing Effort to
Promote Civil Society in Russia

James Richter

When the Soviet Union collapsed in 1991, the industrial countries of Western Europe and North America committed themselves to helping the new Russian state transform itself into a stable market democracy. As part of this commitment, multilateral and governmental assistance agencies, as well as private donors, allocated hundreds of millions of dollars to Russian nongovernmental organizations (NGOs) to promote civil society (defined here as a realm of voluntary organizations situated between the household and the state).[1] A robust civil society of this definition was widely believed to be necessary to consolidate democratic reforms. Participation in voluntary associations independent of the state, it was thought, would instill habits of mutual trust among the citizenry necessary to solve common problems without direct state intervention. It would empower ordinary citizens to articulate their demands to governmental agencies more effectively and to mon-

The author thanks Douglas Blum, Alla Kassianova, Mikhail Troitskiy, Rick Fawn, and Michael Bradshaw for the useful comments and suggestions on drafts of this chapter.

itor these agencies to ensure accountability. Finally, it was hoped, such associations, supported with outside help, would create a constituency for reform in Russia that would facilitate its entry into the community of democratic states.

Unfortunately, the results never did live up to the rhetoric. Though by 2002 more than 450,000 social organizations had registered with the Ministry of Justice, the majority of these were very small, often short-lived, and not very active.[2] The most visible and effective NGOs depended heavily on outside assistance and often tailored their priorities and practices to meet donors' expectations rather than local needs. Now that many of the biggest outside donors, such as the U.S. Agency for International Development and the Soros Foundation, have cut their funding to Russian NGOs, many of them are struggling for existence. Meanwhile, the Vladimir Putin administration has made a concerted effort to contain and control Russian civic life within tight parameters, and it particularly has targeted those NGOs receiving foreign aid.

The Civil Society Regime: A New Policy Agenda

The multilateral effort during the 1990s to strengthen civil society was not limited to Russia but was part of a larger project to promote democracy and "good governance" in developing and democratizing countries all over the world. This "new policy agenda" was in part an optimistic response to democratic reforms in Latin America and the collapse of the Soviet empire, but it was also a recognition that the neoliberal economic policies of the 1980s needed some adjustment.[3] In keeping with neoliberalism, the new strategy continued to privilege market mechanisms over governmental policy as the most efficient means to attain economic growth. Governments needing financial assistance were still required by the International Monetary Fund and the World Bank to implement structural adjustment policies that would reduce the state's capacity for economic intervention, remove bureaucratic obstacles to efficiency and growth, and free the individual to make more rational and efficient decisions in a global marketplace.

Unfortunately, in many cases these policies impoverished the most vulnerable segments of society without producing the economic growth needed to compensate or mitigate such suffering. Local actors, it turns out, did not respond "rationally" to impersonal market signals as much as they did to the opportunities, loyalties, and obligations arising from complex local networks of political and personal ties. As a result, many local governments lacked the political capacity or will to implement the policies fully. Even when they did, the outcomes were different from what was expected.

By the early 1990s, the international development community came to the conclusion that market-oriented policies would work best in the context of "good governance," defined as more transparency, more governmental efficiency, respect for individual human rights, and a tolerance for political pluralism.[4] In this context, civil society would act as a supplement to the market, outside the state. It could supply social services to the poor more efficiently than could government agencies, create a constituency for reform to make the policies more politically viable, and monitor state agencies to ensure transparency.

One of the central assumptions behind the project was that voluntary associations would build "social capital," a term defined by Robert Putnam as "features of social organization, such as trust, norms and networks, that can improve the *efficiency of society* by facilitating coordinated actions."[5] According to this argument, voluntary associations instill the norms of trust, tolerance, and cooperation to allow individuals to solve problems of collective action and to perform essential social functions without government help. Conforming to neoliberal assumptions, civil associations are applauded not because they promote justice or social solidarity but because they provide rational, egoistic individuals with the tools they need to increase the "efficiency" of society and maximize their gains without state intervention.[6]

When Putnam spoke of civil society, however, he had in mind a Tocquevillean society with overlapping networks of associations both formal and informal, political and merely social. Such overlapping networks could not be created from the outside, and the assistance agencies did not claim to do so. Instead, they defined their operational goals as creating an infrastructure of professional NGOs that could serve as a basis for mobilizing popular participation on a broader scale. The type of citizen empowered by the donors' policies and practices, therefore, was not necessarily the tolerant, trustful, cooperative, individualist citizen whom Putnam envisioned. These traits were certainly not discouraged, but as a practical target they were superseded by the more immediate demand to create professional organizers who would help sustain a network of Western-style advocacy organizations. Assistance agencies invested huge amounts of money toward building "human capital." They instructed local activists in the ways of the professional "Third Sector," invited them to conferences and seminars, and linked them to the Internet. These professionals, it was thought, would then be in a better position to pressure local governments to conform to the ideals of democracy and good governance.

Encouraging local activists to adopt Western organizational models without the political, social, or economic environments to support them, however, ensured that these organizations would remain dependent upon Western support.[7] Meanwhile, assistance agencies generally neglected the informal associations and organizations indigenous to local societies; in some cases, in fact, they actually preferred creating new organizations simply because they were easier to monitor and control.[8] As Thomas Carothers argues, "Aid providers often imagine the NGO advocacy sector as a pristine domain, free of the murky ties and tensions of ethnicity, class, clan, and political partisanship that make the political fabric so messy and difficult to deal with."[9]

The Regime in Russia

The effort to build civil society in Russia diverged very little from this universal model. The agency representatives who arrived in Russia in the early 1990s to promote civic organizations had worked mostly in the developing world and had little or no knowledge of Russian history, language, or culture. They understood, of course, that the problems facing Russia differed from the problems of other countries where they had worked. Russia was not less developed or underdeveloped; it was "misdeveloped."[10] Even so, they applied to Russia many of the same concepts, strategies, routines, and technologies they also used to deal with development. One women's activist with whom I spoke, for example, maintained that some of the very early arrivals had worked from manuals designed to help civic organizations in the developing world, with little accommodation for the Russian context; one of these manuals recommended women's literacy projects in a country where literacy is over 95 percent.[11]

As elsewhere, the assistance agencies approached Russian civil society as an empty page they needed to fill with organizations of their own devising. As it happens, Russian civil society was indeed quite weak. The Soviet regime had not recognized a public sphere autonomous from the Communist Party, and it had allowed few public spaces where people could communicate without official mediation. The social organizations that did exist —such as the Communist Youth League (Komsomol) and the Trade Unions or the Women's Councils—were usually hierarchical, centralized, and dominated by the Communist Party. Most Russians understandably regarded them with suspicion.[12]

Yet this bleak assessment of Russian associational life does not tell the entire story. The skepticism toward official organizations, for example, was widespread but by no means universal. Many people regarded these organizations—or at least some of them—as a space where people could get together, have some fun, or even do some good.[13] In many cases, the networks and habits of service within these organizations survived the collapse of communism, and they could have been used as a resource for building an autonomous public sphere.[14] The Women's Councils under the Soviet Women's Committee, for example, reconstituted themselves as the Union of Russian Women after 1991 and, in an alliance with other women's organizations, won representation in the Russian parliament between 1993 and 1995. Women's Councils in Dubna, Voronezh and Ivanovo, among others, even served as the basis for new organizations independent of the Union of Russian Women.[15]

In addition, there were pockets of genuine autonomy even under the Soviet regime. These included informal networks of dissidents that formed the basis for human rights organizations in the post-Soviet era, as well as the *Druzhiny po okhrane prirody* (Brigades for the Protection of Nature), an independent network of biology students who helped maintain and protect Russia's nature preserves, and who later formed the basis for the Russian environmental movement.[16] Russians also participated in informal, loosely organized subcultures and networks, such as the "hippies" in Saint Petersburg in the 1970s and 1980s.[17]

For the most part, though, the assistance agencies did not seek to build on these indigenous structures. They did work with some of the smaller, less organized, but more independent and "democratic" networks—including a few small independent labor unions, some dissident networks, and the Druzhiny—and they encouraged these activists to adopt the forms and practices more common to organizations in the West. But they dismissed the official organizations as subservient to the Communist Party, and they had no capacity to work with the informal networks. Most often, the assistance agencies sought to create new organizations from scratch.

One of the first things that the assistance agencies did upon their arrival in Russia was to distribute small seed grants (somewhat indiscriminately) to get as many local organizations started as quickly as possible. Many of these early organizations did not outlive the term of their first grant. The next stage, therefore, was to train the more successful organizers from this pool so that they could maintain an organizational infrastructure for a Third Sector over the long term. The agencies funded seminars and training on issues of organizational structure and management, with topics such as governance and leadership, fund-raising, and creating a public image. And the agencies also supported projects to strengthen networks among local activists. They sponsored conferences, helped connect regional organizations to the Internet, and funded the production and dissemination of newsletters. Finally, the agencies began to fund the more successful organizations to carry out this work for themselves, creating resource centers that would help train and advise other organizations in Russia. In a few cases, such as the Consortium of Russian Women's NGOs, the donors created an umbrella organization to coordinate the activities of other women's organizations throughout the country.[18]

These recruits into the Third Sector quickly learned about the kinds of organizations and projects that would receive support. First, the organizations had to have characteristics common to professional advocacy organizations based in the United States or Western Europe: a charter, a mission statement, a business plan, an office, and a professional staff including, at least, a director and an accountant. Second, they must write a proposal couched in the specialized language of the development community. Ideally, this proposal would offer a specific, finite project with a specific statement about expected results and a detailed budget. Many assistance agencies, particularly governmental agencies, tended to favor projects that could be easily evaluated using quantitative measures—for example, the number of people who attended a workshop or training session, the number of organizations hooked up to the Internet, the number of newsletters distributed—rather than evaluating the quality of such connections. When qualitative narratives were required, they often emphasized success stories that the granting organizations could then take to their own governing bodies. Some donors required site visits and other forms of qualitative evaluation that fostered a more productive dialog, but in most cases there were too few resources for an in-depth analysis.[19]

These efforts to promote civil society did achieve some notable successes. First, participation in the civil society regime often shaped the local activists' sense of self. Access to new contacts and new ideas transformed their vision of their past and present, as well as their future. Thanks to Western help, they learned new skills in organizational management, public relations, and lobbying, or even such mundane skills as how to operate a computer. Armed with such skills, they attained the status of director, expert, consultant, legal adviser, or service provider. Second, these professionals sustained networks constituting a small public sphere, autonomous from the state, which promoted international norms from within Russian society. In a society that had for so long been dominated by the state, this was no small accomplishment.

Still, these small networks never penetrated deeply into Russian society. They remained an enclave community speaking with each other in a language filled with terms like "capacity building" and "training of trainers," which had little or no meaning to the general public. They met the same people at numerous conferences and seminars, and they communicated in e-mail discussions that rarely reached people not connected to the Internet. As one women's activist told me, tongue only slightly in cheek, "the only Russian men I talk to nowadays are taxi drivers."[20]

This isolating effect of foreign assistance has been observed by scholars and activists working in different social, political, and economic contexts.[21] When local resources are scarce, encouraging organizations to have offices and paid staff guaranteed their dependence on Western funding. Such dependence in turn fostered a "project mentality," in which professional organizers became adept at using standardized methods and procedures to produce measurable results in discrete projects over a short period of time but did not spend time reaching out to the population and cultivating the kinds of relationships characteristic of civil society.[22] As one environmental activist in Lipetsk argued, "The expenditures on mobilizing human resources don't pay for themselves."[23] When organizations looked for new members of their staff, moreover, they often looked more for applicants' technical skills rather than a commitment to principles.[24]

In Russia, however, the Third Sector's isolation stemmed not simply from its foreign origins but also from attitudes and practices rooted in Russian society. Russia, it turns out, was not a blank slate but a social landscape crowded with the remnants of Soviet rule, leaving little room for independent social organization. The individuals who chose to occupy these constricted spaces were not the rational, atomized individuals assumed by neoliberalism, moreover, but members of an endangered elite who looked to the Third Sector to reconfigure their identities in a rapidly changing social environment. Though many proved quite willing to adopt the ways of a Third Sector professional as their own, they still had to constantly negotiate their new occupation with their participation in other social fields, including personal networks of friends and family. Despite the efforts of the global civil society project to create professionals, therefore, local dis-

courses and practices inevitably seeped into the informal activities of the
Third Sector organizations, sometimes reinforcing the stated mission of the
organization, sometimes capturing the organization to meet local agendas,
and most often ending up as some combination of the two.

The State and Society in Russia

The civil society project approached Russia with very different notions
about the relation between state and society, and between the public and private realm, than the ones that organized most Russians' lives. Civil society,
as promulgated by international assistance agencies, presumed a clear distinction between these realms and assumed that the Third Sector would
work in complementary and ultimately harmonious ways with both state
and market actors.[25] In Russia, however, the relation between state and society continues to be shaped by the Soviet regime's efforts to control access
to social resources. As many scholars have noted, this overweening presence of the state left many Russians looking to retreat from the hypocrisy
and surveillance of the public realm into what was deemed to be a more au-
thentic, private world of friends and family.[26] This sharply perceived dichotomy between public and private was then mapped onto an equally sharp
distinction between "the state, understood as a powerful 'they' who ran the
country, and the family, the private 'us' who sacrificed and suffered."[27]

The problem was that the lines between "us" and "them" were never
quite clear; the government official and the victim of the authorities were
often one and the same person playing different roles in different contexts.
As Gal and Kligman argue, these different roles had very different rules;
"the private 'us' and the public 'them' were understood to operate according to different moral principles. The cultural imperative to be honest and
ethically responsible to those who counted as the private 'we' contrasted
with distrust and a tolerance for duplicity and manipulation in dealings with
'them.' "[28] This dual set of principles made it legitimate, even expected, for
people to appropriate time and resources from their public role in order to
expand their room for maneuvering in the private sphere. This happened at
every level of Soviet society, from the clerk at the grocery store to the
provincial Communist Party secretary.

The collapse of communism did little to change this state of affairs and
much to reinforce it. Officially, the new Russian government under Boris
Yeltsin aspired to reduce the role of the state and integrate Russia into the

international community. It welcomed the rise of independent social organizations and created a legal basis for their existence. But in practice, particularly in the regions, government agencies and officials continued to control social resources and, as before, would often divert these resources to pursue private agendas. This made the operational environment for Russian NGOs difficult. Independent social organizations had few sources of local funding available to them, and tax laws tended to discourage charitable giving; in many regions, independent social organizations found it difficult to find office space without government connections. Bureaucrats and legislators found little reason to consult local NGOs, and even when they did the impact of this input was lost in the incoherence of official institutions. Finally, the continued corruption and sense of powerlessness reinforced the popular perception of the public sphere as a realm where only criminals prospered. Rather than looking to the government or advocacy organizations to seek public remedies for social ills, therefore, many Russians as before looked to their own personal networks for solace and protection.[29]

This state of affairs cramped the space for civil society; on one side, it was crowded out by governmental institutions that still controlled access to most available social resources; on the other, it was avoided by citizens who looked for "private" solutions to social ills. Rather than creating a network of overlapping associations spreading throughout the polity, therefore, advocacy organizations instead occupied the nooks and crannies of the Russian social landscape where conditions were most favorable.[30] Thus, the success of independent social organizations in Russia varied widely across the regions, depending on the inclinations of the local government and the activity and connections of a few individuals. Nizhnii Novgorod, for example, had very active and effective environmental organizations, in large part because the former governor, Boris Nemtsov, began his political career as an environmental activist during perestroika. Both Ivanovo and Yekaterinberg, conversely, had little or no activity on environmental issues but active women's organizations, thanks to the energies and political connections of influential women.

The Professionals

Given that the space for public activism was so limited, what do we know about the people who were drawn to the Third Sector? As elsewhere, the civil society project in Russia recruited overwhelmingly from members of the Russian elite, particularly those whose position was threatened by new economic realities. Women, for example, constituted a disproportionately high percentage of the Third Sector's population. Because women had been generally excluded from politics and business during the transition period, the Third Sector remained the only public sector area available to them. Work in the Third Sector also proved a more congenial environment for women than business or politics, with less corruption and less violence.[31] As one activist put it: "Politics is so dirty that you have to play dirty to stay in it. Most women work in the Third Sector. It should be kept an honorable sector."[32] The Third Sector's emphasis on providing support rather than making decisions also fit nicely with traditional notions of femininity; and, like other feminized forms of labor, work in the Third Sector was generally less visible and less lucrative than work construed as masculine.

The Third Sector also drew heavily from the creative intelligentsia, such as academics, journalists, and engineers.[33] Under the Soviet regime, the creative intelligentsia had always been supported by the state and enjoyed considerable status in society as a result of their education and cultural refinement. This segment of the elite, like much of the rest of Soviet society, considered political life tawdry, but they could distance themselves from that world by presenting themselves as professionals making valuable contributions to society untainted by the stain of political compromise and hypocrisy.[34] When they did venture into the realm of politics and policy, moreover, they often framed their arguments in abstract notions of morality and philosophy rather than the messier world of practical politics. The rhetoric of the biology students in the Druzhiny, for example, described their efforts to protect nature preserves in terms of protecting sacred space, which, as Weiner observes, "effectively shut themselves off from the more mundane environmental concerns of non-professional Soviet people."[35]

The economic and social changes after the collapse of communism had undermined the social position of these elites. They now received little material support from the state, and their cultural prestige was devalued as well. For these members of the elite, the Third Sector offered an opportunity to apply the knowledge, skills, and connections they had accumulated during the Soviet period within a new sphere of public action. They had the cultural dexterity to interact with Western foundations in a way the donors recognized and appreciated. Given that many of the new arrivals did not speak Russian, a knowledge of English was particularly useful, serving as the "convertible currency" of public advocacy in Russia.[36] The director of a Resource Center in Nizhnii Novgorod, for example, had been an English teacher with little experience in social activism when she was recruited into the Third Sector in the early 1990s.[37] And it is remarkable how many prominent members of the Third Sector in Moscow during the 1990s had worked earlier at the USA and Canada Institute of the Soviet Academy of Sciences: the director of the Russian Consortium of Women's NGOs; the director of the Citizen's Foundation, an NGO Resource Center; two presidents of the Moscow Social Scientific Foundation; and the head of the Russian office of the MacArthur Foundation.

Intellectual elites were drawn to Western models of advocacy not only because of career opportunities but also because it enabled them to maintain, in slightly altered form, their identity as nonpartisan experts above the tainted, even criminal spheres of business and politics.[38] In the Third Sector, they became part of a network of professional advocates, with its own specialized language and rituals, that extended beyond Russian borders and set them apart from the rest of Russian society. As under Soviet rule, the international Third Sector enabled them to advance abstract principles of global governance, such as sustainable development, equal rights for women, or children's rights, without spending too much time on grittier realities, such as local chemical waste dumps, homeless children, or domestic abuse.[39]

The transnational connection with the West was a crucial element in the Third Sector's attraction among this segment of the elite, particularly during the early post-Soviet era. During this period, the West was often regarded as a standard of "normal" life, in contrast to the discredited ways of the Soviet past. Because Western ways were often considered to be more rational or efficient than Russian ways, their identity with the West enabled these elites to maintain, again in slightly altered form, their self-image as the competent professional. Their privileged relation to Western ways also endowed these members of the elite with a new and pertinent form of cultural capital: If culture and education no longer provided the status they once had, the familiarity with Western ways again allowed them to distinguish themselves as part of Russia's future.

Participants in the Russian women's movement, often isolated within local communities, were particularly likely to orient themselves toward transnational connections and practices to distinguish themselves from the rest of society. At seminars for the Independent Women's Forum, observes Rebecca Kay, "speakers were apt to lament the 'backwardness' of Russian women and the 'low level of their consciousness' in a language that clearly distanced themselves and their select audience from that mass. Instead, they allied themselves with their 'Western sisters,' several of whom were often present in the room."[40]

As one might expect, this orientation provided the activists little incentive to connect with other sectors of society, particularly with the semiofficial networks left over from Soviet social organizations. Valerie Sperling, for example, cites one "independent" woman activist who dismisses Valentina Fedulova, then the leader of the Union of Russian Women, as "a lady of the nomenklatura."[41] Another woman characterized the members of the Women's League, an independent organization but with membership drawn from more traditional social activists, as "the same old Party functionaries. What was there has remained. They have repainted themselves."[42] In this case, therefore, the isolation of the Russian women's movement was not simply the consequence of the donors' practices. Russian feminists themselves had an interest in disparaging other forms of women's activism in Russia, for it preserved their own self-image (as well as their privileged access to transnational donors).

To their credit, the U.S. Agency for International Development and other donor agencies responded to the isolation of the Russian Third Sector with a new strategy designed to encourage wider networks. They placed greater emphasis on funding organizations outside the capital cities of Moscow and Saint Petersburg and showed less interest in funding advocacy activities in favor of projects that provided services directly to members of the population, such as youth organizations, psychological counseling services for victims of domestic abuse and sexual assault, and the like.[43] This shift in emphasis brought civil society efforts increasingly in contact with a different set of the elite. This second group included people who had been involved in Soviet-era organizations, such as the Women's Councils or the Trade Unions, and who sought to maintain their activities throughout the transition. This group of organizers, for the most part, gained access to global civil society regime not through intellectual dexterity but through continuing ties to local government officials.[44]

Not surprisingly, the elites coming from more traditional social organizations were less likely to conform to the expectations of a Third Sector professional. They generally received less funding from international agencies and were more likely to derive their status and resources from within the networks and practices of local members of the elite. As a result, they tended to value outside donors more narrowly in instrumental terms, as improving their standing among (and funding from) local officials.[45] Unlike the members of the elite drawn from the intelligentsia, the official members of the elite were more likely to be involved in service and charitable organizations than advocacy groups. They usually defined this service in paternalistic terms, however, and so—like the members of the elite from the intelligentsia, though for different reason—they generally did not encourage wide public participation in the political process.

The campaign to create crisis centers for victims of domestic violence illustrates the characteristic responses of the two types of elite members.[46] Though a few women's activists in Russia had targeted domestic violence in the early 1990s, the concept of domestic violence as a social issue came almost entirely from the United States and Western Europe. In the late 1990s, the assistance agencies identified the topic as a priority among issues related to women and gender. The campaign also reflected the donors' shift in emphasis away from advocacy groups in the capitals and toward service organizations in the regions. The primary aim of this campaign, at least in its initial phases, was to help create and coordinate hotlines and crisis centers throughout Russia, where victims of domestic violence could find emotional support, psychological and legal counseling, and, in a very few cases, shelter.

By most indicators, the campaign was a substantial success. By 2002, the umbrella organization, the Association of Crisis Centers, had more than sixty affiliates across the country.[47] More important, the association provided a space where activists with roots in the Soviet intellectual class found common ground with activists connected with regional authorities.[48] Still, differences persisted. The assistance agencies and Third Sector activists drawn from the intelligentsia were much more likely to view the crisis center movement through a feminist lens, focusing on domestic violence as reflecting and reproducing a patriarchal society and expressing the hope that the crisis centers would raise women's consciousness. The activists drawn from the traditional Soviet networks, conversely, tended to view their mission as preserving families in distress, which included not only domestic violence but also unemployment, alcoholism, and other issues.[49] In other words, whereas the donors hoped the campaign might empower women to question prevailing gender roles, the more official groups, often working closely with local governments, sought to help women fulfill their traditional roles more effectively.

In short, Russian activists could not entirely distance themselves from the logic and practices of Russian society. Even among those members of the elite who prided themselves on their ability to adopt Western ways, local attitudes about the relation of state and society, and of private and public spheres, continued to shape their behavior. Several of the activists spoke of their relation to the donors in ways that echoed the practice of public dissimulation in the Soviet sphere. One activist explicitly compared the practice to Soviet times: "I tailor this project according to the policies of the funds so I can get funding. This is a mutual game, understandable to both sides. People adjusted early. We learned to play these games during socialism."[50] Another stated that "we have to speak in two languages: one with the donors and another among ourselves."[51]

The informal networks so prevalent in Russian society during the Soviet era also pervaded the Third Sector. At times, personal loyalty within the group reinforced the bonds between activists within and between organizations and fostered a greater sense of group solidarity.[52] Local knowledge of informal relations and practices also enabled local organizers to resist the pressures from donors and adapt the assistance agencies' rhetoric, priorities, and strategies to better suit local conditions. But such informal networks could also undermine efforts to promote civil society if they became self-serving cliques that distributed resources according to personal loyalty. Janine Wedel describes how such cliques can use their contacts with foreign donors to become gatekeepers between assistance agencies and other local organizations.[53] In Russia, for example, at least some local activists complained that the resource centers funded by Western assistance agencies, rather than offering information, advice, and other resources freely to other organizations, offered it only to organizations they favored. Some local organizers even complained of a new *nomenklatura* of Third Sector organizations that used their contacts with foreign donors to influence the distribution of grants.[54]

Putin and *Gosudarstvennost*

If the civil society project in Russia enjoyed any success in the 1990s, it was made possible because the Russian government under Yeltsin welcomed foreign assistance as part of its professed goal to integrate Russia more fully into the community of liberal democracies. Under Yeltsin, therefore, the state's official rhetoric presumed a separation between state and society more or less along the lines of liberalism, even if the practices of government officials belied such rhetoric. Since Putin became president, however, and particularly during his second term of office, the Russian government has sought to redefine the relation between state and society to reassert the sovereign status of the state over society. As part of this effort, the Putin administration has systematically targeted those areas of society where an independent voice remained possible—including the parliament, the political parties, the press, and the Third Sector—paying particular attention to NGOs funded by outside sources. This attack on foreign-funded NGOs, ironically, gives credence to the argument that a robust civil society would be a bulwark of democracy against efforts to restore authoritarian rule, even though the Russian Third Sector has so far been unable to offer any meaningful resistance.

Putin's style of rule reflects a philosophy of governance with its own distinctive notions about the boundaries between state and society, the public and the private. For lack of a better term, I describe this philosophy here as *gosudarstvennost*."[55] The concept of *gosudarstvennost* has deep roots in Russian history.[56] Unlike the liberal state, *gosudarstvennost* does not consider the state to be a regulatory body that ensures the self-regulating mechanisms within society will run smoothly. Rather, it sees the state as an entity separate and autonomous from society, an embodiment of the collective will of the nation. The state should stand aloof from the bickering of partisan politics, directing society (from above) in the interests of the whole. The interests of the state, then, are both separate from and must take precedence over popular concerns. Individuals are free to pursue private interests as long as they are not seen to impinge upon the public sphere. Interests that do impinge upon the public sphere should be harmonized with the interests of the collective and rendered compatible with the overall mission of the state.

Harley Balzer, in an article on "managed pluralism," describes how Putin's conception of the boundary between the public and private realms translates into policy.[57] According to Balzer, Putin recognizes the need to encourage popular initiative if Russia is ever going to restore its status as a great power in an increasingly global economy, but he seeks to orchestrate and constrain this initiative within boundaries consistent with the interests of the state. The state does not "attempt to dictate a single political, religious or cultural 'norm' in complex societies," but it does seek "to restrict the palette to shades and hues compatible with familiar landscapes."[58]

Putin's approach to civil society clearly follows this model of managed pluralism. On the one hand, his rhetoric consistently has acknowledged the importance of civil society in modernizing Russian society. In his State of the Nation speech on May 26, 2004, for example, he praised the "thousands of citizens' associations and unions working constructively in our country," and he declared that it was "necessary gradually to transfer to the non-state sector the functions which the state should not carry out or is incapable of carrying out efficiently."[59] He also has acknowledged that it would be unproductive, perhaps even impossible, to construct such a strong society "from above."[60]

Yet Putin has always conceived of civil society as helping to strengthen state structures rather than potentially working against them. First, he has suggested that civic organizations could perform functions that the state cannot perform, or cannot perform as well, particularly in the delivery of social services. Second, he has called upon civic organizations to act as a conduit or, more accurately, a transmission belt that can mobilize support for government policy, consult with state officials on how to implement government policies, and monitor local and regional officials to minimize corruption.[61] Thus, NGOs who help the state enforce its laws more effectively—for example, NGOs working to educate enforcement agencies on domestic violence or the trafficking of women, to preserve existing natural areas, or to monitor conditions in Russian prisons have had relatively few problems working with the authorities.

Those organizations that transgress approved boundaries, however, and particularly environmental and human rights organizations, have been targeted by Putin and his allies not simply as hostile to administration policies but also as alien forces outside the body politic, serving foreign interests. In a press conference for foreign journalists on January 31, 2006, for example, Putin reiterated his support for NGOs as "an important constituent part of society as an organism," but he warned that "we do not want them to be run by puppet masters from abroad."[62] The campaign against foreign-funded NGOs particularly escalated after the "Orange Revolution" in October 2004, which many Russian officials believe had been arranged by pro-democracy groups funded by the United States. In July 2005, for example, Putin told the Council for Facilitating the Development of Civil Society Institutions and Human Rights that "Russia will not allow its public organizations to receive foreign financial assistance."[63]

Since that time, the Putin administration has introduced several measures designed to harness civic activism in service to the state. One of the most notable was the creation, in late 2005, of the Public Chamber (Obshchestvennyi Palata), a corporatist arrangement that allows select members of Russian civil society to consult regularly with state authorities on the formation and implementation of policy, usually social policy. The ostensible functions of this chamber are to articulate to the authorities the "needs and interests" of private citizens and public organizations, to provide public expertise on laws and regulations, and to execute "public control" over executive powers at the federal, regional, and local levels. During its first year of existence, it gained some credibility among the public for its advocacy against xenophobia and its intervention in a property dispute between the Moscow City Duma and the residents in the district of South Butovo.[64] Yet the structure of the body makes it unlikely that it will ever pose a significant challenge to the priorities of the president.[65] Forty-two of the Public Chamber's members are appointed directly by the president, and these forty-two then help select the remaining eighty-four. Its recommendations do not hold the force of law, and it is financed from the budget of the presidential administration in the Kremlin.

A second measure was a new law that Putin signed on January 10, 2006, creating a Federal Registration Center to monitor and control the activities of domestic and foreign NGOs in Russia. This body was given extensive powers to refuse registration of new NGOs and to initiate a judicial process to close foreign NGOs if they are deemed to "threaten the sovereignty, political independence, territorial integrity, national unity and self-identification, cultural heritage and national interests of the Russian Federation." In addition, the center is required to monitor foreign-funded NGOs to ensure they are not engaged in any activities that conflict with the "political independence of the Russian Federation."[66]

So far, a year after the Federal Registration Center legislation was signed, the law has caused major bureaucratic headaches and delays for foreign-funded organizations, but most have been allowed to continue their work. There have been at least two exceptions, however: the Russian-Chechen Friendship Society was shut down after it refused to remove a board member accused of extremism; and the Moscow-based office of the Russian Justice Initiative, which helped two Chechen brothers in a successful case against Russia at the European Court of Human Rights, was refused registration in January 2007.[67] There is no guarantee that the law will not be used even more aggressively in the future.

No doubt, Putin's campaign against foreign-funded NGOs reflects a real, if exaggerated, fear that they might become a rallying point for popular displeasure with his regime. But the fear in itself proceeds from his conception of the Russian state as the embodiment of the collective will. Such a vision of state-society relations requires a conception of society as an organic whole with clear boundaries corresponding to those of the state's rule.

In such a vision, dissenters logically must be seen as outside the body politic, as alien forces seeking to undermine the integrity of society from within. Connecting dissenters with foreign "puppet masters" vividly captures their outsider status, as well as the threat it represents. Unfortunately, these organizations' dependence on Western funding, their isolation, and their orientation toward global norms have made them vulnerable to such attacks.

Conclusions

What does this account of the civil society project tell us about Russia's relation to a globalizing world? The project was an attempt to create a network of advocacy organizations and individual professionals in Russia that would constitute a constituency for deeper economic and political reform, anchoring the country more firmly in the community of advanced liberal democracies. To achieve this goal, however, the project applied a universal model of promoting civil society that was informed by neoliberal assumptions about states, markets, and societies but was ill suited to Russian realities. First, the model presumed a clear distinction between state and society, and it assumed that the retreat of the Soviet state would leave a clear field that would allow organizations from the grassroots to flourish. As we have seen, however, the Russian landscape was crowded with official and semiofficial organizations left over from Soviet rule that still retained control over most social resources. By seeking to create organizations from scratch, rather than engaging the existing structures and networks on their own terms, the assistance agencies found themselves constrained within narrow segments of the postcommunist social landscape. The attempt to model these new organizations along the lines of professional advocacy groups found in the West, without the legal, financial, or social environments to support them, even more ensured their isolation.

Indeed, the presumption that one could create such organizations along Western lines presupposed a population of potential activists who could somehow abstract themselves from the local social environment to conform to the norms and practices of the Third Sector. In fact, many Russian recruits into the Third Sector did prove to be highly competent professionals who, for both instrumental and principled reasons, adopted the ways of the Third Sector as their own. But they were also operating within the frame of local norms, expectations, and practices. For them, participation in the

Third Sector could not be understood simply as a means to a principled end; rather, the transnational connections of the Third Sector ensured that such participation would be loaded with additional implications for one's social status and one's relation to the rest of Russian society. Moreover, most activists were not the atomistic individuals presumed by neoliberal models but looked to personal networks to insulate themselves from the devastating effects of the transition. Inevitably, such informal networks would shape the organizational practices in the Third Sector as well, often in ways that contradict the ethos of impersonal professionalism and impedes the organization's ability to make a greater impact.

As a result, the Third Sector, which was supposed to consolidate democracy and prevent a return to authoritarianism, found itself unable to resist President Putin's efforts to reassert the sovereignty of the state over Russian society. On the one hand, the efforts to create a Third Sector that conformed to neoliberal assumptions ensured that the advocacy organizations under its protection remained isolated from society and dependent on its support, making it easy for Putin to depict them as alien influences in Russian society. When the Western donors withdrew their financial support earlier this decade, the advocacy organizations had few resources left with which to wage effective resistance. But the problems of the Third Sector stemmed not only from their connections outside Russian society but also from their position within that society. Some of the new activists, after all, were attracted to the Third Sector precisely because it offered them a way to distinguish themselves from the rest of Russian society. Moreover, given the continued dominance of state institutions within Russia's regions, in particular, it is unlikely that they would have any more resources or strategies available to them without Western assistance.

In short, then, one can probably fault the civil society project in Russia for not reaching out to existing networks in structures in the early days of the transition. But the chief reason for the project's failure lies not in the practices of the Western assistance agencies or the predispositions of Russian activists. Rather, the key problem seems to have been the failure to reform Russian political and economic institutions more deeply during the 1990s, particularly in the regions, thereby giving the current administration the material with which to reassert state power.

In this respect, the fate of the multilateral civil society project points to a much greater dilemma facing Russia today. Putin hopes to restore the sovereignty of the Russian state, both domestically as the embodiment of col-

200　　　　　　　　　*James Richter*

lective will and internationally as a great power. He cannot do both. To achieve his international goals, he must be able to integrate Russia into the world economy and develop individual initiative with links to the outside world. His domestic goals, meanwhile, require a vision of Russian society as an organic body with clear boundaries with the outside world. To the extent that the state needs to patrol these boundaries to meet domestic needs, it will fail in securing international goals, and vice versa.

Notes

1. Marina Ottaway and Theresa Chung, "Toward a New Paradigm," *Journal of Democracy* 10, no. 4 (1999): 106.
2. Sarah Henderson, *Building Democracy in Contemporary Russia: Western Support for Grassroots Organizations.* (Ithaca, N.Y.: Cornell University Press, 2003), 42.
3. Michael Edwards, and David Hulme, "Introduction," in *Beyond the Magic Bullet: NGO Performance and Accountability in the Post–Cold War World,* ed. Michael Edwards and David Hulme (West Hartford, Conn.; Kumarian Press, 1996), 2; M. Robinson, "Governance, Democracy, and Conditionality: NGOs and the New Policy Agenda" in *Governance, Democracy and Conditionality: What Role For NGOs?* ed. A. Clayton (Oxford: International NGO Training and Research Centre, 1993), 1–15.
4. Edwards and Hulme, "Introduction"; Robinson, "Governance, Democracy, and Conditionality."
5. Robert D. Putnam, *Making Democracy Work: Civic Traditions in Modern Italy* (Princeton, N.J. : Princeton University Press, 1993), 8, cited by William Walters, "Social Capital and Political Sociology: Re-Imagining Politics," *Sociology* 36, no. 2 (2000): 377–79; the quotation here is on 379. The emphasis is from Walters.
6. Walters, "Social Capital and Political Sociology."
7. Steven Sampson, "The Social Life of Projects: Importing Civil Society to Albania," in *Civil Society: Challenging Western Models,* ed. Chris Hann and Elizabeth Dunn (New York: Routledge, 1996), 121–42.
8. Ottaway and Chung, "Toward a New Paradigm," 112.
9. Thomas Carothers, *Aiding Democracy Abroad: The Learning Curve* (Washington, D.C.: Carnegie Endowment for International Peace, 1999), 212.
10. Janine Wedel, *Collision and Collusion: The Strange Case of Western Aid to Eastern Europe, 1989–1998* (New York: St. Martin's Press, 1998), 21.
11. Interview, Elvira Novikova, Moscow, May 1998. I have used Novikova's name here because she explicitly allowed me to do so. Without such explicit permission, I have withheld the names of other interviewees.
12. Though this argument has been made by many observers, the best empirical work establishing such mistrust can be found in *The Weakness of Civil Society in Post-Communist Europe,* by Marc Morje Howard (Cambridge: Cambridge University Press, 2003), 125–27.
13. Similar arguments about positive civic experiences in the semiofficial organizations can be found in "The Shifting Meanings of Civil and Civic Society in Poland," by

Michal Buchowski, in *Civil Society,* ed. Hann and Dunn, 79–98; Sarah Henderson, *Building Democracy in Contemporary Russia: Western Support for Grassroots Organizations* (Ithaca, N.Y.: Cornell University Press, 2003), 37; Valerie Sperling, *Organizing Women in Contemporary Russia: Engendering Transition* (Cambridge: Cambridge University Press, 1999), 189.

14. Howard, *Weakness of Civil Society,* 127–29.

15. Henderson, *Building Democracy,* 95.

16. Douglas R. Weiner, *A Little Corner of Freedom: Russian Nature Protection from Stalin to Gorbachev* (Berkeley: University of California Press, 1999), 312–39.

17. Oleg Kharkhordin, *The Collective and the Individual in Russia* (Berkeley: University of California Press, 1999), 313–17.

18. Valerie Sperling, *Organizing Women,* 241–44.

19. E.g., the Ford Foundation was known among Russian activists for its careful, qualitative evaluations. Because such evaluations demanded so much effort on their relatively small staff, they tended to give a few large grants rather than many small ones. Speech by Mary McAuley, director, Moscow Office, Ford Foundation, delivered at the opening session of a meeting of the Association of Crisis Centers, Moscow, May 21, 1998.

20. Interview, women's activist (name withheld), Moscow, May 12, 1998.

21. See, e.g., the work of Emma Mawdsley, Janet Townsend, Gina Porter, and Peter Oakley, *Knowledge, Power and Development Agendas: NGOs North and South,* NGO Management and Policy Series 14 (Durham, U.K.: INTRAC, 2002). For similar conclusions regarding foreign assistance to postcommunist countries, see Sarah E. Mendelson and John K. Glenn, eds., *The Power and Limits of NGOs* (New York: Columbia University Press. 2002).

22. Henderson, *Building Democracy,* 100–19.

23. Sergei Fomichov, "Yeshcho raz k voprosu o krizise" (Once more on the question of crisis), *Tretii put'* 29 (1993): 6.

24. Mawdsley et al., *Knowledge, Power and Development Agendas,* 69.

25. Jude Howell and Jenny Pearce, "Civil Society: Technical Instrument or Social Force for Change" in *New Roles and Relevance: Development NGOs and the Challenge of Change,* ed. David Lewis and Tina Wallace (West Hartford, Conn.: Kumarian Press, 2000), 75–88.

26. Vladimir Shlapentokh, *Public and Private Life of the Soviet People: Changing Values in Post-Stalin Russia* (New York: Oxford University Press, 1989); Susan Gal and Gail Kligman, *The Politics of Gender After Socialism: A Comparative-Historical Essay* (Princeton, N.J.: Princeton University Press, 2000); Kharkhordin, *The Collective and the Individual.*

27. Gal and Kligman, *Politics of Gender,* 41.

28. Ibid., 50–51.

29. Howard, *Weakness of Civil Society,* 127–29.

30. On the limited space available to activism allowed by state and social structures in Russia, see Laura A. Henry, "Orienting Organizations: Creating Space for Activism in Post-Soviet Russia," paper presented at annual meeting of American Political Science Association, Washington, September 2005.

31. Valerie Estes, "Lessons in Transition: Gender Issues in Civil Society Development," *Give & Take: A Journal on Civil Society in Eurasia* 3, no. 2 (Summer 2000): 5–6.

32. Interview, women's activist (name withheld), Moscow, May 15, 1998.

33. Much of the argument in this section is drawn from the work of Julie Hemment but has been augmented by my own observations in the field. See Julie Hemment, *Empowering Women in Russia: Aid, NGOs and Activism* (Bloomington: Indiana University Press, 2007); and Julie Dawn Hemment, "Global Civil Society and the Local Costs of Belonging: Defining Violence against Women in Russia," *Signs: Journal of Women in Culture & Society* 29, no. 3 (Spring 2004): 1–26.

34. E.g., it is interesting to note that many leading Soviet officials who had made their career within the ranks of the Communist Party urged their sons and daughters to avoid politics and pursue an academic or technical career.

35. Weiner, *Little Corner of Freedom*, 434.

36. Natalya Abubirikova and Maria Regentova, untitled and unpublished manuscript, 1996, 14; cited by James Richter, "Evaluating Western Assistance to Russian Women's Organizations," in *Power and Limits of NGOs*, ed. Mendelson and Glenn, 72.

37. Interview, Evgeniya Verba, director, NGO Resource Center, Nizhnii Novgorod, May 29, 1998.

38. Again, this argument draws heavily from the ethnographic work of Hemment, *Empowering Women in Russia.*

39. Henderson, *Building Democracy.* A similar tendency was noted among environmental NGOs in Central Asia by Erika Weinthal and Pauline Jones Luong, "Environmental NGOs in Kazakhstan: Democratic Goals and Non-Democratic Outcomes," in *Power and Limits of NGOs*, ed. Mendelson and Glenn, 161.

40. Rebecca Kay, *Russian Women and Their Organizations: Gender, Discrimination and Grassroots Women's Organizations, 1991–1996* (New York: St. Martin's Press, 2000), 181.

41. Sperling, *Organizing Women*, 186. Similar antipathies could be found within the environmental movement; interview, Svet Zabelina, environmental activist, Moscow, May 1999.

42. Sperling, *Organizing Women*, 184.

43. Carothers, *Aiding Democracy Abroad*, 227–31.

44. An interesting discussion of the role of intellectuals in postcommunist transitions, who base their status upon technical expertise and cultural dexterity, and the "bureaucrats" who continue to rely on personal networks, can be found in *Theories of the New Class: Intellectuals and Power,* by Lawrence Peter King and Ivan Szelenyi (Minneapolis: University of Minnesota Press, 2004).

45. Henderson, *Building Democracy,* 102.

46. Hemment, "Global Civil Society"; Henderson, *Building Democracy,* 146–48.

47. Interview, Irina Khaldeyeva, president, Association of Crisis Centers, Saratov, May 2003.

48. Richter, "Evaluating Western Assistance."

49. Hemment, "Global Civil Society"; Henderson, *Building Democracy.*

50. Interview, women's activist (name withheld), Moscow, May 12, 1998.

51. Interview, women's activist (name withheld), Moscow, May 5, 1998.

52. Hemment, *Empowering Women in Russia.*

53. Wedel, *Collision and Collusion,* 83–120.

54. Kay, *Russian Women and Their Organizations,* 187–206; Richter, "Evaluating Western Assistance."

55. Other discussions of this term, which for lack of better choices might be trans-

lated into English as "statism," can be found in "Civil Society and the Challenge of Russian Gosudarstvennost," by John Squier, *Demokratizatsiya* 10, no. 2 (2002): 166–83.

56. An intellectual history of Russian concepts of the state can be found in "What Is the State? The Russian Concept of *Gosudarstvo* in the European Context," by Oleg Kharkordin, *History and Society* 40 (2001): 206–40.

57. Harley Balzer, "Managed Pluralism: Vladimir Putin's Emerging Regime," *Post-Soviet Affiars* 19, no. 3 (2003): 189–227.

58. Ibid., 191.

59. A transcript of this speech can be found at Johnson's Russia List, no. 8225, http://www.cdi.org/russia/johnson/2004-state-nation.cfm.

60. Vladimir Putin, "Speech at the Civic Forum, November 2001," cited by Marcia Weigle, "State and Civil Society from Yeltsin to Putin," *Demokratizatsiya* 10 (2002): 136.

61. Georgii Satarov, "Russia's Government Launches Dialogue on Civil Society Issues," *Russia Journal* 4, no. 24 (June 22–28, 2001), http://www.russiajournal.com/printer/weekly4798.html, cited by Weigle, "State and Civil Society," 133.

62. "Vladimir Putin's Annual News Conference for International Journalists," RTR Russia TV, Moscow, January 31, 2006, as translated by BBC Monitoring and republished in Johnson's Russia List, 2006-30, February 1, 2006, available at http://www.cdi.org/russia/johnson.

63. "Putin Does Not Allow Russian Politicians to Receive Foreign Money," *Noviye Izvestiya,* July 21, 2005. Republished in Johnson's Russia List, July 22, 2005, available at http://www.cdi.org/russia/johnson.

64. "Popular Public Chamber Seen as Possible Prototype for Other Bodies," Gazeta.ru February 8, 2007. Commentary signed Gazeta.ru: "Chamber of Complaints and Proposals: In Some Ways the Role of the Public Chamber Is Similar to the Role of Literaturnaya Gazeta during the Stagnation Era," Accessed through Johnson's Russia List, no. 32, February 9, 2007, available at http://www.cdi.org/russia/johnson.

65. For an excellent account of the Public Chamber and its institutional limitations, see Nikolai Petrov, "Obshchesvennaya palata: Dlya vlasti ili dlya obshchestva? (Public Chamber: For those in power or for society?), *Pro et Contra* 10 (2006): 40–56.

66. The citations from the law are taken from Jeffrey Thomas, "US Says Russian NGO Law Does Not Meet Human Rights Commitments," U.S. Department of State Bureau of International Information Program, January 27, 2006, republished in Johnson's Russia List, 2006-26, January 28, 2006, available at http://www.cdi.org/russia/johnson.

67. The report on the Russian-Chechen Friendship Society can be found in "Russian Court Backs Closing of Chechen Rights Group," by Peter Finn, *Washington Post,* January 24, 2007. A report on the Russian Justice Initiative can be found in "Registration Service Denies Chechen Legal Aid Group," *Moscow Times,* January 26, 2007, cited by David Johnson's Russia List, no. 19, January 26, 2007, available at http://www.cdi.org/russia/johnson.

Part II

Globalization and Foreign Policy

8

Going "Relativistic": The Changing Vision of "Just International Order" in Russian Foreign Policy

Mikhail Troitskiy

Morality is a poor practical guide to foreign affairs. However, power politics in its pure form has been equally deplored by the developed world of democratic states. Walking the narrow path between these two extremes, a policymaker looks for stable principles that fall short of moral altruism or excessive self-restraint but provide enough psychological comfort, can be successfully "sold" to the public, and can be defended in the face of domestic or international criticism. The principle of a "just" foreign policy fits well in this niche exactly because it meets the demands for a reasonable compromise between power and the ideal.

Concepts of justice need to be more in themselves than a smokescreen or decoy offered by cynical politicians to their naive constituencies. Even if initially introduced into foreign policymaking to mislead potential critics, the notion of justice in its applied form soon becomes deeply incorporated into the country's self-perception and international identity. It is mainly through identity politics that the notion of justice translates into the foreign policy "habits" and "inclinations" of a state.

Historically, the idea of justice resonated strongly with Russian culture. From Pushkin to Dostoevsky to Tolstoy, much of classical Russian nineteenth-century literature revolved around the notion of justice and its psychological and social repercussions. But apart from the elusive features of the "Russian soul," there seem to be more down-to-earth explanations for the impact of justice concepts on the country's international conduct. Such explanations invoke Russia's crisis of identity after the end of the Cold War. This crisis brought about the need for points of reference in constructing a new Russian identity. Although no dramatic break with the Soviet identity eventually occurred, justice turned out to be an important fallback in formulating the new features of the "democratic Russia's" identity and, consequently, in defining the country's patterns of international conduct.

Justice concepts are especially powerful in raising an actor's self-assessment—something that is badly needed in times of identity crisis, when witch-hunters are seeking out those responsible for the collapse of the previous identity. It is also in times of crisis that countries become especially concerned with their external image. Because they need international recognition of their emerging identity, they stress their past roles as providers of "common international good." And self-perceptions of these roles constitute the core of "international justice" concepts cherished by the country's policymakers and public. Yet when the comfort of a clear identity is recaptured, foreign policy becomes more pragmatic and, consequently, less reliant on justice concepts. Once a more or less comfortable niche for a country is found, policymakers realize that the problems they face in the real world often require "unjust" policies and treatment of other actors. This makes the case for the implementation of justice principles more difficult to defend and diminishes the salience of justice rhetoric in the country's public discourse.

Justice reappears on the scene as a principle motivating foreign policy when a state begins to seek favorable changes in the status quo. Strong arguments are usually needed to justify assertive policies aimed at improving a state's standing vis-à-vis other states, and justice can be a handy diplomatic instrument in limiting external resistance to one's expanding influence.

The purpose of this chapter is twofold. First, it analyzes the mechanisms whereby justice concepts affect foreign policy decisionmaking. Second, it seeks to substantiate the hypothesis that the salience of justice concepts tends to decrease as a state overcomes its identity crisis. The foreign policy of Russia—a country that suffered a severe identity crisis in the 1990s—provides a remarkable testing ground for this hypothesis. I argue that the influence of "justice discourse" on foreign policy was diminishing in Russia as the country was consolidating its post–Cold War identity.

The Past as a Moral Guide to the Future: What Is Justice in International Politics?

Hedley Bull defined justice in terms of the *distribution of resources* or *conduct*. He wrote that justice "is a particular kind of right conduct, viz. conduct in which persons are treated fairly, or given the rights and benefits that are due to them."[1] In a similar vein, he regarded a just distribution of resources to be a *"fair" distribution.* To make a step further, one needs to single out the abstract yet specific principles of "fairness" in distribution or conduct.

Let us assume that the notion of justice finds expression in an actor's (A) behavior vis-à-vis another actor (B). Then the principles of "just treatment" will arguably include:

1. *Reciprocity.* All other things being equal, B deserves from A the same treatment that A was receiving from B in the past. For example, just treatment implies gratitude for services rendered in the past.
2. *The "general past record"* of B as recognized by A. If A's experience of treatment from B is absent, too limited, or too mixed to be used by A as a guide in dealing with B, the whole "past record" of B can be referred to in determining what kind of treatment to which B is "entitled." This principle, which can be viewed as a "diffuse" form of reciprocity, equally applies to a "fair distribution" among a group of actors. In such a case, other things being equal, the share each actor gets depends on her merit defined, for example, by her previous contributions to the common cause.
3. *Certain inherent features of B.* Judgments on whether B is "good" or "bad" and hence what treatment B deserves often hinge on B's nature or acquired properties that have not affected A-B relationship to date. For example, if A and B are humans and have not had any prior interaction, B's nature as a human being, who enjoys the right to life and dignity, can define the boundaries of "fair" treatment of B by A. Yet sometimes, it is exactly the opposite: Treatment will be "unfair" if it is a function of certain inherent features of B. In the case of humans, such features can include sex, race, or other properties that a human is not able to choose. In the international community of states, for example, the legal understanding of justice implies that if a dispute between two states is consid-

ered by an international court, the size and the relative national wealth or strength of the armed forces of each party should not be taken into account by the court when ruling on the case.

4. If the first three principles are met, the fairness of treatment is reinforced by A's *consistency in policy and observance of unswerving principles* in dealing with B. This factor plays a crucial role in defining the moral image (and hence the extent of righteousness) of A as an actor seeking to influence B. If A's guidelines in treating B used to comply with the first two criteria, a change in those guidelines could testify to egoism, opportunism, and irresponsibility on the part of A. Conversely, adherence to a "fair" status quo is a reliable criterion of "justice" because there were precedents. Shifting away from this status quo risks breaking the justice principle.

Given our definition of justice and "just behavior," what are the alternatives to the justice-based principles of action and decisionmaking? One can point out at least two other principles that have considerable intersections with each other and with the justice principle but are still not identical. The first principle is premised on the current balance of forces between A and B. A treats B in a purely rational way that reflects A's ultimate power (or lack thereof) over B. In other words, in any interaction or distribution, everyone gets what she can. As an illustration, some Russian pundits have maintained, commenting on the purportedly thankless U.S. policy toward Russia in the aftermath of the terrorist attacks of September 11, 2001, that the West does not understand the notion of gratitude but rather takes what it can at each particular moment.[2] Such comments demonstrate that Russia never pursued a "pure" balance-of-power strategy in its post–Cold War international relations. Russian policymakers needed to explain (more to themselves than to the outside world) that their actions were morally sound and met the international standards of justice.

The second alternative principle puts the formal norms existing in a society at the core of decisionmaking about mutual treatment or the distribution of resources. It is easy to note that formal norms (e.g., those stipulated by law) can deflect from the commonly accepted meaning of justice. Most sociologists would maintain that formal laws tend to reflect reciprocity. However, it is exactly because justice involves more than reciprocity (see the four determinants of "fair" treatment defined in the list above), formal norms can contradict the meaning of justice for a particular case. Therefore, in certain situations, norm-based treatment of B by A will be different from justice-based treatment. The Russian political tradition, manifest in the country's foreign policy at all stages of identity formation, implies a "selective" approach to the observance of norms. Here justice again serves as a concept defining Russia's attitude to a particular norm. For example, the sense of injustice among decisionmakers under President Vladimir Putin pushed Moscow toward claiming access to retail natural gas networks and oil-processing facilities in the Western countries—major buyers of Russian natural resources. The prospect of Russia becoming a "raw materials appendage" to the Western economies—that is, a simple seller of oil and natural gas—was brushed aside as fundamentally unjust because it perpetuated the technological gap between Russia and the West. The concept of an "energy superpower" that crystallized in Russian foreign policy thinking in the mid-2000s demanded a "fairer" distribution of revenue than was otherwise generated by Russian natural resources.

To sum up, by putting justice at the center of the decisionmaking process, an actor or a group of actors attributes primary importance to what happened in the past or the inherent nature of other actors, as opposed to the current status quo or an ideal state of affairs as enshrined in law.

A coherent theory of the role of justice in foreign policymaking should not only stipulate *why* the "justice factor" is important but also show *how* the meanings of justice affect foreign policy and provide a clue as to where such ideas come from. A full-fledged theory of justice applications to foreign policy falls beyond the scope of this chapter. I limit my theoretical deliberations to arguing that the meaning of justice comes to bear on foreign policy in the realm of a country's self-identity. An essential part of self-identity is what the state thinks it deserves from other actors, what it feels it is allowed to do internationally, and what it is entitled to vis-à-vis other states. It is this aspect of self-identity whereby the meaning of justice finds a way to affect policymakers' thinking about their country's natural interests and necessary policies. All three guiding principles that define "fair treatment" come into play here: past record, "normative consistency," and reciprocity (on a case-by-case basis). Policymakers construct a justice-ridden image of their own country mainly from ideas of their country's past achievements as well as from their assessment of themselves as consistent promoters of the "common international good."

During the 1990s and the early 2000s, Russia has been an illustrative example of a justice-laden approach to the formulation and execution of foreign policy guidelines. In the following section, I explore how the meaning of justice informed Russia's post–Cold War self-identity during the emergence of the country's statehood. Once that process (though incomplete) came to a halt at the beginning of the 2000s, the influence of justice concepts on the making of Russian foreign policy began to crumble, but it then resurfaced during Putin's second term as president. This claim, in its turn, is substantiated in the final case study section of this chapter.

The Meaning of Justice as an
Identity-Shaping Force in Russia

The abstract principles of "just treatment" materialized into the features of Russia's post–Cold War identity through commonly accepted interpretations of several historic events and tendencies along with specific assets of the Russian state, as well as widespread theoretical ideas and constructs. These interpretations and ideas helped the Russian foreign policy community—which encompasses the political leadership, foreign policy bureaucracy, mainstream experts, and journalists—to define what Russia deserved and, consequently, to what it was entitled in world affairs. Let us briefly examine each of the six pertinent factors.

The first factor is the crucial role played by the Soviet Union in the victory over Nazism and the sacrifices made by the Russian people in World War II. Having played a crucial role in defeating Nazi Germany, Russia (formerly the USSR) has since enjoyed moral authority, which justified Russia's aspirations to international leadership. This factor not only was instrumental in shaping the justice discourse among Russian experts and policymakers in the 1990s but also continues to play an important role in the mid-2000s.

The second factor is the peaceful dissolution of the Soviet bloc in Central and Eastern Europe and the subsequent self-destruction of the USSR in the late 1980s and early 1990s. As the successor state to the Soviet Union, Russia naturally expected the West to acknowledge its goodwill to do away with Cold War hostilities and make a number of important concessions in 1989–91, such as agreeing to the reunification of Germany and German membership in NATO or cooperating with the United States in resolving a number of conflicts in the developing world (Afghanistan, Nicaragua, Angola, etc.). Though in the West the events of 1989–91 were regarded as an indisputable victory in the Cold War, mainstream Russian political discourse never fully acknowledged Russia's defeat. Sergey Kortunov, an influential Russian expert and policymaker, wrote in 1998: "The historical truth is that the Soviet communist system imploded and collapsed due to its internal tensions. . . . The collapse of the Soviet system was primarily an internal process, natural and inevitable."[3]

The third factor is Russia's role as a Eurasian power whose existence and integrity guarantee the stability of the vast Eurasian territory and whose natural resources the international community (including both Western and Asian economic giants) is doomed to rely upon and will increasingly need in the future. Echoing the views of Halford MacKinder, Eduard Pozdnyakov, a prominent Russian representative of the "geopolitical school of thought," concluded in 1992 that "a stable world is inconceivable without geopolitical power balance," ensured by Russia, which "controls the world's Heartland."[4] This implies a deeply rooted, if not often articulated, view that Russia provides a crucial "bridge" linking East and West and stabilizing their mutual relations. An essential part of the country's mission is to maintain that bridge "in order" and ensure access to it—yet with due attention to Russia's own national interests. Hence, if Russia disintegrated or its state institutions weakened to the extent that proper management of its territory was not possible, then much of the international community—and especially, its most developed part—would suffer. As the then–chief of President Putin's staff, Dmitriy Medvedev, once opined, in comparison with such a scenario, "the collapse of the Soviet Union could look like a child's game."[5] Although criticized by Russia's prominent geographers and social anthropologists (see chapter 11 in this volume by Solovyev), the view of Russia as one of the few geopolitically pivotal states providing stability on the world scale has been widely accepted by the Russian public and extensively played upon by populist politicians.[6]

The fourth factor is Russia's posture as a major nuclear power. In this capacity, Russia, on one hand, provides strategic stability by balancing the United States and—potentially—Chinese nuclear capabilities and, on the other hand, contributes to nonproliferation efforts as a nuclear-weapon state party to the Nuclear Non-Proliferation Treaty of 1968. A country's possession of nuclear weapons automatically promotes it to the highest ranks within the international community—not only because these weapons constitute a formidable military deterrent but also because having them places special requirements on the responsibility of the nuclear state's leadership.

The fifth factor is Russia's and the Warsaw Pact's history of an "equal relationship" with the United States and NATO during the Cold War. According to conventional wisdom, the Soviet Union and its allies were treated "equally" by the West thanks primarily to their significant military power and political influence, which matched and in some areas exceeded NATO's capabilities. As long as Russia managed to preserve its principal components of state power—that is, the nuclear deterrent and most of its geopolitical resources—it deserved to be treated as an "equal counterpart" by the West, even after the end of the Cold War.

"Equal treatment" implied, first, according priority to Russia's concerns in relations with the West and, second, managing these relations in direct communication between Russia and the United States or other great powers—leaders of the Euro-Atlantic community. For example, during the first half of the 1990s, Russia was reluctant to deal in high-politics issues (e.g., NATO enlargement) with smaller international actors, such as countries of the former Soviet bloc.

The sixth factor is Russia's outstanding contribution to the world's cultural heritage and the resulting spiritual authority of the Russian state as the embodiment of a profound civilization. This tenet not only asserted the important role that Russian culture and language play around the globe (clearly, an uncontestable point) but also implied equal rights to existence for all cultures, with no exception for Western and, particularly, American value systems. Such conceptions, which are quite popular among the makers of and experts on Russian foreign policy, are generally in line with common sense. However, in Russian political discourse, they are often overstated, their main thrust being not to support cultural diversity around the globe but rather to reject the applicability to Russia, as a unique, "self-sufficient" civilization, of American or European political traditions and institutional designs.

Viewing American leadership in the international arena as inescapable, quite a few Russian observers pointed to the inability of the United States to put forth a set of ideas and values that could soothe the sharp contradictions within the international community. In the 1990s, it was popular to argue that America did not possess, as Kortunov expresses it, "the moral, spiritual, cultural and historical assets that are more necessary than pure military or economic power . . . for a country that wants to act as a dominating and unifying force for the new civilization." A required contribution to the spiritual authority of the world leadership group, as Kortunov and the philosopher Eduard Batalov maintained, could be made by Russia—a country with a highly respected culture and profound history.[7]

To sum up, at the initial stage of identity formation, post-Soviet Russia viewed itself as a great power representing a distinct, outstanding cultural system. It voluntarily embarked on political transformation, which led to a temporary decline in its influence. Because this transformation was regarded as an act of goodwill aimed at enhancing international security, the Russian foreign policy community felt that the country continued to deserve "equal treatment" from the United States and its allies. This feeling was reinforced by the availability of such assets as nuclear arms and abundant natural resources, whose importance as Russia's trump cards was somewhat exaggerated. Even if Russia acknowledged that it was lagging behind the West in economic development or diplomatic influence, its foreign policy community believed that the West (and particularly the United States) would not be able to sustain its preponderance in world affairs due to the inevitable logic of power balancing.[8] Russian politicians viewed their country as a weakened yet ultimately reemerging power center that would be courted by both East and West in their quest for global influence.

During the 1990s and especially in the second half of the current decade, these "justice-informed" components of the Russian international identity played an important role in the formulation of concrete doctrines and policies. A few examples further illustrate this point. (The impact of Russia's perception of international justice on its concrete foreign policy actions is considered in greater detail in the concluding case study section of this chapter.)

The sixth factor noted above combined with multipolarity theories to shape a Russian version of the "multipolarity doctrine." This doctrine, in its normative part, regarded hegemony as intrinsically unjust—because no country can win enough credit (by contributing to the world's well-being or any other past achievement) to claim the right to dominate or even lecture the rest of the international community. The multipolarity doctrine further argued that the world hegemon must pursue multilateral policies and abstain from imposing its will on other members of international community. Acknowledging that such a scenario was highly unlikely given the United States' military preponderance and dominant political and economic resources, Russia pledged to contribute to the formation of a multipolar world, which implied a clear choice for a balancing (rather than bandwagoning) policy toward the United States.

Yevgeniy Primakov, the Russian foreign minister in 1996–98 and one of the founding fathers of the Russian multipolarity doctrine, argued that "the evident unwillingness of most states to put up with a world order shaped by only one country" gives Russia extended opportunities "to play a leading role in international relations."[9] Given Russia's unique natural resources and geopolitical advantages and the widespread dissatisfaction with the

unipolar world, it would be quite natural for Moscow to embark on a multipolar course, that is, to assist in creating and possibly lead coalitions that
would seek to balance the United States. During the second half of 1990s,
multipolar rhetoric was one of the cornerstones of Russia's international
agenda.

On a regional scale, Russia was claiming the right to become integrated
into multilateral European and Euro-Atlantic security and, possibly, economic institutions. This should have followed from a fair recognition of
Russia's being part of Europe and was regarded as a benefit that the West
had to guarantee to Moscow for consistent pursuit of democratization and
economic reforms.[10] Russia proposed organizing the core of European security architecture in the form of consultations among Europe's great powers, possibly involving the United States as a member of the Conference
(since 1995, Organization) for Security and Cooperation in Europe.[11]

Russia also sought to preserve an important component of its "just influence"—the prestige of the United Nations—and argued for an increase in the
UN's role in maintaining international security. On the issue of Security
Council reform, Russian leadership, up to the late 1990s, was opposed to the
admission of any new permanent members to the Security Council because
such move could siphon away Russia's influence within the council.[12] However, under President Putin, who at the initial stage of his presidency dismissed much of the Yeltsin-Primakov justice rhetoric, Russia adopted a more
positive stance on admitting Germany, India, or even Japan, because this
could (1) win Russia important concessions from the states Russia promoted
as would-be permanent Security Council members and (2) enhance the prestige of the UN, which had been steadily declining over the 1990s.[13]

The "Relativistic Drift" of the Early 2000s:
Factors of Change

Since Russia's emergence as an independent state distinct from the USSR
and the prerevolutionary Russian Empire, Russia has been undergoing intense "socialization" under the influence of various realities. The new Russian identity has thus been maturing under the influence of factors which, as
it has turned out, often work against "justice universalism"—by "convincing" the foreign policy community that a consistent application of justice-
ridden concepts to substantiating a foreign policy course could actually
contradict Russia's interests. Consequently, a decade after 1991, Russia's

"mature identity" was much less interwoven with the discourse of justice that it was at the initial stages of identity formation. As a new identity was emerging and justice concepts receded, Moscow began changing previously uncontested official views on a number of substantive foreign policy issues.

Two of these issues are explored below in case studies that illustrate the contrast between the Yeltsin-Primakov justice-ridden approach of the late 1990s and President Putin's initially more pragmatic ("relativistic") vision of "international justice." These case studies, however, need to be preceded by an analysis of the perceptions and ideas that, in the course of Russia's "socialization," weakened the imprint of international justice concepts on the Russian identity. As Russia's international socialization was progressing, the country's foreign policy community was acknowledging a number of realities about the emerging characteristics of international relations, Russia's objective place in the world, and the country's interests. During the 1990s, the Russian political leadership and foreign policy bureaucracy had to accept five realities in particular. Let us look at each.

The first reality was that Russia was irreversibly weakened after the collapse of the USSR and the end of the Cold War, while the United States rose to the position of the only superpower, whose edge in military strength, technology, and economic well-being was rapidly increasing. This naturally led to doubts about whether Russia could expect "equal treatment" from the West. Such doubts began to emerge even among liberal-minded experts sometime in 1994–95. Aleksey Arbatov, at that time one of the most pro-Western and influential members of the Russian foreign policy community, wrote in 1994: "Russia will never enjoy the position of an equal [partner] either in NATO or in the European Union. . . . This will mean Russia will only be able to play secondary roles while remaining a key member in any conceivable Euro-Atlantic security system."[14]

Discussions about Russia's changed status in international affairs reached their climax in 1996–97. At that point, as the political scientist Tatiana Shakleina observed, "Most experts of various political orientations acknowledged a decline in Russia's status as well as in the resource base of its foreign policy"—a development that required the elaboration of a new "realistic external strategy." Further debate on such a strategy was won by the analysts who maintained that "Russia should not aspire to the status of a global power."[15] A few years down the road, President Putin unambiguously stated that Russia could no longer afford competing with other great powers in faraway regions or for the benefits of secondary (or purely ideological) interest. The official Foreign Policy Concept of the Russian Federation, signed by the Russian president in June 2000, acknowledged that "expectations for . . . an equal and mutually beneficial partnership between Russia and the outside world did not come true."[16]

The second reality was that Russia had to reassess threats to its national interests and recognize the need for at least tactical cooperation with the United States in combating these threats, including armed separatism in Chechnya and tensions with countries accused by Russia of closing their eyes to or even supporting the Chechen separatists, such as Georgia, Turkey, and several Arab states. As long as combating Chechen separatists (which had been necessary since 1999) required military means and warnings to other states of the serious consequences of supporting the rebels, Russia had to waive many of its earlier objections to U.S. counterterrorism policies carried out with limited respect for other states' sovereignty. Russia supported the American anti-Taliban campaign in Afghanistan in 2001, and in 2003 it ultimately watered down its criticism of the United States–led intervention in Iraq aimed at toppling Saddam Hussein. At the same time, as John Ikenberry observed, Putin skillfully negotiated concessions from the West in return for Russian support of the Afghan campaign.[17]

The third reality was that an "absolutist" interpretation of justice actually limited Russia's freedom to maneuver in its foreign relations. Russia needed to retain flexibility in determining its official position not only to tackle new security challenges but also to explain its support for a number of separatist regimes in regions crucial to its interests, such as the Transnistrian Republic, Abkhazia, and—since 2003—South Ossetia. Russian policymakers started taking it for granted that too many countries relied in part on "double standards" in their relations with the outside world. This, in turn, significantly constrained the policymakers' ability to use justice concepts in asserting Russia's rights in the international arena.

The fourth reality was that the Russian foreign policy community failed to rally potential allies behind the Russian conception of justice in the 1990s. The Russian vision of a just world order and its regional components turned out to be insufficiently attractive on the whole to other great powers or to most countries in Russia's neighborhood—the former Soviet republics. These republics either chose to pursue a balanced course (and, toward the end of the 1990s, an increasingly pro-Western course)—in the case of Ukraine, Azerbaijan, Georgia, Moldova, and Uzbekistan until 2005—or to promote their own views on the goals of partnership with Russia—in the case of Belarus—which were, however, too radical for Russia to accept. The end of the Kozyrev era marked the acknowledgement that, if a new Russian identity ever matures, it will not be fully Western. The bankruptcy of Kozyrev's admittedly "idealistic" approach to formulating Russia's interests, amplified by the West's (and especially America's) perceived disregard for Russian concerns, significantly undermined the justice discourse.

The former Soviet allies in Central and Eastern Europe opted for integration into NATO and the European Union immediately after the collapse of the Warsaw Pact—no matter how much this strategy would cost them in relations with Russia. In the early 1990s, Moscow still expected that these countries would seek to "restore their ties with Russia because [further] damaging these relations, especially in the economic domain, [could] complicate . . . economic modernization and transition to market institutions."[18] However, such countries as Poland, Hungary, and the Czech Republic (and later the Baltic states) coped with the challenges of their transition to the extent of being able to join the EU without restoring an alliance or even partnership with Russia.

The fifth reality was that Russia could not endorse any of the alternative "strong" conceptions of international justice. America-centrism, anti-Americanism, antiglobalism, or any kind of religion-based radical conception was too eccentric to underlie the foreign policy of a regional power that seeks to position itself in a balanced way vis-à-vis the only superpower—uninterested and unable to either build a formal alliance with the hegemon or to openly challenge it. Starting in 2000–1 and at least until late 2004, Russian foreign policymakers watered down their multipolarity rhetoric directed against "American dominance" and President Putin expressed Russia's commitment to reforms and development in accordance with Western patterns of economic and political organization and governance.

To sum up, Russia's established identity as a midrange power seeking to retain as much freedom of action as possible pushed its politicians (consciously or unconsciously) toward a "relativistic" approach in applying international justice principles to formulating the country's foreign policy agenda. As a result, Russia departed from an "absolutist" interpretation of justice—makers of foreign policy ceased insisting on a uniform application of norms, rules, and procedures that defined justice for them, but they acknowledged that these norms could be interpreted differently depending on the situation. As a consequence, Moscow became more willing to budge on those issues on which, in the past, no concessions from the Russian side could have been contemplated.

Justice rhetoric resurged during President Putin's second term in office, which started in May 2004. By that time, the issue of reciprocity again became key to the justification of Russia's foreign policy choices. In 2000–1, Russia arguably embraced Western-style liberal reforms and began to make attempts to become more attractive to foreign investment. It also provided almost unconditional support to the America-led "war on terrorism," and it acquiesced to the abrogation of the Anti–Ballistic Missile Defense Treaty of 1972 and the second round of NATO expansion. Moscow tried hard to get its position on Chechnya across to Western audiences (see chapter 10 in this volume by Fawn) and made clear that it wanted a continued rapprochement with NATO and the EU in their respective spheres of competence.

Yet the Russian assessment of Western response to this bid for partnership fell short of satisfaction. Russia's mainstream politicians and analysts complained about "unfair" (i.e., not reciprocal) treatment by the West, which failed to appreciate Russia's friendly posture during the first two years of Putin's presidency. Evidence to substantiate that point was found in such moves by the West (notably, the United States) as the continued criticism of Putin's ostensibly undemocratic domestic policies, the sponsoring of mass protests that led to regime changes in Georgia and Ukraine, and the lack of willingness on the part of the European Union to ease visa regimes with Russia.

As the debate over Iraq and subsequently American involvement in the "colored revolutions" in Russia's immediate neighborhood were heating up, Russian foreign policy discourse recaptured much of the justice rhetoric of the 1990s. Explaining Russia's growing cooperation with China or policies designed to limit U.S. involvement in Central Asia, the Caucasus, and Eastern Europe, Russian pundits criticized the West for "unfair" anti-Russian policies as well as its inability to compromise. A good illustration of this most recent trend, which it is still perhaps too early to analyze in depth, is the change in Russia's mainstream attitude toward globalization—the third case study presented in the following section.

Case Studies in International Justice and Russian Foreign Policy

For Russian foreign policymakers, the meaning of justice played an important role in defining Russia's position on a number of key foreign policy issues and influenced the formation of Russia's strategy vis-à-vis major international actors. Here, I present three illustrative cases: the evolution of Russia's approach toward NATO enlargement, the ups and downs of Russian-American relations after the Cold War, and Russia's changing view of globalization during President Putin's two terms in office.

NATO Enlargement

One of the best examples of how the diminished role of international justice as an identity-shaping force affected Russia's official position on concrete foreign policy issues is the country's evolving attitude toward NATO enlargement. Russia's initially high expectations for an easy accession to or at least close partnership with Western economic and political institutions, including NATO, were reflected in the Russian Foreign Policy Concept of 1992—the first detailed, official document issued by the Foreign Ministry that set guidelines for Russia's relations with the outside world. It noted the importance of "intensification of contacts [with NATO] on both bilateral and multilateral levels and interaction with NATO bodies in strengthening peace and security."[19] In the early 1990s, Russian politicians also deemed it possible to "ensure a most tight connection between the EU, NATO, Western European Union, and the emerging security architecture under the aegis of the CSCE [Conference on Security and Cooperation in Europe],"[20] expecting that these Western institutions would agree to subordinate their security policies to the CSCE's pan-European yet very loose structures.

These hopes, grounded in Russia's mainstream perception of international justice, continued to inform its official position on European security issues until the mid-1990s.[21] Consequently, in 1994–97, the eastward expansion of NATO became one of its primary negative concerns: The West was acting "unfairly" in trying to impose NATO as the core European security institution instead of nonexclusive structures, such as the CSCE.[22] The Russian National Security Concept adopted in 1997 argued that "the plans to enlarge NATO to the East are unacceptable to Russia because they pose a threat to Russia's national security."[23] It further claimed that "the expansion of NATO to the East and its emergence as the dominant politico-military force in Europe threaten to . . . divide the continent, which is extremely dangerous at a time when . . . multilateral peace-support mechanisms are insufficiently effective."[24]

A revised version of the National Security Concept, issued in 2000 by the Putin administration, still maintained that "the consolidation of military blocs and alliances, especially NATO expansion to the East," was one of "main threats [to Russia's interests] in the international arena."[25] This document, however, was principally conceived and developed well before

Putin, who signed it in January 2000, became acting president of the Russian Federation.

Just as Russia's reliance on international justice concepts diminished after 2000–1, so too did its criticism of NATO enlargement and the Alliance itself. After the terrorist attacks of September 11, 2001, President Putin stated: "Over 40 years Russia and NATO eyed each other with suspicion and anger. . . . I think that now we are entering an era of substantive and practical cooperation." He added that "if NATO transforms into a political organization, we will certainly review our attitude towards the enlargement."[26] Similarly, in the spring of 2004, he expressed only a mild criticism of NATO enlargement by saying that "a mechanical expansion of NATO does not help to combat the threats we are facing." Downplaying Russia's dissatisfaction even further, he added that he hoped "NATO enlargement will promote trust in Europe and the whole world and will serve as a [new] element of international security."[27] Several months later, Russian foreign minister Sergey Lavrov reiterated that position when he told an Egyptian newspaper that "realizing that Russia and NATO pose no threat to each other, we do not regard the expansion of the Alliance as an obstacle to continuing our collaboration . . . and to moving toward a genuinely cooperative model of European security."[28]

Russian-American Relations, 1992–2005

Another remarkable example of how ideological shifts in Russian foreign policy course have affected the country's external strategy is Russia's changing official attitude toward relations with the United States. Since the end of the Cold War, this attitude has passed through three major phases, which could be tagged the "early Kozyrev," "Primakov," and "Putin" approaches.

Russia's first foreign minister, Andrey Kozyrev (1991–96), identified Russia with the West (at least, in the long run) and consequently saw no alternative to developing a close partnership or even alliance with the United States. This view was initially endorsed by President Boris Yeltsin, who instructed his foreign policy bureaucracy in 1992 to direct Russian foreign policy at helping the country's economic and political reforms. During the first two years of Russian statehood, Yeltsin and Kozyrev were ready to make concessions to the United States on various important international issues in exchange for unequivocal support from Washington for Yeltsin's transition strategy for Russia. Moreover, the "early Kozyrev" approach was based on the assumption that an unconditional partnership with the United

States would help achieve a stable and democratic world order, which was at that time considered one of Russia's primary foreign policy goals.

This approach was severely criticized by Kozyrev's opponents, who argued, for example, that a partnership with the United States should not come at the expense of other Russian interests, such as influence in the post-Soviet space. These critics maintained that Washington was in fact squeezing Russia out of its historical "spheres of influence"—the Balkans and "near abroad"—which should have become the main focus of Russia's foreign policy instead of the United States.[29] These analysts and politicians finally got the upper hand in 1996, when Yevgeniy Primakov replaced Kozyrev as the Russian foreign minister.

As a consequence, Russia's approach to relations with the United States toughened radically in light of the rising popularity of Primakov's "multipolarity doctrine." Not only did Russia adopt a more assertive stance vis-à-vis Washington, but Russia's official National Security Concept of 1997 did not even mention relations with the United States among Russian foreign policy priorities, which included enhancing integration within the Commonwealth of Independent States, cooperation in combating transnational crime, and strengthening collective security mechanisms. The authors of the National Security Concept also maintained that "how well Russian interests will be served in the international arena depends largely on Russia's relations with major powers and integration blocs."[30] To compensate for a cool-down in Russian-American relations, Moscow moved to a more active policy vis-à-vis the European Union. The Russia-EU Partnership and Cooperation Agreement, signed in June 1994, came into force in December 1997. During the second half of the 1990s, Russia and the EU pursued active talks over the implications of EU enlargement for Russia's relations with would-be EU members from Central and Eastern Europe. In 1999–2000, the Russian Foreign Ministry and the European Commission published documents outlining strategies for mutual relations.

Russia's preoccupation with the EU as well as its unnecessarily harsh criticism of U.S. policies ended in mid-2001, when President Putin showed clear signs of departure from the "multipolar world" rhetoric that was so dear to Yeltsin in his final years in the Kremlin. After meeting with President George W. Bush in June 2001 and, most markedly, after the terrorist attacks of September 11, Putin not only endorsed much of the U.S. approach to security policy but also returned a commitment to close relations with Washington to the top of the Russian foreign policy agenda.[31]

On the wave of cooperation in the antiterrorist campaign, Russia and the United States got over their contradictions on the future of anti–ballistic missile defense and the second round of NATO expansion. In May 2002, the two presidents signed a Joint Declaration on New Strategic Relations as well as a Strategic Nuclear Potentials Treaty, which was to create a formal basis for mutual arms reduction efforts until 2012. The importance of co-operation with the European Union was, at the same time, somewhat down-played, especially after a bitter row over the status of Russia's Kaliningrad exclave and Russia's economic ties with the EU after its enlargement.

Having accepted Russia's identity as a regional yet Eurasian (i.e., "trans-continental") power, President Putin realized that good relations (though, indeed, something short of an alliance or even full-fledged partnership) with the United States were the sine qua non for retaining Russian influence in Eastern Europe, Central Asia, and even the Caucasus. Moreover, support-ing the United States–led "war on terrorism" required considerable flexi-bility in construing international legal norms, which used to constitute one of the cornerstones of the Russian conception of international justice. Gen-erally, changes in this conception were not only the precursors but also the necessary conditions for shifts in Russian-U.S. relations to occur during the decade and a half after the end of the Cold War confrontation.

These relations, however, started to sour in 2003–4 as a new wave of jus-tice rhetoric emerged in the Russian foreign policy discourse. As in the 1990s, the return of "justice" resulted from the feeling that Washington was not making reciprocal moves to reward Moscow's support for the "war on terrorism" and readiness to put up with the abrogation of the Anti–Ballistic Missile Treaty of 1972 and the second wave of NATO enlargement, which was finalized in early 2004. Divergences over Iraq and the "colored revo-lutions" in the Russian neighborhood, and continued criticism by the United States of Putin's internal policies, led many influential politicians and ex-perts in Moscow to conclude that Washington was again acting unfairly by denying Russia much of what the United States allowed itself to do both do-mestically and in the international arena.

Russia's Evolving Views on Globalization, 2000–5

The evolution of Russia's mainstream views on globalization provide a good example of how a particular international trend moved a long way from being perceived as a "fair," beneficial phenomenon to an "unjust," se-lective instrument that the only superpower uses to advance its interests in the world. Early in Putin's presidency, a moderately positive perspective on globalization dominated the Russian mainstream political discourse. Whatever the scholarly meaning of globalization may encompass, it was widely acknowledged in Russia that globalization implied not only increased openness to foreign economies and extensive opportunities to conduct business abroad but also stronger competition in Russian internal markets, which would become increasingly accessible to foreign companies. Putin made it clear in 2001 that "we [Russia] should not be afraid of globalization" because "there is nothing worse than isolation, which is disastrous for any country and its economy."[32] He added, as late as June 2004, that "there is no country that could rely only on its own economy and not be affected by outside developments. This is impossible in the age of globalization."[33]

Russia's official Foreign Policy Doctrine, signed by President Putin in June 2000, stated that "under globalization, Russia's economic development is unthinkable without the country's deep involvement in the world economy."[34] In his early years as Russian president, Putin also stressed, on a number of occasions, that Russian companies will need to adapt to the increasingly competitive environment of both domestic and international markets. Boosting the "competitiveness of the Russian economy" became one of the core slogans of the "early Putin," who clearly sought to encourage Russian economic agents to increase efficiency and review the range of products and services they were offering to both Russian and foreign customers.

The start of the "war on terrorism" highlighted yet another meaning of globalization for Russia. This perception was focused on international security threats that have either emerged or been magnified in the globalized world but also create a security agenda that Russia, the West, and the rest of the world need to address cooperatively. A commonly accepted list of these threats features megaterrorism (which has become possible due to terrorists' expanded range of means of communication, proliferation of knowledge, and technological advances), the proliferation of weapons of mass destruction (especially when combined with terrorism), trafficking in drugs and human beings, and the spread of infectious diseases. For example, in April 2000, President Putin pointed to "international terrorism and organized crime, militant separatism, and illegal trade in arms and drugs" as the most dangerous threats in the globalized world.[35]

This school of thought about globalization recommended strengthening international cooperation and coordination on security policies among most powerful actors and their main regional allies. In 2002, Putin noted that the "threats that have emerged in the age of globalization [require] a new 'philosophy of partnership' based on a firm legal basis, respect to others' interests and the equality of rights."[36] The Declaration of the Heads of State of the Shanghai Cooperation Organization Member Countries, signed in Moscow in May 2004, stated that because "no country can isolate itself from the transnational threats that have emerged in the era of globalization, . . . there is no doubt that comprehensive cooperation to combat these threats should be developed at both regional and global levels."[37] More recently, an official spokesperson for the Russian Foreign Ministry stated in an article outlining Russia's basic foreign policy orientations: "The contradictory nature of globalization focuses our attention on the search for concerted efforts to respond to the new challenges because it became evident that no single state or even group of states, irrespective of their economic potential and military might, can combat . . . transnational threats to security and stability, threats that have a bearing on all members of the international community."[38]

Integration with Russia's neighboring states was seen as one of the most effective responses to the challenges of globalization. Addressing a meeting of high-ranking representatives of Kazakhstan, Belarus, Ukraine, and Russia—countries that launched, in 2003, a project to establish a Single Economic Space—President Putin reminded the stakeholders that "however difficult it could be to advance on the way towards the Single Economic Space, . . . the objective world-economic trends, caused by the so-called globalization, will put us on that track."[39]

Through such a lens, the United States was viewed as a partner in combating the negative implications of globalization. The "common threats" philosophy in Russia received a strong impetus after the 9/11 terrorist attacks. So did the Russian-U.S. partnership, which now had a common security agenda.

This agenda, however, did not result in the consolidation of a long-lasting U.S.-Russian alliance. Disputes over Iraq, regime changes in the Russian "near abroad," and the fate of Russian democracy brought about a certain disillusionment over the implications of globalization for Russia. It became increasingly fashionable to point out the "uneven nature" of globalization, which can become a blessing for one country and a curse for another. As particularly unfair, Russian analysts and politicians noted the fact that the United States was unwilling to agree to constraints on its own sovereignty while trying to limit the sovereignty of other states. It was argued in Russia that Russia had the same rights as the United States to manage its internal affairs and retain a free hand in foreign policy.[40] According to a number of observers, after a series of regime overthrows in the post-Soviet space in 2003–5, top Russian policymakers decided to call for a "consolidation of elites" against various destructive external (and internal) forces.[41]

These events markedly changed the tone of Russia's official view of globalization. Concern over national sovereignty started to outweigh positive spin-offs of globalization in the eyes of the Russian political elite, who feel that control over key socioeconomic and political levers may well slip out of their hands. The shift in Russia's response to globalization toward stronger protectionism in politics and the economy has reflected the changing perspective on the "fairness" of globalization. In 2005, globalization was no longer viewed in Russia as an "objective phenomenon" equally harmful or beneficial to most countries across the globe. The dominant view in the middle of the decade was that of the selective nature of globalization, harnessed (if not directed) by the West to its global cause.

Conclusions

By the end of 2005, Russia's adherence to justice principles in formulating its foreign policy options had come full circle. Kozyrev's "idealist" policies and later Primakov's "national-interest-based" approach were formulated against a backdrop vision of the "fair treatment" to which Russia was entitled from the outside world. As Russia's international socialization was progressing and the acceptance of its midrange power status was growing, mainstream politicians and experts adopted a more "relativistic" approach toward the discourse of justice. By the mid-2000s, Russia's growing resources allowed its leadership to step up efforts aimed at preserving the country's positions in the world and expanding its influence in neighboring regions such as Central Asia, the Caucasus, and Eastern Europe.

These trends, along with the disappointment about the failure of the alliance with the West in the wake of 9/11, may be bringing the justice discourse back to the agenda for Russia's dialogue with the outside world. So far, examples of this change include Moscow-backed pressure on the United States to downsize the American military presence in Central Asia (which is "fair," given Washington's insistence on the withdrawal of Russian troops from Georgia and Moldova) and reprisals on the United States for its "unfair" criticism of the allegedly undemocratic elections in Chechnya and Belarus (given America's own involvement with the less-than-transparent elections in Afghanistan and Iraq).

The return of justice discourse to the foreign policy rhetoric of a country with a relatively robust identity and increasing resources may occur because of the country's rising self-assessment and ability to dictate rules in the games where it has a stake. A powerful actor can assume more responsibility for the developments around it. This naturally gives it grounds for asking for "fair" compensation—not only in the form of the satisfaction of its own demands but also in other actors' consent to consider it a legitimate mediator or even a "judge." Here, justice-based arguments initially come into play. Once a country feels strong enough to project power abroad, it may seek to impose its own rules of the game in its sphere of influence—for example, to resolve conflicts among third parties, to find ways to enhance regional security, or to reshape trade relations. Judges or mediators need to offer their vision of justice, and if one is not yet in existence in the form of long-standing norms, it should be built up from scratch. In such a case, justice-based arguments can help promote the rules that an outside power seeks to establish.

An analysis of international justice perceptions on the part of Russian political elites provides a good explanation for a number of important Russian foreign policy trends. A student of justice rhetoric and its applications cannot claim an exhaustive account of a country's foreign policy conduct. However, the process of exploring applications of the justice discourse to foreign policy opens a vast research agenda. Russia provides a remarkable case, allowing us to observe how a country's inclination to resort to justice-based arguments depends on the degree of its "socialization," that is, the maturity of its external and internal international identity. As has been shown in this chapter, norms-based and power-based explanations draw a far less original, if not misleading, picture of the evolution of Russian foreign policy since 1991.

At the same time, "static" investigations into the role of justice discourse for a country not experiencing identity transformation can also enrich the constructivist paradigm. It is important to further explore the sources of the meaning of justice used by policymakers, how it affects decisionmaking, and how it depends on the position of a state in the international hierarchy. The task is formidable given the fact that policymakers rarely call a spade a spade, that is, refer to justice by its own name. One must employ a precise definition of justice and strong interpretative skills to unveil the references to the meaning of justice that may be deeply hidden in a country's public discourse.

Notes

1. Hedley Bull, *Justice in International Relations* (Waterloo, Ont.: University of Waterloo, 1984), 2.

2. See, e.g., the presentation by a prominent Russian historian, Anatoliy Utkin, at the "Gorbachev Foundation" conference on "Perestroika: 20 Years Down the Road," *Moskovskiy komsomolets,* October 28, 2004.

3. Sergey Kortunov, *Imperskie ambitsii i natsional'nyye interesy: Novye izmereniya vneshnei politiki Rossii* (Moscow: Moscow Science Foundation, 1998), 150.

4. Eduard Pozdnyakov, "Geopoliticheskiy kollaps i Rossiya," *Mezhdunarodnaya zhizn',* August–September 1992, 14–15.

5. Interview with Dmitriy Medvedev, head of administration for the president of the Russian Federation, *Ekspert,* April 4, 2005.

6. Solovyev quotes V. Kolosov and R. Turovskiy, who called the notion of Russia as the "geographical center of world politics" an essentially flawed and misleading concept.

7. See Sergey Kortunov, *Rossiya: Natsional'naya identichnost' na rubezhe vekov* (Moscow: Moscow Science Foundation, 1997), 20; and Eduard Batalov, *Russkaya ideya i Amerikanskaya mechta* (Moscow: Nauka, 2001).

8. This perception was supported by manifold international relations theories pointing to the instability and transitory nature of bipolar and, especially, unipolar international systems. In line with political scientists who argued that such systems cannot last long and will be inevitably succeeded by multipolarity, influential Russian policymakers, during the 1990s and even later on, sometimes went as far as to call multipolarity "the God-blessed international order." This effectively implied that any distortion in the equal distribution of power would run against the will of God.

9. See, e.g., Yevgeniy Primakov, "International Relations on the Eve of the 21st Century: Problems and Prospects," *Mezhdunarodnaya zhizn'* (International Affairs), October 1996, 3–13.

10. The 1992 Russian Foreign Policy Concept stated that it was necessary to "covert Russian-European partnership ties into concrete measures and arrangements"; i.e., at that point Russia expected the West do deliver on its praise for Russian democratization and market reform efforts. These achievements, however, needed to get a clear acknowledgement in the form of shared institutions or other long-term arrangements where Russia had to enjoy an equal treatment. See "Kontseptsiya vneshney politiki Rossiyskoy Federatsii 1992" (1992 Russian Foreign Policy Concept), officially published in *Diplomaticheskiy vestnik,* January–February 1993, 13.

11. As was mentioned in the 1992 Foreign Policy Concept, "Russia's interest is to promote . . . and further institutionalize the Conference on Security and Cooperation in Europe . . . [in order to] turn it into the fundamental block of the emerging international society architecture." *Diplomaticheskiy vestnik,* January–February 1993, 12.

12. The 1992 Foreign Policy Concept warned against "encroaching upon the time-tested basic principles of UN functioning" and continued: "Our interests will not be served by attempts to revise the UN Charter, the composition and the working principles of the Security Council." Russia only supported noninstitutionalized "involvement of large regional states in decision making at the Security Council." *Diplomaticheskiy vestnik,* January–February 1993, 21.

13. See, e.g., the official Russian Foreign Ministry document titled "Issues in Reforming the [UN] Security Council" and dated July 17, 2005, available at http://www .ln.mid.ru/. Although Russia continued to argue against an "excessive enlargement" of the Security Council, the document stated that "Germany, Japan, India and Brazil . . . could be worthy candidates for seats on the Security Council once it is expanded."

14. "Interesy Rossii v SNG," *Mezhdunarodnaya zhizn'*, September 1994, 27.

15. Tatiana Shakleina, *Rossiya i SShA v novom mirovom poryadke* (Moscow: ISKRAN, 2002), 182–83.

16. Kontseptsiya vneshnei politiki Rossiyskoy Federatsii 2000, officially published in *Diplomaticheskiy vestnik*, August 2000, 3.

17. G. John Ikenberry, "American Grand Strategy in the Age of Terror," *Survival*, Winter 2001–2, 30–31.

18. *Diplomaticheskiy vestnik*, January–February 1993, 10.

19. Ibid., 14.

20. Ibid., 17.

21. Russia's first foreign minister, Andrey Kozyrev, believed in 1994 that "trust can not be unilateral. We [Russia] have the right to expect that the United States will disregard skeptical warnings about the need to 'keep an eye' on Russia." According to Kozyrev, the primary element of Russian-American partnership should be "the mutual recognition [by the United States and Russia] as likeminded states committed to common democratic values and norms of the United Nations and CSCE." While Russia had made its way to partnership with the West, Kozyrev was expressing disappointment with "the continued existence of institutions embodying our common values yet still excluding Russia, such as [Group of Seven] and NATO." Andrey Kozyrev, "A Strategy of Partnership," *Mezhdunarodnaya zhizn'*, May 1994, 9–10.

22. Western reluctance to pay tribute to Russia's record of reforms and reciprocate her friendly attitude toward the West was harshly criticized, e.g., by a former Soviet ambassador to the GDR: "Right after the ideological confrontation was quickly and radically overcome, Russia started to behave as an informal yet full-fledged ally of the West. Russia has joined forces with the West to prevent any complications that could threaten the mutual rapprochement on the Continent (. . . as an ally, Russia had plenty of obligations, but no rights whatsoever). At first, the West was accepting Russia's commitment to the 'Western cause' with enthusiasm, then—with irony. It regarded Russia's behavior as her unilateral concession that did not require reciprocity. Ultimately, the West started to take Russia's rejection of her own national interests for granted and deny Russia any right to depart from such position. Igor' Maksimychev, *How the Beginning of NATO Enlargement Threatens Russian Security* (Moscow: Institute of Europe, Russian Academy of Sciences, 1998), 8.

23. "Kontseptsiya natsional'noy bezopasnosti Rossiyskoy Federatsii 1997" (1997 Russian National Security Concept), officially published in *Diplomaticheskiy vestnik*, February 1998, 10.

24. Ibid., 20.

25. "Kontseptsiya natsional'noy bezopasnosti Rossiyskoy Federatsii 2000" (2000 Russian National Security Concept), officially published in *Diplomaticheskiy vestnik*, February 2000, 6.

26. *New York Times*, October 4, 2001.

27. Russian Television Channel 2 news program, April 8, 2004, http://www.vesti.ru/ news.html?id=52880.

28. Russian Foreign Ministry official Web site publication, http://www.mid.ru, July 23, 2004.

29. See, e.g., *Komsomol'skaya Pravda,* March 19, 1992.

30. "Kontseptsiya natsional'noy bezopasnosti Rossiyskoy Federatsii 1997," 6.

31. One of the best analyses of "ideological shifts" in Russian foreign policy, including those affecting Russian-American relations, can be found in Igor Zevelev, "Russia and the U.S. at the Turn of the Century: 'Anarchy, the Mother of Partnership'?" *Pro et Contra,* Autumn 2002, 72–85.

32. President Vladimir Putin, "Responses to Questions from Participants of the Asia Pacific Economic Cooperation Business Meeting," October 19, 2001, http://www.kremlin.ru/text/appears/2001/10/28672.shtml.

33. President Vladimir Putin, "Remarks at the Press Conference after Meeting with Islam Karimov, President of Uzbekistan," Tashkent, June 16, 2004, http://www.kremlin.ru/text/appears/2004/06/72919.shtml.

34. The quotation is from "Kontseptsiya vneshnei politiki Rossiyskoy Federatsii 2000," http://www.scrf.gov.ru/documents/25.html.

35. Acting President Vladimir Putin, "Greeting Address to the 'South–South' Summit in Havana," June 12, 2000, http://www.kremlin.ru/text/psmes/2000/04/31270.shtml.

36. President Vladimir Putin, "Speech at the Presentation of Credentials Ceremony," Moscow, September 26, 2002, http://www.kremlin.ru/text/appears/2002/09/29470.shtml.

37. "Declaration of the Heads of State of the Shanghai Cooperation Organization Member Countries," Moscow, May 29, 2003, http://www.kremlin.ru/interdocs/2003/05/29/1349_type72066_46275.shtml.

38. A. V. Yakovenko, "Russia: A Policy of Peace and Progress," *Vneshneekonomicheskiye svyazi,* October 2004, 27.

39. President Vladimir Putin, "Introductory Remarks at the Meeting of the High-Level Group (Russian, Belarus, Ukraine, Kazakhstan)," Moscow, July 25, 2003, http://www.kremlin.ru/text/appears/2003/07/49314.shtml.

40. See a detailed analysis of this trend in Russian foreign policy thinking in *Power and Influence in US-Russian Relations: A Semiotic Analysis,* by Igor' Zevelev and Mikhail Troitskiy, Essays on Current Politics 2 (Moscow: Academic Educational Forum on International Relations, 2006), http://obraforum.ru/pdf/Semiotics-US-Russian-relations-WP2.pdf.

41. See, e.g., *Vedomosti,* April 26, 2005.

9

Socializing Baltic Sea States into a Security Community: Aspects of Globalization

Erik Noreen

Globalization is one of the most discussed concepts among social scientists. Just like power, justice, or security, it has become one of these "essentially contested concepts" that "generate unsolvable debates about their meaning and application."[1] This is not the place to take part in the academic debate on globalization as a theory, historical process, ideology, or whatever it might be delimited to. It is, however, important to notice that the concept of globalization has also been widely discussed in Russian academic circles in the new millennium, and it has often been used by leading policymakers. Among the former group, there has been a tendency to focus on its negative effects and on Russia. This critique has ideological undertones, for it depicts a threat image that "characterizes present-day globalization as 'Atlanticist,' a new form of enslaving most of humankind."[2] Policymakers, conversely, are indeed inclined to use the term as a background condition to various problems and threats in world politics, such as international terrorism, poverty, and epidemics. However, globalization is not only presented as a context for negative developments in world affairs and in Russia; it also signifies a challenge, because it "takes humanity to a new development level of civilization."[3]

The Midget and the Giant in the Baltic Sea Area

In this chapter, I take my point of departure in the conceptualization of Richard Sakwa, who bases his definition on a general conception of globalization (which is in line with that used by Hedetoft in chapter 1 of this volume) but applies this reasoning to a postcommunist reality:

> The whole world becomes embroiled in a single set of social relations. When applied to the former communist countries, this suggests the universal applicability of some sort of integral "transition" process where the shift to market is accompanied by a common set of economic and social norms. It also has political effects, and the assumption is that the creation of a liberal democratic order is "the best possible shell" for capitalism, as Lenin put it.[4]

This chapter focuses on one certain aspect of globalization as it is defined above, namely, international socialization, or more precisely, *transition* in terms of communication and learning processes. The aim of the chapter is thus to analyze how globalization has influenced relations between states in the Baltic Sea area in terms of communication, learning, and the development of social identities within the framework of international socialization. I have, moreover, delimited the study to two states within the region, Estonia and Russia. These countries are of particular interest because they represent contrasting cases on this regional basis. In their roles as the *midget* and the *giant* bordering the Baltic Sea, they have a critical relationship due to the historical record of a half century of Soviet/Russian annexation. To highlight the relationship between a former annexation power and its victim during the postoccupation period might be considered a critical case—a litmus test— of whether the region has any prospects of becoming socialized into a prestage of a *security community,* aiming at developing "dependable expectations of peaceful change" among its population.[5]

This chapter, furthermore, concentrates on issues and aspects that I suggest are important for how interstate relations have developed not only between Estonia and Russia but also for the region by and large. One key question is how their images of each other have developed in the post–Cold War era. This question raises a number of further ones. How do the policymakers of the neighboring states socially identify themselves in terms of belonging to Europe or the Western world? Who is the "Other," and how could this Other be characterized? From an Estonian point of view, the process of leaving the tyrannous Soviet Union for democracy in Europe should be interpreted within the context of finding a new post–Cold War identity, as well as regaining the interwar identity as an independent European state. How, then, is Russia assessed within the process of forming a collective Estonian "self"? To what extent do Estonians assess Russia as a threat? Corresponding images in Russia may at first glance seem absurd. In what respect should Russians ever have considered a small Baltic state as a military threat? This question becomes less peculiar when one looks at this state in the context of being a NATO member, and it is well known that the policymakers in Moscow have made such assessments, at least since the middle of the 1990s, when the Baltic states started to express their wishes to join NATO.

In this chapter, I argue that in spite of disagreements over interpretations of the past—including whether Estonia was annexed or occupied by the Soviet Union, and whether the naturalization process of residents of with undetermined citizenship in Estonia is handled according to prevailing standards of human rights—there are striking similarities in how the languages of security and social identities have developed in Russia and Estonia, and that this change in discourse indicates that policymakers in both Moscow and Tallinn are involved in a process of international socialization—one which is interwoven with globalization, and which works itself out through a shared process of communication and learning. Though expressions of a common European identity are more apparent in Tallinn than in Moscow, I suggest that a fairly slow progression of international socialization is under way throughout the entire region.

The main objects of analysis of this chapter are the views of the respective governments in Estonia and Russia—it is thus a study of the political elites' discourses. Although an investigation of a popular discourse would be relevant in illustrating and comparing any discursive gap between a public and an elite discourse, such a gap is not the focal point here. Rather, in focus are the official governmental discourses in Moscow and Tallinn, respectively. This choice is based on the logic of centrality and appropriateness, meaning that among all different entities of the assemblage called the political elite, ministries such as the Ministry of Foreign Affairs, Ministry of Defense, and the Presidential Office, are selected, because these are the most central actors in formulating each respective security policy line after the Cold War.

The chapter is organized as follows. In the next section, the language of security in Estonia and in Russia, respectively, are analyzed; in particular, I look at how policymakers in these states have presented threat images in the new millennium. Thereafter, I focus on how international socialization and the development of identities, in varying degree, have affected Estonia and Russia as they have become Europeanized. A critical case in point is brought to the fore, namely, the question of the Russian minority in Estonia—the most troublesome issue of contestation between Tallinn and Moscow.

Strategies of the Midget

Estonia is the midget of the Baltic Sea area. Its population has recently been estimated at 1.3 million, whereas Russia's population is more than hundred times this number, about 143 million in 2006. Estonia's total land area is roughly the size of New Hampshire and New Jersey combined, whereas Russia is the largest country on Earth. The post–Cold War history of Estonia can be divided into three phases: the *proto-independence* mobilization during the last years of Soviet occupation, the first years of *formal independence,* and the *state-building phase.* The first phase of proto-independence started at the end of 1988 with the "singing revolution," when popular movements began to openly manifest demands for a politically independent Estonia. Already in this period, a language law was initiated, which established the "status of Estonian as the sole official language of national and local government."[6] An essential foundation for Estonian national identity had thereby been laid. This period ended in August 1991, when the provisional Estonian government declared its country's de jure independence.

The second phase of independence was initiated thereafter and completed in August 1994, when the Russian government, after drawn-out negotiations, withdrew all its troops from Estonian territory. Like the other Baltic countries, Estonia was now de facto independent. The period was characterized by tension between the Estonian government and those organizations that tried to mobilize the Russian-speaking minority, which at the start of the 1990s made up about a third of the Estonian population. The tension was fueled by the Citizenship Law of 1992, which excluded the Russian settlers from immediate influence on important political instances in Estonia.

The last completed phase could be characterized as a *state-building* phase, that is, a phase of economical, societal, and political consolidation. This period extended over almost a decade and ended in 2004, when Estonia became a member of NATO and the European Union. The years that preceded those historic events were characterized by the Baltic states' attempts to prove themselves ready to become ideal nation-states, not only in terms of economic progress but also in the way they handled certain political and societal problems. A problem of the latter kind was obviously the Russian-speaking minority issue. The Estonian government's handling this minority issue was carefully scrutinized not only by organizations such as the EU and the Organization for Security and Cooperation in Europe, but also by the Russian government.

At the turn of the millennium, we can discern a shift in Estonia's attitude toward its Russian-speaking minority. There was a clear tendency to acknowledge that Estonia after the occupation really had become a multicultural and multiethnic society. In March 2000, the government approved a State Integration Program. A cornerstone of this policy was to obtain "a significant reduction in the number of persons without undetermined citizenship, a substantial breakthrough in teaching the Estonian language and full participation of non-Estonians in Estonian society at all levels."[7] This policy found fertile ground in Washington and Brussels, as it eased the way to both EU and NATO membership.[8]

In spite of the detente between Moscow and Tallinn at the turn of the millennium, a vast majority of the Estonian public opinion assessed Russia as a threat against the Estonian state. According to opinion polls on threat perceptions, 60 to 78 percent of the Estonian people perceived the Russian state as an ominous force in relation to Estonia, a proportion that had not significantly changed since the 1990s.[9] The question then becomes, How did the Estonian policymakers frame the threats with reference to Russia? What else, if anything, did they refer to in terms of being a threat to Estonian national security?

An account of the Estonian political elite's threat images after the Cold War based on quantitative and qualitative text analyses has been given elsewhere.[10] In these studies, a paradox was found: The military threat from a former occupant—although this is being assessed from a historical point of view rather than from current conditions—creates Estonia's interest in NATO membership. This membership, in turn, contributes to the precedence of soft threats rather than hard ones on the Estonian security policy agenda; that is, it focuses on nonmilitary, unconventional threats rather than military, conventional ones.

If we look somewhat more closely at the development of policymakers' presentations of threat images over time, it is fairly obvious that soft security language increased immediately after the Russian troop withdrawals in 1994, almost concurrently with more direct statements on the necessity of Estonian NATO membership. Moreover, references to any immediate military threats directed toward Estonia became increasingly rare after 1994. The tendency to prioritize softer at the expense of harder threats, and to emphasize threats based on structural factors rather than on actors (read Russia), seems somewhat to correspond with the expressed prospects of becoming a member of the Western alliance.

References to terrorism were, not surprisingly, very frequent in speeches and statements after the terrorist attacks of September 11, 2001. Literally speaking, there was an explosion of allusions to terrorism in comparison with the period that preceded these events. In the regularly held "Guideline" speech addressed to the Estonian Parliament in October 2001, terrorism was mentioned forty-nine times.[11] In the corresponding speech held in the autumn of the previous year, nothing was said about terrorism.[12] This tendency to stress terrorism every time threat issues were brought up also continued for some period of time.

The closer came the crucial decision as to whether the new group of Central and Eastern European countries would join NATO, the more prevalent in Estonian statements were the more inclusive views vis-à-vis Russia. Thus, it was pointed out, for both international and domestic audiences, that cooperation with Russia was necessary, within the framework of the security policy architecture, in which Estonia would become a natural building block. It was emphasized that "in order for NATO to be an effective and successful security and defense organization, intensive co-operation is essential between the United States, Europe, and third countries, including Russia."[13]

Previous research has been all too quick to assume that the Russian Other is the only determinant in understanding both Estonia's images and its actions. A study of Estonian political discourse—which explores how the elite categorize themselves, their state, and the world surrounding them—reveals on the contrary that the *dynamics* of collective identity formations provide a feasible explanation of the dynamics of threat framing.[14] From this perspective, the Estonian wish to join the EU and NATO is not solely guided by a perceived Russian threat but is rather driven by a desire to reestablish bonds with Western political culture. It is also stressed in the Estonian discourse—predicating Estonia as industrious and modern—that the country intends to join international organizations to have a say in various international issues, rather than only using them as a means of protection.[15]

The assumption concerning Estonia's ongoing antagonistic relationship with Russia, or its Russian-speaking minority, could thus be qualified. Much has happened since; for example, the Estonian foreign minister in 1994 drew a parallel between the Russian government's relations with the Russian-speaking minority in Estonia and Hitler's program of protecting the so-called *Volksdeutsche* living outside the boundaries that then constituted Germany.[16] Although this is an example of rhetoric, this kind of verbal politics gives a sense of how relations between states develop, as well as how the domestic contexts within a state evolve. The integration policy initiated by the end of the 1990s indicates the introduction of an alternate Estonian discourse.

However, the widespread protests over the relocation of a bronze statue of a Soviet soldier in Tallinn in spring 2007 indicates that other discourses still circulate. This is hardly surprising, since—as of early 2007—there are still some 120,000 Russian-speaking residents in Estonia with undetermined citizenship, who neither have the right to vote in parliament elections nor to become employed within the civil service sector. The unemployment rate of this ethnic group is more than twice that of Estonian citizens.[17]

Responses by the Giant

NATO could certainly be considered as one of the traditional threats from the Russian policymakers' point of view. Hence, the alliance was once created as a response to the presumably aggressive union within which Russia was the principal actor. That is, the *origins* of NATO, rather than its current intentions, fuel the image of a threatening alliance.[18] Accordingly, surveys in the latter half of the 1990s show that some 60 percent of Russia's political elite perceived the "spread of NATO in Eastern Europe as a security threat."[19] Indeed, the enlargement of NATO to post-Soviet territories might have seemed almost provocative in the eyes of Russian leaders, in particular when considering the historical perspective of the Baltic states as "a gate for both Western aggressions against Russia, and Russian invasion against the West."[20] Nonetheless, there is a fairly broad consensus in the literature on Russian security relations in Northern Europe that this "area is not a very important priority for Moscow." The Kremlin policy makers are far more concerned with the risk of losing territories in the South or East than with any NATO enlargement in the West.[21]

Although the politicians' negative views vis-à-vis NATO expansion have
been fairly manifest all throughout the post–Cold War era, we can certainly
discern nuances. The rather complex and somewhat contradictory framing
of the NATO problem is well captured in an interview with Vladimir Putin
in October 2000:

> We are against NATO's expansion. Personally, I do not quite understand
> NATO's present role. Indeed, NATO was established to counterbalance
> the Soviet Union and the Eastern bloc that was created by the Soviet
> Union. Today there is no Eastern bloc. In fact, even the Soviet Union is
> no more. In other words, the reasons that brought NATO to life are no
> longer there. Yet NATO exists. It not only exists, but it is expanding,
> moreover, towards our borders. As you know, some time ago, several
> months ago, one of your colleagues, your American colleagues, asked me:
> "Do you allow for a possibility of Russia joining NATO?" I replied: "Yes.
> Why not?" And very soon we got an answer—true, an unofficial one, but
> it sounded at a sufficiently high level—that nobody in NATO was ex-
> pecting Russia. But if nobody is expecting us there, why should we re-
> joice at the expansion of NATO and NATO's approach to our borders?[22]

The skepticism against NATO is clearly voiced, and there is a tendency
to depict the organization as a way-outdated Cold War phenomenon. However, there are also incentives among the policymakers to strengthen the cooperation between Russia and NATO. A chain of cooperative steps since the
1990s rather points toward a pro-NATO view.[23] Putin's "Yes. Why not?" to
Russian NATO membership might at least indicate that the Alliance is not
perceived as being threatening to Russia.

Notable here is that the Russian government's attitude toward NATO
during the 1990s was not always entirely negative. In the literature, there
have so far been a few attempts to describe the Russian foreign policy discourse vis-à-vis NATO, which reveals a far-from-clear pattern of distinguished waves.[24] To briefly summarize, one could claim that from 1994,
when NATO's intentions for an eastward expansion became more or less
established, to the spring of 2004, when seven new members joined NATO
in a "fifth wave of NATO enlargement," Russian decisionmakers watched
the process from outside, expressing their concerns to varying extents.[25]

However, looking at the discourse of 1994, one could at first argue that a
form of consensus existed between Russia and NATO, at least regarding cooperative efforts between the two of promoting peace and security. In line

with this discourse, Boris Yeltsin's foreign minister, Andrei Kozyrev, stressed the importance of establishing good relations with the West, arguing that "both Russia and the NATO members are like-minded nations. We belong to one and the same democratic community of nations." Due to these shared democratic ideals, Kozyrev also denounced the idea that the West would pose any form of threat remotely similar to the ones of the Cold War.[26]

Nevertheless, this situation would turn out to be somewhat more complicated than what appeared initially. Russia faced difficulties in balancing the role of simultaneously being a great power—maintaining geopolitical influence—and being an open, democratic, and modern society. This resulted in a somewhat distrustful Western view of Russia, and it served as an obstacle to one of the central aspects of the NATO-Russian relationship—the one of an equal partnership. Kozyrev claimed that because the development of Russian internal and external affairs did not "fit the usual Western criteria and stereotypes, some analysts cannot accept the idea of a strong Russia." This, in turn, led to a form of "lagging partnership" between the two camps, and "while elements of cooperation exist on some concrete issues, a mature strategic partnership has yet to emerge."[27] Kozyrev did not, however, abandon his pro-West stance altogether, and his somewhat mixed message and inconsistent policies eventually led to his forced resignation.

Kozyrev's replacement, Yevgenii Primakov, advocated a somewhat different approach. Though claiming to want to maintain good relations with the West, he clearly voiced the idea of Russia being a great power, and he aimed to make Russia "one of the influential centers of a multipolar world."[28] With regards to NATO, he was less amiable than his predecessor, stating that it was "absolutely inadmissible" for Russia to have any of the ex-Soviet republics, including the Baltic States, join the Alliance.[29] These antiexpansionist sentiments increased around the time of the Kosovo crisis in 1999, where, in particular, the Russian military leadership stressed an increased threat from NATO, something that "was facilitated by the fact that NATO's action in the Balkans was widely perceived across Russia's political spectrum as an act of aggression."[30]

The anti-NATO language following the Kosovo crisis within Russian military circles was also an indication of harsher tunes against NATO among civil policymakers. For instance, in the National Security Concept of 2000, some aspects of NATO policy were recognized as being threatening to Russia, that is "the strengthening of military-political blocks and alliances, above all NATO's eastward expansion."[31] Already, however, this policy document—which to a large extent was a product of the Yeltsin administration (albeit published under Putin)—above all else emphasized another threat, which was to become the main threat image of the international security discourse in the coming years: "Terrorism represents a serious threat to the national security of the Russian federation. International terrorism is waging an open campaign to destabilize Russia."[32]

This focus on international terrorism as a threat represents a fundamental shift in Russian security policy, especially when considering the previous corresponding policy document from 1997. This document did indeed address international terrorism as a threat, but rather as one among other international problems, such as transnational crime and ethnonational interests.[33]

Previous research has been eager to stress that the external shock of September 11, 2001, caused a fundamental shift in Russian security policy, particularly in relation to the United States and the West. It is reasonable that the Russian government took advantage of this window of opportunity, particularly to convince the United States to "join forces to confront together the dangerous threats and challenges that humanity will face in the twenty-first century."[34] Moreover, the tragedy of 9/11 might have helped Putin convince his domestic audience that his pro-Western shift was necessary.[35] However, the attempts to make this shift dependent on the effects of 9/11 are somewhat exaggerated by the literature, especially when it is stated, with reference to Russian strategic thinking, that "after 11 September, . . . a new outgroup emerged: international terrorism."[36] In this context, it is worth noting that the Russian government had warned the West against this outgroup already early in 1999 in connection to the Kosovo crisis:

> Can European people take advantage of the emergence of a center of Islamic extremism on the continent? Why don't Americans understand that backing extremist Muslims in Kosovo amounts to helping a new Bin Laden to emerge? . . . Does Europe need the constitution of a centre of Islamic extremism, a centre of weapons and drug trafficking?[37]

When browsing through the hundreds of references to the term "threat" stored at Russian government's Web sites at the turn of the millennium, it is obvious that the policymakers much more frequently refer to terrorism rather than conventional threats, such as missiles, nuclear weapons, and NATO.[38] When explicitly mentioning threat, it is obvious that the Russian government prefers to highlight other issues than, for example, NATO. This becomes apparent ten days before 9/11. When the Russian president is asked why he has difficulties in accepting that the Baltic states would join

NATO, he replies in a fairly prophetic manner: "What problems is NATO solving? Protecting from whom? For the real threat today is terrorism, the spread of narcotics, organized crime, the traffic in arms. That is what really can threaten us today."[39]

The skepticism against NATO per se has obviously been toned down at the turn of the new millennium. Moreover, the 9/11 events have convinced the greatest of the powers of something that Moscow continually has asked for; namely, a strengthened cooperation aimed at combating international terrorism—the threat of all threats.

The emphasis on the *international* aspects of terrorism was apparent in Russian statements before as well as after the 9/11 events: The militant extremism has expanded beyond the Asian region, and the Osama bin Ladin–led network is characterized as a globally destructive force that threatens international peace and general values. As Eduard Solovyev argues in chapter 11 of this volume, it is occasionally stressed that Russia in population composition, spirit, culture, and prevalent religions is a European country, although it is also emphasized that Russia is "the natural bridge between Europe and Asia."[40] To characterize Russia as primarily European places the Federation in the same in-group as the other states in the European–North Atlantic region; they are presupposed to be subjected to the same threats from international terrorism. Because of its strategic location, the Russian discourse predicates Russia as being an especially important and responsible actor within the Western in-group:

> Terrorism is a worldwide pain, and an analogy involuntarily suggests itself that Russia, which is now on the frontline of the struggle against international terrorism in Chechnya and Central Asia, is saving the civilized world from the terrorist plague just as it saved Europe from a Tatar-Mongol invasion in the 13th century through its own suffering and deprivations.[41]

Due to this framing of terrorism as an international matter, it is no surprise that when texts after 9/11 are scrutinized, they in essence contain the same message—albeit even more emphasized—as previously.[42] In addition, the "Chechnya problem" has been framed as being a part of a larger threat of international terrorism, particularly during the second Chechen war. It is, for example, emphasized that the centuries-old Chechnya problem above all else should be characterized as a fundamentalist invasion: "International terrorists have openly—quite openly—declared their intention to establish a fundamentalist state on the territory between the Black and the Caspian Seas—the so-called khalifate, or the United States of Islam."[43]

Unfortunately, the rest of the international community appears not to understand this matter and subsequently does not share the Russian view on Chechnya. Instead, the officials of the Russian government have been "forced during each visit abroad to answer unpleasant questions about Chechnya." Although the 9/11 events have to some extent created an increased understanding of the Russian position, "double standards still exist [and a] certain circle of persons have deliberately made the criticism of Russia for the events in Chechnya their pet subject."[44] With regard to the threat that religious fundamentalists pose, there is a clear sense of "us" against "them" in the discourse, and Russia is presented as belonging to the European-Western in-group, standing vis-à-vis the Muslim out-group.[45]

Threat Image Trends

To sum up the language of security in Tallinn and Moscow, the tendencies to downplay any threats from NATO in general and NATO enlargement in particular are discernable in Russia in the new millennium, whereas Estonian policymakers have toned down any threat from Russia since the 1990s. Moreover, both states have broadened their threat image agendas since the mid-1990s in line with the security policy language of the Western world. In other words, they have begun to focus on nonmilitary threats such as organized crime, drug trafficking, and environmental threats, as well as—of course—terrorism (also see chapter 12 in this volume by Fenenko). The focus on the latter threat is apparent in Russia before the 9/11 events, due to a series of terrorist incidents initiated already as a consequence of the first Chechen war. Hence, the threat image of terrorism, which Russian leaders prefer to frame with international overtones, is nevertheless based, first and foremost, on domestic experiences. The same cannot be said about threat framing in Estonia. Before 9/11, terrorism is considered to be *one* of several threats on the broadened security agenda; but after the terrible incidents in the United States, there is an explosion of allusions to terrorism, a trend that has declined substantially since 2003.

As shown from speeches and interviews in the new millennium, Estonian policymakers are not particularly concerned about Russia *in terms of being a threat,* which is remarkable against the historical background that Estonia was occupied by Russia for about a half century. Turning to Russia, NATO could certainly be considered a threat because the Alliance was once created as a response to the presumably aggressive union within which Russia was the principal actor. Nonetheless, NATO is rarely brought up by Russian policymakers in the context of a threat. Instead, in both states, international terrorism, organized crime, drug trafficking, and so on are framed as severe threats.

Thus, there seem to be interesting similarities in the way the language of threat has developed in Russia and Estonia, and one may wonder whether there are any ambitions among policymakers in Moscow and Tallinn to develop a common understanding of not only what is threatening but also what is threatened in terms of values and identities. Would it be possible to develop a security community between such extreme cases such as Russia and Estonia? Or, for that matter, is it even possible to develop a security community in the Baltic Sea area? In trying to answer these questions, we need to consider that the development of a security community is a process of long-term learning that involves a fairly slow progression of international socialization.

International Socialization and Developing Identities

During the past decade, there has been a fairly lively academic discussion on the development of security policy in the Baltic Sea area. Several studies have focused on the roles and positions of the Baltic states as well as Russia within the European and North Atlantic security policy context. In particular, the Baltic states' prospects of becoming NATO members, and Russia's attitude toward this enlargement process, were in focus. We can discern a tendency, especially during the 1990s, to more or less explicitly analyze these states' security policy options in realist terms.[46]

It has also been argued that fear and stereotyped images of Russia among Baltic policymakers are the driving forces behind their security policy choices. The memory of the half-century Soviet occupation was lurking in the dark, implying that the policymakers' wish to join NATO was based on lessons learned from history.[47] The image of threats from Russia was almost self-evident. However, at the end of the 1990s, there were observations concerning Baltic leaders' appreciation of "softer" security threat images.[48] In the latter half of this decade, policymakers in, for example, Tallinn began to present threats differently. Apparently there were other issues than Russia to be concerned about, even in a security policy context.

In addition, the concept of *identity* began to show up fairly frequently in various studies of Baltic security.[49] Concurrently, an interest in the notion of identity could be discerned in studies of Russian security policy.[50]

Identity exists on several different levels of analysis—from individual to national and regional levels. The most important category in terms of affecting national security, and thus the one discussed here, is *collective or social identity.* The creation of a collective identity occurs within a defined social sphere, and it is mainly sensed when contrasted with other external identities. The constellation of an identity—the *in-group*—as well as its relations with external groups, is, however, neither static nor constant but must instead be regarded as a highly dynamic process.[51] For instance, who is included in a certain group and the basis for this inclusion/exclusion can change greatly over time. The same can be said about the in-group's relations with any external group, *the out-group*. What is important to note, however, is that although the relation between the in- and out-group is often characterized by difference, this difference does not necessarily imply conflict. It is not the existence of two contrasting groups per se that creates negative assessments of each other. Instead, as so-called social identity theory implies, it is the constitution of the groups themselves that brings about conflict.[52]

Two contrasting assumptions can be derived from this theory. On the one hand, it has been suggested that in a group attempting to strengthen its sense of collective identity, the more strongly members identify with each other, the more negative will be their attitudes vis-à-vis external groups. In other words, the in-group, under these circumstances, is more apt to depict the out-group as a threat, and in extreme cases this antagonism may lead to conflict. On the other hand, it is assumed that a strong feeling of identity is necessary and healthy for individuals. Units with a well-developed sense of social identity, in terms of who they are ("we are Russians"; "we are Estonians," etc.) are more apt to invite and include external entities into their collective identity formation ("we are Europeans"). According to this assumption, states can "learn additional 'social' . . . identities above and beyond the state, creating 'concentric circles' of group identification."[53] Whereas the former identity construction is often determined by the way the in-group distances itself from the out-group, often defined in terms of "we are *not* as the other," the latter identity construction concerns what "we admire and strive to become."[54]

Empirically, both assumptions fit sequentially in the process of building the nation-state. In the 1990s, the Estonian government was, for example, eager to stress what it did not belong to anymore, that is, anything like the Eastern Hemisphere centered on Moscow. Russia was consequently depicted as a threat against Estonia. As identity strengthened among Estonians and the self-esteem of this national entity increased, there was no longer any reason to emphasize a Russian threat based primarily on historical experience. Estonians were rather socialized into the European context; they adopted a focus on other threats, for example, terrorism and environmental pollution, perhaps even in collaboration with the former occupying power. By analogy with the security community approach, we may suggest that if the we-feelings—that is, mutual sympathy and loyalty—among the population of a state have matured to a certain extent, the prospects of developing dependable expectations of "peaceful change" with other states are better than if the we-feelings were poorly developed in the state in question.[55]

In line with the assumptions of social identity theory, I propose that the more developed the sense of collective identity between the citizens of a state, the more inclined they will be to become socialized into larger social identity formations, such as being "Europeans." It may not be too farfetched to conclude that state identity is more developed in Estonia than in Russia, although the existence of some 120,000 so-called stateless persons in Estonia somewhat contradicts the argument.[56] However, the point here is not whether *all* people living within the state's territory hold the same identity, which would be fairly unrealistic. Rather, the assertion here is that *ethnic Estonians* tend to have a highly cohesive identity. Russia is far more problematic in this respect, in the sense that this extremely vast country, hosting some 140 million Russian citizens, makes up an agglomeration of different cultures. The difficulties are related to the development of a formal collective Russian identity, or rather a Russian *state* identity, meaning that the Russian state is to be considered host "to a range of different identities, making up a complex whole."[57]

However, one possible unifying factor should be noted here: the previously mentioned norms connected to Sakwa's definition of globalization, that is, the values that emanate from Western political culture within the framework of a liberal democratic order.[58] The recurrent struggles between various political camps in Russia, be it in the name of Euroasianists or Slavophiles vis-à-vis Atlanticists or Westernizers, might determine the limits on how far-reaching socialization processes can develop from Moscow's point of view.[59] Although the Russian government under Putin could be characterized as being bureaucratic-authoritarian, due to inter alia historical traditions, the *main* direction during the one and a half decades of the reborn Russian state has been one of democratization according to Western standards. Despite severe setbacks, such as the restrictions on the liberty of the press in connection to the Chechen conflict, Russia could still be considered a student of Western democracy, albeit (especially during Putin's second administration) a disobedient student.[60] Globalization is especially relevant in this context, because it is likely to increase the intensity and institutionalization of relationships linking Russia and the West, thereby facilitating the process of socialization.

Europeanization and the Russian-Speaking Minority

When former Russian foreign minister Igor Ivanov emphasized that "Russia belongs to Europe not only geographically, but also by the very nature of its culture and civilization" and continued to talk about "threats or challenges (that) currently face Europe," he also managed to articulate that not only "we as Europeans" are facing the same threat, but also that "our values" are threatened by "them," that is, Islamic fundamentalists.[61] This is one example of the Russian tendency to frame post-Soviet Russia as a *European* power, which implies an increased interaction with the EU (including Estonia). Now the question is how language is put into practice. Is there any correspondence between talking and acting?

This is not the place to provide a detailed description of the "complex and comprehensive partnership covering almost all policy areas and issues" that has developed between Russia and the EU during the last fifteen years, because this has been done thoroughly elsewhere.[62] Still, there is the somewhat overlooked controversial issue of the Russian-speaking minority, the hottest and most frequently debated bilateral issues between Estonia and Russia since the troop withdrawals in 1994. In Moscow, the authorities have not been satisfied with the Estonian way of handling this question.[63] Russia's role as a watchdog for the Russian minorities was intensified during the months that preceded the Baltic states' entrance into the EU in May 2004. A case in point was the positive reactions in Moscow to the EU's monitoring assignments vis-à-vis Estonia's Russian minority policy, that is, to "further promote integration of the Russian minority by, in particular, continuing to increase the speed of naturalization procedures and by taking other proactive measures to increase the rate of naturalization."[64] "We hope"—as it was expressed in an official statement from Moscow—"that, with the active participation of the EU, it is possible, even in the coming months, to ensure some real shifts in the improvement of the situation of the Russian-speaking communities of these countries (Estonia and Latvia)."[65]

What is notable here is that the Russian authorities had much more confidence in the EU than in the Baltic governments concerning the destiny of the respective minorities in the Baltic states. When Russia and the EU finally signed an accord extending the partnership and cooperation agreement between the two, in April 2004, Moscow was all in all essentially satisfied with the references, albeit vague, to the protection of human and minority rights in the Baltic states.[66] Baltic EU membership could from this perspective be seen as a guarantee that the Estonian integration policy was moving in the right direction, from a Russian—as well as from a European—point of view. The enlargement of the EU was actually, from Moscow's point of view, considered to be beneficial as regards the Russian minority issue or, as the chairman of the Duma Foreign Policy Committee put it:

> In the context of the EU enlargement, in particular the problems we have in relations with the Baltic states, Russia now gets new levers of influence. While in the past discussions related to the Russian-speaking minorities in the Baltic nations were held in a bilateral format and with organizations which could only issue recommendations on that situation—I mean the [Organization for Security and Cooperation in Europe], the Council of Europe—shifting those issues to the EU level, in our opinion, gives us certain prospects, and I think Russia will energetically raise those issues in its dialogue with the EU. At least parliament members plan doing this in the framework of the parliamentary cooperation committee formed by Russia and the European Union.[67]

Other statements from Russian government officials point in the same direction. The EU is a partner with which Russia could cooperate concerning the crucial and fairly complicated issue of Russian-speaking minorities' rights in the Baltic states.[68]

Toward a Security Community?

At the end of the Cold War, Estonia perceived Russia as a threat and Russia perceived NATO as a threat due to its historical past. These stereotypes were based on lessons from history rooted in peoples' minds and, as we have seen, in particular opinion polls, indicating that these cognitive factors seem to have influenced individuals' threat images. Still, already in the beginning of the post–Cold War period, there were indications of a socialization process in which both Estonian and Russian policymakers identified themselves positively with, above all else, the EU. This chapter has shown an increasingly explicit consistency in the way policymakers in Estonia and Russia are framing social identity, in terms of "we belong to the European family." Still, the language of identity and norms within the context of the process of Western socialization is more apparent in Tallinn than in Moscow. Whereas Russia's part in this process is more restrained, Estonians are more eager to adapt to nearly everything that is European and Western in outlook.

We might, however, also take into consideration the triggering dramatic events, for instance, the terrorist attacks in Moscow, New York City, and Washington that caused policymakers in both Estonia and Russia to resolutely replace threat images of the Cold War with those of international terrorism. This language of security, often followed by related threat images such as arms and drug trafficking and organized crime, is indeed a globalized language in the sense that it reaches the extension of social relations around the globe. Still, common assessments of threat are not sufficient but may well be, in Adler and Barnett's conceptualization, a "precipitating" condition for the development of a security community.[69]

There are pros and cons regarding the judgment as to whether the relationship between Estonia and Russia really is developing in the direction of a security community. On the one hand, there have recently been several indications of tension when it comes to the verbal climate between the two. Accordingly, Estonia has been accused for its "rigid position" vis-à-vis the Russian-speaking minority. That is, there is the fact that this group of noncitizens is still estimated at about 10 percent of the population of Estonia in the first place, but there are also "insinuations of bad treatment" of the group as such.[70] Disagreements remains on this issue, and Estonian representatives respond by referring "to all EU standards for the protection of human rights and minority rights" to which they "clearly subscribe." Although Russia and Estonia continue to argue about the Russian-speaking minority,[71] there are, conversely, still signs of a long-term improving, neighborly relationship. One example is that high-level diplomacy has become fairly routine in the twenty-first century, as compared with the 1990s, when visits in the respective capitals at a ministerial level were almost nonexistent.[72] In a well-researched study by Ingmar Oldberg, the following conclusion is drawn with regard to future prospects for the Baltic Sea area, focusing on the role of the Russian-speaking minorities:

As for the Baltic states, NATO and EU memberships will not only promote their economic development and European identity. They can also feel more secure from Russian pressure and develop ties with Russia that are profitable to them. Many Balts know Russia well and speak Russian. The Russian-speaking populations, especially people engaged in business, tend to be more EU-centric (Eurorussians) than the titular nations, at the same time as many have old contacts with [members of the Commonwealth of Independent States]. The Baltic states can thus become some kind of bridge between Europe and Russia and contribute to integrating Russia into Europe. The Baltic countries also have strong interests in promoting European unity and progress.[73]

There are other examples beyond the area of high politics that are sometimes indicated by regional press reviews:

Last week I witnessed a trend that gave me a positive view of relations between Russians and the ethnic Russians and Balts in the Baltic states. While traveling with Saint Petersburg businesspeople on a trip to Estonia, it became clear that in spite of disagreements between politicians in Moscow and Tallinn, ordinary people, businesses especially, are making a huge effort in getting closer to each other. They want to show their goodwill, which is the only way to achieve mutual advantages.[74]

These very different examples indicate that a socialization process is under way in the Baltic Sea region, in the sense that people of various nationalities to an increasing extent interact and communicate. And this is actually happening *in spite of* differences of opinion concerning interpretations of the past—whether, for example, Estonia was annexed or occupied by the Soviet Union, or whether language tests are relevant and fair instruments to determine citizenship. As has been suggested in a recent study, "a security community is neither conflict-free nor power-free. Its distinctive features are that its internal conflicts are solved peacefully, and that power is expressed by means short of physical violence."[75]

Notes

1. Barry Buzan, *People, States, and Fear: An Agenda for International Security Studies in the Post-Cold War Era,* 2nd ed. (Boulder, Colo.: Lynne Rienner, 1991), 7; Justin Rosenberg, *The Follies of Globalisation Theory: Polemical Essays* (London:

Verso, 2002); J. Weldes, "Globalisation Is Science Fiction," *Millennium–Journal of International Studies* 30, no. 3 (2001).

2. Julia Rozanova, "Russia in the Context of Globalization," *Current Sociology* 51, no. 6 (2003): 652. Also Mikhail Ilyin, "Studies of Globalization and Equity in Post-Soviet Russia," *Communist and Post-Communist Studies* 37, no. 1 (2004): 71–83.

3. Sergey Lavrov, *Democracy, International Governance and a Future World Pattern,* Ministry of Foreign Affairs of Russia, December 27, 2004, available at http://www.mid.ru. Also see Yuri Fedotov, "Statement by Deputy Minister of Foreign Affairs at the Ministerial Segment Meeting of the 60th Session of the United Nations Economic and Social Commission for Asia and the Pacific," Ministry of Foreign Affairs of Russia, April 27, 2004, available at http://www.mid.ru; Vladimir Chizhov, "Remarks by Russia's Deputy Minister of Foreign Affairs at the Conference 'Wider Europe: New Agenda,' Bratislava, March 2004," Ministry of Foreign Affairs of Russia, March 20, 2004, available at http://www.mid.ru; and Igor Ivanov, *The Iraq Crisis and the Struggle for a New World Pattern,* January 19, 2004, Ministry of Foreign Affairs of Russia, 2004, available at http://www.mid.ru.

4. Richard Sakwa, "Russia and Globalisation: Concluding Comments," in *Russian Transformations,* ed. Leo McCann (London: RoutledgeCurzon, 2004), 211.

5. Emanuel Adler and Michael N. Barnett, *Security Communities,* Cambridge Studies in International Relations 62 (Cambridge: Cambridge University Press, 1998), 7; Karl W. Deutsch, *Political Community and the North Atlantic Area: International Organization in the Light of Historical Experience* (Princeton, N.J.: Princeton University Press, 1957); Unto Vesa and Frank Möller, *Security Community in the Baltic Sea Region? Recent Debate and Recent Trends,* Occasional Paper 88 (Tampere: Tampere Peace Research Institute, 2003); Alex J. Bellamy, *Security Communities and Their Neighbours: Regional Fortresses or Global Integrators?* (Basingstoke, U.K.: Palgrave Macmillan, 2004).

6. David J. Smith, "Minority Rights, Multiculturalism and EU Enlargement: The Case of Estonia," *Journal of Ethnopolitics and Minority Issues in Europe,* no. 1 (2003), available at www.ecmi.de.

7. *State and Society. Integration Framework. The State Integration Programme 2000–2007,* 2003, http://www.riik.ee/saks/ikomisjon/programme.htm.

8. Ronald D. Asmus, *Opening NATO's Door: How the Alliance Remade Itself for a New Era* (New York: Columbia University Press, 2002), 228–38.

9. After almost a decade of peaceful relations with Russia, a majority of Estonian citizens still assessed the former occupying power as a threat to their state. Nonetheless, more recent polls indicate another trend. Between 2000 and 2004, the percentage of Estonians believing in the probability of being attacked from another state steadily decreased from 33 to 12. *Estonia Today: Support for NATO Membership,* Estonian Ministry of Foreign Affairs, April 2005, available at http://www.vm.ee; Richard Rose, *New Baltic Barometer IV: A Survey Study,* Studies in Public Policy 338 (Glasgow: University of Strathclyde, 2000).

10. Erik Noreen, "Verbal Politics of Estonian Policy-Makers," in *Threat Politics: New Perspectives on Security, Risk and Crisis Management.,* ed. Johan Eriksson (Aldershot, U.K.: Ashgate, 2001), 88; Erik Noreen and Roxanna Sjöstedt, "Estonian Identity Formations and Threat Framing in the Post–Cold War Era," *Journal of Peace Research* 41, no. 6 (2004): 733–50.

11. Toomas H. Ilves, *Main Guidelines of Estonia's Foreign Policy. Address to the Riigikogu,* Estonian Ministry of Foreign Affairs, October 25, 2001, available at http://www.vm.ee.

12. Toomas H. Ilves, *Developments in the Main Directions of Estonia's Foreign Policy. Address to the Riigikogu,* Estonian Ministry of Foreign Affairs, October 12, 2000, available at http://www.vm.ee.

13. Kristina Ojuland, "Address by Estonian Foreign Minister at the Danish Institute of International Affairs, Copenhagen," Estonian Ministry of Foreign Affairs, April, 12 2002, available at http://www.vm.ee; Eiki Berg, *A Lively and Active Foreign Policy,* Estonian Ministry of Foreign Affairs, 2003, available at http://www.vm.ee.

14. Noreen; and Sjöstedt, "Estonian Identity Formations and Threat Framing." For another perspective, see, e.g., the realist-influenced anthology *Bordering Russia: Theory and Prospects for Europe's Baltic Rim,* ed. Hans Mouritzen (Aldershot, U.K.: Ashgate, 1998), but also constructivist contributions, e.g., Merje Kuus, "Toward Cooperative Security? International Integration and the Construction of Security in Estonia," *Millennium–Journal of International Studies* 31, no. 2 (2002): 297–317; and Merje Kuus, "European Integration in Identity Narratives in Estonia: A Quest for Security," *Journal of Peace Research* 39, no. 1 (2002): 91–108. Also cf. Alexander Sergounin, "The Russia Dimension," in *Bordering Russia,* ed. Mouritzen.

15. Kuus, "Toward Cooperative Security?"; Kuus, "European Integration in Identity Narratives in Estonia"; Pami Aalto, "Revisiting the Security/Identity Puzzle in Russo-Estonian Relations," *Journal of Peace Research* 40, no. 5 (2003): 573–91; Noreen and Sjöstedt, "Estonian Identity Formations and Threat Framing."

16. Juri Luik, "Statement at the Swedish Institute of International Affairs, Stockholm," Estonian Ministry of Foreign Affairs, March 2, 1994, available at http://www.vm.ee. Even if a speculative analogy like this did not occur very often in official statements, it occurred repeatedly in the media. See, e.g., the daily *Postimees,* August 21 and September 25, 1994.

17. "Estonia Today Citizenship," Fact Sheet, April 2007, Press and Information Department, Estonian Ministry of Foreign Affairs, available at www.vm.ee.

18. Interview with Alexander Pikayev, director, Center for International Security Studies, Moscow, May 17, 2005. Also see, Charlotte Wagnsson, *Russian Political Language and Public Opinion on the West, NATO and Chechnya: Securitisation Theory Reconsidered,* rev. ed. (Stockholm: Stockholm University and Department for Strategic Studies, Swedish National Defense College, 2000).

19. William Zimmerman, *The Russian People and Foreign Policy: Russian Elite and Mass Perspectives, 1993–2000* (Washington, D.C.: Princeton Paperbacks, 2002), 91–92. One population poll reveals that, in spite of the 9/11 incidents, which might have bridged any gap between the former superpowers, 57 percent considered NATO expansion as a threat to Russia in late September 2001. The share had significantly increased since 1997 (47 percent) (Public Opinion Foundation Database, 2001).

20. Alexander A. Pikayev, "Russia and the Baltic States," in *The Baltic States in World Politics,* ed. Birthe Hansen and Bertel Heurlin (Richmond, U.K.: Curzon Press, 1998), 137.

21. See Sergounin, "Russia Dimension," 16–17; and Andris Spruds, "Perceptions and Interests in Russian-Baltic Relations," in *EU Enlargement and Beyond: The Baltic States and Russia,* ed. Helmut Hubel (Berlin: Arno Spitz GmbH, 2002).

22. Vladimir Putin, "Interview with French TV Channels TF-1 and France-3," RFI Radio Broadcasting Corporation and ORT TV Channel, Moscow, Ministry of Foreign Affairs of Russia, October 23, 2000, available at http://www.mid.ru.

23. Wagnsson, *Russian Political Language and Public Opinion,* 81–82.

24. Thomas Ambrosio, "From Balancer to Ally? Russian-American Relations in the

Wake of 11 September," *Contemporary Security Policy* 24, no. 2 (2003): 1–28; Dmitri Trenin; and Bobo Lo, *The Landscape of Russian Foreign Policy Decision-Making* (Moscow: Carnegie Moscow Center, 2005).

25. Denis Alexeev, *NATO Enlargement: A Russian Outlook,* Conflict Studies Research Centre: Russian Series 04/33 (London: Defence Academy of the United Kingdom, 2004).

26. Andrei Kozyrev, "Russia and NATO: A Partnership for a United and Peaceful Europe," *NATO Review* 42, no. 4 (1994), http://www.nato.int/docu/review/1994/9404-1.htm.

27. Andrei Kozyrev, "The Lagging Partnership," *Foreign Affairs* 73, no. 3 (1994): 60. These claims turned into discursive practice in November 1994, when Kozyrev picked a tougher stance toward the West and refused to sign previously agreed Partnership for Peace documents with NATO. Richard Sakwa, *Russian Politics and Society,* 2nd ed. (London: Routledge, 1996), 280.

28. Quoted by Bobo Lo, *Russian Foreign Policy in the Post-Soviet Era Reality, Illusion, and Mythmaking* (Basingstoke, U.K.: Palgrave Macmillan, 2002), 59.

29. Quoted by Johan Matz, *Constructing a Post-Soviet International Political Reality: Russian Foreign Policy Towards the Newly Independent States 1990–95* (Uppsala: Acta Universitatis Upsaliensis, 2001), 252.

30. William D. Jackson, "Encircled Again: Russia's Military Assesses Threats in a Post-Soviet World," *Political Science Quarterly* 117, no. 3 (2002): 391.

31. "Russian National Security Concept, 2000," signed by President Vladimir Putin on January 10, 2000, http://www.russiaeurope.mid.ru/russiastrat2000.html.

32. Ibid.

33. "Russian National Security Blueprint, 1997," http://www.fas.org/nuke/guide/russia/doctrine/blueprint.html.

34. Quoted by Ambrosio, "From Balancer to Ally?" 7.

35. Lilia Shevtsova, "Political Leadership in Russia's Transformation," in *Russia's Engagement with the West: Transformation and Integration in the Twenty-First Century,* ed. Alexander J. Motyl, Blair A. Ruble, and Lilia Shevtsova (London: M. E. Sharpe, 2005), 103.

36. Ambrosio, "From Balancer to Ally?" 7–8.

37. Quoted by Colin Guillaume, "Russian Foreign Policy Discourse during the Kosovo Crisis: Internal Struggles and the Political Imaginaire," in *Questions de Recherche* 2 (Paris: Science Po, 2004), 25.

38. There is more on this in "Threat Framing and Socialization: Focusing on Estonia and Russia in the New Millennium," by Erik Noreen, in *Security Strategies, Power Disparity and Identity,* ed. by Olav F. Knudsen (Aldershot, U.K.: Ashgate, 2007).

39. Vladimir Putin, "Interview Granted by the President to the Finnish Newspaper *Helsingin Sanomat,*" Ministry of Foreign Affairs of Russia, September 1, 2001, available at http://www.mid.ru. A principal difference between opinion polls and the texts that are scrutinized in this chapter is that a majority of the survey participants, when asked if they consider NATO as a threat, answer in the affirmative; none of this is apparent in the documents from the Russian government. Rather, policymakers prefer to talk about other issues, such as international terrorism and Islamic fundamentalism, in terms of threat. However, the survey studies also indicate that when participants are free to choose among several potentially threatening issues, it is not "military threats from other nations" that worry them but rather drug-addiction, crime, terrorism, low living standards, corruption, the situation in Chechnya, etc. Public Opinion Foundation Data-

base, Russia, January 16, 2003, http://www.fom.ru/report/map/; cf. Wagnsson, *Russian Political Language and Public Opinion.*

40. See Sergei Ivanov, "Speech at the 37th International Security Conference on the Theme 'Global and Regional Security at the Start of the 21st Century,'" Ministry of Foreign Affairs of Russia, February 13, 2001, available at http://www.mid.ru. Also see Vladimir Putin, "Statement in Connection with the Explosion of Pushkin Square, Moscow," Ministry of Foreign Affairs of Russia, August 11, 2000, available at http://www.mid.ru. Alexander Losyukov, "Moscow's Policy: Neither a Western Nor an Eastern Tilt," *Diplomat Magazine,* no. 4 (2001). Putin, "Interview Granted by the President to the Finnish Newspaper *Helsingin Sanomat.*"

41. Ivanov, "Speech at the 37th International Security Conference."

42. Vladimir Putin, "Remarks by President Vladimir Putin of Russia in the Bundestag of the Federal Republic of Germany Berlin," Ministry of Foreign Affairs of Russia, September 25, 2001, available at http://www.mid.ru.

43. Ibid.

44. Anatoly Safonov, "'The Chief One on Terrorism,' Interview Granted to the Newspaper Moskovskiye Novosti," Ministry of Foreign Affairs of Russia, October 25, 2001, available at http://www.mid.ru.

45. Igor Ivanov, "Remarks by Minister of Foreign Affairs, Münich, December 10, 2003," Ministry of Foreign Affairs of Russia, available at http://www.mid.ru; Vladimir Putin, "Interview with National Public Radio, the US Radio Station, New York, November 19, 2001, Ministry of Foreign Affairs of Russia, available at http://www.mid.ru; Valentina Matviyenko, "Statement at the 31st Session of the General Conference of UNESCO," Ministry of Foreign Affairs of Russia, October 18, 2001, available at http://www.mid.ru; Safonov, "'Chief One on Terrorism.'"

46. See, e.g., Philip Petersen, "Security Policy in the Post-Soviet Baltic States," *European Security* 1, no. 1 (1992): 13–49; Birthe Hansen; and Bertel Heurlin, *The Baltic States in World Politics* (Richmond, U.K.: Curzon Press, 1998); Hans Mouritzen, ed., *Bordering Russia: Theory and Prospects for Europe's Baltic Rim* (Aldershot, U.K.: Ashgate, 1998); and Andrus Park, "Russia and Estonian Security Dilemmas," *Europe-Asia Studies* 47, no. 1 (1995): 27–45.

47. Mouritzen, *Bordering Russia,* 8–9; also see Mare Haab, "Estonia," in *Bordering Russia,* ed. Mouritzen, 109–29.

48. C. Archer and C. Jones, "The Security Policies and the Concepts of the Baltic States: Learning from Their Nordic Neighbours?" in *Stability and Security in the Baltic Sea,* ed. O. F. Knudsen (London: Frank Cass, 1999).

49. See, e.g., Aalto, "Revisiting the Security/Identity Puzzle"; Kuus, "European Integration in Identity Narratives in Estonia"; Merje Kuus, "Sovereignty for Security? The Discourse of Sovereignty in Estonia," *Political Geography* 21, no. 3 (2002): 393–412; Vahur Made, "Estonia and Europe: A Common Identity of an Identity Crisis?" in *Post–Cold War Identity Politics. Northern and Baltic Experiences,* ed. Marko Lehti and David J. Smith (London: Frank Cass, 2003); Noreen, "Verbal Politics of Estonian Policy-Makers"; Noreen and Sjöstedt, "Estonian Identity Formations and Threat Framing."

50. See, e.g., Viatsheslav Morozov, "The Baltic States in Russian Foreign Policy Discourse: Can Russia Become a Baltic Country?" in *Post–Cold War Identity Politics,* ed. Lehti and Smith; Alla Kassianova, "Russia: Still Open to the West? Evolution of the State Identity in the Foreign Policy and Security Discourse," *Europe-Asia Studies* 53, no. 6 (2001): 821–39; Ted Hopf, *Social Construction of International Politics: Identities and*

Foreign Policies, Moscow, 1955 & 1999 (Ithaca, N.Y.: Cornell University Press, 2002); Wagnsson, *Russian Political Language and Public Opinion;* and Michael C. Williams; and Iver Neumann, "From Alliance to Security Community: NATO, Russia, and the Power of Identity," *Millennium: Journal of International Studies* 29, no. 2 (2000): 357–87.

51. Alexander Wendt, *Social Theory of International Politics* (Cambridge: Cambridge University Press, 1999); Hopf, *Social Construction of International Politics.*

52. Wendt, *Social Theory of International Politics,* 241.

53. Ibid., 242. Also see Mark Schafer, "Cooperative and Conflictual Policy Preferences: The Effect of Identity, Security, and Image of the Other," *Political Psychology* 20, no. 4 (1999): 829–44; and Tobias Theiler, "Societal Security and Social Psychology," *Review of International Studies* 29, no. 2 (2003): 249–68.

54. Trine Flockhart, " 'Complex Socialization': A Framework for the Study of State Socialization," *European Journal of International Relations* 12, no. 1 (2006): 89–118.

55. Deutsch, *Political Community and the North Atlantic Area.*

56. "Europe / Document NDEG 2363/2364: EU Enlargement," Agence Europe, March 24, 2004, available at http://global.factiva.com.

57. Ted Hopf, "Introduction: Russian Identity and Foreign Policy after the Cold War," in *Understandings of Russian Foreign Policy,* ed. Ted Hopf (University Park: Pennsylvania State University Press, 1999), 6–8. And see Wagnsson, *Russian Political Language and Public Opinion,* 40–42.

58. Vincent Pouliot, "The Alive and Well Transatlantic Security Community: A Theoretical Reply to Michael Cox," *European Journal of International Relations* 12, no. 1 (2006): 119–27.

59. See, e.g., Motyl, Ruble, and Shevtsova, *Russia's Engagement with the West;* Richard Sakwa, "The 2002–2004 Russian Elections and Prospects for Democracy," *Europe-Asia Studies* 57, no. 3 (2005): 369–98; Trenin and Lo, *Landscape of Russian Foreign Policy Decision-Making.*

60. Quoted by Sakwa, "2002–2004 Russian Elections," 391.

61. Ivanov, "Remarks by Minister of Foreign Affairs, Münich." For a statement in the same direction by the Russian president, see, e.g., an article by Vladimir Putin, "Nya skiljelinjer riskerar att bildas i Europa" (Risk of creating new borders in Europe), in the Swedish *Dagens Nyheter* (Daily News), November 22, 2006, where he states that "Russia is historically and culturally a natural part of the 'European family.' "

62. Stephan Kux, "European Union–Russia Relations: Transformation through Integration," in *Russia's Engagement with the West,* ed. Motyl, Ruble, and Shevtsova, 171. Also see Rikard Bengtsson, *The EU as a Security Policy Actor: Russian and US Perceptions,* Research Report 36 (Stockholm: Swedish Institute of International Affairs, 2004), 35; and Viatsheslav Morozov, "Russia in the Baltic Sea Region: Desecuritization or Deregionalization?" *Cooperation and Conflict* 39, no. 3 (2004): 328.

63. Alexander Yakovenko, "Statement Regarding Likely Adoption by Estonian Parliament of Aliens Law Amendments, 17.12. 2003," Ministry of Foreign Affairs of Russia, available at http://www.mid.ru.

64. "List of Main Claims and Recommendations as Regards the Rights of National Minorities Offered by International Organizations and NGO to Estonia (Reference Paper), 18.12.2003," Ministry of Foreign Affairs of Russia, available at http://www.mid.ru.

65. "Russian MFA Information and Press Department Commentary Regarding the Human Rights Situation in Latvia and Estonia," Ministry of Foreign Affairs of Russia, available at http://www.mid.ru.

66. "EU/Russia Protocol on Extending PCA to Ten Accession Countries Signed, Due to Joint Declarations, 28 April 2004," Agence Europe, 2004, available at http://global.factiva.com.

67. "Press Conference with State Duma Committee for Foreign Affairs, Chair Konstantin Kosachev, May 19, 2004," Federal News Service, Russia, available at http://global.factiva.com.

68. "Kremlin Insider Gives Upbeat Account of EU-Russia Talks: Interview with President Putin's Aide Sergey Yastrzhembskiy, 22 May 2004," BBC Monitoring Former Soviet Union, available at http://global.factiva.com.

69. Adler and Barnett, *Security Communities.*

70. E.g., see "Russian Parliamentarian Suggests Ways to Improve Relations with Baltic States, 30 August 2006," BBC Monitoring Former Soviet Union, available at http://global.factiva.com; Yulia Andreyeva, "Russia Aims Effectively to Ensure Ethnic Russians' Rights, 24 October 2006," ITAR-TASS World Service, available at http://global.factiva.com; "A Look at Estonia's Minority Question, 1 November 2006," *Baltic Times,* available at http://global.factiva.com.

71. Yelena Volkova, "RF Calls on Estonia to Grant Political Rights to Ethnic Minorities, 7 March 2006," ITAR-TASS World Service, available at http://global.factiva.com.

72. "Estonia and Russia: Important Visits and Meetings, 06 October 2005," Estonian Ministry of Foreign Affairs, available at http://www.vm.ee.

73. See Ingmar Oldberg, *Reluctant Rapprochement: Russia and the Baltic States in the Context of NATO and EU Enlargements* (Stockholm: Swedish Defense Research Agency, 2003), 72 and Morozov, "Russia in the Baltic Sea Region," 328.

74. See "Last Week I Witnessed a Trend," *Saint Peterburg Times,* June 24, 2005; and "Eastern Parts of Estonia Are Highly Interested in Investments from Russia," *Saint Petersburg Times,* June 28, 2005.

75. Vincent Pouliot, "The Alive and Well Transatlantic Security Community: A Theoretical Reply to Michael Cox," *European Journal of International Relations* 12, no. 1 (2006): 125.

10

Chechnya, the Council of Europe, and the Advocacy of Human Rights in the Toughest of Cases

Rick Fawn

We will not allow anyone to provoke us into adopting primitive, anti-Western policies.
—Russian foreign minister Sergey Lavrov, September 1, 2005

The Russian-Chechen conflict conjures images of some of the most ruthless brutality in postcommunist Europe. The Council of Europe (CoE), by contrast, typifies noncoercive normative values in world politics. In other words, this intergovernmental body practices the softest aspects of contemporary European politics. What could be the connection between the conflict and the CoE? How can that seemingly limited, even oxymoronic

The author gives immense thanks to Douglas Blum for inviting him to participate in the project that led to this book, and for invaluable insights and suggestions throughout its duration. Members of the project also provided interesting and important observations, some of which are expressly incorporated here. Two anonymous referees offered helpful comments. Andrew Williams kindly read a revised version of this chapter. The Kennan Institute was most helpful in organizational matters.

relationship be juxtaposed against the biggest (if ill-defined) buzzwords of current world politics: globalization, identity, and security?

Each of these three words invokes a voluminous and contentious literature. Precisely because the CoE is a value-laden institution, CoE membership also indicates how members and would-be members see themselves. As is argued in this chapter, Russia has been willing to partake in and conform to CoE practices in some respects but not others. In addition, despite both presumptions and analysis to the contrary, the chapter argues that the CoE has had subtle but important influence on Russian conduct of the wars in Chechnya. CoE membership, therefore, has had both domestic and international costs for Russia. Russia nevertheless remains involved in the CoE because of the crucial symbolic and identity functions its membership serves. This relationship, therefore, also provides understandings of the ambiguities that arise from the relationship among globalization, security, and identity.

This chapter first considers the content of Russian-CoE relations by assessing manifestations of globalization in Europe. Second, it outlines the CoE's significance for Russia. It also indicates the difficulties of applying human rights norms to the Russo-Chechen conflict, thereby acknowledging the extraordinary circumstances that the Russian government and security services face. Third, on the basis of the literature on international human rights practice, it hypothesizes three ways in which human rights norms may still influence the Russo-Chechen conflict. Fourth, it indicates, even in this most difficult case, how the CoE has some influence over the conduct of the conflict. Fifth, it considers how Russia has interpreted and used CoE criticism, demonstrating trade-offs between identity and interests. The chapter closes with brief observations from this case about the interaction of security, identity, and interests.

The Context: Globalizing Processes in Europe after the Cold War

The end of the Soviet Union has meant the expansion over space and the intensification of the processes of globalization. Parts of Russian society and economy have undergone unprecedented exposure to or integration into global processes. This phenomenon has brought, as elsewhere, challenges for existing values. Part of globalization is the smoothing out, the standardization of practices, from the choice of basic consumer goods to fundamental questions of geocultural belonging. Post–Cold War globalization is a period of adaptation and of rejection; states and societies are conforming—or not—to larger sets of values.

This process of adaptation has been particularly pronounced in the postcommunist space, with foreign policies that express geocultural goals and preferences. For states now in the European Union and NATO, the "return to Europe" was their fundamental objective. This cannot be taken lightly. Though these countries sought to teach Western decisionmakers of their rightful place *back* in Europe, they nevertheless had to meet Western requirements. Hindsight—that, by 2007, ten postcommunist states would be members of the European Union and NATO—must not diminish the uncertainty these governments faced in seeking membership and having to confront standards largely set outside their control.[1]

If globalization is the contraction of space and time, the expansion of interconnections between peoples, then institutionalization in Europe is globalization at its most intense, even if those processes are also a reaction to aspects of globalization. The member states of EU institutions have overtly codified the norms and practices that define their collective association. In turn, Europe's process of creating a common identity has been fundamental to achieving its own security. It is the incarnation of the idea that likeminded (small-r) republican polities will banish the use of force from the menu of choice. However, the European (small-c) community may be said to have arisen, a common understanding of security and identity now seems inseparable. States that lack common conceptions of security, with those also being integral to their identity, are unlikely ever to become members.

The European coalescence of identity and security derives from and requires several elements. Powers must no longer have grand (for which read "global") ambitions; instead, to be European is to be content with the status quo and, at best, a middle power (as individual states, not necessarily as a conglomerate). We think immediately of Britain and France, with their (small) nuclear arsenals and UN Security Council vetoes. But ambitions to be greater than middle powers jar badly in Europe and are anyway short lasting. It is also true that some European countries find themselves drawn into legacies of empire, as occasionally occurs between Britain and Spain over Gibraltar. These few incidents underscore how past great power status and empire are at odds with (and get submerged in) European values of negotiation, conciliation, and preference for the status quo.

These traits also explain European concern—albeit still selective—over Russian behavior in the "near abroad." One of the CoE's demands on Russia for membership was that it cease distinctions in its references to and treatment of former Soviet republics from other states. The implication may be that the more Russia behaves in a "proto-imperial" or "neo-imperial" way toward its post-Soviet neighbors,[2] the less it can be "European."

This is not to say that the interpretations of Russian interests in the near abroad are wrong. Russian policymakers interpret or objectively face different security concerns from their Western counterparts, and they generally decide to confront them differently. Russia faces different understandings of identity and security in dealing with Europe, but with synergy: "Europe" is a different form of security and a different understanding and operationalization of sovereignty.

The European Union cannot have a monopolistic definition of "Europe." We should perhaps recall the surprise, even anger, that communist-era Central European dissidents expressed when the then–European Community had unilaterally appropriated that name for a small part of the continent. The government and the peoples of Russia can offer other definitions of "Europe." In contrast to Soviet ideology's "really existing socialism," the EU can be said to have created a "really existing Europe," with terms of membership and, therefore, also of exclusion.

Russia can reject that process and/or continue to offer its own definitions of Europe. Doing so, however, will simply underline the gulf—existential, legal, bureaucratic, and material—among these different conceptions of "Europe." Russia's size and history are of course inseparable from its ability to integrate with Europe. Russia may not be so much a part of anything but rather a unique entity.[3] The more one accepts arguments for Russia's uniqueness, the greater the distance between it and Europe. Different justifications for the use of violence may also stem from the residue of great power status or of geocultural uniqueness. The use and justification of violence in the Chechen conflict can separate Russia from Europe.

It is also essential to understand that few question the threat that Russia has faced from Chechen violence. As has been said, no Western government has acknowledged the Chechen claim to independence, and, when they have been made, criticisms of the Russian campaigns routinely carry condemnations of Chechen atrocities.[4] The norm is that indiscriminate violence anywhere by anyone is unacceptable.

The intensified globalization that is European integration presents choices and trade-offs. As innocuous as it may appear, the CoE is the initial entry point for deciding how states see their sources of security and thus their identity. A state's desire for CoE membership indicates its intentions to express its political values. More practically, the CoE has been the antechamber for deeper integration into European institutions. No postcommunist state has entered the EU without first gaining CoE membership. But before we assess the CoE's impact, it is necessary to establish a framework for assessing the impact of international human rights norms.

Measuring Identity and Security through Human Rights in the Conflict between Russia and Chechnya

Measuring international human rights pressure on Russian behavior in Chechnya is the toughest test case and can be the most revealing. Russia faces tremendous threats in duration or nature from Chechen violence that are incomparable to terrorism in the West. Transposed to the United States, Chechen terrorism in the past decade might look thus: In 2004, two passenger planes flying from Washington are destroyed by suicide bombers, just a week after an explosion on the Washington subway kills ten commuters; and in 1999, residential areas of Washington and Baltimore are bombed, killing 300. In addition, various civilian sites have been attacked by sometimes dozens of assailants and hundreds have been taken hostage, including a Florida school in 2004, a Washington theater in 2002, and two hospitals in Alabama in separate attacks in 1995 and 1996, where in just one case two-thirds the number of victims of the terrorist attacks of September 11, 2001, are taken hostage, and in those two attacks, civilian deaths number in the hundreds.[5] This analogy excludes numerous lower-scale attacks.

Apart from the frequency of attacks, also significant is the targeting of the quintessentially "innocent": hospitals and schools. The Beslan school siege of September 2004—in which about a thousand civilians were taken hostage for three days, including hundreds of children—is rightly called "a nadir in the annals of terrorism."[6] The attacks of October 2005 in Kabardino-Balkaria suggested that the geographic scope of violence was widening. The Parliamentary Assembly of the Council of Europe (PACE) rapporteur for Chechnya, Andreas Gross, noted on October 21, 2005, "We have to be aware that the focus is now broader, that it's not only Chechnya, the Chechen conflict now touches four, five, six republics."[7]

Chechen atrocities prompt Western conclusions that "according to any traditional or universally accepted version of the laws of war, Russia's legal right to prosecute this war is incontestable."[8] That said, numerous Western nongovernmental organizations, some Russian analysts, some Western governments, and many international organizations have challenged *the way* Russian measures are implemented against Chechen terrorism. It is also generally recognized that the indiscriminate use of violence as a counterterrorism measure is itself counterproductive. The perpetrating state risks discrediting its own values, a process that has beset the United States in some of its antiterrorism measures since 9/11.[9]

To ask how international human rights norms, particularly those of the CoE, work regarding Russian responses to Chechen violence is not in itself a criticism of Russian responses. Rather, it is an assessment of a *process* that is occurring. In fact, as this section argues, exerting human rights norms consistently and effectively in the Chechen case is an unlikely scenario—precisely because of the threats and the horrific violence involved. Yet dialogue about human rights in the Chechen campaign has occurred, and some concrete measures have resulted.

What limits the ability of international human rights norms to succeed? First and foremost, the literature on the conditionality of human rights points out that international pressure depends on the susceptibility of that state. Though any discussion of power should be placed in relative and relational terms, Russia's relative lack of susceptibility is already contoured by "objective" facets of international power, including its geographic and demographic preeminence in Europe, its sizable armed forces, its continuing nuclear capability, and its permanent seat and veto on the UN Security Council.[10] It is also relatively insulated against economic sanctions. Its economy is not fully integrated into world markets, which makes sanctions (the utility of which generally is at best unproved) pointless, apart from being politically unlikely. That part of the Russian economy most integrated into world markets is also that upon which Western Europe most depends: energy.[11] The Russian-European energy relationship might best be described as codependency.[12] European sanctions on Russian fuel remain extremely unlikely. Already, in January 1995, Russian foreign minister Andrey Kozyrev noted: "Common sense tells [us] that the USA or the EU will not adopt economic sanctions against Russia."[13] The EU became more outspoken against Russian manipulation of energy supplies in later 2006, but the long-term impact seems questionable.

Second, the literature on the acceptance of international human rights finds least compliance when significant security issues are at stake. Even before the "global war on terrorism," the Bill Clinton administration attached substantial importance to cooperation with Russia and sought not to allow the first Chechen campaign to disrupt relations.[14] Few Western commentators or policymakers, especially since 9/11, make light of the implied threat and the actual damage caused by Chechen extremists. Indeed, this is essential to appreciate in any analysis of questions of human rights and the Russian government's efforts to deal with the Chechen crisis.

Third, domestic actors seem essential to a positive response to international human rights pressure. But Russia is challenged by having an underdeveloped civil society. The following is representative of Western assessments of civil society in postcommunist Russia: "The hopes for the imminent flourishing of a civil society that would be as developed as those in established democracies were disappointed in the 1990s, as nongovernmental organizations struggled to continue their existence under extraordinarily difficult conditions," and Putin "has sought to decrease the degree of pluralism in the Russian political system, and it has become increasingly apparent that he wants civil society to be an adjunct to a monocentric state," which is "a contradiction in terms."[15]

More specifically, when an issue is framed in security terms, as Chechnya has been, the importance of security agencies is prioritized. That almost always means the minimization or exclusion of such domestic civilian actors. The importance of Chechnya cannot be overstated; since the mid-1990s, "Chechnya has become the great defining issue of Russian statehood and the test of Russian military power."[16] Putin enunciated the stakes in Chechnya bluntly for Western consumption: "If we don't put an end to this [Chechen violence and separatism], Russia will cease to exist," and doing so is "a question of preventing the collapse of the country."[17]

Cognizant of these severe challenges to achieving compliance with human rights norms, we now proceed to a framework for detecting and assessing the CoE's influence on human rights.

The Framework: How Human Rights Norms May (Still) Influence Russian Action in the Chechen Conflict

A growing literature is mapping the impact of international human rights norms on domestic state practice.[18] That literature's conclusions may be too optimistic or universalistic, claiming for instance that democratization has been "increasing in strength and robustness."[19] Regardless, we need also to study cases of partial compliance or noncompliance with international norms.[20] Russia has been recognized as a case in which "conditions that scholars have identified as necessary and sufficient for the spread of international norms" exist but where their diffusion is hampered.[21]

We need, therefore, to assess what impact the CoE (and other international organizations) may have on this most challenging case. This study focuses on the CoE because, as stated above, it is primarily normative and lacks material incentives or sanctions. Though in principle it can make recommendations to bodies with material power, such as to the European Bank for Reconstruction and Development, in practice it has not done so, for political reasons.[22]

The questions asked and techniques applied in assessing normative influence may take three broad forms. First, we can ask why states seek membership in institutions that assert human rights criteria that could contradict national policy. It may be that at this level states agree to membership terms for other, self-serving reasons. This could include participation in a large policy game or an expression of geocultural belonging—that is, in the case of postcommunist Europe, not being excluded from any institution and of showing a state's membership in that geocultural space. Whatever the reasons for joining, concessions are made in principle, including the exposure or even subordination of domestic law to international practice. The concessions the state makes "spiral" so that it is forced to make more.[23] The Russia/Chechnya case is all the more useful because outside pressure for human rights compliance has generally been seen as weak toward Russia. At the end of the first campaign, international attitudes toward the Russian invasion were deemed "weak, lax and confused." For its part, Russia avoided "any adverse consequences for itself from its conduct."[24] The CoE has been considered possibly the most "hypocritical" of international actors toward Russia over Chechnya by having admitted it as a member.[25] Similarly, Russia's leading human rights organization, Memorial, called the CoE's decision to accept Russia unfortunate.[26]

On the basis of such assessments, this case presents an even greater challenge for human rights discourse; the spiral model sees states accepting some international practices, which in turn have further impact. Countries generally observe international law, and even when they abrogate it, they make considerable efforts to justify that breech.[27] As one foreign commentator observed, Russia "recognizes the centuries-old international legal canon of *pacta sunt servanda*—obligations must be followed. Respect for international law and primacy of international obligations over domestic laws are emphasized in the 1993 Constitution of the Russian Federation, and the law on the international agreements of the Russian Federation, approved in 1995, is based on the conscious fulfillment of obligations."[28] Of course, many states ignore their international commitments, and a prominent school of international relations simply dismisses international institutions for exerting "minimal influence on state behaviour."[29]

Nevertheless, governments can eventually be snared or "entrapped" by the language to which they have agreed, and this is the second point of examination. Because of such a government's resistance, compliance is also likely to manifest itself only subtly and over time. In hindsight, the Helsinki Accords are seen as having had a substantial impact on East European dissidents and, if more slowly, also on their communist governments. This process creates language that governments become obliged to use and to which detracting entities can turn to legitimate their claims. Once in power, East European dissidents praised the Conference on Security and Cooperation in Europe (CSCE), and some sought to make it the cornerstone of their foreign policy.[30] At least one American cold warrior, Central Intelligence Agency director Robert Gates (who also succeeded Donald Rumsfeld as U.S. secretary of defense) assessed the CSCE's influence thus: "The Soviets desperately wanted the CSCE, they got it, and it laid the foundations for the end of their empire."[31] Institutions can have one set of attractions or benefits for a state but ultimately create other consequences.

The emergence of human rights (where they are not already integral to the polity and society) works best when there is pressure from outside *and* from below.[32] As Sarah Mendelson indicates, the West, and the United States in particular, have invested substantial resources to develop Russian civil society. The Chechen case gives indications of how civil society has been developing and how outside entities, such as the CoE, have fostered it, even when the issue is framed in extreme security terms.

Third, stemming directly from the consequences of the previous point, is how domestic actors can become empowered. By ratifying international agreements, governments incorporate that legislation into domestic law and create domestic legal frameworks for the operationalization of international practice. How do these points of examination work in the relationship between Russia and the CoE over Chechnya?

The Framework in Practice

Although Russia has relations and agreements with many post–Cold War bodies, the CoE is the only European institution to which Russia has successfully applied for membership. To assess both the importance of the CoE and its impact, this section considers five issues: first, influence from the value of membership; second, influence from within the organization and its mechanisms; third, sanctions, including suspension; fourth, the creation of domestic institutional and legal structures; fifth, physical access to the conflict zone; and sixth, overall accountability.

Influence from the Value of Membership

The CoE's foremost importance rests on it being an expression of values. It is called the antechamber to "Europe," and CoE membership is based on evidence of democracy, the rule of law, and the establishment of provisions for the fulfillment of human rights. In 1993, one scholar of human rights wrote that the CoE was a "very strong human rights regime."[33] Another called the CoE "the most prestigious organization in the fields of human rights protection and the safeguarding of democracy in Europe."[34] Czechoslovakia's postcommunist president, Václav Havel, called the CoE Europe's "political, legislative and ideological centre."[35]

What did Russia see in the CoE when it first applied for membership in May 1992, almost from the outset of the existence of the Russian Federation? We cannot discount what can be called foreign policy experimentation in the early 1990s. New or politically emancipated states (and Russia could count as both) tried various forms of foreign policy—and the many regional groupings, some with longevity and substance, others without, are a testament to it. Russia may have applied to the CoE as something to try. As *The Economist* wrote in 2003, "Russia, unlike Groucho Marx, will join any club that will have it as a member."[36]

Russian statements, however, suggest that the CoE has a purpose for Russia. Former Russian foreign minister Igor Ivanov wrote that "membership in the CoE helps establish and strengthen institutions of democracy and law in Russia and supports basic human rights and freedoms."[37] Other officials have said that CoE membership indicates a "European" identity for Russia, but they also saw it as a means to regulate the domestic behavior of *other* states, particularly regarding the treatment of national minorities. The first point expresses identity; the second indicates interests.

Through wanting CoE membership, Russian officials have shown the importance of the principles of democratic and legal norms, which can have an unintended internal impact. The domestic importance of this was indicated in the Russian media. When Prime Minister Yevgeniy Primakov deposited Russia's ratification of three key CoE treaties, some media wrote that Russia had achieved not only one of the main requirements for admission to the CoE but also a means of advancing legal protection of its citizens and of establishing a unified legal and democratic zone in Europe.[38] Russia was knowingly binding itself to international agreements on human rights and was thereby seeing itself as part of Europe. After years of CoE criticism, this sentiment was reiterated in 1999 by Deputy Prime Minister Valentina Matvienko: "It is not only economic aid that is important to us. We also need the appreciation of the fact that Russia is part of Europe, part of the world community, and that it takes a common road, if with difficulty, and is striving to become a full-fledged member of the European family."[39] When Russia began its six-month chairmanship of the CoE's Council of Ministers in May 2006, the CoE officially stated of Lavrov's opening comments that he underlined his country's approach to the CoE "as an important European cooperation mechanism aimed at building a Europe without dividing lines and the establishment of a single European legal and humanitarian space."[40]

CoE membership affirmed the values of European identity that the Russian government wanted to express; but it was also seen as a type of security provider. The two need not be trade-offs; but when they seem to clash, security policy prevails over identity. Here, suffice it to say that Russian leaders and the media have recognized that the CoE provides legality in Europe and that, in doing so, it provides security and stability across the continent and transforms it into a single legal and humanitarian space.[41] Regardless of the precise balance between the security and identity motivations behind a state's decision to seek membership in an international organization, once joined, that organization is likely to exert some influence on domestic practice. Certainly this view has governed the CoE's thinking about admitting Russia (and certain other postcommunist states): More positive influence can be achieved by having the target state in than out.

Some of a state's nonnormative interests in joining and accepting a normative regime's practices may also "snare" it into human rights norms. Perhaps unintentionally, Russia has made commitments through CoE membership, and the practical sides of it can eventually have a palpable effect. This has certainly been seen to have occurred with Russia in the Organization for Security and Cooperation in Europe (OSCE). That organization became "active in the former Soviet Union, but when Russia, in the name of consensus, agreed to the establishment of the new OSCE regime, it scarcely considered that its own territory would soon be host to a mission."[42]

The CoE's influence has also occurred in other areas. The Federation Council's deputy speaker, Vasiliy Likhachev, who has also been a member of Russia's delegation to PACE, explained in 1997 that despite Russian objections to the council's fierce criticism regarding the death penalty, "we should proceed from the premise that we must discharge the obligations we have assumed in view of the priority of international law over national legislation."[43] Though parts of Russian society and government were committed to retaining capital punishment,[44] nonetheless, ultimately "Russia's international obligations trumped death penalty advocates."[45] More recently, Putin's signature of the decree placing Federal Security Service detention centers under the penitentiary system was described as a measure that ensured that the rights of suspects and convicts were maintained according to PACE recommendations.[46]

Influence from within the Organization and Its Mechanisms

The CoE can impose punitive measures against member states. PACE can ask member states to bring cases against other states. Indeed, the nongovernmental organization Human Rights Watch asked CoE member states to make a claim against Russia in the European Court of Human Rights. Though this provision has not been exercised, it indicates the first level of accountability resulting from membership.

In addition, PACE also issues recommendations and resolutions criticizing the behavior of members. These are in the public domain and are intended to generate pressure on recalcitrant governments by mobilizing domestic and transnational pressure. They give balance in the recognition of threats to and the rights of the Russian state, but they also highlight and condemn its transgression of agreed-on international norms. Consider the boldness and clarity of PACE's Recommendation 1444 (2000), "The Conflict in Chechnya," which states:

> The Assembly condemns, as totally unacceptable, the current conduct of military operations in Chechnya with its tragic consequences for large numbers of the civil population of this republic. As a result of this indiscriminate and disproportionate use of force, innocent noncombatants in Chechnya are suffering most serious violations of such fundamental human rights as the right to life, the right to liberty and the right to security.

Such statements can simply be dismissed as "words." They are nevertheless a public indictment of behavior and a reinforcement of the principle that the Russian Federation has signed international commitments on the use of force. Of course, enforcement seems necessary for these to have greater impact.

Sanctions, Including Suspension

For noncompliant states, the incentive to comply comes from an explicit threat of suspension from PACE and, thereafter, to recommend expulsion from the CoE. This is an attempt to influence the compliance calculations of national elites.[47] In the case of PACE, these identified failures by Russia led to suspension. PACE's move has been criticized as insufficient, which implies a belief that PACE has greater capacity. Regardless, relative to what the CoE had done previously, the move to suspend the Russian Federation was unique in its fifty-year history.[48] The Jamestown Foundation, experienced in supporting Soviet-era dissidents, called the move "politically gutsy."[49] The drawback, elaborated below, is when the target government (and also, but not necessarily, society) believes these criticisms to be misguided or less costly than the required policy change. The Russian delegation's response to the resolution was to denounce it and to leave PACE.

Finally, the CoE can suspend members. Apart from waiting for membership for three years, consideration of Russia's application was formally suspended in February 1995 because of the Chechen war. The CoE ultimately decided that it could have more influence over a state's behavior by admitting it. This is a choice of strategy, and the CoE could have had less influence on Russian practice if it had not been admitted.

Views on that strategy aside, PACE suspended Russia's voting rights in April 2000. It reinstated them less than a year later, again prompting debate about influence from inside or outside the body. Russian foreign minister Ivanov called the restoration of Russia's voting rights a "justice," which suggests that the intended penalty of suspension was ignored. He added, however, that "we are not evading the problems that exist in the North Caucasus, but the justice is in seeing that the Russian leadership is doing all it can to find a political solution for the problem."[50] This nevertheless suggests, in muted form, an acknowledgement by Moscow had that it was obliged to undertake a *political* strategy regarding the conflict and to limit the nature and use of force, of which it has been accused of not doing.

The Creation of Domestic Institutional and Legal Structures

Apart from requirements of membership itself and the risks of sanction within the CoE, Russia has also had to sign and enact international requirements as domestic law. A basic requirement of membership is ratification of the Convention for the Protection of Human Rights and Fundamental Freedoms (also known as the European Convention on Human Rights, or ECHR), which Russia did in May 1998. This means that the signatory country must allow any citizen to lodge claims of that state's noncompliance with European law. As is discussed below, the residents of Chechnya have exercised this provision to file allegations of human rights abuse. Russia has also had to agree to ratify, and thus again make into domestic law, the Convention on the Prevention of Torture. CoE membership has also opened the possibility for actors within Russia to seek and secure assistance on technical matters that can in the future limit the use of force. This includes assistance from forensic science in determining the causes of civilian deaths.

Physical Access to the Conflict Zone

In addition to the measures that can be, and at times have been, taken regarding human rights abuses in the Chechen campaign, Russian membership in pan-European bodies has limited its ability to control access to the conflict, and thus its foreign presentation. Both the OSCE and the CoE have been given admission to Chechnya for monitoring purposes (to be sure, the time and movement are controlled, in part because of genuine security concerns). We can ask of the CoE what Christer Pursianen did of the OSCE: "Why did Russia openly violate certain commonly accepted OSCE rules? Why, after a period of negotiation, did Russia nevertheless allow the OSCE to become a legitimate party in conflict management in its own territory in the form of a long-term permanent mission?"[51]

Such physical presence contrasts with the situation of the UN, whose human rights commissioner, Mary Robinson, was refused entry into Chechnya. Russia perhaps sees the CoE as less powerful or significant (in terms of public attention); but this access still allows the CoE to make what it wants of its findings). The CoE has gained various forms of access and accountability. In April 2000, with fighting under way, Foreign Minister Ivanov consented to the inclusion of CoE representatives in the Bureau of the Presidential Envoy on Human Rights and Liberties in Chechnya. Ivanov advised the CoE that its representatives would have "use of every existing possibility for the freedom of travel and access to the local population, while observing only security restrictions." Of course "security restrictions" could curtail movement, but the principle remains important. Indeed, some

PACE members who traveled to Chechnya said that, once there, as much as Russian officials may have wanted otherwise, they saw human rights violations for themselves.[52] In some specific cases, access resulted in releases. Walter Schwimmer, the CoE secretary-general, praised the work of three CoE experts who were permitted to work with the Russian president's human rights envoy to Chechnya in July 2000; he said they were instrumental in *freeing* twenty detainees from the Chernokozovo detention center. Furthermore, these releases were reported in the Russian media.[53]

Although CoE officials had to "observe the confidentiality of individual files," their CoE status ensured that they could "freely report" to the CoE secretary-general.[54] Apart from that particular arrangement, PACE's commissioner for human rights, Alvaro Gil-Robles, and its rapporteurs on Chechnya, Rudolf Bindig of Germany and Andreas Gross of Switzerland, have visited the republic regularly and have publicized their findings. From the outset of his election as human rights commissioner, which coincided with the second Russian campaign in Chechnya, Gil-Robles requested access to Chechnya. Even with the war having begun, Foreign Minister Ivanov granted him access to Chechnya. Gil-Robles recounted that his request was "not an easy decision" for Ivanov and that "all the necessary assistance was given."[55] Gil-Robles has visited Chechnya several times since, as have the PACE rapporteurs, who have provided regular and arguably substantial public record of Russian (and other) activities. For example, the rapporteurs noted in June 2004 after another visit that more than 100 people had been killed in Chechnya, and more than 170 have disappeared or been kidnapped so far that year. These measures create public awareness, and that is a form of accountability.

Overall Accountability

More tangibly, as Russians have written, threats of sanctions from the CoE (and the OSCE) have been seen to make the Kremlin "need to show that it is law abiding." The arrest and trial in 2000 of regimental commander Colonel Yuri Budanov for the murder of a Chechen girl is given as evidence, as was the court ruling exonerating Russian Radio Liberty correspondent Andrei Babitsky.[56] That the Russian government chose in 2002 not to continue the OSCE's Assistance Group in Chechnya suggests that it was having an impact. Indeed, three Western analysts asserted that "Western media and policy elites" have not acknowledged "Russian official attempts—albeit limited and inadequate—to address human rights abuses by Russian forces."[57] Given the limits on what a norms body can do, it is significant that "the Council of Europe has investigated problems in Chechnya and engaged in the most extensive dialogue with Russian authorities over them."[58] Similarly, a 2001 study found that "the most intensive interaction with the Russian Federation over Chechnya is now with the Council of Europe."[59]

CoE membership can lead to the creation of institutions or practices that in turn heighten accountability. For example, when fifty-two bodies were found, Nurdi Nukhazhiyev, the Chechen Republic's chairman of the committee for defending Russian citizens' constitutional rights, wanted a bureau for forensic medicine, and one that would be independent. He asked for assistance from the commissioner of human rights of the CoE, which offered equipment and expert training.[60]

The CoE also provides a legal framework for domestic groups to use. In addition to cases mentioned where the Russian government is perceived to have acted differently, or tried to make retrospective amends because of international legal agreements, on some occasions Russian citizens have employed the new legal structures. The ECHR, which, as noted above, Russia had to ratify as part of its agreement to enter the CoE, gives legal recourse to citizens outside their country if their state fails to provide domestically. There is therefore both a mechanism for recourse and built-in pressure on governments to serve their citizens. In February 2005, the European Court of Human Rights, which included one Russian judge, delivered three judgments that found that the right to life given in Article 2 of the ECHR had been violated by the Russian state. It also ruled that Article 13 had been violated because no effective remedy for these claims was provided before Russian courts. The court also awarded damages of €35,000 and legal costs to the Russian citizens who brought the charges regarding their murdered relatives.[61]

It is impossible to know exactly how these measures may have moderated the application of force in Chechnya; it may be that many more people are alive because of them. That even a few soldiers, or the Russian state itself, are held to account may moderate future behavior, and this also suggests the emergence of a framework that Russian authorities must address.

In this light, Matthew Evangelista argues against perceptions that after 9/11 Western governments all muted their criticism of Russian human rights abuses in Chechnya. Apart from State Department reports critical of Russia, he refers to the CoE, which he previously said had had no impact on Russia, stating that it was keeping "up the pressure."[62]

We cannot expect categorical, immediate change in Russian practice because of CoE statements. Instead, as has been outlined, this work assesses influence in what would be the least-likely case of such influence and which also notes that any such influence works over time. The extent to which we can detect some changes will come from how Russian officials react to CoE criticisms.

Russian Responses to CoE Pressure

This chapter suggests that security and identity in an interdependent or even globalized world means a convergence of the two. How the Russian government has reacted to CoE pressures can be illustrative of trade-offs between identity and security. The extent to which the two coincide—or differ—on issues and how they present their cases indicates the quality of the divide on values.

The starting point is an assumption that the CoE represents political values that European states share or to which they have had to adapt. In the post–Cold War era, the CoE was expected to have a "significant impact" on human rights practice in many postcommunist states—or at least, for the human rights scholar Jack Donnelly, the ones that are considered "more progressive."[63] This view might be supported by the commonality of values among Central European states and the CoE. Where divergences occurred —such as in the treatment of Russian-speaking minorities in Latvia and Estonia or of Roma in the Czech Republic—the applicant states ultimately accepted international organization opinion and implemented legal changes. (Russian policy, however, disagrees that sufficient measures have been undertaken for Baltic Russians.[64]) Postcommunist states ultimately met criticisms and also asserted that their and Western institutional political values corresponded.

Russian membership in the CoE at first signaled the same. In retrospect, the Russian government may have valued CoE membership when it was more than simply an expression of identity; it provided normative values *to* Russia, and these could be translated into efforts to secure interests. There is nothing wrong with that in principle; it again raises questions of interpretations of identity and security.

"European values" have been deployed by Russia as standards for other European states. Boris Yeltsin saw practicality for Russia in the CoE's values. As the Duma was set to ratify the CoE conventions in March 1996, Yeltsin told Russian delegates to PACE "to use in full measure the European parliamentary rostrum for the defense of the rights of the Russian-speaking population of the Baltic" and elsewhere. Foreign Minister Primakov proceeded similarly throughout 1996, stating specifically that CoE membership would help Estonia to end its double standards.[65] Primakov also advised CoE foreign ministers that Russia expected it to apply consistent and energetic measures to safeguard the rights of Russian minorities.[66] The Russian parliamentarian Aleksandr Shokhin further demonstrated Russia's expectations. In April 1998, he demanded that CoE standards be applied to Russians in Latvia: "We must, after all, make it clear to Latvia that what is being done there does not conform to any of the international conventions."[67]

Again, the European peace project is based on a common understanding of identity and security; and if, perhaps belatedly, European institutions, including the CoE, felt that Russian minorities in Estonia and Latvia had lost rights and acted to have them reinstated. Legitimate claims must be seen to receive appropriate treatment. Russian Federation Council deputy speaker and Russian PACE delegate Likhachev found otherwise: "But at the 48th session we met with a serious lack of understanding. Some delegations adopted an extremely rigid stance [against our] very sensible arguments . . . in favor of real democratic guarantees for the rights of the Russian-speaking population of the Baltic."[68]

When differences arose between the CoE and Russia, the former was presented as hostile to and/or ignorant of Russia. As an example, after one year's membership in the CoE, Likhachev objected that the CoE exuded "anti-Russian ideas." He elaborated: "Our country is not known, it is not trusted, [people are] still afraid of it."[69]

The Chechen issue has been more telling, as it invokes principles of sovereignty. In an enormous departure from Westphalian statehood, European integration has ultimately meant that all domestic law becomes subservient to supranational law. By contrast, Russia has responded to CoE criticisms of its handling of Chechnya with reassertions that sovereignty remains internal. Likhachev simply interpreted the CoE's role as clear-cut: that relations with Chechnya are an inter-Russian and interfederal matter.[70] When PACE voted in 2000 to remove Russia's voting rights, the Russian Duma issued a memorandum that called Chechnya an internal matter. Chechen president Alu Alkhanov said in March 2005: "There's no need to show us or teach us how to live our lives because the establishment of the state authorities is nearly finished and the process is taking place in strict accordance with the Constitution which, in terms of content, is as good as any even those recognized as highly democratic in any state in the world."[71]

Apart from rhetorical statements, Russia has been seen even to play with the institution in practice. Generally, Russia was seen to behave accordingly over in the first campaign: "Whenever criticism grew stronger, or a loan or membership in an international organisation was in danger, Russia merely announced a cease-fire—which it could later ignore—to receive what it wanted."[72] The CoE demanded a cease-fire in its November 1999 resolution, which went unheeded.[73] It deemed force reductions in Chechnya in January 2001 as an improvement in Russia's conduct of the war, and one done in response to international criticism. But these withdrawals were not permanent; even worse, it was thought repression increased afterward.

If that is a subversion of international normative pressure in policy, the same may occur with the use of language. In responding to CoE criticisms, the Russian government has often made reference to the same laws that the CoE was using to criticize it. In these cases, the Russian government is not rejecting the arguments outright or the validity of the laws. It is giving some legitimacy to them even in reinterpreting their meaning. In assessing the parallel case of Russia's participation in the OSCE, Pursiainen suggests that the Russian government may not have even made cost/benefit calculations of noncompliance in its behavior in Chechnya. Ultimately, however, "the costs of violation seemed to grow day by day" and "Russia's compliance with the OSCE's demands to participate in conflict management . . . went far beyond what it had agreed to in any document."[74]

As Jeffrey Checkel has observed from extensive first-hand study of the CoE, the body works generally on the basis of what can be called "low-level influence," and over time.[75] This process relies on the use of language, and while subtle, successes are to be found. Russian officials have generally tried to show either that CoE practices or recommendations have been consciously adopted by their government or that the CoE's ethos even parallels that of Russian reform. Thus, for example, Sergei Glotov, a member of the State Duma and once the head of the Russian delegation to PACE, wanted the Russian government to ask for the CoE's legal advice generally and to have amendments to the State Constitution reviewed by the CoE.[76] The Russian press considered overall reforms under the Primakov government to parallel those prescribed by the CoE.[77] This creates a normative framework in which, over time, general expectations of the CoE could become more commonplace. In addition, CoE membership itself creates an environment in which Russia is obliged to listen to criticism. PACE resolutions are particularly relevant to this process. Even after criticisms of Russian practice by PACE, A. I. Vladychenko, secretary of the Interdepartmental

Russian Commission on Council of Europe Affairs and deputy director of the Department of General European Cooperation in the Russian Ministry of Foreign Affairs, wrote that Russia had become influential in the CoE and held leading posts in PACE, and he deemed the CoE to be "the lynchpin of Greater Europe."[78]

The emergence of human rights (where they are not already integral to the polity and society) works best when there is pressure from outside *and* from below.[79] The CoE is seen by Western observers as substantiating this second dimension. For example, though he was critical of the CoE's leniency toward Russia, William Jackson still notes that "PACE committees have provided a forum for Russian human rights groups to raise issues in Strasbourg."[80] And Checkel determines that the CoE's practice of off-the-record talks among members that a combination of soft and hard influence is most effective, but he nevertheless concludes "under certain conditions 'talk' can promote compliance."[81] This is generally disregarded by Russian observers, but Konstantin Kosachev, leader of the Russian parliamentary delegation to PACE and head of the State Duma Committee on International Affairs, announced on June 27, 2005, that a roundtable meeting would be held in Grozny and that the idea came from a PACE session.[82] What comes practically from this remains to be seen; it nevertheless gives official testimony that the CoE imparts practical ideas. Even though critical of the CoE, Chechen president Alu Alkhanov said in March 2005 that he was "grateful to the Parliamentary Assembly of the CoE for its activities aimed at ensuring human rights are observed in whatever country of Europe."[83]

Conclusion

The CoE represents important geocultural values for Russia; membership has been sought accordingly. CoE membership could be used to provide tangible security benefits—that is, identity and security converged on some issues areas, particularly concerning Russian minority rights.

This suggests that a quid pro quo is required for identity and security to be mutually reinforcing. From a Russian perceptive (both governmental and societal), the CoE has lost credibility and utility because it is perceived to have become one-sided. This was already occurring in the mid-1990s. Ivanov bluntly declared: "The admission of Estonia to the CoE, despite dubious civil rights standards, whilst the first Russian application was rejected, appeared to many Russians as a double-standard."[84] But the perception has been reinforced over Chechnya, with, for example, the CoE giving an audience to Chechen terrorists (the CoE perspective is that it wants fairness in hearing each side and that peace comes from trying to determine, and then meet, any legitimate claims on all sides).

Indeed, Russian officials frequently indicate that the CoE does not demonstrate enough (or any) respect for or understanding of Russian circumstances and that the West has double standards in recognizing and responding to terrorism. This view was reiterated after the July 2005 terrorist bombings in London. As Taus Dzhabrailov, the chairman of the Chechen State Council, stated: "The West refuses to draw parallels between the terrorist acts in the U.S., Great Britain, and Russia." He continued, "Western politicians attempt to find different explanations and definitions for the terrorist acts in Russia, stating that the fight against terrorism must be put within certain margins. However, if the blasts destroy subway stations or buildings in Europe or the U.S., they unanimously call them acts of terror committed by international terrorists."[85] Similarly, Yury Sharandin, the chairman of the Federation Council committee on constitutional legislation, noted after those bombings: "It is no secret that Europe pursues a policy of double standards on terrorism." He added that the CoE had been unable to adopt an international convention on combating terrorism for several years.[86] That views builds on what other Russian officials have said. In 2002, for example, Shaid Djamaldayev, chairman of the Consultative Council for the Chechen Republic, expressly said the CoE and Co-chairman Lord Judd were "pursuing a policy of double standards." He added that the CoE listens to one side in the conflict and ignores the "positive proposals" of the (Moscow-supported) Chechen government, and that the PACE used Chechnya as "an instrument to exert political pressure on Russia."[87] From a Russian perspective, the CoE is guilty of double standards in the application of minority policy generally, in Chechnya specifically, and in its terrorism policy.

For some Russian observers, the CoE has discredited itself in Russia by having come (or been seen) to concentrate only on Chechnya. Whether this is objectively true, for present purposes, is irrelevant. It is perception that matters, and that perception is strong. As one Russian professor of international relations declared in 2005, "speaking for the Council of Europe in Russia now is like shooting yourself."[88]

In 1996, the CoE knew that Russia (and other postcommunist states) had not met conditions for membership. Instead, the CoE's thinking was that more change—in other words, more compliance—could be achieved in these polities by admitting them and working with them from within. This suggests that the CoE operates on the principle of acknowledging differences and then working to change practice through dialogue. On a tactical note, Checkel writes positively of off-the-record small-group sessions at the CoE in which policies for which a state is or might be criticized are worked through and comparisons made to now-solved problems in older member states. Some West European parliamentarians involved in PACE meetings with Russian officials in the mid-1990s insist that the CoE was effective because it included Russia and it talks *with* Russian representatives, whereas all other international organizations talk *to* them. Doing so, according to the PACE members involved in talks with Russian officials over Chechnya even in the second campaign, have had some impact on Russian thinking.[89] CoE representatives emphasize that they are responsive to Russia; Russian observers ask, by contrast, whether the CoE itself is "learning."[90]

A chasm exists between Russian perceptions of how the CoE operates and what its members, and analysts thereof, contend. Regardless, or to encourage as much change as possible, the CoE would be wise to play fully on perceived benefits to its members and to link changes. Skeptical of the CoE's utility, Russian observers suggest that the CoE would be better appreciated within Russian society if it pursued (again) efforts to stop abuses of recruits in the army.[91] For his part, Human Rights Commissioner Gil-Robles called the hazing practice *dedovshchina* "horrible" and noted that for some recruits "every single moment . . . is subject to harassment, humiliation and violence."[92] Even so, this suggests that the CoE's efforts are too ineffective or unrecognized in Russia, or both. One may have very good grounds to reject CoE criticisms; such a position still indicates a divergence in political identity. That also fits with suggestions that Russian foreign policy thinking views human rights norms not as something in themselves but routinely as a guise for pure realpolitik.[93]

This chapter began with a quotation from Russian foreign minister Lavrov. In the same speech, he stated: "In conditions of globalization, the border between external and internal resources for defending national interests is erased, and no country, however powerful, can attain its goals without international cooperation."[94] This underscores Russia's desires for interconnections with the wider world; the initial quotation indicates that these links are meant to be first and foremost to the West. Part of those interconnections are a limitation as to how one conducts affairs within one's boundaries, including in the most guarded realm of sovereignty: dealing with threats that are perceived as fundamental challenges to state interest.

This chapter has outlined, on the basis of some major writing on international human rights conditionality, that getting Russia to abide by any international human rights norms regarding Chechnya would be remarkable. It has applied three hypotheses regarding how human rights pressure could occur and indicated six ways in which this may have happened.

In examining Russian responses to CoE criticism, it also showed distinct trade-offs by Russia between security and identity. But it also suggests that for human rights norms to work most effectively, the totality of the target country's interests and identity must be recognized. The risk remains that the target state may find the changes demanded inappropriate and reject them wholesale. The combination of a consistently firm line against human rights abuses with verbal and practical recognition of other areas of human rights that the interlocutor considers important will offer a greater chance of an overall effect. The degree of compliance and the validity of the language used to challenge unaccepted norms reveals the extent of convergence or divergence between identity and security. In Russia's challenging case, more convergence has occurred than might have been expected, and the impact of those changes may only be fully felt years from now.

Lavrov's statement suggests, first, that Russian foreign policy is fundamentally Western and, second, that non-Western forces are attempting, and not succeeding, in transforming it into something "primitive" and non-Western. By contrast, the interplay between the Russian Federation and the CoE indicates that different conceptions of "Europe" and of the "West" exist, and that mutual learning and adaptation are required, if those conceptions are to meet in practice. In this toughest of cases for international human rights norms, Russia has shown some modest but surprising cases of socialization, sometimes unintentionally. This chapter also suggests that some of the changes that Russia has allowed because of its relationship with the CoE will have further, unintended influence, emboldening human rights norms within that polity. For the time being, however, security policy largely trumps expressions of identity.

Notes

1. I attempt to give an overview of this process in "The East," in *The Geopolitics of Euro-Atlantic Integration,* ed. Hans Mouritzen and Anders Wivel (London: Routledge, 2005), 128–48.

2. A leading example was given by Zbigniew Brzezinski, "The Premature Partnership," *Foreign Affairs* 73 (1994): 67–82. A recent study ascribed "imperialism" to Putin's foreign policy even more broadly. See Janusz Bugajzki, *Cold Peace: Russia's*

New Imperialism (Washington, D.C.: Center for Strategic and International Studies, 2004).

3. See Vladimir Baranovsky, "Russia: A Part of Europe or Apart from Europe?" *International Affairs* 76 (2000). A useful categorization and analysis of contending Russian foreign policy views is given by Margot Light, "In Search of an Identity: Russian Foreign Policy and the End of Ideology," *Journal of Communist Studies and Transition Politics* 19 (September 2003): 42–59.

4. This is, of course, a subjective matter. But resolutions examined for present purposes by major international organizations castigated Chechen violence. As discussions with Russian observers indicate and some of the discussion below suggests, such statements are nevertheless considered insufficient. In addition, Russian officials and politicians have vigorously objected to Western governments and international organizations be willing to meet with Chechen representatives that the Russian Federation considers to be terrorists.

5. The analogy obviously includes the Beslan school siege in September 2004; the Moscow subway bombing that killed 10 commuters on August 31; the bombing, a week earlier, of two planes from Moscow to Sochi and Volgograd, killing a total of 90 people; the three-day Moscow theatre siege on October 2002; four bombings of apartment blocks in Moscow and Volgodonsk in September 1999, killing over 300 residents; the 1995 hostage-taking on 300 people in a hospital in Budennovsk, Dagestan; and a similar event at a hospital in Kizylar, Dagestan, in January 1996, in which 2,000 people were taken hostage.

6. Andrew Meier, *Chechnya: To the Heart of a Conflict* (New York: W. W. Norton, 2004), 3.

7. Interview with RFE/RL on October 21, 2005. See http://www.rferl.org/features article/2005/10/C7CF10AC-261F-4F8C-BA2D-2A0CC1F65FD6.html.

8. Anatol Lieven, "Chechnya and the Laws of War," in *Russia's Restless Frontier: The Chechnya Factor in Post-Soviet Russia,* ed. Dmitri V. Trenin and Aleksei V. Malashenko with Anatol Lieven (Washington, D.C.: Carnegie Endowment for International Peace, 2004), 212.

9. Nye writes, e.g., "Damaging to American attractiveness is the perception that the United States has not lived up to its own profession of values in its response to terrorism" and "It remains to be seen how lasting such damage will be to America's ability to obtain the outcomes it wants from other countries." Joseph S. Nye Jr., *Soft Power: The Means to Success in World Politics* (New York: PublicAffairs, 2003), 59, 60.

10. Yeltsin considered these "objective" features of Russian powers for Russia to be immune from Western criticism in its conduct of the first Chechen war. He replied to criticisms from Clinton in 1999 with "It seems he has for a minute, for a second, for a half-minute, forgotten that Russia has a full arsenal of nuclear weapons" (cited in *Financial Times,* December 10, 1999).

11. The EU receives 20 percent of all its natural gas from Russia. *The Economist,* November 15, 2003, 48. Some countries are much more dependent.

12. Fiona Hill, *Beyond Co-Dependency: European Reliance on Russian Energy,* United States–Europe Analysis Series (Washington, D.C.: Brookings Institution Press, 2005).

13. *Rossiyskay gazeta,* January 28, 1995, cited by Christer Pursianen, "The Impact of International Security Regimes on Russia's Behavior: The Case of the OSCE and

Chechnya," in *Understanding Russian Foreign Policy,* ed. Ted Hopf (University Park: Pennsylvania State University Press, 1999), 153.

14. See Gail W. Lapidus, "Contested Sovereignty: The Tragedy of Chechnya," *International Security* 51 (1999).

15. Alfred B. Evans Jr., "A Russian Civil Society?" in *Developments in Russian Politics 6,* ed. Stephen White, Zvi Gitelman, and Richard Sakwa (Basingstoke, U.K.: Palgrave, 2005), 112.

16. Jacob W. Kipp, "Putin and Russia's Wars in Chechnya," in *Putin's Russia: Past Imperfect, Future Uncertain,* ed. Dale R. Hespring (Lanham, Md.: Rowman & Littlefield, 2005), 205.

17. Vladimir Putin, *First Person: An Astonishingly Frank Self-Portrait by Russia's President Vladimir Putin* (New York: PublicAffairs, 2000), 140.

18. A strong indication of how international pressure has improved domestic human rights is given by Thomas Risse, Stephen C. Ropp, and Kathryn Sikkink, eds., *The Power of Human Rights: International Norms and Domestic Change* (Cambridge: Cambridge University Press, 1999).

19. Thomas Risse and Stephen C. Ropp, "International Human Rights Norms and Domestic Change: Conclusions," in *Power of Human Rights,* ed. Risse, Ropp, and Sikkink, 260.

20. See the conclusion of Sonia Carendas, "Norm Collision: Explaining the Effects of International Human Rights Pressure on State Behavior," *International Studies Review* 6 (2004). Her article also provides a useful synthesis of recent literature from which this chapter benefits.

21. Sarah E. Mendelson, "Russians' Rights Imperiled: Has Anybody Noticed?" *International Security* 26 (2002): 40.

22. See the Bank's Charter. Its Web site currently states: "The mandate of the EBRD stipulates that it must only work in countries that are committed to democratic principles." Political conditionality, however, does not seem to be a major consideration in loans. The EBRD does seem sensitive to environmental lobbying, but that is not comparable to political norms and does not relate back to the CoE. The lack of connection between political criticism and financial sanction against Russia is a problem in achieving any change in policy. Even though PACE heavily criticized Russian actions in Chechnya in early 2000, Stanley Fischer made clear that the International Monetary Fund would not punish Russia. See Matthew Evangelista, *The Chechen Wars: Will Russia Go the Way of the Soviet Union?* (Washington, D.C.: Brookings Institution Press, 2002), 148.

23. See Thomas Risse and Kathryn Sikkink, "The Socialization of International Human Rights Norms into Domestic Practices: Introduction," in *Power of Human Rights,* ed. Risse, Ropp, and Sikkink, 1–38.

24. Svante E. Cornell, "International Reactions to Massive Human Rights Violations: The Case of Chechnya," *Europe-Asia Studies* 51 (1999): 97.

25. Sebastian Smith, *Allah's Mountain's: The Battle for Chechnya* (London: I. B. Tauris, 2001), 226.

26. Members of Memorial wrote in English: "The UN Commission on the Elimination of Racial Discrimination asked that all those who had violated human rights or humanitarian norms during the conflict in Chechnya, be held responsible. Unfortunately, these demands were not backed by the Council of Europe, which in January 1996 in-

vited Russia to become a member of that organization. In the opinion of the authors, the decision of the Council of Europe does not bear relationship to the real situation prevailing in the Russian Federation." See O. P. Orlov, A. V. Cherkasov, and A. V. Sokolov, "The Violation of Human Rights and Norms of Humanitarian Law in the Course of the Armed Conflict in the Chechen Republic: A Report of the Human Rights Center Memorial," http://www.memo.ru/hr/hotpoints/chechen/checheng/fin_rep.htm.

27. See Hedley Bull, *The Anarchical Society* (London: Macmillan, 1977), 137, 138.

28. Pursianen, "Impact of International Security Regimes on Russia's Behavior," 111–12.

29. John J. Mearsheimer, "The False Promise of International Institutions," *International Security* 19 (Winter 1994–95): 7.

30. This draws from work in progress by the author.

31. Quoted in Daniel C. Thomas, *The Helsinki Effect: International Norms, Human Rights, and the Demise of Communism* (Princeton, N.J.: Princeton University Press, 2001), 257.

32. For a non-European case, see Alison Brysk, "From Above and Below: Social Movements, the International System and Human Rights in Argentina," *Comparative Political Studies* 26 (1993): 259–85.

33. Jack Donnelly, *International Human Rights* (Boulder, Colo.: Westview Press, 1993), 82.

34. Hans Winkler, "Democracy and Human Rights in Europe: A Survey of the Admission Practice of the Council of Europe," *Austrian Journal of Public and International Law* 47 (1995): 171. Writing in 1995, he prefaced these comments with: "Nobody can say yet whether the Council of Europe will be able to remain what it has been."

35. Cited by Catherine LaLumière, "The Council of Europe's Place in the New European Architecture," *NATO Review* 40 (1992): 12.

36. "Seal of Disapproval: Russia's Need to Belong," *The Economist,* November 15, 2003, 48.

37. Igor S. Ivanov, *The New Russian Diplomacy* (Washington, D.C.: Brookings Institution Press, 2002), 99.

38. Reported in *Rossiiskaya gazeta,* May 22, 1998.

39. ITAR-TASS, January 28, 1999.

40. Press release—293(2006), "Chairmanship of Committee of Ministers: Russian Federation Presents Its Priorities," Strasbourg, May 19, 2005, https://wcd.coe.int/View Doc.jsp?id=1002429&BackColorInternet=F5CA75&BackColorIntranet=F5CA75&B ackColorLogged=A9BACE.

41. See the commentary in *Rossiiskie vesti,* September 3, 1997.

42. Pursianen, "Impact of International Security Regimes," 136.

43. *Rossiiskaya gazeta,* March 29, 1997.

44. This is discussed comparatively in Rick Fawn, "Death Penalty as Democratisation: Is the Council of Europe Hanging Itself?" *Democratization* 8 (Summer 2001): 69–96.

45. Robert Sharlet, "In Search of the Rule of Law," in *Developments,* ed. White, Gitelman, and Sakwa, 137. This assessment can certainly be challenged, but it is an example of thinking that Russia complies with some external human rights norms.

46. RIA Novosti, July 13, 2005.

47. See Jeffrey T. Checkel, *Compliance and Conditionality,* Arena Working Paper 18, 2000, http://www.arena.iuo.no.publications/wp00_18.htm.

48. For such a view from international human right advocacy, see Leo Zwaak, "The

Council of Europe and the Conflict in Chechnya," *Netherlands Quarterly of Human Rights* 18 (2000): 181.

49. "Council of Europe Action Serves as Reprimand for Chechnya," *Jamestown Foundation Monitor* 6, no. 70 (April 7, 2000), http://www.jamestown.org/publications _details.php?volume_id=23&issue_id=1759&article_id=17069.

50. Quoted on Interfax, January 26, 2001.

51. Pursianen, "Impact of International Security Regimes on Russia's Behavior," 110.

52. This is based on a summary of experience and observations given by the former Dutch parliamentarian Hanneke Gelderblom-Lankhout, who was part of several PACE delegations to the Russian Federation and who in that capacity visited Chechnya several times during the 1994–96 conflict; interview, November 4, 2005.

53. ITAR/TASS, July 24, 2000.

54. Reported on Interfax, April 5, 2000.

55. "Report by Mr Alvaro Gil-Robles, Commissioner for Human Rights, on his Visits to the Russian Federation 15 to 30 July 2004 19 to 29 September 2004. For the Attention of the Committee of Ministers and the Parliamentary Assembly," sections 323 and 324, p. 68, http://www.coe.int/T/E/Commissioner_H.R/Communication_Unit/Documents/pdf.CommDH%282005%292_E.pdf.

56. See Trenin, Malashenko, and Lieven, *Russia's Restless Frontier,* 142–43.

57. Fiona Hill, Anatol Lieven, and Thomas de Waal, *A Spreading Danger: Time for a New Policy towards Chechnya,* Policy Brief 35 (Washington, D.C.: Carnegie Endowment for International Peace, 2005), 5.

58. Pamela A. Jordan, "Russia's Accession to the Council of Europe and Compliance with European Human Rights Norms," *Demokratizatsiya* 11 (2003): 289.

59. Asbjørn Eide, "Chechnya: In Search of Constructive Accommodation," *Leiden Journal of International Law* 14 (2001): 441.

60. ITAR-TASS, August 16, 2005.

61. This is not to say that bringing such as case is easy; human rights groups noted that death threats and violence can occur against who do so or so intend. Nevertheless, more than 100 other such cases are pending.

62. Evangelista, *Chechen Wars,* 181, 150.

63. Donnelly, *International Human Rights,* 141.

64. The EU-Russia summit communiqué in 2003 lacked reference to Chechnya because Putin insisted on mention of "abuses" of the rights of Russians in Latvia. *The Economist,* November 15, 2003.

65. ITAR-TASS, May 3, 1997.

66. ITAR-TASS, May 2, 1997.

67. Interfax, April 8, 1998.

68. *Rossiiskaya gazeta,* March 29, 1997.

69. Interfax, April 25, 1997.

70. *Rossiiskaya gazeta,* March 29, 1997.

71. "Chechen President Outlines Acceptable Topics for PACE Meeting," Interfax, March 18, 2005.

72. Cornell, "International Reactions to Reactions to Massive Human Rights Violations," 97.

73. Resolution 1201 (1999), Conflict in Chechnya.

74. Pursianen, "Impact of International Security Regimes," 148.

75. Checkel, *Compliance and Conditionality.*
76. ITAR-TASS, September 25, 1998.
77. ITAR-TASS, January 28, 1999.
78. A. I. Vladychenko, "Rossiya-Sovet Evropy: Opyt dvukh let sotrudnichestva," *Mezhdunarodnaya zhizn* 4 (1998), http://www.coe.ru.koi/05zagl.htm, cited Jordan, "Russia's Accession to the Council of Europe," 286.
79. For a non-European case, see Brysk, "From Above and Below."
80. William D. Jackson, "Russia and the Council of Europe: The Perils of Premature Admission," *Problems of Post-Communism* 51 (September–October 2005): 24.
81. Checkel, *Compliance and Conditionality,* 18.
82. ITAR-TASS, June 27, 2005.
83. "Chechen President Outlines Acceptable Topics for PACE Meeting," Interfax, March 18, 2005.
84. Quoted in *Financial Times,* March 18, 1995.
85. RIA Novosti, July 29, 2005.
86. RIA Novosti, July 8, 2005.
87. ITAR/TASS, February 15, 2002.
88. This was an observation made at the Moscow meeting.
89. This is from a summary of experience and observations of the Dutch parliamentarian Hanneke Gelderblom-Lankhout; interview, November 4, 2005.
90. This is from comments made at the Washington meeting.
91. This is from comments made at the Moscow meeting.
92. "Report by Mr Alvaro Gil-Robles," section 374, 78.
93. See Viatcheslav Morozov, "Resisting Entropy, Discarding Human Rights: Romantic Realism and Securitization of Identity in Russia," *Cooperation and Conflict* 37 (2002): 409–29.
94. Quoted in "Foreign Minister Vows No Anti-Western Path for Russia,'" *RFE/RL Newsline* 9, no. 167, part I, September 2, 2005.

11

Russian Geopolitics in the Context of Globalization

Eduard Solovyev

In Henry Kissinger's definition, geopolitics is an "approach that pays attention to the requirements of equilibrium."[1] In practice, geopolitics is a convenient label for a variety of theories that concentrate on geographic factors, both as primary influences and as ostensibly imperative guides for action. The enduring "plot" of this discipline is the global balance of power and the future of strategic advantage in an anarchic world. Indeed, its main emphasis is on power, and its research goal is to understand the causes of the rise and fall of state power in international relations. This is why some scholars have characterized geopolitics as a branch of political realism.[2] Yet traditional geopolitics, as compared with realism, is often much more reductionist in its emphasis on using state size and geography to explain state behavior, and in its search for solutions to global problems.

This chapter analyzes the uses of geopolitical thought in Russia under the pressure of globalization and in the situation of transforming Russian identity. Objectively, globalization (as Hedetoft notes) challenges traditional understandings of spatial relations—and indeed, space is crucial for geopolitical analysis. Yet, depending on how globalization is subjectively construed, its specific implications may vary considerably for Russian geopolitical thinkers. I begin with a brief overview of the assumptions typically shared by geopolitical analysts in Russia. Next, I consider the role of geopolitics for elements of the political opposition as well as for official Russian thought and policymaking, particularly with respect to the notion of polarity. I conclude with some reflections on Russia's quest for a unifying identity and its relationship with the geopolitical.

Shared Assumptions of Russian Geopolitical Thinkers

Traditional or formal geopolitics is often criticized for its attempts to represent "timeless truths" and for its concern with certain "insights" and "prophecies."[3] In Russia, however, these general tendencies are combined with an inordinate degree of Russocentrism, especially with regard to the role of Russia in Eurasia. As Kolosov and Turovski argue, such Russocentrism has created a false image of the country "as the key to global stability and the geographical center of world politics,"[4] and it has also contributed to other idealized notions of Russia's "mission." In particular, the idea that Russia constitutes the strategic axis of Eurasia is one of the most popular geopolitical myths.[5] However, it is the geopolitical school's reductionism and simplicity, as well as its pretension to provide clear and unambiguous answers to complicated questions about the modern world, that have attracted a wide array of post-Soviet Russian scholars and politicians.

To begin, it should be stressed that modern Russian geopolitics is a kind of political discourse, one overloaded with normative judgments and/or suffering from a certain "naive Machiavellianism," consumed with fabricated images of political space and a desirable place for Russia in world politics. This sort of vision is closely linked to the ideological demand for geopolitics in Russia, which is another reason for its popularity. The reductionism of geographical determinism has created an opportunity for policymakers to use geopolitics as a tool to explain their motivations and foreign policy priorities. As a result, geopolitical terminology is now being used by both state officials and representatives of the opposition. Among the most famous "geopoliticians" of modern Russia are well-known political figures like Vladimir Zhirinovskiy, Aleksey Mitrofanov, and Gennadiy Zyuganov.[6] After the disintegration of the USSR, preserving the territorial integrity of the state became an extremely urgent task for Russia (becoming, in fact, the idée fixe of Russian politics). The geopolitical thesis about the importance of direct control over territory was widely accepted during this time.

Furthermore, certain principles of traditional geopolitics were adopted in Russia for psychological and even rehabilitative purposes for its population. With the disintegration of the USSR, in a time of weakness and deep crisis of state and social institutions, geopolitical conceptions assigning Russia a particular role and providing it with a particular mission in the world (Russia as an axis region in Eurasia, as a key actor for preserving a world balance of power, etc.) had not only a mobilizing but also, in some sense, a therapeutic effect. This geopolitical argument became a means of sublimating post-imperial psychological problems for Russian citizens.

During the past decade, political thinkers in Russia have imagined different geopolitical scenarios for the past, present, and future of Russia and the world order. These geopolitical scenarios may be divided into two main camps, based on the scholars associated with them. The first camp consists of the political opposition of any sort (including those espousing so-called liberal geopolitical thought, patriotic leftist geopolitical constructions, and a wide range of patriotic right-wing scenarios), whereas the second consists of official geopolitical thinkers.

The Geopolitical Thought of the Russian Political Opposition

The appeal of geopolitics to the Russian extreme right and left can be explained by persistent, long-established stereotypes of their political agendas—the idea of the eternal and inevitable confrontation between Russia and the West, and the necessity for Russia's military and political self-sufficiency in order for it to survive in the constantly threatening environment. On the left and right patriotic flanks of the Russian political spectrum, there are at least two main geopolitical tendencies—Neo-Eurasianism and communist geopolitics. In addition, liberalism has often made extensive use of geopolitical concepts.

Neo-Eurasianism

Elementy magazine and the newspaper *Zavtra* (formerly *Den*) became the main advocates of Neo-Eurasianism in the Russian mass media, and Aleksandr Dugin emerged as its primary theoretician. Dugin's supporters believe that the configuration of world politics is defined by the principal dualism of, and confrontation between, sea-based and land-based empires. The two main civilizations—Eurasianism versus Atlanticism, according to this point of view—are fundamentally irreconcilable, although the degree of their confrontation and the balance of power between them may vary from one historical period to another.

Aleksandr Panarin has developed his own alternative version of Neo-Eurasianism. He offers a more philosophically and politically refined interpretation of Neo-Eurasianism.[7] The primary objective for him is to transform the unipolar world order into something else, either a multipolar or a bipolar structure. He views Russia's main objectives to be the restoration of a *system of checks and balances* on a world scale and the prevention of a purely hegemonic model of world order. Though not sharing Dugin's somewhat mystical vision of Eurasia, Panarin believes in constructing scenarios of the world's development, or "futurist projects," for the purpose of achieving the identified objectives. In his futurist project, Russia must develop multilateral contacts with India, China, and the Muslim states to restore its political position and to undermine Western global hegemony.[8] For him, globalization is closely tied to the new "social asymmetry" or even "new global segregation," according to which all humanity is divided into categories of a "powered center and exploited periphery."

Neo-Eurasianism has not earned a serious place in the Russian political process. But it indirectly influences the geopolitical ideologies of Russian Communists and geopolitical populism.

Russian Communist Geopolitics

Communist geopolitics emphasizes such notions as *derzhava* (great power), "socialism," and Russian statehood. The Communists present Russia's long history as a coherent and continuous process, and they draw a straight line from the fifteenth-century "gathering of Russian lands" to the calls by the Communist Party of the Russian Federation (CPRF) for a revival of the Soviet empire. They view the relationship between Russia and the West in primarily confrontational terms, and they insist that Russia must resist the unipolar trends in global politics, which are perceived as the "dictatorship of the United States and NATO."[9] Even at the beginning of the twenty-first century, the resolutions passed at CPRF congresses continue to be grounded in the ostensible inevitability of confrontation between the West as a whole and the rest of humanity. Zyuganov, the leader of the CPRF, has argued that "socialism is the modern form of Russian patriotism."[10] Russian Communists are trying to form a united front of patriotic forces to battle against "cosmopolitan capital" and the liberal government of President Vladimir Putin, who has betrayed their ideals. From Zyuganov's point of view, Russia has fallen into a new phase of social and political crisis because of Putin's irresponsible "liberal" domestic and foreign policies.

At this point, the CPRF's attitudes toward globalization are absolutely predictable. Thus, during the Seventh Congress of the CPRF (held in December 2000), a special resolution was adopted, titled "About the Treatment of Imperialistic Globalization." Globalization was interpreted in this document as a contradictory process. On the one hand, globalization leads inevitably to the intensification of integrative trends in the economic, scientific, and informational realms. But on the other hand, modern capitalism uses these trends to establish a so-called new world order. As the process is developing now, this "ensures the interests of imperialism in an epoch of the dominance of transnational capital," leading to "global apartheid," and to the establishment of a division of all humanity into the "golden billion" and the oppressed and exploited majority of the planet's population. The CPRF called for solidarity in the confrontation against "imperialistic globalization," including a stand for the preservation of state sovereignty, the territorial integrity of political communities around the world, and the preservation of the "cultural and national originality (distinctiveness) of all peoples."[11]

Moreover, Zyuganov stands firmly against Russia's participation in any antiterrorist coalition to support "President Bush's antiterrorist war." This war is an "aggression aimed at the enforcement of U.S. positions in the region of the Middle East to the detriment of Russia's main geopolitical interests."[12] The main geopolitical task for Russia, according to this assessment, is to create a system of checks and balances on a global scale.

The Geopolitics of Russian Liberals

From the point of view of many liberal-minded politicians, experts, and officials in Russia since the collapse of the Soviet pole of the bipolar world, the international system has become unipolar. Russian liberals perceive unipolarity as the *global and collective leadership* of the West in world politics. From their point of view, obvious objective factors favor the unprecedented concentration of influence and power in the states that make up the unipole. In the early 1990s, Russia's main goal was to gain access to the most important official unipolar institutions (and perhaps even informal institutions, like the Group of Seven) in the shortest amount of time and then to realize its vital interests through them.[13] If successful, according to this viewpoint, Russia would become a member of the elite club of modern states that holds the power to develop the rules of the game in world politics. The global interests that Russia shared with the West were considered to be primary and realizable through the collective efforts of the unipolar states, while other national interests could be pursued separately or by bargaining quietly within the unipole.

In some respects, this policy worked. However, Russia's inclusion in the unipolar institutions or cooperation with such institutions has been painfully slow, due to the weakness of the West's willingness to cooperate with feeble, downtrodden Russia. The pace was too slow, and neither Russia nor the West managed to take advantage of various opportunities that have since passed.[14] The pace has also been too slow to allow Russian liberals to earn credit for the validation of their political course. As a result, the geopolitical thought of Russian liberals has changed. This is tied closely to their need for a positive public image and increased electoral popularity.

Preserving Russia's national sovereignty and restoring its status as a strong power were popular ideas following a decade of the state's decline, national humiliation, and the default of its economic system. At the beginning of the 2000s, Anatoliy Chubays put forth the idea of a renewed liberal empire (a Russian liberal empire, which could find a new mission in promoting democracy and protecting human rights in post-Soviet states). According to Chubays, such an interpretation of the Russian mission in the modern world would allow Russians to completely rethink the very foundations of their foreign policy:

> [With] the strategic advantage of the creation of a ring of great democracies in the Northern Hemisphere—the United States, a united Europe, Japan, and a future Russian liberal empire—Russia would achieve its natural place and unique role in the world—to complete the ring and to make up a new system of economic, military, and political agreements that could preserve its interests inside the ring and all over the world. Then Russia would be able, on an equal basis and in cooperation with partners, to stand for freedom and order all over the planet.[15]

And yet, the geopolitical way of thinking is not prevalent among Russian liberals. This appears to be related to their views of globalization. In general, Russian liberals welcome economic globalization because it involves the long-distance flows of goods, services, financial resources, and information, as well as the perceptions that accompany market exchange. They believe that, on a profound level, globalization affects the consciousness of individuals and their attitudes toward culture, politics, and personal identities. From this viewpoint, the main task for Russia is to take part actively in globalization processes.[16] At the same time, it is necessary to stress the fact that for many Russian liberals, globalization is synonymous with *growing interdependence.* Accordingly, globalizing threats demand united efforts from the whole world community. American leadership in the style of "follow or get out of the way" aggravates Russian liberal disappointment with U.S. policy and paves the way for a more critical "pragmatic liberalism."[17]

Thus, geopolitical rhetoric was an integral part of the opposition's ideology (the communist-nationalist faction) and/or a convenient means for ideologically manipulating a public disoriented by the reforms of the early 1990s. In the late 1990s and the beginning of the twenty-first century, however, these ideologized constructs no longer had a significant impact on Russian politics. A much more important role was played by the set of perceptions about the place and role of Russia in contemporary world politics, which might be called official geopolitics.

Official Geopolitics: The Concept of a Multipolar World

Although the opposition could avoid worrying about whether their conclusions and assessments were realistic (the important thing to them was coming up with slogans attractive enough to win over a demoralized public confused by the changes taking place), foreign policy professionals could not. Analysts in the government, the Ministry of Foreign Affairs, and the Office of the President, as well as political officials themselves, gradually understood the need to form their own geopolitical vision, one that was distinct from both the liberal interpretation of geopolitical issues and the geopolitical traditionalism of the communist and nationalist opposition.

This situation arose due to the intellectual shift from the idealism of the Mikhail Gorbachev era and the liberal overtones of Boris Yeltsin's avant-gardism toward political realism. Of course, it would have been much easier for Russia to bear the blow to its prestige in the early to middle 1990s if it had been discussed not only in terms of the loss of Russia's superpower status but also in terms of the decline of power politics in general. The highly popular view in Russia (and not just among the liberal intellectuals) that power politics was a thing of the past, and that the use of force in politics was impermissible and clearly anachronistic, found expression in the utterly unviable projects and plans of the Gorbachev era: total disarmament, the dismantling of the Soviet Bloc structures, the creation of new security mechanisms based on cooperation and global management, and the like. However, Western politicians were openly skeptical of such concepts as early as the 1980s. In the 1990s, NATO did not see any reason to dissolve (merely to show its goodwill), and the Western countries openly demonstrated their intention to continue pursuing their own national interests as well as the corporate interests of Western civilization, rather than ignoring these interests simply because Russia was having trouble pursuing its own.

As paradoxical and naive as it may sound, many members Russia's political elite (including those of a liberal and democratic persuasion) were disappointed by the West's exploitation of the dividends of the end of the Cold War, even as Moscow bore the heavy burden of spending on demilitarization and life support for the disintegrating Russian Federation. However, the real detonator for the conceptual changes in the perception of world politics was the beginning of NATO expansion. This expansion was seen by many experts and politicians in Russia in geopolitical terms—both as an eastward expansion of the contiguous area of U.S. military and political supremacy and as an attempt to exploit the weakening of Russia in order to make permanent geopolitical inroads into Eurasia. The response was formulated in the spirit of political realism and based on geopolitical designs (including the concept of Russia's special role in the "near abroad" countries—Russia's "Monroe Doctrine" for the post-Soviet region). At the same time, the changes taking place in world politics (defining contemporary international relations as unipolar or multipolar) were also viewed in geopolitical terms. As a result, Yevgeniy Primakov became the "official mouthpiece" for geopolitics, first as minister of foreign affairs and then as prime minister.

After the collapse of the bipolar world, many countries began searching for their place in the changing world in the context of the profound transformations in international relations. This was doubly difficult for the Russian Federation, which regarded itself as the heir to the USSR in world politics, despite the fact that it had lost its superpower status and was being forced to enter a period of adaptation to the new conditions in international relations. Russia's overall situation worsened in the 1990s, because with the collapse of the Soviet Union it lost a significant portion of its economic, demographic, and military resources. The Russian Federation possessed a significant amount of latent security potential inherited from the USSR (nuclear weapons, competitive military technology, etc.) and significant political influence (a permanent seat and veto on the UN Security Council, a special role in the post-Soviet region, etc.). However, in the course of the reforms, Russia was transformed relatively quickly from a superpower into a country with open borders, a weak army, an unstable economy, and a lack of reliable allies. Russia also fell further behind the leading countries in technology, information, and economic strength, and it grew more dependent upon other centers of power in the modern world. Moreover, it became increasingly unable to set an independent foreign policy agenda, respond to challenges, and counter the new and diverse threats to its national security.

Under these conditions, Russia began focusing more attention on an issue that was directly linked to an understanding of the structural factors in world politics. The disappearance of one of the superpowers left the United States and its allies in the position of the only "pole" in the modern world, based on almost unprecedented military might; unique economic, scientific, and technological capabilities; and the role of the dollar as the world currency. In the early 1990s, this situation was implicitly reflected in the 1992 Foreign Policy Framework of the Russian Federation, which noted that "the West is ceasing to be a military and political concept in the traditional sense of power, but it remains one of the most important centers of the world economy, international relations, and the global process of civilization."[18] Russia's development of comprehensive relations with Western countries and its attempt to incorporate itself into the global center of the "civilization process" defined its priorities in foreign policy.

Official views changed noticeably as a result of NATO's expansion, its operations outside its area of responsibility (particularly in the Balkans), and disappointment over the West's role in Russia's reform process. From an implicit recognition of the fact of the unipolar world and an attempt to align with the single pole, the Russian leadership shifted its position in the mid-1990s to a doctrine of multipolarity and began to distance itself from the United States and the other Western countries. Geopolitics as a type of ideological discourse was required in these conditions to justify this change in policy. Geopolitical rhetoric made it possible to express in clearly normative terms the inevitability of a multipolar world and, therefore, the need to diversify Russian foreign policy and make it multifaceted.

In fact, the initial statements of these ideas contained nothing more than rhetoric. Primakov, the new minister of foreign affairs, tried only to outline the conditions for comprehensive cooperation with Western countries, which did not seem at all unreasonable to most members of the Russian political elite.[19] The first condition was to eliminate the danger of new dividing lines on the European continent. This was the cause of Russia's negative reaction to NATO expansion, the attempts to make NATO the basis for a new security system, and the tendency to marginalize Russia in the European security system (Moscow clearly recognized that there was no place in NATO for Russia). The second condition was that unilateral decisions were unacceptable, particularly in areas adjacent to the Russian Federation, regardless of how attractive such unilateral decisions and actions might be from a tactical standpoint. Ultimately, they would only spur rivalry and introduce chaos and an element of unpredictability in international relations. The third condition was the democratization of international economic relations and an end to the practice, with only weak justification under international law, of imposing economic sanctions on individual companies or entire groups of countries. The fourth condition was to create a real cooperative spirit (rather than a transatlantic corporate approach) in actions by the international community, at least in areas like security, conflict resolution, disarmament, and strengthening the humanitarian and legal components of the system of contemporary international relations.

It is clear from the above that from the beginning, the concept of multipolarity was loaded with normative judgments and essentially contained the set of views held by the Russian political establishment regarding a "just and democratic world order." But later, as the relationship with the United States and the other Western countries became more complicated following the Kosovo campaign and the cooling of Western leaders' attitudes toward President Yeltsin and his policies, Russia's multifaceted foreign policy orientation was reinforced with political action (joint political declarations with China, the formation of the Shanghai Cooperation Organization, etc.) and was expressed in Russia's defining foreign policy documents. The new Foreign Policy Framework of the Russian Federation, adopted in 2000, even asserted that the Russian Federation will strive to "form a multipolar system of international relations" that truly reflects the many faces of the modern world and the variety of interests within it.[20] It also stated that Russia wishes to create a stable system of international relations based on the principles of equality, mutual respect, and mutually beneficial cooperation. The framework noted in particular that "the world order of the 21st century should be based on mechanisms for resolving key issues collectively, on the supremacy of law, and on thorough democratization of international relations."[21] "Considering our history, intellectual resources, size, wealth of natural resources and finally, the level of military development, Russia will not agree with the position of a 'leading' country; it will assert itself in the role of an independent center in a multipolar world,"[22] said Primakov, one of the key ideologues of multipolarity.

In general, the official position was that a multipolar world began to develop after the end of the Cold War. However, a "pole" like China, with its stable economic growth rate of nearly 10 percent growth and steadily increasing share of world gross domestic product, should not be underestimated. Moreover, a center of economic power such as the European Union cannot be ignored. Despite the fact that the military and political future of the EU has become more uncertain following the failure of the referendum on a common European Constitution, it is clear that economic integration in the EU is irreversible. One way or another, the EU will continue to develop as one of the world's poles. And despite the commonality of democratic institutions, conflicts and problems in transatlantic relations will only increase over time. Likewise, it would be foolish to ignore the growing political and economic weight of India.

The concept of multipolarity is often interpreted as an attempt by Russia to prevent the United States from solidifying its role as the leader of the modern world—at any price (the price being a loss of sovereignty "in favor of" China or the EU). In fact, however, the motivation and intellectual underpinnings for the emergence of the concept were completely different. The primary issue for Russia in the 1990s was its failure to integrate into modern Western relationships and institutions on its own terms, that is, quickly (or even better—immediately) and with its high-level international status intact (recognizing the United States as the overall leader). There was also an obvious attempt to assume a position "alongside America," as a "preferred partner" but not a client of the United States. Both Yeltsin and his foreign minister, Andrey Kozyrev, tried to establish a preferential relationship with Washington based on an equal partnership, but these efforts failed back in 1992, when President George H. W. Bush rejected as groundless Yeltsin's politically naive proposal to create a formal alliance between Russia and the United States.

Primakov subsequently revised the Kozyrev legacy, and—contrary to widespread opinion in the West—maintained a policy of openness toward the outside world and cooperation with the West. He simply attempted to strengthen Russia's position in the dialogue, relying on the largely virtual but ostensibly special alliances with countries like China and on Russia's "natural" position of leadership within the Commonwealth of Independent States (CIS). Ultimately, he was too optimistic about the strength of Russia's position in the CIS and the viability of the CIS as an organization through which Russia could act as an intermediary between the West and "outside players." He also miscalculated the level of anti-Americanism and, correspondingly, the opportunities to exploit the potential of the leading Asian powers in this area. As a result, he was not successful in bolstering Russia's position in bargaining and negotiating with the West. In fact, Aleksei Bogaturov was right on target when he noted that

> under Foreign Minister and then Prime Minister Primakov, Russia's foreign policy evolved "along two parallel planes: the declared policy and the real policy." On the level of declared policy, Moscow played the role of global opponent, a "non-threatening counterweight" to the United States. In reality, Russia acted as an American partner even after 1996, albeit in a rather unique partnership (consistent with geopolitical parameters and cultural and historical particulars) in which Russia is more stubborn, easily offended, and demanding than would be typical of, say, Canada or Great Britain.[23]

These features of official Russian policy have led some to speak of the rise of "Russian Gaullism."

Putin's rise to power fundamentally changed this paradigm, at least at first glance. However, a more penetrating look reveals points of continuity and even a certain cyclical nature in policy. The terrorist attacks of September 11, 2001, allowed Russia to make one more attempt to become integrated into the institutional structure of the transatlantic community on terms acceptable to it, that is, quickly (almost immediately) and with its high-level international status intact. Moscow acknowledged American preeminence by providing all possible support to the antiterrorist campaign in Afghanistan, including by using its influence on the Northern Alliance in the country and by not reacting to American activism in Central Asia. The pragmatically minded members of the political establishment, including those in the military and security agencies, were ready to consent to American leadership—to the extent that this raised the hopes of the Russian elite for acquiring a real voice in the new security system taking shape on the European continent, for the rapid integration of Russia into a reformed NATO as a reward for cooperation, and for thus gaining a stake in the international organizations and institutions that are developing the new rules of the game in the global arena.

History has no patience for the subjunctive mode. But in this case, the counterfactual method is called for. The problem is whether the West has an adequately inclusive strategy and the ability to summon the initiative and political will to deepen cooperation and at the decisive moment. If President George W. Bush had made the decision in October 2001 to actually transform NATO into an operational management body for an international coalition to fight terrorism, and if he had taken the initiative and accepted Russian membership in a truly rejuvenated NATO, Russia would very likely have responded positively. Accepting Russia at the initiative of the West, at the same time or before accepting other Eastern European countries, would probably have satisfied the Russian elite. However, the West demonstrated once again that it does not have an inclusive strategy with respect to Russia. Its entire strategy consists of supporting geopolitical pluralism in the post-Soviet region or attempting to use Russia's resources and political influence to resolve some of its own foreign policy problems.[24]

As a result, a significant portion of the Russian elite interprets the further expansion of NATO in geopolitical terms (as a means of expanding the American sphere of influence into Eastern Europe), despite repeated statements by Russian officials that NATO's expansion does not pose a direct threat to the Russian Federation. The majority of midlevel analysts, as well as those in the military and security agencies, operate on the principle of political realism, which holds that NATO's intentions may change but its capabilities remain. And it is already at Russia's borders. Moreover, the West—especially NATO itself—has become much less popular among the general public in Russia. After the beginning of the Iraq war (2003), the idea of Russia joining NATO was supported by only 5 to 10 percent of its population, whereas the creation of a counterweight to NATO was supported by 10 to 23 percent (depending on how the question was phrased).[25]

A number of scholars (Dmitriy Trenin, Bobo Lo, et al.) believed that the problems of multipolarity were becoming less significant during President Putin's time in office and that geopolitical calculations and views were moving into the background of official policy. These assertions are correct, but they do not fully reflect reality. In geopolitical terms, Russia's interests have been "localized" and "regionalized." Its long-term foreign policy interests involving humanitarian issues and economic relationships have been concentrated primarily in the CIS. The CIS countries are seen as a foreign policy priority, a zone for the expansion of Russian capital, a source of labor, and a security buffer for Russia. What has changed is Russia's means of pursuing its interests. Economic, political, and cultural-informational methods have replaced military and political interventionism. Putin's Russia has abandoned the world ideological mission (whether liberal or communist), proclaiming itself a "sovereign democracy." Once again, a multipolar structure in international relations is considered preferable. However, though the

Russian leadership has advocated for its position firmly and fairly consistently, it has done so without being too shrill (as often happened in Yeltsin's time) and without much fanaticism. The new geoeconomic approach and the pragmatic focus on domestic affairs and problems was a turning point in political strategy. The new Russia is not isolating itself from the outside world, but it is primarily concerned with its own issues rather than leading the revolutionary camp, as the USSR did, or acting as an uncompromising advocate for liberal values, as the Yeltsin regime tried to do. At least this is how a significant portion of the Russian political elite perceives the situation.

Indeed, this is exactly why the elite does not understand or is even irritated by accusations of neo-imperialism, new expansionism, "pipeline imperialism," and so on. Plans to significantly diversify the supply routes of Russian energy and energy resources were unveiled as part of an ambitious Russian energy plan published in 2003 (by 2020, Russia plans to attract up to $700 billion in investment in the fuel and energy sector).[26] It was obvious that to reduce political risks, Russia would actively develop alternative routes to supply energy resources to the European market. Moreover, Western and Russian experts generally recommend diversifying energy supply routes in order to maintain the stability of the world energy market. In their opinion, "expanding the system of energy security by constructing additional routes to transport energy resources is in the interest of all countries as well as foreign investors."[27]

However, as soon as Russia announced its plans to build a gas pipeline on a new route (e.g., the North European gas pipeline), there was a negative, almost hysterical reaction in several European capitals. Similarly, when Russia raised the prices of its energy resources to a level that was still lower than the average European prices ($220 vs. $250 per thousand cubic meters), after announcing that it no longer wished to subsidize the Ukrainian economy to the tune of $3 billion to $5 billion a year (depending on the level of European energy prices), there was a nervous reaction from the United States and a number of European countries, along with new accusations that Russia was attempting to resurrect its imperial might, crush democracy in neighboring countries, and so on. These steps of the Russian government may, of course, be interpreted geopolitically and offensively, as many Western observers have been inclined to do. But from another perspective, they reveal a radical turn in Russian policy toward the CIS; they signal a real recognition of independence on the part of these states. As long as the Russian elite viewed the reintegration of post-Soviet space as possible and desirable, this had to be reconciled with Russia's de facto donor position. In contrast, a demand "to pay the bill" means that the Russian elite have essentially renounced the idea of reintegrating post-Soviet space.

Unlike the incompetent Yeltsin, who loved to shock the world and his own public with his behavior and outrageous statements, Putin has not been carried away by harsh rhetoric. Rather, he is ready to act consistently and clearly in defending Russia's national interests. He does not scare the West into thinking that "Russia is moving East" or try to create his own Eurasia, but he is actively looking for alternatives to Russia's dependence on Western countries, including by diversifying energy export routes. He is attempting to create a new geopolitical situation in which the West and the East (especially China) would be forced not so much to pressure Russia as to compete for its resources. That is why he seeks to position the Russian Federation as a stable and predictable "energy power." The problem is that the concept of a multipolar world ceases to be merely a figure of speech in this new geoeconomic sense. This concept is gradually being fleshed out by a new reality of tactical political alliances with a number of Asian countries, and by the expansion of gas and oil pipeline networks to the East. And if Russian-Western relations worsen, the West may actually lose Russia—not as a democracy but as a partner and natural ally against the new challenges and threats raised by globalization.

Geopolitics and Identity

Political and socioeconomic modernization assumes a significant change in identity (or identities).[28] However, the formation of a new identity (or identities) involves a search for ways and methods to make the imperatives of modernization organically consistent with the imperatives of preserving historic forms of cultural identity.

One of the key manifestations of this crisis in identity was and still is the crisis of national identity experienced by the citizens of Russia. Throughout the 1990s, according to public opinion polls, up to 30 percent of the population of Russia still identified with the Soviet state; that is, they considered themselves Soviet people (among older groups, this proportion reached 70 percent). In this environment, playing upon people's perceptions and emotions was an effective way for the opposition to win votes. The opposition saw the geopolitical ideology and a certain type of geopolitical discourse as a powerful method of forming a new Russian identity, which made it possible to exploit existing stereotypes. Indeed, the question of which civilization Russia belongs to remains one of the key issues for Russian public consciousness. This helps explain why contemporary geopolitical theory is so popular in the country, and why Samuel Huntington's book *The Clash of Civilizations* is practically a desk reference for many Russian politicians. In both the academic literature and political commentary, lively debates continue over whether Russia is the periphery of Europe and an outpost of European culture in the East; or a part of Asia, sometimes striving for Europeanization; or an independent civilization in itself, unique or (depending on the interpretation) synthesizing features of East and West.

During the crisis and subsequent collapse of the Soviet Union, many intellectuals and members of the political elite began to look for a way out of this dilemma, based entirely on Western models and formulas for organizing political and economic life. The failure of the reforms conducted under the direct patronage of Western experts by the team of young reformers under President Yeltsin led to disillusionment among a significant portion of the public.[29] This gave rise to an increase in skepticism about the Western model of development as a whole, and its applicability to the situation in Russia in particular. Demand grew for a great power policy, based not on common human (which really meant Western) values but on Russia's interests, considering its national and cultural identity. This mood was most clearly reflected in the results of the last parliamentary elections, in which the "pro-Western" right-wing parties (SPS, "Yabloko") went down to crushing defeat, not even reaching the 5 percent threshold. To some extent, this situation is related to the deep stereotypes that Russians have about self-identification, according to which the country and society are seen as a unique state and culture that is developing on a path that is different from the countries of the West. The revived interest in religion is a significant factor in this as well.[30] But the current policy will have the biggest impact on the course of events. This explains the wave of mistrust and alienation toward the West that, according to public opinion polls, arose again in the Russian public consciousness at the turn of the century.[31]

However, it would be an exaggeration to say that we are dealing with the emergence (or reemergence) of an anti-Western psychological complex among Russians. In terms of values, Russia is not an "alternative" to the West. Modern Russia incorporates a fluctuating combination of common international and historically unique Russian values. On the whole, they are typical of the values of an industrial society. The differences that exist are unlikely to interfere with cooperation or partnership with the West.

A sore spot, however, remains the place and role of democratic values, and whether the political elite and the general public believe in them. Many foreign observers note that the level of social pluralism has declined in Russia since 2000, and that more and more authority in foreign policy and foreign trade is being concentrated in a small group of people in the government and the presidential administration. This is actually occurring, and it is an alarming trend that causes much lively political discussion within Russia. Nonetheless, it is clear that a real pluralism of interests—regional, economic, corporate, and the like—is continuing to develop in Russia. And these interests are being advanced.

At the same time, during the past decade the preference for Russia to have "its own path" of development has spread among the general public. According to a poll by the Public Opinion Foundation in 1999, the majority (60 percent) of respondents believed that in terms of its traditions and culture, Russia is a unique country, different from both Europe and Asia.[32] However, nearly half of those polled considered themselves Europeans. A similar situation arose three years later, also demonstrating that the Russian public consciousness contains various and sometimes rather contradictory identities, with very diverse historical, geographical, geopolitical characteristics.[33] Isolationist, anti-Western views are actually not typical of most supporters of Russia's "own path." Among those who wanted Russia to following its own special path of development, the majority (60 percent) supported the continued expansion of economic, political, and cultural ties and becoming closer to the West in general, and only 18 percent supported a reduction in such contacts.[34]

Growth in nationalism in contemporary Russia can be interpreted in different ways. In fact, the traditional identity in the last decades of the Russian Empire and during the seventy-plus years of the USSR was *a supranational, imperial* identity. As one observer expresses it, "Russian identity (which is, strictly speaking, identity with a state rather than a nation) was historically determined by the specific way in which power was organized in the Eurasian area."[35] The emergence of ethnic and cultural nationalism and the formation of a national state are in this sense a break with the prior tradition of the supranational, imperial identity. The shift from unconditional unity with the West toward the logic of national interest does not represent the authoritarian whim of the Russian leadership. Rather, it reflects the transformation of Russia from a supranational, missionary, and imperial state to a national state, and the need for a positive national philosophy that accompanies this change.[36] In this sense, objective sociocultural processes in Russian society are liberating the public consciousness from the nominally universal or even cosmopolitan, but essentially imperialistic, notions typical of the Soviet era.

Russian society finds itself sandwiched between two very contradictory demands: the need to complete the process of political modernization (i.e., creating the basis for social institutions and a civil society), and the need to adapt to new trends of globalization. Russia is clearly not among the leading nations in the globalization process. But it has also ceased to be a closed society. Foreign trade now makes up more then 40 percent of gross domestic product. It is therefore impossible for Russia to separate itself from the process of globalization and its attendant communications capabilities; commercial, financial, and informational networks; and cultural exchanges —and this creates tremendous additional pressure.

At the same time, the effects of globalization are far from unambiguous. On the one hand, as one scholar notes, "ideas, images, lifestyles, behavioral models, and consumption patterns are spread around the world more quickly than ever. They form the new soil in which the seeds of civil society are falling."[37] But on the other hand, in some contexts, these trends are capable of hindering as well as promoting the transition to democracy and the political modernization of the country. They make it harder for Russian society to escape from its current identity crisis. In other words, without forming a new national identity (i.e., a set of beliefs defining the Russian political community) and without choosing a particular path of development, the structures of civil society that are being created in Russia will still float above the "national soil" and only imitate, within certain enclaves and nongovernmental organizations, the structures of civil society in more developed countries.[38] In this context, it is understandable that the Putin administration is attempting, although not always consistently, to create effective state institutions and foundations for local government. This strategy leaves less room for "civilizational," "Eurasian," and other ideologized geopolitical approaches, with all the mythology that goes along with them.

Notes

1. Henry Kissinger, *The White House Years* (Boston: Little, Brown, 1979), 914.

2. Pavel A. Tsygankov, *Mezhdunarodnyie otnosheniya* (Moscow: Mezhdunarodnye otnosheniya, 1996), 157.

3. See John Agnew, *Geopolitics: Re-Visioning World Politics* (London: Routledge, 1998); Gearoid O. O'Tuathail, *Critical Geopolitics: The Politics of Writing Global Space* (London: Routledge, 1996); and Gearoid O. O'Tuathail, "Understanding Critical Geopolitics: Geopolitics and Risk Security," *Journal of Strategic Studies,* June–September 1999, 107–24.

4. Vladimir A. Kolosov and Ruslan F. Turovskiy, "Predisloviye," in *Geopolitich-*

eskoye polozheniye Rossii: predstavleniya i real'nost', ed. Vladimir A. Kolosov (Moscow: Art-Kur'er, 2000), 22.

5. See Eduard Solovyev, "Geopolitics in Russia: Science or Vocation?" *Communist and Post-Communist Studies,* January 2004, 85–96.

6. Vladimir V. Zhirinovskiy, *Posledniy brosok na Yug* (Moscow: Floriant, 1996); Aleksey Mitrofanov, *Shagi novoy geopolitiki* (Moscow: Izdatel'stvo Russkiy Vestnik, 1997); Gennadiy A. Zyuganov, *Za gorizontom* (Moscow: Informpechat', 1995); Gennadiy A. Zyuganov, *Geografiya pobedy* (Moscow: N.p., 1997).

7. See Aleksandr S. Panarin, *Iskusheniye globalizmom* (Moscow: Russkiy Natsional'niy fond, 2000).

8. Aleksandr S. Panarin, "Ontologiya terrora," in *Geopolitika Terrora* (Moscow: Aktogeya Tsentr, 2002), 45–51.

9. Zyuganov, *Geographiya pobedy,* 243.

10. *Politicheskiy otchet Tsentral'nogo Komiteta KPRF VII s'ezdu* (Moscow: ZAO Gazeta Pravda, 2000), 27.

11. See *Ocherednye zadachi KPRF* (Moscow: ZAO Gazeta Pravda, 2000), 49–51; and Gennadiy A. Zuganov, *Globalizatsiya: Tupik ili vykhod* (Moscow: ZAO Gazeta Pravda, 2001), 29. See also Gennadiy A. Zyuganov, *Globalizatsiya i sud'ba chelovechestva* (Moscow: Molodaya gvardiya, 2002), 126.

12. Gennadiy A. Zyuganov, *Globalizatsiya i sud'ba chelovechestva* (Moscow: Molodaya gvardiya, 2002), 126.

13. See Andrey V. Kozyrev, "Strategiya partnerstva," *Mezhdunarodnaya zhizn',* May 1994, 3–12.

14. See Vladimir P. Lukin and Anatoliy I. Utkin, *Rossiya i Zapad: Obschnost' ili otchuzhdeniye?* (Moscow: SAMPO, 1995).

15. Anatoliy Chubays, "Missiya Rossii v XXI veke," *Nezavisimaya gazeta,* October 1, 2003.

16. See Viktor L. Sheynis, "Rossiyskaya vneshniaya politika pered vyzovami globalizatsii," in *Obshchestvenno-politicheskiye sily Rossii i Zapada i problemy globalizatsii,* ed. Nikita V. Zagladin and Kirill G. Kholodkovskiy (Moscow: IMEMO, 2002), 92–105.

17. See Irina Kobrinskaya, "Pragmaticheskiy liberalism vo vneshney politike," *Otkrytaya politika,* August 7–8, 1997; Grigoriy Yavlinskiy, "Tri uroka Balkanskogo krizisa," *Obshaya gazeta,* June 8–14, 1999; and Alexey Arbatov, *Bezopasnost': Rossiyskiy vybor* (Moscow: Mezhdunarodnye otnosheniya, 1999).

18. "Kontseptsiya vneshney politiki Rossiyskoy Federatsii, 1992," in *Vneshnyaya politika i bezopasnost' sovremennoy Rossii, 1991–2002,* vol. 4 (Moscow: ROSSPEN, 2002), 21.

19. See Yevgeniy M. Primakov, "Mezhdunarodnye otnosheniya nakanune XXI veka: problemy i perspectivy," *Mezhdunarodnaya Zhizn',* October 1996, 3–13.

20. "Kontseptsiya vneshney politiki Rossiyskoy Federatsii, 2000," in *Vneshnyaya politika i bezopasnost' sovremennoy Rossii, 1991–2002,* vol. 4, 111.

21. Ibid.

22. Yevgeniy M. Primakov, "Moskva i Vashington: nuzhny doverie i sotrudnichestvo," *Rossiya v global'noy politike,* November–December 2005, 177–78.

23. Aleksey D. Bogaturov, "Rossiya i Amerika: Ot neizbiratil'nogo partnerstva k izbiratel'nomu soprotivleniyu," *Mezhdunarodnaya Zhizn',* June 1998, 16.

24. See Zbignev Bzhezinskiy, *Velikaya shakhmatnaya doska* (Moscow: Mezhdunarodnye otnosheniya, 1999).

25. *Obshchestvennoye mneniye–2004* (Moscow: Levada-Tsentr, 2004), 155.

26. See "Energeticheskaya strategiya Rossii do 2020," http://www.minprom.gov.ru/docs/strateg/1/.

27. Jan H. Kalicki and David L. Goldwyn, *Energy and Security: Toward a New Foreign Policy Strategy* (Washington and Baltimore: Woodrow Wilson Center Press and Johns Hopkins University Press, 2005), 161. On this problem, also see Nodari Simoniya, "Neft' v mirovoy politike," *Mezhdunarodnye protsessy,* September–December 2005, 4–17.

28. Valentina G. Fedotova, "Modernizatsiya i Globalizatsiya," in *Megatrendy mirovogo razvitiya,* ed. Vladimir Inozemtsev (Moscow: Ekonomika, 2001), 91.

29. The main manifestations of this failure were a 40 percent fall in GDP through the mid-1990s, the crash of the Russian stock market, and the collapse of the ruble during the default in 1998.

30. See Anastasiya V. Mitrofanova, *Politizatsiya pravoslavnogo mira* (Moscow: Nauka, 2004).

31. See Vladimir V. Lapkin and Vladimir I. Pantin, *Geoeconomicheskaya politika i global'naya politicheskaya istoriya* (Moscow: Olita, 2004); Vladimir V. Lapkin and Vladimir I. Pantin, "Obrazy Zapada v soznanii postsovetskogo cheloveka," *MEiMO,* July 2001, 68–83; Vladimir V. Lapkin and Vladimir I. Pantin, "Transformatsiya natsional'no-tsivilizatsionnoy identichnosti sovremennogo rossiyskogo obshchestva: Problemy i perspektivy," *Obshchestvennye nauki i sovremennost',* January–February 2004, 64–75.

32. "Dannye Fonda Obshchestvennoye Mneniye, 1999," http://www.fom.ru/reports/frames/of19990501.html.

33. See Vladimir A. Kolosov, ed., *Mir glazami rossiyan: mify i vneshniaya politika* (Moscow: Institute of the Public Opinion Foundation, 2003).

34. *Obschestvennoe mneniye 2002—po materialam issledovaniy* (Moscow: VTsIOM, 2002), 157.

35. Yuriy A. Melvil', "Liberal'naya vneshnepoliticheskaya al'ternativa dlya Rossii," in *Vneshniaya politika i bezopasnost' sovremennoy Rossii,* vol. 1 (Moscow: ROSSPEN, 2002), 334.

36. For more detail, see Alexey D. Bogaturov, "Natsional'noye i nadnatsional'noye v rossiyskoy politike," in *Ocherki teorii i politicheskogo analiza mezhdunarodnykh otnosheniy,* ed. Alexey D. Bogaturov (Moscow: NOFMO, 2002), 253–65.

37. Ilya B. Levin, "Grazhdanskoye obshchestvo na Zapade i v Rossii," in *Grazhdanskoye obshchestvo v Rossii: Struktury i soznaniye,* ed. Nikita V. Zagladin (Moscow: IMEMO, 1998), 31.

38. See Leonid S. Mamut, "Grazhdanskoye obshchestvo i gosudarstvo: Problema sootnoscheniya," *Obshchestvennye nauki i sovremennost',* September–October 2002, 99–100.

12

Globalization, Identity, and Changing Understandings of Security in Russia

Alexey Fenenko

External military threats were problems of central importance for Soviet security concepts in the 1970 and 1980s.[1] During this period, views of Soviet-American deterrence underwent a series of transformations based on emerging theories of "realistic nuclear war" (1960s), "flexible response" (1970s), and "limited nuclear war" (the first half of 1980s). More recently, an increased focus of attention on globalization has led to a new political and public discourse in Russia, as themes connected with economics, social problems, national identity, and religion have overshadowed military fears.[2] This was in stark contrast to the traditional (pre-Gorbachev) Soviet conception, which tended to equate security with the absence of military conflict. Indeed, by the 2000s, official Russian military thought declared that external military threats had become less acute.[3] As a result, in Russian political discourse, the notion of "security" has gained a wider meaning; that is, it has come to include economic, ecological, ethnic, and social dimensions.

This chapter explains how and why such a change has occurred, by exploring the security environment in which Russia finds itself, as well as the objectives discernible in Russian security policy and the adaptations that these objectives require. I conclude with some speculations about the challenges facing Russia in the area of security, in the context of globalization.

Globalization and the New Security Environment

In the middle of the 2000s, globalization forms a new environment for international security. This is true in six important ways. The first is *the changing conception of "international security."* The idea of "international peace and security" was one of the central issues addressed by UN documents in the 1940s. Then, and for much of the remainder of the twentieth century, the term "international security" meant the absence of global interstate war, or a system of international agreements and institutions based on the idea of preventing global war.[4] Today, it refers to the interaction between traditional (states) and new actors (nongovernmental actors and corporations). As a result, the language of security has been transformed to include new ideas, such as a "global antiterrorist coalition," "nation building" in "failed states," and "horizontal networks" of Islamist organizations as well as criminal groups—from drug-dealers and illegal suppliers of fissile materials to shadow financial associations.[5]

The second way in which globalization forms a new environment for international security is *the "socialization" of the security environment.* In the 1930s and 1940s, European and American politicians regarded the "state" as an integral and united community. Questions such as "What is the United States?" or "What is Germany?" made no sense, because states had stable interests, stable foreign politics, and an internal consensus about key international problems.[6] By contrast, in the 2000s experts tend to analyze a state's foreign policy according to the interests of key social groups; for example, they tend to believe that bureaucratic and business groups have different foreign policy priorities.[7] Indeed, increasingly, it makes sense to conduct such analyses, because one of globalization's effects is precisely to fragment society, and to establish close ties between elites or interest groups that transcend national boundaries. States thus join in the new security environment as components of global networks—not as a united and integral community.

Third, *the notion of "ethnic-social processes" increasingly overshadows the conception of the "national idea."* The national idea refers to a specific concept generated by a synthesis of liberal and conservative ideologies in the nineteenth century, when European states were based on the idea of the "absorption" of small ethnicities by larger, titular nations.[8] In the twentieth century, the national idea maintained the state's integrity, because it affirmed both the unity of ethnic groups living within the state's territory and the right of "titular nations" to play a leading role in the state's domestic and foreign policies. But after the 1980s—when the USSR, Yugoslavia, and Czechoslovakia all collapsed—the state began losing its national integrity, as many small ethnic groups formed their own states (Slovenia, Slovakia, the Czech Republic, Croatia, Bosnia and Herzegovina, Macedonia, Latvia, and Lithuania), in the process reviving prenational or medieval collective identities.[9] Moreover, some experts suggest that states are losing their national unity owing to large-scale migrations from Africa, Asia, and South America.[10] The upshot is that globalization creates objective problems for multiethnic states.

Fourth, the new international security system suggests *the "renaissance" of military power.* Liberal concepts of the 1970s affirmed the decline of the military factor and the rise of various institutional factors in the global power structure.[11] By contrast, today we can observe a certain reemergence of military power, albeit in a nontraditional form, as the latest wave of the technological revolution creates new types of highly accurate weapons systems. As a result, we are seeing new rationalizations for the use of military power: (1) humanitarian intervention, (2) attacks on terrorist bases, (3) intervention designed to prevent the collapse of state institutions, and (4) counterproliferation actions.[12] War with Islamist networks requires small, mobile military groups able to act far from state borders. The new type of interstate wars is likely to take the form of intense conflicts between aircraft and the antiaircraft defense systems. Indeed, it is difficult to forecast the result of highly accurate weapons systems development and the effect of experiments on nuclear arms modifications.

Fifth, in the 2000s, *the economic factor has become not only crucial but also nonsubstitutable.* In the nineteenth and twentieth centuries, the leading economic development model was "rapid modernization." Any state could introduce a mass mobilization system and, simply by generating ever-increasing material inputs, could achieve a large-scale industrial system within a relatively short time. Today, such modernization is becoming practically impossible; instead, the new technological revolution (often mistakenly called the "scientific-technical revolution"[13]) is essential for states wishing to achieve modernity. As a result, there may be a "constant" technological gap between developed and underdeveloped states.

References to the technological success of China, India, and other South and East Asian states are commonplace.[14] Though this is true, their industrialization is different from the old, rapid modernization of the German Empire (1870s), the Russian Empire (1880s), Japan (1890s), Italy (1900s), and the USSR (1930s). First, the "new industrial powers" do not create "closed" or "isolated" financial and industrial systems. The elites of these states see themselves as working toward, rather than against, the formation of a global economic space, in contrast to German and Soviet elites in the first half of the twentieth century. Second, their industrialization does not create technological alternatives to Western military leadership. These states buy Russian, American, and European military technologies; they do not create their own, original high-technology systems. By contrast, the old, rapid modernization model aimed precisely at creating a competitive military industry.

Sixth, *the "energy factor" is again acquiring priority among international security factors.*[15] Today, we can observe a kind of restoration of the situation of the nineteenth century, when the main sources of industrial growth were coal, iron, and gold. In the 2000s, it has become clear that the rise of a postindustrial economy depends directly on the amount of energy consumption.[16] One of the priorities for international politics thus becomes the struggle for oil, gas, and uranium. However, the unprecedented rise in oil prices increases profits for the monarchs of the Persian Gulf, which in it turn increases the financing of transnational Islamist networks. The growth of uranium mining and the recycling of military plutonium provide conditions for an expanding nuclear black market, which increases the likelihood of nuclear proliferation, including to transnational terrorist networks.[17] As a result, analysts are becoming aware that the energy factor, while crucial, is also fraught with threats to international security.

In sum, globalization establishes new parameters for Russia's security, which in turn lead to a number of fundamentally new objectives:

- to create an effective defense mechanism against "network attacks";
- to prevent the disaggregation of Russian foreign policy;
- to prevent ethnic separatism;
- to build effective military forces able to efficiently solve new military problems;
- to develop a new strategy of economic security that combines breakthroughs in modernization with economic profitability; and
- to draw appropriate conclusions from the negative effects associated with the current international energy system.

In the 1990s, Russian security experts mainly feared the development of a new model of governance that involved a limitation of sovereignty.[18] In the 2000s, the possible disintegration of the state (i.e., the disaggregation of state institutions as well as state weakness) as well as the proliferation of weapons of mass destruction take first place in Russian security concerns. These trends have not yet become key issues for Russian political discussion. But in 2004 and 2005, the preconditions for a new Russian security strategy began to appear.

The New Parameters and New Objectives for Russia's Security

Two general orientations in security research can be observed in Russia today. The first can be called "statist." According to this trend, Russian foreign policy and Russian security policy must be regarded as a single system, based on a unified conception and characterized by coordinated interaction between different institutions.[19] By contrast, the second orientation (which can be qualified as "liberal") views Russian security not as an integrated system but as the interaction of distinct groups of actors: the state bureaucracy, business communities, analytical centers, and mass media structures. Each group of actors has its own interests, which often intersect with the interests of transnational financial and industrial groups.[20] Thus, "Russian security" emerges as the result of interactions among all these actors. Globalization processes have accentuated the differences between these orientations concerning Russian security strategy. In this respect, we can discern three important tendencies, having to do with sovereignty, institutional fragmentation, and ethnic nationalism.

First, reflecting on problems of "globalization" and "international politics," Russian analysts increasingly discuss the restriction of sovereignty by various external factors and processes, as well as the influence of transnational actors on interstate policy.[21] In the 1990s, analysts tended to focus on the positive aspects of globalization, which were assumed to include the reduction of military threats. In the 2000s, however, analysts tend to emphasize the emergence of new threats, especially the activities of terrorist organizations and criminal networks.[22] Unlike in the United States, the "network problem" is not yet the main focus of analysis for Russian experts.[23] It is true that many Russian analysts express concerns that the Muslim regions of Russia might be targets of ideological expansion on the part of radical Islamists.[24] Unfortunately, however, these experts have tended to restrict their analysis of the network problem to this issue, notwithstanding the activities of criminal groups and separatist movements in certain regions (especially the Northern Caucasus).[25] Key Russian documents still give priority to threats posed by "unfriendly external coalitions" rather than the threat of domestic and/or transnational networks.[26]

Second, in the 1990s and early 2000s, a tendency toward the institutional fragmentation of the security environment caused new problems for Russian security. As European and American analysts observed, Russian foreign policy actually comprised a combination of distinct "foreign policies" conducted by the Russian Foreign Ministry, the presidential administration, and lobbies representing the interests of oil and gas, the military, and so on.[27] Thus, in the course of key foreign policy discussions about the Bosnian crisis and NATO enlargement, different Russian institutions (e.g., the Ministry of Foreign Affairs, Ministerstvo Inostrannikh Del; the Ministry of Defense, Ministerstvo Oborony; and the Foreign Intelligence Service, Sluzhba Vneshney Razvedky[28]) starkly opposed one another. Russian experts, too, were of course deeply conscious of the lack of coordination between Russia's security institutions, and they worried that this programmed Russian foreign policy for a chronic lack of success.[29] Moreover, it raised the possibility of "playing on the contradictions" inside the Russian security system, because any action that was not objectively beneficial for Russia might be justified on the grounds that it merely caused a negative reaction from certain domestic groups. (For example, during NATO's two enlargements, some European representatives insisted that the Kremlin's negative reaction was caused not by Russian strategic interests but by a lack of civil society in Russia.) Russian experts therefore became concerned that foreign actors might be able to impose measures that were detrimental to Russian security.[30]

During the 2000s, the state's institutional coordination has undoubtedly become stronger. However, it should be noted that there are objective problems associated with this process. That is, globalization creates an environment in which the interaction of social actors often takes place beyond the state's borders. As a result, government institutions can potentially cooperate, on their own, with various transnational groups. This raises the prospect of renewed institutional fragmentation at some point in the future.

Third, the rise of "ethnic nationalism" affects the security politics of all multiethnic states, including Russia. It is here that Russian elite see the most serious danger. On the one hand, the Russian state system is based on the principles of federal and territorial division. On the other hand, the "national republics" inside Russia have their own public administration systems, and in this way there are unified (or "aggregated") communities.[31] However, viewing the state as a combination of ethnic regions implies a decentralization of Russian administration. This problem was of central importance for Putin's three major reforms: the formation of presidential districts in May 2000, the transformation of membership in the Federation Council in July 2000, and the canceling of elections for regional governors in September 2004.[32] The "decentralization threat" remains a popular theme in Russian political commentary, albeit less so than in the 1990s.[33]

Thus, at present, we observe the development of a several trends arguably related to globalization in Russian security analysis. However, their practical significance depends largely on their fit with the new international security environment and the kinds of adaptations that this requires.

Russia's Adaptation to the New Security Environment

Alongside the tensions generated by globalization with respect to domestic cohesion and security policymaking, the new global environment objectively decreases Russian security capabilities. As a result, the Russian political-military elite find it difficult to fit into the developing international security system.

Sovereignty and Military Factors

It took some time for observers to recognize this situation. In the first half of the 1990s, most of the elite (with the exception of radical communists and nationalists) and analysts perceived the developing environment in a positive light.[34] Russian foreign policy was influenced by the prevailing liberal outlook, according to which Moscow could afford to make one-sided concessions to its Western partners.[35] The idea of partnership agreements between democratic countries also prevailed.[36] It seemed that the Russian government agreed to accept the new ideas regarding self-limitations on sovereignty. As an example, Russia agreed to negotiate with the United States about the future of the Soviet nuclear arsenal, and with the International Tribunal with regard to the former Yugoslavia in 1993.

But by the early 1990s, one could already observe a rehabilitation of the "military threat" notion. The strategy of "Gorbachev's new vision" (1986–90) was based on the idea of giving up the concept of war as a political tool.

During this period, Russian analysts were concerned about the "axis of instability" along the southern border of the Commonwealth of Independent States (CIS), from Afghanistan to the Muslim regions of the CIS.[37] The idea of "limited war" was regarded as a possible tool for maintaining Russia's security. But by the second half of 1990s, the Russian political and military elite had become aware that this new idea of limited sovereignty might also be dangerous for Russia. After NATO's military interference in the Bosnian crisis (in the summer of 1995), Russian analysts came to the conclusion that, under certain conditions, Russia itself might become a target of the "new interventionism."[38] Discussions over NATO enlargement convinced many of the Russian elite that the new center of international governance— the Group of Seven–NATO complex—still did not regard Russia as an equal partner. As a result, by the end of 1990s, one could observe—in Russian publications as well as official Russian documents—a renaissance of ideas regarding external military threats.[39]

It is noteworthy that at this very time, Russian analysts increasingly were discussing the new role (or restoration) of the military factor.[40] In particular, as mentioned above, analysts tended to be concerned with the threat of regional wars with transnational Islamist networks. The events in Afghanistan and Central Asia showed that in case of dramatic developments, Islamists could occupy the territory of states neighboring the CIS (and possibly even one of the CIS countries), use the territory as a base for aggression, and cooperate with Islamist networks inside Russia. In such a situation, Russia would be forced not only to undertake military actions in Central Asia and the Caucasus but also to support secular political regimes in the Central Asian states that were allied with Russia.[41] Therefore, in the context of globalization, when choosing between "soft-power" and "hard-power" mechanisms, the Russian elite still favor the latter.

The increased emphasis on the military was also connected with a renewed focus on deterrence as a complex of preventive measures against any possible foreign threat.[42] In 1996, analysts began writing about a purported new role for nuclear weapons, including their use as an effective instrument in defense of state sovereignty.[43] Indeed, an important role belongs to the discussion of the rise of new "nuclear factors" in international politics.[44] Since the end of 1990s, Russian experts have argued that a lowering of the "nuclear threshold" has taken place, resulting from both the acquisition of nuclear arms by new powers and the wishes of established nuclear states (the United States, and potentially France and the United Kingdom) to develop new types of nuclear systems. In this context, Russian analysts fear that foreign political-military elites may come to see the notion of "limited nuclear conflict" as potentially advantageous.[45] Analysts also suggested the idea of using conventional military power against separatist movements, and, after NATO's operation in Yugoslavia (1999), they focused attention on the new role of highly accurate weapons systems.[46] Thus, the new military tendencies were perceived to potentially enhance as well as threaten national security.

At the same time, there were concerns about Russia's ability to meet military challenges. On the one hand, this should not be exaggerated. Despite the widespread, lingering opinion that Russian military forces are in decay, Russia occupies the second position internationally (after the United States) with regard to military expenditures and numbers of weapons.[47] However, the Russian army is mobilized based on recruiting. As in the past, it is influenced by an extensive interstate war model based on mass mobilization, including the mobilization of industry. Many Russian experts believe that such a system is not effective for modern problems.[48] Consequently, analysts are gradually becoming aware of the "social weaknesses" of the Russian army (including corruption and mass avoidance of military service), which are caused by the fact that there has been no need for the mechanism of extensive war for more than half a century.[49]

Partly as a result of such concerns, beginning in the first half of 2000s, the Russian elite started to consider changes in the new security environment to be "inevitable" ones, which Russia needed to accommodate. Supporting the United States and NATO antiterrorist operation in Afghanistan, the Russian elite admitted the possibility (and in some cases, the necessity) of "limited sovereignty." By agreeing to NATO's military presence in the CIS, Russian politicians essentially rejected the concept of "sphere of influence," inherited from the nineteenth century, which assumed a monopoly for great power military presence.[50] In addition, by accepting America's unilateral abrogation of the Anti–Ballistic Missile Treaty, Moscow acknowledged the necessity of transforming the arms control regimes inherited from the Cold War period.

It is true that in the Council of Europe and the Organization for Security and Cooperation in Europe, the Russian delegations have angrily rejected outside interference in domestic political affairs. However, Moscow agreed to discuss Russian domestic problems, which was quite different from the positions taken by China, the Central Asia states, and India. Beijing has not agreed to participate in international negotiations on Xinjiang and Tibet. Tashkent and Astana have not agreed to take part in international discussions about the situations concerning their national diasporas. All in all, then, the Russian political-military elite started to see their country as a part of a new international security system, one based on the idea of a united defense mounted by allied states against transnational threats.

In this connection, it should be noted that the concepts of "sovereignty" and "spheres of influence" are often equated in Russian political discourse.[51] But this is because many experts understand sovereignty as the sovereignty of "great powers" in the nineteenth century. In fact, however, "spheres of influence" is actually a quite different idea than sovereignty. According to the traditional notion, great powers had the right to restrict the sovereignty of failing states. Thus, in the nineteenth century, the "great status" of the French, Russian, and British empires suggested a limitation of China's, Turkey's, and Egypt's sovereignty.[52] In other words, these empires created spheres of influence whereby they limited the sovereignty of other states. In contrast, today most Russian analysts agree with the idea that the CIS states can have independent political and military contacts with other "centers of power" (e.g., China, the United States, European states).

Modernization and Energy Resources

In addition to the ways in which globalization bears on the role of traditional military factors and sovereignty concerns, it is also useful to point to globalization's affect on strategies of modernization and energy policy, both of which are key issues for Russian security. With regard to the first, for the past three centuries, the Russian political-military elite have preferred the "rapid modernization" model. This idea suggested a combination of two things: (1) the state must have five basic production branches (mining, oil, metallurgy, machinery, energy system); and (2) the agriculture system must be able to meet the population's food demands. Today, however, Russian experts are becoming aware that it is impossible to keep up with the world's high-technology leaders by these means.[53] In the 2000s, the dominant idea is to choose a successful development project and spearhead its effective realization within the world economic system. Such an approach contradicts traditional Russian security concepts, which were based on established ideas of industrial and military power.

With regard to the second issue, the rise of the energy factor provides new economic opportunities for the Russian Federation. Russian analysts more often argue that the "energy" factor is as important for national security as is the nuclear one.[54] Russia thus appears as one of the key energy partners for European countries (and potentially for the United States and China). The high profitability of oil and gas gives Russia a chance to realize a relatively successful economic project: to become one of the main fuel providers. This promises to give Russia greater access to financial resources and also strengthens its position in the international political system. As a result, we have seen the development of an "energy security concept." Much as in the United States or the United Kingdom, this deals with the establishment of a beneficial pricing policy and secure means for exporting oil and gas. In Russia, however, energy exporting is also regarded as a way of improving the country's foreign policy position. The gas conflict with Ukraine at the end of 2005 and in early 2006 provided an obvious example of this approach to energy trade. The assumption that Russia is a potential "energy superpower" strongly influences attitudes regarding the country's role in the international political system.

At the same time, the energy factor has also increased the role of resource-mining regions within the political system of the Russian Federation. Because the Russian budget depends largely on energy exports, the resource-mining regions of the North and Siberia have begun to demand special status in the Federation. In 1998–99, the "Siberian Accord" project appeared, within which the governor of Krasnoyarskiy Kray (Aleksandr Lebed) and the governor of Khakasiya (Aleksey Lebed) sought to play the leading role. In the mid-2000s, negotiations over the export of northern Siberian energy resources to China, Japan, and potentially the United States created a new mechanism for consultations between the federal center and these regions.[55] The prospect of developing a new system of "special" relationships between the Kremlin and the most important economic regions cannot be excluded.

Future Challenges for Russian Security

In the middle of the 2000s, Russian analysts began discussing a number of completely new problems, which in the future might pose difficulties for the Russian security system. Four key problems may be highlighted here.

The first problem is the creation of a "new nuclear environment." On the one hand, the cooperation of Russia and United States in the field of nuclear nonproliferation is slow and very difficult.[56] The Russian government as well as Russian firms cooperate with Iran, Syria, North Korea and India—the very states that Washington defines as the key nuclear and missile proliferators. The Kremlin perceives American calls for limiting such cooperation to be an element of a new "containment strategy" for Russia. Similarly, official Russian reactions to the Indian and Pakistani nuclear tests in 1998 and North Korea's nuclear test in 2006 were quite moderate. The reason for this stance is that some Russian politicians and military figures tend to think that missile proliferation may in fact limit American hegemony in a globalizing world.[57]

Conversely, by 2004 American and European experts as well as the mass media began discussing three new nuclear problems: (1) the collapse of states in South, Central, and East Asia and the Middle East (and probably in Africa), most of which have arsenals of weapons of mass destruction; (2) international control over the nuclear arsenals of "failed states"; and (3) control of the fissile materials by international programs and institutions, which could inhibit the proliferation of nuclear technologies.[58] By contrast, Russian analysts argue that the idea of joint control over nuclear fissile materials would impose limitations on Russia's sovereignty.[59] After the Bratislava summit (February 2005), Russian public opinion and even some analytical centers began to discuss a new danger: What if counterproliferation strategy was eventually applied to Russia?

It is interesting to recall that the problem of providing security for fissile materials is an old issue in U.S.-Russian relations. In 1991, Washington proposed the Nunn-Lugar initiative—that is, to provide financial assistance for Russia's nuclear disarmament. In the spring of 1995, Russia and the United States signed two documents calling for American financial support for the transportation of Russian nuclear materials. But in the early 1990s, Russian public opinion evaluated this cooperation as being helpful, rather than as foreign control over domestic nuclear capability.[60] The problem thus has a psychological, rather than an objective, realpolitik character. It seems likely that some influential Russian political actors disagreed with key new nonproliferation agreements (e.g., the Additional Protocol of the International Atomic Energy Agency, 1997, UN Resolution 1540), according to which the "old" nuclear states must create an *international* limitation system of nuclear fissile control.[61] These agreements create problems for private nuclear business, especially for private contracts with the main state proliferators (Iran, North Korea, and Pakistan). This is why such problems concern not only Russia but also the other nuclear states, especially China and France.

The second new security problem concerns the *results of the new military doctrine,* which assumes the possibility of preventive military operations on other countries' territory. This problem appears to be analogous to the United States' conception of a "global antiterrorist war." However, it may bring about certain changes in Russian politics. In the 1990s, Moscow built its relationship with the CIS states based on the rejection of overt foreign pressure.[62] More recently, however, Russia has started to perceive the CIS states as a potential source of military problems. From August to September 2002, the Russian government declared that Russia was entitled to conduct air raids in the Pankisi Gorge—a remote part of Georgia where Chechen separatists had allegedly set up bases.[63] On October 2, 2003, Russian minister of defense Igor Ivanov declared that preventive attacks to counter potential aggressors would henceforth be an important part of Russian military doctrine.[64]

On the one hand, hypothetical Russian operations could bring the hope of independence to these as-yet-unrecognized "states." On the other hand, the central governments of CIS states (Georgia, Moldova, etc.) could start military operations to counter what are perceived to be separatist movements. In any case, however, the fact is that this new military strategy will reinforce political-military tensions during the post-Soviet area. Nevertheless, the very emergence of this military strategy reflects the fact that the Russian elite consider network terrorism—the key factor explicitly justifying such military intervention—to be not only a social-political problem (as it was in 1990s) but also a military problem. The tendency to revive the concept of "limited war," which first surfaced in 1993, is related to this development as well.

The third new security problem may be regarded as an "ideological" one. In the middle of the 2000s, Russia faced the new phenomenon of "colored revolutions"—that is, a number of politically revolutionary changes in CIS states. It is almost universally recognized that one driving force behind the upheavals in Georgia and Ukraine was to dissociate the nation from Russia. The underlying sources of this political turmoil remain difficult for Russian analysts to understand; many suspect that they represent a sort of "ideological project" that is supported by certain foreign (including CIS) states and that has anti-Russian potential. Partly for this reason, since the end of 2004, many Russian experts have concluded that the consolidation of Russian security requires the development of a coherent information strategy.[65] This, in turn, reveals certain changes toward the role of information in security issues.[66] Thus, a key task facing Russia is to develop a viable information project, one capable of merging the rising tide of ethnic nationalism with Russia's own interests. Indeed, this is linked to the development of a concept of informational security more broadly, including the potential use of the mass media (especially electronic) to create a positive image of the country.[67]

It is interesting that in speaking about the events in Georgia (November 2003), Ukraine (December 2004), and Kyrgyzstan (March 2005), Russian and American experts prefer to use metaphorical images—"Rose Revolution," "Orange Revolution," and "Tulip Revolution," respectively. The political agendas of these revolutions are still very difficult to define. However, we can now conclude that these revolutions

- did not lead to the democratization of the political system (in Georgia, a regime based on the personal power of Eduoard Shevardnadze was replaced by a regime based on the personal power of Mikhail Saakashvili, whereas in Ukraine the main opponent of redistributing power in favor of the parliament is President Viktor Yushchenko, who himself rose to power in the Orange Revolution);
- created an environment for (re)criminalization (suffice it to recall that corruption scandals dominated the news in Ukraine throughout 2005);
- were not directed against the "nomenclature" political class in general— the new leaders who came to power in Georgia, Ukraine, and Kyrgyzstan (and the people who tried to come to power in Azerbaijan in 2005) had held senior positions in the previous administration.

However, the situation changes when we view the "colored revolutions" as primarily nationalistic movements. It is no coincidence that they occurred in countries with imbalanced relations among ethnic groups and unresolved interethnic issues, left over from the political (and often military) conflicts of the early 1990s.

Since the Soviet republics declared independence in 1991, the political elites in most of the new post-Soviet nations have sought to built alliances with nationalist forces by proclaiming ideas like the creation of a "Greater Georgia," a "Greater Azerbaijan," the "Ukrainization of Ukraine," and the like. But at that time, these attempts were unsuccessful. The hard-line nationalists (e.g., Gamsakhurdia and Elchibei) were overthrown in military coups d'état; the moderates (Kravchuk, Ter-Petrosyan, Shushkevich) were defeated in elections in the mid-1990s. By 2000, these nationalistic projects, which sought to sever relations with Russia and suppress ethnic minorities, once again found themselves in opposition to the leadership in the majority of the new post-Soviet nations.

The "colored revolutions" radically changed this situation. In the spring and summer of 2004, the Georgian authorities essentially revoked the autonomy of Adzharia and dramatically escalated its conflicts with Abkhazia and Southern Ossetia (areas that had acquired de facto autonomy as a result of the bloody conflicts of 1991–93). In 2005, the new Ukrainian leadership ruled out any possibility of creating a Southeastern autonomous area or a Donetsk Republic, which could have been formed based on existing distinctions between Russian-speaking and Ukrainian-speaking areas. Similarly, a policy of "widespread penetration of the Ukrainian language" (which is seen as a return to the radical "Ukrainization" of 1992) ignores not only the rights of the Russian-speaking population but also such integral parts of Ukraine as the Hungarian minority in the Transcarpathia, predominantly Rumanian North Bukovina, the Jewish community in Odessa, and the Transcarpathian Rusyns (a separate Russian-language ethnos in the Transcarpathia that traditionally associated its self-determination not with Russia or Poland but with Austria-Hungary and, later, Slovakia and Hungary). Thus, there is a renewed threat of interethnic conflicts of the type seen in the early 1990s.

The above tendencies place three problems before Russia. First, nationalization processes in the CIS states have the potential to disrupt the existing ethnic balance and lead to armed interethnic conflicts. Second, Russia has essentially incurred a new mission—the protection of Russian diasporas in the CIS countries, which inevitably has negative effects on Moscow's relations with the new (national) elites of these states. Third, the very foundation of independence for these countries is based on the goal of breaking away from Russia. Should they come to fruition, these tendencies could fundamentally alter geopolitical relations in the post-Soviet region and raise the prospect of the disintegration of the CIS.

Paradoxically, another potential future security problem is energy. As discussed above, most Russian experts today (including Putin) regard energy resources as perhaps the key resources for Russian security as a whole.[68] However, in 2004–6 the possibility was raised in Russian publications that the country's energy potential might become exhausted in ten to fifteen years. This notion quickly gained currency, for several reasons. Some experts pointed to low levels of investment in prospecting and drilling oil and gas wells in the northern and east regions of Russia. Others noted the low profitability of North Siberian output (an observation that goes back to the end of the nineteenth century), due to the necessity for high investments in heating infrastructure and the lack of open ocean ports. Still others observed that by the 2000s the national atomic energy system had reached capacity. As a result, Russian analysts have increasingly argued that the contribution of energy resources to Russian security should not be overestimated.[69]

Alexey Fenenko

Some European and American experts like to apply the term "Dutch disease" to Russian conditions (i.e., the ideas that certain sectors of the state's economy may be harmed by rising currency values resulting from oil exports).[70] Indeed, following the Russian bank crisis in the summer of 2004, even Russian observers started suggesting that the main danger facing the economy was not a possible decrease in oil prices (as in the middle 1980s and late 1990s) but rather a surplus of oil revenues. It is clear that the export of energy resources can be both a source of profit and a potential problem for Russian economic and social security. Thus, among Russian analysts, one detects a small but crucial shift toward reconsidering the role of the energy factor in the overall system of Russian priorities.

Finally, another shift taking place in Russian security publications in the 2000s is that the topic of "foreign military threat" is gradually being superseded by other, *nontraditional* security problems—that is, "transnational terrorist networks," "nuclear proliferation," "drugs trafficking," and various other internal threats (which are considered to reveal the lack of an effective defense security system). Most Russian analysts (excluding radicals on the right and left) agree with the proposition that Russian security strategy will be effective only if Russia is able to coordinate effectively with European states and the United States. However, the new international security system is based not on the idea of defending states *from other states* but on the idea of defending states *from transnational actors* (e.g., Islamist networks). This problem has become one of the main topics in Russian security discourse.

Conclusions

The new security environment is causing new problems for Russia. In part, this is because the presence of transnational threats elevates the importance of protecting the general interests of society, whereas over the past three hundred years the main priority for Russian elite had been protecting state sovereignty. Moreover, as we have seen, the global social environment tends to integrate states gradually, in their constituent parts, as independent institutions and elite groups. Finally, changes in the perceived distribution of power are having a profound effect on Russian identity.[71] For the first time since the nineteenth century, Russian society does not feel itself to be one of the leading industrial countries (at or near the level of European countries and the United States) but rather perceives itself as one of the largest supplier of key natural resources, along with the countries of the Persian Gulf, Central Asia, and possibly Canada, Australia, and South Africa (the uranium states). This new Russian identity demands a new security policy. At the same time, the inertia of the "old" thinking is still too great. The Soviet security conception was based on the threat of a recurrence of the script of 1941. To some extent, the new Russia has rejected or at least substantially modernized this conception. But at times, notions of security problems appear to be based on the ideas of an even earlier period, dating back to the end of the nineteenth century. Russia's integration into the new global security environment thus stands as one of the key tasks facing the Russian elite in coming decades.

Notes

1. *Vtoraya Mirovaya Voyna: Itogi i Uroki* (Moscow: Voyenizdat, 1985), 387–412; Aleksey Arbatov, *Voenno-Strategicheskiy Paritet i Politika SShA* (Moscow: Politizdat, 1984); Andrey Kokoshin, *V Poiskakh Vykhoda: Voenno-politicheskie Aspekty Mezhdunarodnoy bezopasnosti* (Moscow: Izdatel'stvo politicheskoy literatury, 1989); Michael McñGwire, *Perestroika and Soviet National Security* (Washington, D.C.: Brookings Institution Press, 1991).

2. Aleksandr Chumakov, *Globalizatsiya: Kontury Tselostnogo Mira* (Moscow: Prospekt, 2005); Marat Cheshkov, *Globalistika kak Nauchnoe Znanie: Ocherki Teorii i Kategorial'nogo Apparata* (Moscow: NOFMO, 2005). Georgiy Shakhnazarov, "Miroporyadok Civilizatsiy?" *Pro et Contra,* Fall 1998, 149–65; Aleksey Bogaturov, "Sindrom Poglosheniya v Mezhdunarodnoy Politike," *Pro et Contra,* Fall 1999, 28–48.

3. Tatiana Shakleina, ed., *Vneshnyaya Politika i Bezopasnost' sovremennoy Rossii: 1991–2002* (Moscow: ROSSPEN, 2002); Aleksey Arbatov, *Bezopasnost': Rossiiskiy Vybor* (Moscow: EPIcentr, 1999); Andrey Kokoshin, *Yadernye konflikty v XXI Veke / Tipy, Formy, Vozmozhnyye Uchastniki* (Moscow: Media Press, 2003).

4. Preamble, Charter for the United Nations, http://www.un.org/aboutun/charter/index.html.

5. Ann-Marie Slaughter, *A New World Order* (Princeton, N.J.: Princeton University Press, 2004); Robert F. Trager and Dessislava P. Zagorcheva, "Deterring Terrorism: It Can Be Done," *International Security,* Winter 2005–6, 87–123; Andrew H. Kydd and Barbara F. Walter, "The Strategies of Terrorism," *International Security,* Summer 2006, 49–80.

6. Alan John Percival Taylor, *Bor'ba za Gospodstvo v Yevrope: 1848–1918* (Moscow: Inostrannaya literatura, 1958), 38.

7. Eduard Solovyev, *Natsional'nye Interesy i Osnovnye Politicheskie Sily Sovremennoy Rossii* (Moscow: Nauka, 2004).

8. Alexey Fenenko, *"Natsional'naya Ideya" i Yeë Evolyutsiya v Tvorchestve Frantsuzskikh Konservatorov XIX veka* (Voronezh: Voronezhskii Gosudarstvennyy Universitet, 2005).

9. Stephan Krasner, "Think Again: Sovereignty," *Foreign Policy,* January–February 2001, 20–29.

10. Ninna Nyberg Sørensen, *The Development Dimension of Migrant Remittances,* http://www.old.iom.int/documents/publication/en/remittances_development_dimensions.pdf.

11. Robert Keohane, *After Hegemony: Cooperation and Discord in the World Political Economy* (Princeton, N.J.: Princeton University Press, 1984).

12. Seyom Brown, *The Illusion of Control: Force and Foreign Policy in the 21st Century* (Washington, D.C.: Brookings Institution Press, 2003).

13. The term "science and technology revolution" (in the sense in which it was used in the late 1950s) implies the creation of new technologies and the application of these technologies in manufacturing. Today's "technological revolution" changes the meaning of "manufacturing" itself. This term is now associated not so much with heavy industry as with information technologies and the mining and processing of minerals. Technological revolutions took place in the 1880s (electrification), the 1920s (conveyor and chemical industry development), and the 1950s (the creation of the nuclear, space, and aero industries). These revolutions were quite intensive, because they changed the quality of production. The postindustrial production system (information technologies, connection systems, and artificial intelligence) are incompatible with centralized planning. Those investing in high-technology production businesses are aware that a final result can be expected not in two to three years (as it was in 1920s), but in fifteen to twenty years.

14. *Entsiklopediya Stran Mira* (Moscow: Ekonomika, 2004), 537–678.

15. Jan Kalicki and David Goldman, eds., *Energy Security: Toward a New Foreign Policy Strategy* (Washington and Baltimore: Woodrow Wilson Center Press and John Hopkins University Press, 2005); Michael Klare, *Blood and Oil: The Dangers and Consequences of America's Growing Petroleum Dependency* (London: Penguin Books, 2005).

16. Lev Zevin, "Natsional'nye Ekonomicheskiye Sistemy v Global'nykh Protsessakh," *Mirovaya ekonomika i mezhdunarodnye otnosheniya,* November 2003, 17–24.

17. Chaim Braun and Christopher F. Chyba, "Proliferation Rings: New Challenges to the Nuclear Nonproliferation Regime," *International Security,* Fall 2004, 5–49.

18. Ivan Maksimychev, "Rossiya kak Sostavnaya Chast' Obsheevropeiskogo Tsivilizatsionnogo Prostranstva," *Obshestvennye nauki i sovremennost',* November–December 1997, 85–96.

19. Aleksey Arbatov, *Bezopasnost': Rossiiskii Vybor* (Moscow: EPIcentr, 1999); *Razoruzheniye i bezopasnost', 1997–1998: Rossiya i Mezhdunarodnaya Sistema Kontrolya nad Vooruzhyeniyami* (Moscow: Nauka, 1997); Yevgeniy Primakov, *Mir Posle 11 Sentyabrya* (Moscow: Mysl, 2002).

20. Nikolay Kosolapov, "Rossiysko-Amerikanskiye Otnosheniya: v Chem Sut' Krizisa?" *Mirovaya ekonomika i mezhdunarodnye otnosheniya,* July 1996, 79–88.

21. Andrey Kokoshin and Aleksey Bogaturov, eds., *Mirovaya Politika: Teoriya, Metodologiya, Prikladnoy analiz* (Moscow: URSS-KomKniga, 2005); Aleksey Bogaturov, "Mezhdunarodnyy Poryadok v Nastupivshem Veke," *Mezhdunarodnye protsessy,* January–April 2003, 6–23; Nikolay Kosolapov, "Yavlenie Mezhdunarodnykh Otnosheniy: Sovremennoe Sostoyanie Ob'ekta Issledovaniya (Vvedeniye v Teoriyu)," *Mirovaya ekonomika i mezhdunarodnye otnosheniya,* May 1998, 98–108.

22. Tsygankov and Tsygankov, eds., *Rossiiskaya Nauka Mezhdunarodnykh Otnosheniy;* Dmitrii Furman, "Vneshnepoliticheskiye Orientiry Rossii," *Svobodnaya mysl',*

August 1995, 3–14; Yurii Fëdorov, "Kriticheskiy Vyzov Dlya Rossii," *Pro et Contra,* Fall 1999, 5–27; Andrey Volodin and Gleriy Shirokov, "Globalizatsiya: Istoki, Tendentsii, Perspektivy," *Polis,* September–October 1999, 83–93; Yevgenii Satanovskiy, "Mezhdunarodnyy Terrorizm," *Mezhdunarodnaya Zhizn',* November 2005, 19–20.

23. One of the exceptions is Eduard Solovyev, "Setevye Organizatsii Transnatsional'nogo Terrorizma," *Mezhdunarodnye Protsessy,* May–August 2004: 71–83.

24. Yuriy Mizun, *Islam i Rossiya* (Moscow: Veche, 2004); Dmitriy Trenin and Aleksey Malashenko, *Vremya Yuga: Rossiya v Chechnye," Chechnya v Rossii* (Moscow: Carnegie Endowment for International Peace, 2002).

25. See Vladimir Dyatlov and Sergey Ryazantsev, *Stabil'nost' i Konflikt v Rossiyskom Prigranich'ye: Etnopoliticheskie Protsessy v Sibiri i na Kavkazye* (Moscow: NOFMO, 2005).

26. "Kontseptsiya Natsional'noi Bezopasnosti Rossiiskoy Federatsii (v Redaksii Ukaza Prezidenta RF ot 10 yanvarya 2000 No. 24)," *Diplomaticheskiy vestnik,* February 2000, 3–13; *Voennaya Doktrina Rossiyskoy Federatsii,* http://www.iss.niiit.ru/doktrins/doktr02.htm; *Doktrina Informatsionnoy Bezopasnosti Rossiiskoy Federatsii,* http://www.businesspravo.ru/Docum/DocumShow_DocumID_15786.html.

27. See the interesting book by German experts, Stefana Kroysbergera, Sabine Grabovski, and Yutty Unzer, eds., *Vneshnyaya Politika Rossii: Ot El'tsina k Putinu* (Kyiv: Optima, 2002); Strobe Talbott, *Bill i Boris: Zapiski o Prezidentskoy Diplomatii* (Moscow: Izdatel'skiy dom Gorodets, 2003); Allen Linch, "Realizm Rossiiskoy Vneshney Politiki," *Pro et Contra,* Fall 2001, 136–40.

28. The first conflict we could observe was in November 1993, when the Foreign Intelligence Service of Russia, headed by Evgeniy M. Primakov, produced an analytical report on the expansion of NATO. The paper was published in the newspaper *Nezavisimaya gazeta* on Novenber 18, 1993. and caused a harsh reaction by the foreign minister of Russia, A. Kozyrev. A similar situation occurred in 1995. In May 1995, the Council for Foreign and Defense Policy of Russia, led by Sergei Karaganovym, prepared an analytical report on the reaction of Russia in connection with the expansion of NATO. This paper was published in *Nezavisimaya gazeta* on June 21, 1995. The document was supported by the Ministry of Defense but has caused resentment of the Ministry of Foreign Affairs.

29. *Strategiya Dlya Rossii: 10 let SVOP* (Moscow: Vagrius, 2002), 24–48; Roy Medvedev, *Vladimir Putin: Chetyre Goda v Kremle* (Moscow: Vremya, 2004); Vladimir Gel'man, "Shakhmatnye Partii Rossiiskoy Elity," *Pro et Contra,* Winter 1996, 22–31.

30. Nikolay Kosolapov, "Stanovleniye Sub'ekta Rossiiskoi Vneshney Politiki," *Pro et Contra,* Winter–Spring 2001, 7–30.

31. See Leokadiya Drobizheva, *Sotsial'nyye Problemy Mezhnatsional'nyh Otnosheniy v Postsovetskoy Rossii* (Moscow: Academia, 2003); Valeriy Tishkov, "Samoopredelenie Rossiiskoy Natsii," *Mezhdunarodnye protsessy* 8 (2005): 17–27.

32. Vladimir Putin, "Televizionnoe Obrashchenie k Grazhdanam Rossii," http://www.kremlin.ru/appears/2000/05/17/0000_type63374_28742.shtml; Vladimir Putin, "Vystuplenie na Vstreche s Predstavitelyami Soveta Federatsii," http://www.kremlin.ru/appears/2000/05/17/0000_type63378_59540.shtml; Vladimir Putin, "Vystuplenie na Rasshirennom Zasedanii Pravitel'stva s Uchastiem Glav Sub'ektov Rossiiskoy Federatsii," http://www.kremlin.ru/appears/2004/09/13/1514_type63374type63378type82634_76651.shtm.

33. *Konstitutsionno-Pravovoy Mekhanizm Vneshney Politiki* (Moscow: MGIMO/

326   *Alexey Fenenko*

ROSSPEN, 2004); Sergey Kortunov, "Prinyatie Vneshnepoliticheskikh Resheniy v Rossii i SShA," *Mezhdunarodnye Protsessy* 5 (2004): 59–70; Dmitriy Trenin, *The Landscape of Russian Foreign Policy Decision-Making* (Moscow: Carnegie Moscow Center, 2005).

34. *Etap za global'nym: Natsional'nye Interesy i Soznaniye Rossiiskoy Elity—Doklad Nezavisimoy Gruppy Ekspertov RNF* (Moscow: RNF, 1993).

35. Andrey Kozyrev, "Strategiya Partnerstva," *Mezhdunarodnaya Zhizn'*, May 1994, 5–15.

36. Andrey Kozyrev, *Preobrazhenie* (Moscow: Mezhdunarodnye Otnosheniya, 1995).

37. Sergey Karaganov, "Budushchee Evropy Stavit Voprosy," *Mezhdunarodnaya Zhizn'*, April 1991, 53.

38. Linch, "Realizm Rossiiskoy Vneshney Politiki."

39. See Vadim Tsymburskiy, "Rossiya-Evropa: Tryet'ya Osen Sistemy Tsivilizatsiy," *Polis*, March–April 1997, 70–71.

40. This problem is analyzed in Andrey Kokoshin, *Strategicheskoe Upravlenie: Teoriya, Istoricheskiy Opyt, Sravnitel'nyy Analiz, Zadachi Dlya Rossii* (Moscow: MGIMO MID Rossii; ROSSPEN, 2003).

41. Georgiy Mirskiy, "Vozvrat v Srednevekov'e?" *Rossiya v Global'noy Politike*, September–October 2006, 8–20; Sergey Luzyanin, *Vostochnaya Politika Vladimira Putina: Vozvrashchenie Rossii na "Bol'shoy Vostok" (2004–2008)* (Moscow: Izdatel'stvo Vostok-Zapad, 2007), 188–210.

42. According to "Kontseptsiya natsional'noy bezopasnosti" (*Rossiiskaya gazeta*, December 26, 1997), "Russian military policy must be based on the principle of realistic deterrence and use of all military power (including nuclear weapons) in response to foreign aggression." For more about this issue, see Aleksey Podberzkin, ed., *Sovremennaya Politicheskaya Istoriya Rossii,* vol. I (Moscow: Fond Dukhovnoe Nasledie, 1999).

43. Vladimir Belous, "Sredstvo Politicheskogo i Voennogo Sderzhivaniya," *Nezavisimoe Voennoe Obozrenie,* September 26, 1996; Nikolay Sokov, "Takticheskoe Yadernoe Oruzhie: Novye Geopoliticheskie Real'nosti ili Starye Oshibki?" *Yadernyi Kontrol',* February 1997, 12–16; *Nestrategicheskoe Yadernoe Oruzhie: Problemy Kontrolya i Sokrashcheniya* (Moscow: Tsentr po Izucheniyu Problem Razoruzheniya, Energetiki i Ekologii Moskovskiy Fiziko-Tekhnicheskiy Institut, 2004), http://www.armscontrol.ru/pubs/NSNW_print_v2d.pdf.

44. See Andrey Kokoshin, Vasiliy Veselov, and Aleksey Liss, *Sderzhivaniye vo Vtorom Yadernom Veke* (Moscow: Institut Problem Mezhdunarodnoy Bezopasnosti RAN, 2001).

45. Aleksey Arbatov and Vladimir Dvorkin, eds., *Yadernoe Sderzhivanie i Nerasprostranenie* (Moscow: Moskovskiy Tsentr Karnegi, 2005), 41, 45; Igor Bocharov, "Yadernaya Politika Administratsii Dzh. Busha," *SShA i Kanada,* October 2003, 16–30.

46. Nikolay Efimov, *Politiko-Voennye Aspekty Natsional'noy Bezopasnosti Rossii* (Moscow: KomKniga-URSS, 2006); Mezhdu Proshlym i Budushchim: Rossiya v Transatlanticheskom Kontekste (Moscow, 2001), 127–276.

47. Aleksey Arabatov, *Posledstviya voiny v Irake,* http://www.ln.mid.ru/brp_4.nsf/2fee282eb6df40e643256999005e6e8c/cc11c224f9cfb977c32570e800312645?OpenDocument.

48. See Aleksey Arbatov and Petr Romashkinn, "Kakie Voyny Rossii po Karmanu," *Nezavisimoye voennoye obozreniye,* April 27, 2001, http://nvo.ng.ru/concepts/2001-04-27/3_vojna.html.

49. Many analysts have argued that these specific problems are related to broader problems of state strength and legitimacy. See Aleksandr Bat'kovskiy and Yevgeniy Hrustalev, "Sistemnye Parametry Perspektivnogo Oblika Vooruzhennykh Sil Rossii," *Mirovaya Ekonomika i Mezhdunarodnyye Otnosheniya,* June 2005, 45–53.

50. Michael Margelov, "Rossiya i SshA: K Voprosu o Prioritete Otnosheny," *Mezhdunarodnaya Zhizn'* 12 (2005): 41–53. See also Intyerv'yu Ministra Inostrannyh Del Rossii S. V. Lavrova "Pervomu Kanalu" Rossiiskogo Televideniya Po Tematike Predsedatel'stva Rossii v "Gruppe vos'mi," Moscow, December 30, 2005, available at http://www.ln.mid.ru/.

51. Sergey Rogov, "Rossiya i SShA: Partnërstvo ili Novoye Otchuzhdeniye," *Mezhdunarodnaya Zhizn'* 7 (1995): 5–14.

52. Antonen Debidur, *Diplomaticheskaya Istoriya Evropy 1814–1878, Vol. II* (Rostov-na-Donu: Fenks, 1994), 489–99.

53. Konctantin Kosachev, "Rossiya Mezhdu Evropeyskim Vyborom i Aziatskim Rostom," *Mezhdunarodnaya zhizn* 12 (2005): 54–67.

54. See: Aleksey Bogaturov, "The Sources of American Conduct," *Russia in Global Affairs* 1 (2005), http://eng.globalaffairs.ru/numbers/10/821.html.

55. A good example of this was Putin's visit to Yakutiya in January 2006. See *Stenograficheskiy Otchet o Soveshchanii po Voprosam Social'no-ekonomicheskogo Razvitiya Respubliki Saha (Yakutiya),* http://www.kremlin.ru/appears/2006/01/06/1419_type63378type63381_100061.shtml.

56. See Aleksey Arbatov, "Romantizm vryemyen holodnoy voiny: Yadernoye razoruzheniye stanovitsya vse menee produktivnym," *Nezavisimoye voyennoe obozreniye* 6 (2004): 4.

57. For a discussion of these problems, see Aleksey Arbatov and Gennadiy Chufrin, eds., *Yadernoe Protivostoyanie v Yuzhnoy Azii* (Moscow: Carnegie Endowment for International Peace, 2005); Aleksey Arbatov and Vitaliy Naumkin, eds., *Ugrozy Rezhimu Nerasprostraneniya Yadernogo Oruzhiya na Blizhnem i Srednem Vostoke* (Moscow: Carnegie Endowment for International Peace, 2005); and Aleksey Arbatov and Vasiliy Mikheev, *Yadernoe Rasprostranenie v Severo-Vostochnoy Azii* (Moscow: Carnegie Endowment for International Peace, 2005).

58. I analyzed this issue in Alexey Fenenko, "Strategiya 'Prinuditel'nogo Razoruzheniya' i Mezhdunarodnyy Biznes," *Mezhdunarodnye protsessy,* September–December 2005: 45–60.

59. Vladimir Ivanov and Mikhail Tolpegin, "Myagkiy Yadernyy Control," *Nezavisimaya gazeta,* March 2, 2005, http://www.ng.ru/events/2005-03-02/1_control.html; Matthew Bunn and Antony Wier, *Securing the Bomb: The New Global Imperatives,* 2005, http://www.nti.org/e_research/report_cnwmupdate2005.pdf.

60. Jemal Orkhan and Mikhail Yakovlev, "Dogovor-prizrak," http://www.versiasovsek.ru/material.php?3071; Strobe Talbott, "*Sovyetnik po Rossii: Vospominaniya o Prezidentskoy Diplomatii,*" http://www.inosmi.ru/print/149348.html.

61. See U.S. Department of State, "The G8 Global Partnership against the Spread of Weapons and Materials of Mass Destruction: Statement by the Group of Eight Leaders," June 27, 2002, http://www.state.gov/e/eb/rls/othr/11514.htm; White House, "Fact Sheet: Proliferation Security Initiative Statement of Interdiction Principles," http://www.whitehouse.gov/news/releases/2003/09/20030904-11.html; and White House, "President Announces New Measures to Counter the Threat of WMD," http://www.whitehouse.gov/news/releases/2004/02/print/20040211-4.html. For discussions about these

328   *Alexey Fenenko*

initiatives in Russia, see Aleksandr Kalyadin, "IBOR: Stanet li Diplomatiya Prinuzh-deniya Sostavnoy Chast'yu Strategii Ukrepleniya Gloabl'nogo Rezhima Nerasprostra-neniya OMU?"; and *Yezhegodnik SIPRI 2004. Vooruzheniya, Razoruzheniya i Bezopas-nost'* (Moscow: Nauka, 2005), 880–93.

62. "Alma-Atinskaya deklaratsiya," Alma-Ata, Kazakhstan, December 21, 1991, in *Sistemnaya istoriya mezhdunarodnyh otnoshenii v chetyreh tomah. 1918–2003*, vol. 4 (Moscow: NOFMO, 2004), 396–97; *Memorandum o podderzhanii mira i stabil'nosti v Sodruzhestve Nezavisimyh Gosudarstv,* Alma-Ata, Kazakhstan, February 10, 1995, http://www.smix.biz/abro.php?id=7802.

63. Vladimir Putin, "Zayavlenie Prezidenta Rossii," http://www.kremlin.ru/appears/2002/09/11/2051_type63374_29426.shtml.

64. "Vystuplenie Sergeya Ivanova na Soveshchanii v Ministerstve Oborony RF," http://old.old.mil.ru/index.php?menu_id=884.

65. Yevgenii Belov and Oleg Putintsev, "SNG v Protivodeistvii Ugrozam Bezopas-nosti i Stabil'nosti," *Mezhdunarodnaya Zhizn'* 11–12 (November–December 2004): 91–105.

66. Dmitry Trenin, "Rossiya i Konets Evrazii," *Pro et Contra,* July–August 2005, 6–17: Andrey Ryabov, "Moskva prinimaet vyzov Tsvetnykh Revolyutsiy," *Pro et Contra,* July–August 2005, 19–27; Aleksey Miller, "Mnogoye Isporchyeno, No Ne Vse Potyeryano," *Pro et Contra,* July–August 2005, 21–28.

67. On the role of the mass media in Russian foreign policy, see Mikhail Kamynina, "Iz Moskvy ni Dnya Bez Strochki," *Mezhdunarodnaya zhizn'* 11 (November 2005), http://www.mid.ru/brp_4.nsf/26a308f48086479ec3256ee70033e346/875c6676bdaaf2 72c32570bd0027f6c1?OpenDocument. The official document addressing this topic, "Kontseptsiya informatsionnoy bezopasnosti Rossiskoy Federatsii," was adopted in the autumn of 2000.

68. A. Dmitriyevskii and S. Serebryakov, "Gazovaya OPEK: Fantaziya ili real'nost'?" *Mirovaya Energetika* 11 (2005), http://www.worldenergy.ru/mode.1349-id.17928-type.html.

69. Aleksey Bogaturov, "Rossiiskiy Dal'niy Vostok v Novyh Geoprostranstvyen-nykh Izmereniyakh Vostochnoy Evrazii," *Mirovaya Ekonomika i Mezhdunarodnye Ot-nosheniya* 10 (October 2004): 90–98; *Strategiya Dlya Rossii,* 609–28.

70. See Vladimir Milov, "Mozhet li Rossiya Stat' Neftyanym Rayem?" *Pro et Contra,* July–August 2006, 6–15.

71. Anatoliy Torkunov, *Evolyutsiya Rossiiskoy Vneshney Politiki* http://www.best referat.ru/referat-71408.html; Sergey Kortunov, "Natsional'naya Identichnost' Rossii: Vneshnepoliticheskoye Izmereniye," *Mezhdunarodnaya Zhizn'* 6 (June 2003): 38–52; "Korona Ushedshei Imperii: Postimperskaya Transformatsiya," *Rossiya v Global'noy Politike* 4 (November–December 2005): 10–89.

13

Conclusion: Links between Globalization, Security, and Identity in Russia

Douglas W. Blum

Globalization, in Ulf Hedetoft's words, "makes [nation-states] into "reactors to transnational processes more than the shapers of those processes, and in the same vein make nation-states and national/cultural identities into defensive, dependent bastions of communication, organization and 'domesticity.'"[1] Of course, the extent to which this is true varies depending on state capacity; the nations of the West, and especially the United States, are able to influence and/or manage globalization to their own benefit. Russia is far less able to do so. In consequence, our analysis of Russian politics reveals profound tensions emerging in the state's attempt to control borders and prevent disintegration, while at the same time seeking to advance economic integration and profitable forms of cross-border exchange.

Likewise, it reveals mounting social strains, leading to widespread anxiety and defensiveness. This is especially evident in response to migration, the still-unsettled conflict in Chechnya, and the associated threat from radical Islam. But it is also increasingly the case in foreign policy, where a number of external threats have become manifest in Russian discourse, including the spread of democratic revolutions and the perceived expansion of American influence. Together, these tensions give rise to a an often strident nationalist discourse, which Hedetoft suggests may function as a compensatory response, designed to firm up the state's flagging position.

What is the domestic social context within which these pressures are expressed, and to what extent is this context itself shaped by globalization? At least one way of thinking about this relationship (as argued by Korotayev and Khaltourina as well as Bradshaw) has to do with how globalization affects demographic change and public health. Although the evolution of this predicament is complex, part of what Andrey Korotayev and Darya Khaltourina describe in chapter 2 does appear to be related to globalization and not simply to the Soviet collapse. This includes pressures for a hollowing out of the paternalistic regime, leading to marked social stratification and the loss of welfare state guarantees. In addition, on a more positive note, the globalizing trend favors a consumption shift toward fewer, lighter alcoholic drinks. And yet, in addition to Russia's peculiar form of alcoholism, the compounding factors to which Korotayev and Khaltourina point, especially intravenous drug use and unprotected sex, suggest that the inimical influences of globalization are likely to win out for the foreseeable future. As others have warned, the concatenation of a looming AIDS epidemic, pollution, and the decline of the state health infrastructure all portend still more severe problems to come for Russian demography.[2] Such trends cannot but have an impact on national identity, especially in light of the dominant Russian self-conception as a regional if not global power.

Obviously, financial globalization—or more specifically, the extent of Russia's integration into international capital markets—also has immense implications for Russian development. In his examination of foreign direct investment (FDI) in chapter 3, Michael Bradshaw finds that its sectoral allocation reveals Russia's failure to become integrated into global production chains. Instead, it reflects investors' interest in gaining access to domestic markets and natural resources. Moreover, he argues that FDI has a potentially major influence on political development, insofar as it is highly concentrated in a small number of regions. Moscow city and oblast continue to have a dominant share (albeit declining from a previously very high level). Aside from Moscow, the distribution of FDI is determined by several characteristics: gateway geographic position, mineral wealth, market size, infrastructure development, policy framework, and status as a regional industrial-financial center. Bradshaw suggests that in these ways, FDI has a significant influence on the overall pattern of wealth distribution and has contributed to the—widening—gap between the richest and poorest regions.

Globalization also has potentially jolting effects on center-periphery relations by promoting changes in regional identity, which in turn is partly a function of a given region's ability to plug into various international flows. This reflects a conscious policy decision: Vladimir Putin's reforms are designed not only to recentralize but also to open the economy to globalization in the form of investment, technology, and information. It should be stressed that this represents a calculated gamble: that the process can be managed to achieve desirable outcomes while avoiding political pitfalls. To some extent, too, the decision to engage rather than try to block globalization appears to be a forced choice. From this perspective, strengthening the power of vertical ties provides a solid institutional foundation for engaging the global economy, thereby promoting modernization while hedging against the dangers of excessive penetration by transnational corporations, overexuberant local borrowing, or political disintegration.[3] The bid, in other words, is to allow globalization to proceed without sacrificing political control in the bargain.

The consequences of pursuing this path are thus highly complex, and they often cut against the grain of hypercentralization. After all, attaining the flexibility necessary to plug into global supply chains inevitably leads to more autonomous forms of local economic activity, which in turn calls for increasingly diffuse arenas of innovation, social and political interfacing, and transnational linkages. Though it is impossible to say just how widespread such attitudes are within the elite, there is clearly some recognition that the prospects for avoiding decline and disintegration hinge on generating sustainable economic development, and that this can only be achieved through technologically driven growth—which requires ceding a higher degree of delegation and decentralization.[4]

Closely related to this is an awareness of the importance of "democracy," in the sense of allowing local actors the initiative to manage taxes and budgetary allocations in line with their economic interests, issues that are obviously sensitive to involvement in international trade and investment. Indeed, the penetration of big business—domestic as well as foreign—into the regions has already resulted in capital movements and other forms of cross-border activity that the center cannot effectively monitor.[5] The result is a persistent anxiety about the possibility that the formation of horizontal ties, both within and beyond Russian borders, might render vertical ties obsolete and ineffectual.[6] In spite of such anxieties, however, this is precisely the path that Putin wishes to tread.

The outcome of this experiment will depend, at least partly, on regional leaders' political skill and ability to wield institutional levers vis-à-vis Putin, the heads of the federal districts, and the central elite. Another question concerns their willingness to take any assertive steps to begin with. Chechnya doubtless looms as a cautionary tale for many would-be separatists, and the new threat of radical Islam in southern, potentially restive areas may also help to dampen regional assertiveness, as leaders are increasingly inclined to look to the center for security.[7] This balance between securitized and desecuritized narratives within Russia today, reflecting the resonance of threat imagery as well as the perceived receptivity of outside actors to Russian integration, will go a long way toward determining whether regional identities become more accommodating or resistant to the center.[8]

Much also depends on the political acumen and negotiating ability of authorities at the central and federal levels. Under Boris Yeltsin, a given region's identity politics, coupled with its ability to contribute to the Federation economically, determined the center's willingness to make concessions. At the same time, there was a great deal of reluctance to allow high levels of cross-national, institutionalized cooperation, on the grounds that this might encourage separatism in the Far East and in regions bordering Europe. Though certain regions, such as Novgorod, did extensively pursue independent foreign economic ties, this was more a reflection of central weakness than national policy. By the late 1990s, however, the central authorities had become more aware of the potential benefits involved in promoting integration, and they even crafted the notion of "pilot regions" (e.g., Kaliningrad and Karel'ya) that were on the forefront of globalization. Albeit with caution, this general approach has continued under Putin. For example, the center has been willing to allow a substantial degree of autonomy for subnational bodies in the conduct of international economic affairs, including regional associations such as the Siberian Accord. Leonid Drachevskiy, presidential envoy to the Siberian Federal District from 2000 to 2004, diplomatically sought to balance the interests of the center with those of the region. On the one hand, he left open the possibility of greater latitude for the region in pursuing economic activities abroad; on the other hand, he worked to replace the independent Siberian Accord with the Federal District Council.[9]

Moreover, one should not discount Putin's resourcefulness—or that of his successors. In many respects, he has been successful in preventing further separatism, both by consolidating the center through institutional reforms and by propounding an embattled, assertive Russian national idea. Though it has not been frequently exercised, the president's power to remove regional leaders who lose his confidence may also ensure a high degree of compliance. And, as a quid pro quo, Putin has allowed essentially loyal authoritarian leaders to stay in power, especially in potentially restive ethnic republics. As Stoliarov argues, the emphasis on conformity and stability under the present clientelist system serves the interests of the established elite.[10] The result may prove to be a surprisingly stable marriage of power and self-interest.

Yet unmistakable pressures have accumulated within the Federation. Were they to continue to mount, the results might be profoundly destabilizing. For this very reason, in fact, authorities in most ethnic regions of the country have tried to manage the identity formation process, so as to limit the potentially centrifugal effects of ethnic cultural revivalism.[11] Thus, as Vodichev and Lamin argue, a key factor in the future evolution of regional identities is the nature of policy decisions in Moscow, and the affect these have on Siberia's place in center-periphery relations. If development and international integration continue to focus overwhelmingly on Moscow, to the virtual exclusion of the regions, then Siberian identification may continue to evolve in such a way that Moscow becomes the dominant Other, with potentially dangerous consequences for Russian national cohesion. Another possible pitfall, to which Bradshaw points, is the new plans for domestic investment, which call for focusing on a small number of "propulsive regions." As Bradshaw observes, these "will not be resource regions," which have been net donors and which have thus contributed to the development of debtor regions. Instead, it appears that these and other donor regions will provide the revenue for these new growth regions. Even if successful, however, this policy may produce destabilizing results. In Bradshaw's words, "If the propulsive regions grow and the resource regions continue to thrive, there is a real danger that the rest of the regions will be left behind and that this will create real social tensions, particularly if that poverty maps onto Russia's potentially explosive ethnic map." This is all the more true if current demographic trends continue, including immigration, ethnic "unmixing," and higher growth rates in largely non-Russian (especially Muslim) ethnic regions.[12]

It is hard to imagine how far such destabilizing trends might proceed. Some have argued that the prospects of outright Russian disintegration remain small for the foreseeable future: There are currently no pivotal regions able to coordinate a united campaign; nor is there much overt separatism on ethnic grounds.[13] And of course, the center's more active efforts to limit regional assertiveness—another response to the colored revolutions—indicate that regional identities may be harder to consolidate.[14] Nevertheless, several areas (Tatarstan, Bashkortostan, Sakha, the North Caucasus, and Siberia) have systematically promoted ethnic identity through institution-alized means (language and history teaching, titular representation, other preferences). Despite the fact that such strategies have proven hard to im-plement successfully, they do help create identity markers that political leaders might use as a basis for resisting the center's authority, particularly where oppositional patterns of identity formation coincide with resource wealth.[15]

For the time being, the situation appears to be one of uneasy equilibrium. Yet this might be unsettled by the deepening of globalization, especially through the emergence of new ideas about the realm of the possible. As Herrera argues, intersubjective ideas delimit the boundaries of regional economies, within given institutional frameworks.[16] To this, one might add that globalization also contributes to the formation of a regional "imagi-nary," that is, a set of meanings and values associated with the region. This potentially includes a new awareness of the prospects for growth through international integration; as Yevgeniy Vodichev and Vladimir Lamin sug-gest in chapter 4, this might contribute to feelings of backwardness and ex-ploitation. Another development related to globalization is increasing social stratification, due to the adoption of market principles in the context of un-even capital flows. This tendency might be expected to become more pro-nounced over time, as various groups in society are differently positioned to take advantage of globalization's opportunities, by virtue of age, education, and training.[17] Nor is this inconsequential from a national identity stand-point, because rapidly widening gaps in social status might well contribute to an erosion of coidentification. Already, according to a study by Vladimir Zvonosky, social-status-based divisions are stronger than a sense of shared national identity in Russia as a whole.[18] In any case, by accentuating the dis-tinctions between "winners and losers," globalization is likely to place ad-ditional strains on Russia's still inchoate national identity. This tendency is also related to center-periphery problems, because, as Bradshaw points out, the distinction between winners and losers is applicable on the regional level as well. If the disparity between developed and underdeveloped regions con-tinues to grow, the combination of ethnic identities, globalization flows, and relative poverty may produce widely destabilizing results.

Of course, invoking a region's place in the outside world, or within Russ-ian foreign policy, may be done for reasons quite unrelated to separatism. In regional identity discourse, one finds cases of the instrumental use of identity tropes, which may resonate with geopolitical thinking or with other strands of the Russian identity discourse. For example, as Humphrey suggests, the idea of Eurasianism may be manipulated by elites in Buryatiya, Tuva, Kalmykiya, Sakha, and Altay as a way to elevate the importance of these republics within Russia, inasmuch as they supply the vital Asian component of this narrative. At the same time, by implication, the bridge metaphor also connects these republics to Europe. Such images carry important identity and legitimacy implications, perhaps designed to increase regional visibility as part of a bid for greater access to resources and outside connections.[19] Not surprisingly, similar ideas are popular among relatively marginal groups, including Turkic and Muslim elites.[20] And the same calculations appear applicable to Vodichev and Lamin's account of Siberian identity claims, which have been caught up with a bid to adopt institutional reforms in order to tap into market opportunities and foreign investment.[21] In these ways, efforts to mobilize a pan-Siberian, territorial identity often resemble bargaining moves in an extended negotiation with the center.

More likely than outright secessionism, then, we might anticipate the unfolding of a delicate game, in which center and periphery attempt to use each other to gain the benefits of integration into the outside world, while limiting the political and economic risks of doing so. And, for the foreseeable future, this process is likely to be marked by significant tension between the center and certain regions, including those that imagine their economies in ways influenced by globalization yet are circumscribed in their ability to engage with this process.

In sum, Putin's approach contains internal tensions, and as currently formulated it remains unclear whether his project can succeed in achieving the coveted blend of control and modernization. As Pravda observes, "It is not simply a matter of Russia competing effectively on world markets. In order to become an integral part of that community, Russia needs to become a 'competition state,' and that requires the kind of pluralist democracy that scarcely fits in with Putin's domestic political agenda."[22] Similar contradictions can be detected in the views of the middling elite, in the form of simultaneous demands for democracy and strong leadership, and for a strong center as well as regional autonomy.[23] These tensions are encapsulated in the notion of "managed democracy," understood as an attempt to achieve control and modernization by muzzling the press, curtailing independent civic organizations, eliminating open electoral politics in favor of appointment or constrained competition, and replacing formal political institutions with informal institutions answerable to the president.[24] In other words, the contradictions of managed democracy do not simply emanate from the center but also express the paradoxical wishes of a large segment of Russian society.

Of course, it would be mistaken to attribute all developments in center-periphery politics to globalization. To some extent, regional and ethnic identity fragmentation is simply an inevitable result of the fall of the USSR, reflecting local responses to the collapse of any coherent organizing structure and unifying idea. It also reflects the inability of the Putin regime (and the Yeltsin regime before it) to articulate a compelling vision of Russian civic identity, despite its repeated efforts to do so. Yet, in keeping with the foregoing comments, there is reason to suspect that the tendency toward fragmentation may be intensified by globalization.

In this regard, the key issue is that globalization requires—and in return, also tremendously augments—financial and institutional integration into the global economy. This in turn carries certain lessons for Russian education, including its ability to foster the growth of a knowledge-based society. As Gennady Konstantinov and Sergey Filonovich point out in chapter 5, there continues to be a great deal of contestation over such matters in Russian educational policymaking. Nevertheless, leading officials (including Putin) have now clearly endorsed further globalization in this area, as symbolized and accelerated by Russia's involvement in the Bologna Process. It follows from Konstantinov and Filonovich's analysis that the trajectory of educational reform is in fact indistinguishable from still more fundamental debates over national identity. As they note, opponents of the Bologna Process —and of the associated changes in higher education—fear not only a "brain drain" but also Russia's cultural and institutional subordination to the West. In addition, one sense that the underlying struggle concerns whether, or how much, to embrace the tendency for full individual autonomy in the area of critical, open-ended problem solving—something that threatens a loss of central control over knowledge production and economic organization. Obviously, such developments are crucial for Russia's prospects of achieving modernization and/or potentially exercising its power—in either hard or soft form. Despite its attractions, however, the prospect of Russian integration into transnational networks and processes has potentially worrisome implications for collective identity.

Ambivalence concerning these issues is evident in Russia's position on plugging into international flows of technology and investment. Indeed, recent trends cast some doubt on Russia's willingness to do so in the foreseeable future. The country remains handicapped in pursuing technologically intensive development, because the lion's share of innovation in its economy continues to be in traditional areas such as fuels, chemicals, and machinery. Furthermore, its domestic investment for research and development is far below that of the United States, Japan, or the European Union.[25] Yet this is as much due to conscious policy choices as to a lack of infrastructure and capital.

A case in point is the Russian government's effort to appropriate the benefits of the Internet for the purposes of economic development, as reflected in the e-Russia program. As pursued under Putin, this program has been implemented along with the Information Security Doctrine, which was signed into law in September 2000. The doctrine connects media policy in general, and Internet policy in particular, to the core "national security" concerns of the state; this involves asserting government control as well as ensuring that the state has a direct role in system engineering and sponsoring pro-Kremlin Web sites.[26] The upshot is a strategy of promoting increased Internet use while also limiting and harnessing it for the state's purposes— very much in keeping with the theme of managed democracy. And of course, this policy is entirely consistent with the identity orientation (discussed below) of Russia as embattled civilizational outpost, beleaguered by radical Islam and hostile forces within the West. Similarly, numerous policy obstacles hamper the development of information technology, including inadequate funding, high tax levels, archaic legislation, and poor enforcement of what legislation does exist.[27]

Another case in point is the defense industry. On the one hand, a number of domestic analysts have argued that the military-industrial complex is capable of playing a key role in enhancing Russian technological proficiency while taking advantage of human capital, which continues to be one of Russia's real strengths.[28] However, as Alla Kassianova discusses in chapter 6, in comparison with Western experience there has been relatively little transnational integration of the Russian military-industrial complex to date. Kassianova's work thus complements Bradshaw's in suggesting why Russia has failed to become more integrated into global production chains. She argues that, to some extent, reluctance to integrate must be understood at the level of the firm, including the outlooks and incentives of individual plant managers—many of whom are wary of immersion in the international economy. And yet, as she also argues, this outcome is also deeply rooted in the institutional legacies of the Soviet past. This is evident in the general absence of transparency and accountability, as well as the reassertion of statist approaches to ownership and economic activity. She notes that the state under Putin has systematically moved to consolidate control over nominally private defense firms and has tried to expand domestic investment in this sector to compensate for lagging foreign investment. And this is happening at precisely the same moment that Western firms (especially within the EU) are becoming increasingly open to outside investment and enmeshed in global production and supply chains.

In this connection, it is worth noting that Russia's posture with regard to military-industrial complex globalization mirrors its overall posture with regard to global flows of trade and capital.[29] Simply put, there continues to be a low overall level of interfirm alliances in most sectors of the Russian economy. Notwithstanding the legitimate concerns that have been raised about the validity of such barometers, the fact that Russia fell eight places (to number fifty-two) in the latest Kearney Report remains troubling in this regard.[30] This fall reflects a drop in FDI on the heels of the Yukos fiasco, a declining share of trade in gross domestic product (concentrated, moreover, in traditional sectors), and an underlying failure to undertake structural reforms. Such trends spur anxiety about Russia's ability to maintain its political influence in the Commonwealth of Independent States (CIS).[31] And as many analysts have noted, despite Russia's longstanding interest in joining the World Trade Organization (WTO) (and its likely accession by the end of 2007), actually taking this step is fraught with ambivalence, because the result is likely to be jolting for the domestic industrial and service sectors.[32] All of this, in turn, implicates the nature of the national identity orientations that are dominant in Russian policymaking circles, as well as related attitudes toward national security and traditional hard power in an age of globalization. For some, joining the WTO means capitulating to the hegemonic American/neoliberal world order, as a result of which Russia's autonomy and security will be gravely compromised.[33]

Another way of gauging the significance of globalization is by thinking through its influence on state-society relations, both in the realm of civil society and center-periphery politics. Obviously, in the new global context, civil society has an increasingly important transnational dimension. This has become an acutely problematic issue in Russian politics, amid reports that as many as 81 percent of "noncommercial groups" received a portion of their funding from foreign sources.[34] As James Richter discusses in chapter 7, anxieties related to this development have been exacerbated by the "colored revolutions," which are widely perceived to have been supported, if not actually orchestrated, by Western states acting through the agency of international governmental and nongovernmental organizations (NGOs). For these reasons, globalization is often viewed as having the potential to create a crisis of authority, insofar as the central state's role in governance becomes diminished relative to the increasing involvement of transnational social actors. In response to these fears, in January 2006 Putin signed into law a bill placing sharp restrictions on outside aid to domestic NGOs. As of this writing, the entire NGO movement has been thrown badly on the defensive and appears vulnerable to counterpressures from above and below.

From the perspective of civil society development, then, globalization—as a (strategically guided) flow of ideas about democracy and social organization—has led to unforeseen outcomes. These include self-serving adaptations by civic activists, as well as contestation by state institutions and society at large. The ensuing reaction against foreign-backed NGOs has contributed to the consolidation of Putin's managed democracy, which reflects a particular view of the state as above society. This view, in turn, translates into efforts to both mobilize and control NGOs, construed as organic expressions of the popular will to be embodied in forms compatible with the state.

Identity Orientations

As this discussion of economic development pressures demonstrates, globalization brings with it a number of dilemmas, including dominant institutions and ideas as well as more turbulent, unstructured flows, all of which impose difficult adjustments on Russia. How these dilemmas are resolved, or at least addressed, has a great deal to do with discourses of identity and related constructions of security. This is not to suggest that cultural or identity factors operate in isolation from practical concerns; on the contrary, identities constitute modes of interpreting and responding to external developments and concrete problems. It is therefore important to understand the basic contours of these identities, including their connections to globalization and security.

As elsewhere around the world, the overall tendency in Russian identity formation is what we may call hybridization, consisting of a combined effort to absorb certain hegemonic practices, while also rejecting their "excessive" or offensive cultural concomitants, and simultaneously asserting a distinct, supposedly indigenous identity narrative. This dynamic is driven by a perceived need to engage globalization with innovative thinking, designed to embrace rationalist models—including market institutions and individualism—while at the same time retaining something quintessentially

Russian in philosophical and ideological terms. The goal is to achieve a unique synthesis of entrepreneurial dynamism and creativity.[35] Yet in these ways the post-Soviet quest for a unifying ideological or identity discourse continues to be deeply problematic. The very demand for such a unifying idea reveals a desire to avoid complete assimilation. At the same time, support for any given identity orientation is constrained by the perceived requirements of modernity and is conditioned by pressures to conform to global institutional practice. Not surprisingly, then, the practice of hybridization often includes a frank acknowledgement of these tensions, as Russian society attempts to reconcile seemingly opposite tendencies.

In addition to drawing on established (domestic) cultural tropes and hegemonic ideas, to a large extent Russian identity formation is also predicated on constructions of the Other in international politics. Repeatedly, such constructions draw on selective readings of history to locate the sources of Russian identity, as defined with reference to Europe and various forces to the east and the south. Efforts to situate the national self in relation to Others have been marked historically by a particular pattern, consisting of pretensions to Europeanness, followed by European snubs, and ultimately by Russia's wounded pride and rejection of Europe.[36] As a result, the idea of a fundamental cleavage between native and Western cultural trajectories has deep resonance in current political discourse. Transposed into the current debate over modernization versus traditionalism, this increasingly takes the form of a split between supporters of decentralized entrepreneurship, on the one hand, and supporters of state intervention and Russia's "unique path" of development, on the other.[37] Obviously, such divergent approaches have important implications for international cooperation as well as domestic governance. Though liberals have succeeded in shaping policy for brief periods, in general—and still today under Putin—the recurrent tendency has been to draw quite different historical lessons from "globalization." Indeed, as Wallander convincingly argues, the typical pattern of Russian policy has been one of keeping globalism at arms length, seeking to benefit through selective engagement while avoiding challenges that might force fundamental changes in key political and economic institutions.[38]

Responding to the pressures of absorption, many Russian commentators have decried the eruption of ideological "chaos" since the Soviet collapse, seeing a cultural vacuum filled by all manner of charlatanism and Western-inspired, harmful delusions. For some, Russian Orthodoxy becomes the default substitute for ideology, as a reaction to the degrading and atomizing effects of Western culture. For many, however, this too is inadequate, inasmuch as it offers no solution to modern social and economic needs.[39] The result is a welter of cross-cutting, often internally ambivalent narratives of Russian identity, ranging from the European and self-confident to the exceptionalist and embattled.

In chapter 9, Erik Noreen emphasizes the importance of the European variant in Russian discourse and policy. As he points out, Russian policymakers have frequently staked a claim to European identity on the basis of cultural commonality, in addition to geographical proximity. Though a far cry from the expression of such "liberal" ideas in the period 1991–93, the notion that Russia shares a common identity with Europe is still often encountered, including in Putin's own rhetoric:

> First of all, Russia was, is, and of course will be, a great European nation. The ideals of freedom, human rights, justice, and democracy, which have been suffered for and achieved by European culture over the course of many centuries, are a defining value orientation for our society. For three centuries, we, together with other European peoples, arm in arm, have gone through the reforms of the Enlightenment, the difficulties of establishing parliamentarianism, municipal and judicial power, and the formation of similar legal systems. Step by step we have moved together towards recognizing and broadening human rights, equal and full voting rights, understanding the necessity of caring for the needy and weak, emancipation of women, and other social gains.[40]

For those relative few willing to consistently articulate a European identity, the idea of far-reaching integration with the West—even if it might be a slow and difficult process—is considered to be "natural" in allowing the enactment of Russia's ostensibly intrinsic character.[41] Such a policy is also considered to be possible because of the absence of external threats. In reality, of course, the prospects of Russia's acceptance into the EU appear increasingly remote. Nevertheless, the identity politics associated with the idea—including its implications for regional security as well as for domestic institutional development—are perhaps as important as the eventuality. In this connection, the key point is that arguments about the supposed need for integration with the EU are only convincing insofar as a European identity is imaginable for Russia.[42] As Rick Fawn argues in chapter 10, this link between identity and institutional affiliation is obvious in debates about the wisdom of membership in the Council of Europe (CoE), but the point holds more broadly as well. Those who regard ties with the West as being essential for Russia's long-term political and security interests also tend to imagine Russia as "the largest European country" with respect to "civilizational and cultural relations."[43]

From this standpoint, the "colored revolutions" are seen as the culmination of nationalist sentiment in the countries concerned, perhaps coupled with globalization's diffuse effects on political orientation and identity. Rather than pointing to outside machinations, such analysts tend to attribute problems in the CIS primarily to indigenous factors and/or to global forces that are not easily controlled and manipulated by outside powers. Obviously, such statements reveal a distinctive set of normative values and self-identity traits. Though they encourage the reader to draw some hard conclusions about the need for Russian political reform, they do not support a shift in orientation away from the West or away from engaging globalization in the form of neoliberal institutionalism.

The prominence of this European (or Western) identity discourse has subsided greatly in recent years, not least owing to the difficulties in gaining membership, or full acceptance, within the institutions constituting European economic and political space. Indeed, much of the tension evident in the Russian stance on cooperation in security matters stems from indignation over being sidelined during the expansions of NATO and the EU. One key source of irritation has been the 2002 EU visa regime regarding the status of the Kaliningrad enclave.[44] This arrangement allows Russian citizens to travel between the enclave and Russia proper only with a special pass, and it is intended to limit unregulated migration as well as illicit flows of security-sensitive items. Other sources of resentment in the past have included being denied quick entry into the WTO (and being required to raise domestic energy prices as a condition for entrance), as well as continued application of the Jackson-Vanik Amendment in United States–Russia trade relations. These perceived snubs have enormous ramifications, because, depending on underlying attitudes and identities, exclusion from membership in leading intergovernmental organizations (IGOs) may be understood either as a reflection of Russia's own shortcomings or as a calculated rebuff by the West.

Those who share a self-understanding of Russian identity as European tend to hold the former view. Thus, as one group of prominent authors asserted, despite the lamentable fact that Russia has not being accepted into certain key international organizations and processes, there were no grounds to blame others. Instead, "The reason for this . . . isolation is not connected to any kind of evil design and is due primarily to an objective reason: the inadequate level of development of our country."[45] Still more rarely, one occasionally encounters a recognition of Russia's complicity in producing this outcome, for example "by demanding a free hand in its foreign and domestic policies, by stipulating its special interests in Central Asia and in the Caucasus, and by defining the EU solely as its security partner in Europe in the context of Russia's mid-term strategy."[46] From this perspective, difficulties in gaining full membership are due as much to prevailing constructions of Russian identity and misplaced assertiveness as to any objective obstacles such as poverty and infrastructural weakness.[47]

For many, however, Russia's difficulties in becoming incorporated into Europe have led to a starkly different identity orientation. That is, the eventual reaction against the Kozyrev foreign policy line must be understood in light of Russia's inability (conditioned by the West) to effectively reproduce an identity consistent with the one articulated by the framers of that policy, that is, as an equally influential and respected member of the international power elite. The early impulse to embrace the West was thereby transformed into disenchantment, with enormous implications for the mainstream discourse of Russian identity. Insofar as inclusion within Western-backed IGOs became viewed as unachievable, so too, Western modes of social and political organization were discounted as desirable goals. Instead, the emphasis shifted toward pursuing a distinctly Russian approach to integration and international security. Accordingly, as reflected in leading official policy statements as well as an important strand of elite discourse, the West—especially Europe—at once constitutes key elements of self and Other.[48] Stylized overtures to the West notwithstanding, this hybrid orientation has in fact become dominant. On this reading, the evolution of Russian foreign policy under Putin reveals a combined emphasis on (limited) collaboration as well as competition with the West, while becoming fully integrated only on a regional or CIS scale.

This renewed focus on the "near abroad" merely accentuated the feeling of vulnerability raised by the political uprisings in Georgia, Ukraine, and Kyrgyzstan. The revolution in Ukraine has especially disturbing implications for Russian identity, because it has a direct impact on the viability of a desired pan-Slavic confederation led by Moscow.[49] In contrast to the European identity outlook, from the standpoint of the Eurasian and geopolitical identities, the imputed goals of such meddling include rolling back the Russian sphere of influence or even undermining the Putin regime. Similar notions repeatedly surface in the form of conspiracy thinking or the tendency to imagine that almost any unfavorable outcome along Russia's post-Soviet path has been cleverly orchestrated by one or another external enemy. Though in their extreme form such ideas have not been openly endorsed by Putin, they are nonetheless given credence indirectly, as demonstrated by the public allegations of spying leveled against Britain in January 2006. Also resonating with the theme of vulnerability, exclusion from leading IGOs may also feed into a sense of inferiority and self-loathing, which constitutes another significant tendency in Russian discourse. Such attitudes are worrisome, as Boris Dubin suggests, insofar as they translate into anti-Western sentiment—partly as a form of projection and blame for Russian inadequacies.[50]

For all the above reasons, the mainstream variant of hybridity in Russian identity formation includes a profound, and seemingly unstable, juxtaposition of cooperative and competitive aspects. For these reasons, too, the prevailing tendency to engage globalization and neoliberalism should not be equated with pacifism or "trading state" priorities. By way of illustration, Sergei Kortunov's work provides a prominent and relatively sophisticated example of such thinking. On the one hand, he acknowledges the primary importance of global economic factors, arguing that they increasingly blur the boundaries between domestic policy (especially democratic and market-oriented reforms) and foreign policy.[51] On the other hand, he questions the legitimacy of Russian borders insofar as they slice off intrinsically Russian lands, which are populated either by the Russian "superethnos" or by various groups (e.g., Armenians or Ossetians) who supposedly yearn to be part of Russia. Consequently, he argues that Russia should be considered the successor to the Russian Empire, and that this perspective should supplant the still-lingering Soviet identity, according to which the former republics should be recognized as having inviolable autonomy. The inescapable implication of such views is to endorse a gathering together of "historical Russian lands."[52]

Such ideas frequently take both a defensive and aggressive form, within a discourse characterized by Eduard Solovyev in chapter 11 as "geopolitical." According to this general orientation, land takes on powerful symbolic qualities, at once defining the nation-state as a distinct entity and providing its core identity traits. This represents a kind of thinking that Vera Tolz refers to as "imaginative geography," or the process through which the vast open spaces of the Russian Empire were transformed into the natural patrimony of the nation-state.[53] For those such as Aleksandr Dugin, territory literally embodies national power and purpose, and to a large extent determines international political dynamics.[54] Such ideas are typically linked to exceptionalist self-imagery, according to which Russia possesses not only unparalleled size and natural resource endowments but also a national character that derives, directly and indirectly, from the land itself. They also provide the basis for claiming a more exalted status than that generally articulated within the mainstream under Putin: that is, as a "great power," rather than merely a "midrange" or "regional" power. In this way, as Solovyev argues, geopolitical thinking reflects—and to some extent compensates for—the enormous collective trauma of the Soviet collapse; that is, it constitutes a "means of sublimating postimperial psychological problems for Russian citizens." It also offers an attractive political solution to the nation's problems, inasmuch as it furnishes a "tool to explain . . . motivation" as well as a way of rationalizing a highly competitive, (counter-) expansionist foreign policy. In sum, geopolitical thought in Russia today is an entire gestalt: at once an analytical perspective and a practical approach, geared toward regaining Russia's rightful centrality in world affairs.

Although these notions have a long pedigree, in their most recent expressions they are tied to battles on and over land, especially Russia's victories over Napoleon and Hitler. In each case the decisive factor was geographic: the enormity of Russia's land mass, the severity of its climate, and the size of its population. Such ideas are also typically bound up with an emotional attachment to land on which Russian blood was spilled, and which has therefore been sanctified.[55] For many thinkers inclined toward similar views, the result is a kind of defensive self-sufficiency, according to which Russia has the capacity to determine its own historical path, remaining physically detached from outside influences and independent by virtue of its inexhaustible resources.[56]

Another form of imaginative geography involves the notion that Russia's geographic patrimony confers a peculiar and unprecedented destiny on Russia, in a way that transcends mundane considerations of wealth, development, or institutional membership. According to the prominent analyst Mikhail Delyagin,

> While Russia is weak, it nonetheless continues to maintain control over a range of unique resources, vital in our modern world—it has a territory for transits between Europe and Asia, unparalleled resources of Siberia and the Far East, and skills in creating novel technologies. . . . [Therefore] the contest of civilizations is likely to take the form of an overt clash —a clash where everyone struggles against everyone else—on Russian

territory, with the clashing sides focused on control over Russia's resources. What is more, the frontline of the civilizational struggle will lie not along the perimeters of Russia's geographic borders but within the sections of Russian society as such. Under such conditions, Russian society becomes a key, or even the backbone, factor of humanity's further development.[57]

Although geopolitical thinking of one kind or another is nearly ubiquitous in Russian foreign policy analyses, it has also emerged as a key part of the language of the opposition. As such, it tends to express a bristling reaction to the prospect of Russia's immersion in a globalized world. By far the most influential variant of this strain of thought is Eurasianism, which, as Tsygankov puts it, "emphasizes Russia's geopolitical and cultural uniqueness."[58] Even in their relatively crude expression by Dugin and others, such ideas have become a respectable vehicle for articulating alternative approaches to domestic and foreign policy.

To be sure, one strand of Eurasianist thought seeks to encourage Russia's assimilation into the global institutional system, on the grounds that Russia constitutes a crucial bridge linking Europe and Asia as well as the Atlantic, Indian and Pacific oceans. This often includes a partial accommodation of integrationist pressures. An example is the idea that Russia should cooperate closely with Western Europe—and against the United States—while still pursuing full integration with the states of the former USSR and Asia.[59] Although such arguments are typically premised on the imperatives of globalization, they also come with a pronounced geopolitical inflection. However, for the most part Eurasianism is expressed in a manner calculated to be incompatible with far-reaching international integration, insofar as it stresses the inviolable separateness of Russian and Western territories. In a related way, for many proponents of Eurasianism, the idea of Russian integration into the EU process implies a form of political and ideological capitulation. Those who share this view claim that Russia's course within the world economy must remain distinct, as shaped by "natural" historical tendencies within the former Soviet space. For example, Degoyev sharply contrasts the Western, liberal mode of economic and political integration with an "objective," historically developed "law" of Russia's centrifugal pull over post-Soviet region. This supposedly requires vertical integration within the CIS space, as opposed to the "European" tendency to develop horizontal ties.[60] As of this writing, the prevailing discourse shows signs of continuing to evolve away from the European identity and toward more exceptionalist and marginalized understandings of self.

Of course, the European, geopolitical, Eurasianist, and prevailing hybrid identity constructs do not exhaust the political spectrum in Russia today. It is still possible to encounter a completely unreconstructed, paranoiac vision according to which any cooperation with the United States merely plays into the latter's offensive military designs.[61] And in keeping with the tandem of policy and identity orientations, this vision is generally associated with a narrow, often mystical, and highly ethnicized construction of Russian identity. It is not, however, entirely marginal in importance. Even some prominent members of the elite express notions according to which the West seeks to undermine Russian security, perhaps by deflecting Muslim terrorists toward Russian targets.[62] Commentators of this ilk tend to express concerns about the penetration of international institutional actors into the areas of political and human rights, viewing them as insidiously Western backed or inspired.

Identity, Foreign Policy, and Institutional Membership

Although the political currency of a given identity may vary according to its anticipated ease of enactment, its underlying constructs remain deeply rooted and slow to change. And, as the foregoing discussion demonstrates, the connection between self-understandings and attitudes toward specific policy questions merely affirms the fact that identity and interests are co-constituted.[63] Specific policy questions offer focal points for the crystallization of discourse, allowing arguments about identity and interest to mingle within the realm of the political and practical, and producing a configuration of support on any given issue. For this reason, too, the prospect of actually achieving a desired outcome matters, because this not only heightens or diminishes the attractiveness of a concrete policy but also affects the viability of identities associated with it.

An important example of this dynamic is provided by the debate over Russian policy toward the EU. Over the past several years, the festering debate over Chechnya (within the CoE and in other forums) has contributed to an increasingly prevalent view of Russia as fundamentally deficient with respect to human rights and democratic values. Partly as a result, despite proposals for building four common spaces (economic, security, legal, and educational-cultural), in practice not much progress has been made, and limits to cooperation seem increasingly likely.[64] Even energy trade seems less likely to facilitate closer integration than it has in the past, especially in view of the pressures exerted on Ukraine through the offices of Gazprom.

Although European dependence on Russia for energy—over 40 percent for Western Europe, and far higher for Eastern Europe—had already led to an interest in diversification,[65] the combination of heavy-handed diplomacy and growing authoritarianism at home has significantly strengthened this desire. As the gap widens between what Mikhail Gorbachev once referred to as "our common European home," and the reality of institutional and functional bifurcation, arguments in favor of integration may lose their validity. That is, as a European identity becomes more difficult to enact, its associated constructs become less resonant in political discourse.

These observations are relevant to the process of socialization within the European framework, which Noreen suggests has had significant effects on Russia's understanding of threats and regional security arrangements. And yet, as Noreen also acknowledges, socialization is never completed but is instead ongoing and fluid. It may well be that recent interactions have shifted the social learning process in a different direction. For example, Russian resistance to the Organization for Security and Cooperation in Europe (OSCE) process has grown steadily since the mid-1990s, especially due to resentments over Kosovo (which was widely construed in terms of OSCE collusion with NATO) and NATO enlargement. Meanwhile, Moscow's efforts to use the OSCE as leverage vis-à-vis Russian-language speakers in Latvia and Estonia have fallen far short of expectations.[66] In the aftermath of the "colored revolutions," fears of contagion accelerated the shift in attitude. This was reflected in the Astana Appeal of September 2004, which flatly rejected the OSCE's political and human rights orientation. Instead, the signatory states (Russia, Armenia, Belarus, Kazakhstan, Kyrgyzstan, Tajikistan, Uzbekistan, and Ukraine) demanded that such activities be eliminated and replaced by an emphasis on terrorism, economic and environmental cooperation, education, tourism, and culture. It is at least conceivable that the OSCE might retain some potential interest for Russia insofar as such changes are actually implemented and its normative political component is replaced by a practical focus on nontraditional security issues. At present, however, the organization is obviously marginalized in the eyes of Russian decisionmakers.

In contrast, the CoE has generally been able to command a certain respect and even a measure of compliance, as Moscow tended to take a relatively restrained response to the CoE's criticisms. And yet the practical benefits of membership were never apparent to many within the policymaking community, especially because the likelihood of full Russian accession into the EU was always slim, and became increasingly slim over time. The CoE is also a quintessentially political and normative institution—just the qualities, in other words, that made the OSCE so odious in Russia's eyes. The puzzle, then, is not why Russia has increasingly moved to distance itself from the organization, but why it has remained a member for so long. As Fawn contends, this is due to the fact that the CoE provided a useful vehicle for enacting a European identity, something that was desirable not only in its own right but also as a prelude to closer EU ties and ancillary benefits. In keeping with Noreen's analysis, too, the CoE has also provided a diplomatic forum for exerting counterpressure on the Baltic states for discriminating against Russian ethnic citizens. In other words, Russia's participation in the CoE has been both a matter of identity per se and an object of pragmatic calculation.

In contrast, the growing wave of hostility toward the CoE tends to express a distinct, non-European identity. Often, too, it reveals disdain for the idea of participating in multilateral governing institutions, which are viewed as a smokescreen for undoing Russian sovereignty, purportedly in Western (especially American) interests. For example, Narochnitskaya attacked the CoE as a "purely ideological organization, a fourth, liberal, International of sorts, resolved to issue 'maturity certificates.'"[67] From this same perspective, Western practices and IGOs are flatly rejected as un-Russian or even antithetical to Russia's spiritual essence. Similarly, any form of institutionalized "transnationalism"—whether led by multinational corporations or left-leaning NGOs—is viewed as imposing upon Russia a set of culturally foreign policies.[68]

Identity and Perceptions of Globalization

Globalization itself evokes a range of different assessments among Russian observers, depending on how the underlying process itself is understood, including its origins as well as its effects on Russia and other key international actors. Those associated with the idea that Russia is essentially a European country tend to naturalize globalization as an objective phenomenon that follows logically from a set of key technological developments. From this same perspective, globalization produces complex syncretions of "glocalized" culture rather than any homogenous outcome. A plethora of political and institutional responses are therefore available to states such as Russia, which seek to find their own way as part of the process.[69] Overwhelmingly, those operating within this intellectual framework endorse integration into the new global economy for reasons of development. As argued by two well-known analysts espousing a European identity, "In the contemporary world the only means of achieving economic success is to accept the rules of the game which have been generated by the global economy, and to take the course of integration into the community of states which share the ideals and values of Western civilization."[70]

In contrast, those who imagine Russia as unique or essentially non-European tend to view globalization as a hegemonic political project. Frequently, this is attributed to the American leadership, and globalization is interpreted as a strategy designed to consolidate American power.[71] The precise mechanisms whereby such control would be achieved are often left unspecified but are generally implied to work through either cultural and/or economic forms of leverage. For example, a common perception is that globalization actually embodies a Western bid to foster cultural homogeneity:

We all know that many people in China, India, Malaysia, many Arab countries, Iran and even Japan resolutely condemn the cultural expansion of the West carried out under the globalization banner. It seems that what President Putin said about the need to "respect the multicolored variety of contemporary civilization" during his recent visits to India and Turkey was a response to the concern and anxiety obvious in Asia caused by the fairly aggressive cultural and information expansion carried out by the West, the United States in the first place. This Westernization campaign is suppressing the national cultures and traditions and replaces the local cultural values with Western mass culture.[72]

It should also be noted that it is possible to find views in between, according to which globalization represents an objective phenomenon, but one that the United States under George W. Bush is attempting to hijack for its own ends. Even those holding a European identity often subscribe to such views.[73] Furthermore, as Mikhail Troitskiy notes in chapter 8, within the mainstream Russian discourse, attitudes toward globalization have shifted, from embracing its opportunities to (increasingly) raising concerns over its myriad security threats.

Globalization and Security

Without doubt, globalization has already profoundly affected Russian security policy. As Alexey Fenenko argues in chapter 12, this is evidenced by a shift toward a broader conception of security itself, as well as an emphasis on "soft" or nonmilitary threats, including combating drugs, human trafficking, money laundering, terrorism, and disease. The impact of this shift in the understanding of threats varies according to issue area; it ranges from the strident and militaristic in the case of terrorism to the more modulated and institutional in the case of migration and disease. Certainly, in neither Russia nor elsewhere has the result been so sweeping as to eliminate the traditional security state and its standard military approach to international problems.[74] Yet such expectations are overblown and simplistic. Instead, in Russia, what we find is a number of inchoate and often contradictory trends, reflecting the fact that both hard and soft categories of threat seem resurgent.

For example, as already suggested, the tide of democratic change carried by the "colored revolutions" is in itself viewed as a threat to social stability by many Russian observers. Migration also falls into this category. Some, such as German Gref, minister of economic development and trade, have made the rational argument that Russia desperately needs to attract immigrants (it has been estimated that 1 million per year would be required to offset the anticipated demographic contraction).[75] Already, the influx of foreign workers has caused significant social strains, and many—including at times Putin—have sounded the alarm about illegal workers and called for implementing a stricter visa regime.[76] And, as Alexeev and Hofstetter argue, globalization contributes to such "immigration phobia" by exacerbating real and perceived state weakness.[77] Much the same might be said about transnational crime; here again, globalization, a lack of state capacity, and illicit flows go hand-in-hand.[78] Indeed, Cooley observes that globalization may be particularly problematic for postimperial states like Russia, with their massive and poorly rationalized security structures, whose rent-seeking behavior (including the illegal cross-border smuggling of weapons and drugs) contributes to undermining the state.[79]

Although some of these "soft threats" threaten physical harm to civilians and infrastructure, they primarily connote challenges to identity and order; that is, the new threats have a nonphysical dimension.[80] Yet traditional, physical threats also linger. With regard to terrorism (a physical threat but in a nontraditional guise), the mainstream discourse portrays a global Islamist enemy, similar to that faced by Russia in Chechnya and Kabardino-Balkaria, often linked to an image of Russia as a beleaguered outpost of Orthodoxy.[81] Many leading officials have therefore called for heightened tactical collaboration with the West to prevent terrorism.[82] Putin himself provisionally accepted NATO expansion as well as U.S. involvement in Afghanistan and Central

Asia after the terrorist attacks of September 11, 2001. Even in Putin's own rhetoric, however, there are clearly limits to how far such cooperation should go, and more recently he has attempted to shorten the acceptable duration of America's presence in Russia's backyard.[83]

Furthermore, as Fenenko argues, the overall thrust of Russian security organization and spending continues to be directed toward military preparedness, especially for mobile, rapid-deployment, and flexible operations designed to interdict nonstate sources of threat. Despite a shift in the direction of soft security issues, then, one still detects a major emphasis on hard power under Putin. This includes traditional forms of power projection, as evidenced by the acquisition of bases in Kyrgyzstan and Uzbekistan, as well as an effort to beef up the Caspian fleet and coordinate its functions with the other littoral states. Nevertheless, with the (marked) internal exception of Chechnya, in recent years—that is, since the early post-Soviet conflicts in Moldova, Tajikistan, and Georgia—Russia has been restrained in its overt exercise of military power. To a significant extent, this appears to be related to external political calculations, especially reputational concerns linked to integration into leading international organizations and into the EU economic space. Though, in one view, such calculations are entirely rational, here again we glimpse the extent to which identity mediates between globalization and security, by heightening the salience of normative constraints on the exercise of hard power.[84]

Still another indicator of the relationship between security, identity, and globalization has to do with cross-border regimes, which have rapidly become more complex to selectively encourage legal trade while curtailing criminal activity.[85] More sharply oppositional tendencies in self-Other representations, associated with geopolitical discourse and anti-Western forms of identification, tend to be bound up with a deep suspicion of globalization. Accordingly, increased transborder flows may be perceived to jeopardize not only domestic security but also identity—and therefore may be used as a justification for re-delineating or closing borders. The purpose of such policing actions, then, is not so much to prevent harmful flows per se but to solidify national identity, perhaps with the additional effect of asserting sovereignty rights.[86] This underscores one of the endemic tensions of globalization: opening or transcending borders as part of international regimes versus maintaining borders, both for practical reasons as well as for their symbolic function in underlining the distinctness of the nation. Indeed, in this context, security has to do with the ability to maintain sovereignty; this in turn requires that the identity of the nation-state, upon which sovereignty rests, be defended.[87] In Russia's case, this means that the tight linkage between national identity and the state becomes securitized in its own right.

Globalization and Sovereignty

As the foregoing discussion indicates, sovereignty concerns—including arrangements for political autonomy and domestic hierarchy—are closely bound up with the themes of globalization, identity, and security. Hedetoft suggests that this is true in four crucial areas: border problems, diminished state capacity despite military strength (as a result of economic decline), the influence of Western states and global institutions throughout post-Soviet space, and pressures to reconfigure sovereignty as autonomy. In fact, the concept of national sovereignty is often formulated by Russian scholars precisely in such a way as to provide a theoretical and policy counterweight to these identity and security challenges, all of which are correctly seen as being imposed by globalization.[88] The yearning for a strong vertical hierarchy is thus tied to a range of desired outcomes for domestic governance and international influence.[89] Seen in this light, Putin's reforms aimed at strengthening the center represent an attempt to uphold the domestic and international foundations of sovereignty.

To be sure, it is possible once more to view Putin's centralizing programs as a rational reaction to the state's weaknesses during the middle to late 1990s, because the absence of stable institutions and enforcement was clearly an impediment to market-based growth. Nevertheless, it should be emphasized that Putin's policies at home and abroad reflect a particular conception of the state, one that is historically rooted in imperial patrimonialism, Soviet centralization, and the negative experience of privatization after the collapse of the USSR. To some extent, as Richter observes, this conception posits a sovereign actor standing apart from, or over, society and able to regulate social processes. And as McDaniel argues, such assumptions are embedded within a longstanding "Russian Idea," according to which the state and ruler represent both the embodiment and the guarantor of power and order.[90]

Such attitudes are also implicated in identity discourse, and therefore inevitably spill over into foreign policy thinking, most obviously in Russian efforts to exert influence throughout the near abroad. The Russian self-identity as a great, or at least regional, power requires a high level of domestic state capacity, including the ability to guarantee domestic order and security. Obviously, it is possible for a state to expand its domestic capacity without also claiming enhanced geopolitical influence. But in Russia these two tendencies are fused, because of the way internal and external rule have developed historically. Even where closer integration with the West is desired, traditional assumptions about Russia's sphere of influence make themselves felt and often appear inseparable from understandings of state strength and domestic order.[91] The result is a persistent tendency not only to retain a high degree of central control but also to viscerally identify with the state, which is viewed as the source and embodiment of national strength.[92]

In addition, the historical insistence on territoriality (discussed above) underscores the importance of traditional Westphalian ideas in Russian political discourse. The nation's sovereignty and security are seen to depend, first and foremost, on its geographic expanse and natural resources. As Fenenko notes, it is ironic that such attitudes have reemerged at a time when globalization and scientific-technical progress render natural resource factors increasingly secondary, at least for states wishing to become fully developed actors within the international economy. Nonetheless, inasmuch as globalization necessarily challenges Westphalian conceptions, it also tends to butt up against powerful assumptions about national identity.[93]

In keeping with this same theme, according to Troitskiy, the early demands for "justice" in foreign relations, which were articulated under Yeltsin, reflected a peculiar combination of vulnerability ushered in by globalization, and (still unconsolidated) national identity as a great power. The particulars of this discourse shifted, becoming far more conciliatory for a time before turning increasingly assertive again after 2003. Yet they consistently expressed certain attitudes about the role of relative hard power and virtue as key influences shaping Russian national identity. According to this discourse, Russia "deserves" reciprocal cooperation in gaining the benefits of preferential trade and investment, dealing with new security threats, forming alliances with other states that seek to avert Americanization, and obtaining promises of U.S. restraint in Eurasia.

On one level, then, Russian demands for justice reflect quite traditional attachments to sovereignty, understood as sole authority over its domestic political order, in the face of globalization. On another level, however, such demands may be seen as part of a quest for a special kind of "sovereignty bargain," according to which Russia would relinquish some degree of control over process in exchange for an enhanced measure of control over certain coveted outcomes.[94] Concretely, with regard to process, this might mean that the state would allow higher levels of decentralization and delegation to IGOs and regional actors, as well as greater liberalization and privatization (benefiting both oligarchs and multinational corporations). The quid pro quo is that the state—and specifically the president's apparatus— should retain authority to make key policy decisions. With regard to outcomes, the goal is to retain some real influence over flows of investment and trade, as well as deference to Russia's security concerns, respect for the rights of co-ethnics in the near abroad, and acceptance into the club of civilized (especially European) states.

The upshot, once again, is an unmistakable sense of ambivalence. After all, despite Russian claims to at least regional power status, prevailing attitudes toward sovereignty reflect considerable anxiety and defensiveness, which in themselves betray a recognition of Russia's backwardness. As was discussed above, it is widely recognized that this backwardness can only be overcome through integration into the international economy—which, however, requires at least some accommodation of American power.[95] And yet, in the perception of many analysts, such accommodation easily blends into submission. For this reason, too, acceptance of the neoliberal system of governance is often tempered by offsetting demands for protectionism. The result is a typical mixture of compliance and resistance. As Hedetoft argues in chapter 1, the forced nature of this compromise demonstrates that responses to globalization are constrained hegemonically; that is, globalization "is increasingly an institutionally orchestrated and designed configuration of forces shifting the symmetrical structure of the international order toward asymmetry and hierarchy." Comparative studies suggestively confirm this point: State approaches that depart starkly from neoliberalism (e.g., redistributive or protectionist policies) are at best disciplined and at worst discursively "demolished" by leading state and institutional actors.[96] In Russia's case, the result is a widespread perception of "objective requirements" impelling the state to observe international norms and practices. Perhaps typically, however, this perception—accurate thought it may be—is coupled with discursive resistance and limited follow-through.

Conclusions

Globalization inexorably affects Russian society, including its economic, political, demographic, and cultural features; but this does not happen in an entirely predictable way. That is, despite some very general similarities, globalization is not a straightforward process having uniform effects but rather is mediated by certain factors that are peculiar to Russia. As Hedetoft contends, some of these factors have to do with a set of unique historical circumstances, including imperial collapse, decolonization, and the need to build new institutions and identities in the very context of globalization. Richard Sakwa also points to other key mediating conditions, including a distinctive style of governance and capitalism.[97] At the same time, globalization is responded to by conscious political actors, even if their agency is discursively and institutionally constrained. The choices they make yield a particular set of domestic and foreign policies, which may be read in part as a response to globalization. The contributors to this book have tried to sketch the complex interplay between globalization, identity, and security, while highlighting the significance of key Russian actors.

Along the way, too, we have repeatedly emphasized the pivotal role played by the state. Yet the state's role is a modulated one, marked by authoritarian impulses as well as various delegative adaptations to global pressures. The result is a combination of seemingly contradictory trends in governance and social organization. These include the following tendencies:

- pursuing both centralized control and managed decentralization in center-periphery reforms, which however stymie regional flexibility and exacerbate centrifugal identity pressures;
- monitoring and often restricting integration in defense-relevant sectors, while also encouraging entrepreneurship and technological progress in other sectors;
- encouraging population mobility and immigration, which are needed for labor markets, while also seeking to manage the strains this places on local capacity and social cohesion;
- promoting top-down youth socialization, while also encouraging educational reform geared to fostering autonomous, "self-organized citizens"; and
- placing increasing restrictions on free speech and assembly, while also encouraging the emergence of (convivial) NGOs that are able and willing to help solve social problems.

In sum, despite various efforts to accommodate and benefit from the democratizing trends within globalization, we note a recidivistic return to "state power" as an ostensible solution to myriad internal and external problems.[98] And yet, the opposing trends should not be trivialized. There is also a powerful current of decentralization under way in Russia today: market tendencies have been widely embraced, but the state plays a large role in dispensing favors and allowing privileged access to trade and property rights. Entrepreneurial forms of economic organization thus coexist with highly concentrated (and often criminalized) structures, which distort competition and inhibit innovation. In all these ways, we observe a typical mix of responses, reflecting how governance and capitalism affect one another, as well as the extent to which their interaction is shaped by globalization.

Collective identity is another key factor affecting, and being affected by, globalization. As we have seen throughout this volume, many of the problems and conflicts associated with Russian national identity formation reflect not only a lack of shared assumptions and ideological orientations but also the ubiquitous challenges of managing globalization. This is not, as is often assumed, because globalization unavoidably erodes national distinctiveness; on the contrary, at least in the medium run, globalization tends to reinforce national particularism. Instead, some of the most important challenges for national identity formation posed by globalization have to do with the tensions that arise between supposedly adaptive modes of political-institutional change and their (often unintended) effects. For example, as Hedetoft notes, globalization tends to lead to a crisis in mass-elite relations insofar as the state scales back entitlement programs. However, other pathways connect these factors as well: mass-elite trust also depends on how sovereignty is reconfigured under the influence of globalization, which in turn is a function of whether the state is perceived to retain a sufficient level of control over desired outcomes. In other words, to what extent are social norms and expectations regarding state intervention allowed to be held hostage to pressures from IGOs and international NGOs? Or, more concretely, who ultimately has authority over freedoms of expression and assembly, appropriate punishments for criminal offenses, capital investment flows, and educational curricula? The answers given to these questions are predicated on identity constructs.

Once again, it is worth stressing that we observe reciprocal effects: Global flows challenge prevailing institutions and national identities, and yet incipient changes in social organization and identity are also highly contested—which helps determine how much Russia is open to global flows.[99] The way in which this takes place in Russia reflects the historical development of state-society relations, which, as already noted, have been characterized by enormous central power and truncated individual autonomy. However, as a result of globalization, such traditional patterns of governance are increasingly offset by changing understandings concerning the appropriate role of the state, which are heavily influenced by external (and increasingly neoliberal) models. The debate between advocates of more Western-oriented versus exceptionalist approaches also turns in part on these issues.

In addition, as a number of the chapters in this volume also attest, much of the discourse surrounding globalization in Russia—including Western and exceptionalist ideas—has to do with external relations. Just as in domestic affairs, a recurrent theme in Russian foreign policy is the demand for control, which is itself a response to insecurities arising from perceived threats in the international environment. Fenenko observes that such threats include new, nonmilitary, and extra-state sources, as well as others that are highly traditional and state based. And, as Noreen, Solovyev, Troitskiy, and Fawn all demonstrate, this Russian proclivity for threat perception is embedded in prevailing identity constructions. On the one hand, we find profound cleavages and abiding tensions between European, Eurasian, and Asian narratives of self, which have never been resolved. On the other hand, these constructs mingle with sharply diverging narratives of key Others, ranging from potentially cooperative to (increasingly) competitive and even hostile forces in the near and far abroad. Such understandings of self and Other matter inasmuch as they shape attitudes about cooperation, competition, and desirable levels of integration with the outside world. The end result, once more, is that globalization has uneven effects in different arenas of domestic and foreign policy; neither capital nor ideas is able to penetrate unproblematically or with predictable consequences.

Still, whatever its uneven and often troubling effects, the flows that constitute globalization cannot be shut out—nor, under Putin, is there any real interest in doing so. Much of the resulting ambivalence is refracted in an ongoing discourse of legitimacy. This discourse expresses a wish to be respected as a civilized—and, in many respects, as a unique and even transcendent actor in international politics—but it also conveys a sense of injured pride and rejection. Likewise, it includes a demand for diplomatic status befitting a nuclear superpower and Group of Eight member, along with the humiliating recognition of age-old backwardness. At home, it articulates a quest for state power, both as a bulwark of Westphalian sovereignty in a globalizing world and as a means of consolidating domestic hierarchy in the face of all challengers—whether in the form of terrorists, oligarchs, or assertive regional governments. Nevertheless, we also find increasing recognition at all levels of the need to delegate authority and foster local initiative, in order to function efficiently in a globalized, market-based context. Finally, the discourse of legitimacy expresses a wish to acquire the institutional and postindustrial trappings of modernity, while at the same time eschewing decadent forms of hyperindividualism and retaining a distinctive national identity.

The attempt to reconcile these disparate, often contradictory trends is never entirely successful. The ensuing frustration—with its mixture of power and weakness, of self-importance and self-doubt—is reminiscent of former prime minister Viktor Chernomyrdin's famous quip: "We wanted something better, but it came out like always." In a sense, he had it wrong; things are irrevocably different, and are in fact always changing, as global flows wash across Russia in all areas of social and political life. They are, in fact, significantly "better," and in some ways also arguably worse, as a result of becoming more integrated, standardized, and modern. Nevertheless, he was also right; there is (as always) a quintessentially Russian quality to the process, as actors seek to reconcile the imperatives of security and identity within the shifting context of globalization.

Notes

1. Ulf Hedetoft, "The Nation-State Meets the World: National Identities in the Context of Transnationality and Cultural Globalization," *European Journal of Social Theory* (February 1999): 71–94; the quotation here is on 89.

2. E.g., see Murray Feshbach, "Potential Social Disarray in Russia Due to Health Factors," *Problems of Post-Communism* (July–August 2005): 22–27; and Theodore Gerber and Sarah Mendelson, "Crisis among Crises among Crises," *Problems of Post-Communism* (July–August 2005): 28–41.

3. Jeronim Perovic, "Regionalisation Trends in Russia: Between the Soviet Legacy and the Forces of Globalisation," *Geopolitics* (Summer 2004): 342–77.

4. E.g., see O. V. Bratimov, Yu. M. Gorskiy, M. G. Delyagin, and A. A. Kovalenko, *Praktika globalizatsii: Igry i Pravila Novoi Epokhi* (Moscow: Infra-M, 2000), 317–18.

5. Robert Orttung, "The Role of Business in Russian Foreign and Security Relations," Policy Memo 351, Program on New Approaches to Russian Security, November 2004.

6. Nikita Pokrovskiy, "V zerkale globalizatsii," *Otechestvennye zapiski* (2003).

7. Eduard Ponarin, "Russian State Nationalism vs. Local Nationalisms: The Case of Tatarstan," Policy Memo, Program on New Approaches to Russian Security, December 2005.

8. Andrey Makarychev, "Pskov at the Crossroads of Russia's Trans-border Relations with Estonia and Latvia: Between Provinciality and Marginality," *Europe-Asia Studies* (May 2005): 481–500.

9. Oksana Antonenko and Kathryn Pinnick, "Russia's Foreign and Security Policy in Central Asia: The Regional Perspective," *Russian Regional Perspectives* (International Institute for Security Studies), 2003, 4–13.

10. Mikhail Stoliarov, *Federalism and the Dictatorship of Power in Russia* (London: Routledge, 2003), 134–59.

11. Marjorie Mandelstam Balzer, Nicolai Petro, and Lawrence Robertson, "Issues of Culture and Identity: 'Cultural Entrepreneurship' in Russia's Regions," in *Frag-

mented Space in the Russian Federation, ed. Blair Ruble, Jodi Koehn, and Nancy Popson (Washington, D.C.: Woodrow Wilson Center Press, 2001), 219–71.

12. Michael Bradshaw and Jessica Prendergrast, "The Russian Heartland Revisited: An Assessment of Russia's Transformation," *Eurasian Geography & Economics,* March 2005, 83–122; Judyth Twigg, *Differential Demographics: Russia's Muslim and Slavic Populations,* Program on New Approaches to Russian Security Policy, Memo 388 (Washington, D.C.: Center for Strategic and International Studies, 2005).

13. Henry Hale and Rein Taagepera, "Russia: Consolidation or Collapse?" *Europe-Asia Studies,* November 2002, 1101–25.

14. Nikolay Petrov, "A Political Fire Brigade in the Regions," *Moscow Times,* April 7, 2005.

15. Bradshaw and Prendergrast, "The Russian Heartland Revisited," 83-122.

16. Yoshiko Herrera, *Imagined Economies: The Sources of Russian Regionalism* (New York: Cambridge University Press, 2005).

17. Igor S. Semenenko, "Globalizatsiya i sotsiokul'turnaya dinamika: lichnost', obshchestvo, kul'tura," *Polis,* January–February 2003, 5–23.

18. Vladimir Zvonosky, "The New Russian Identity and the United States," *Demokratizatsiya,* Winter 2005, 101–14.

19. Caroline Humphrey, " 'Eurasia,' Ideology and the Political Imagination in Provincial Russia," in *Postsocialism: Ideals, Ideologies and Practices in Eurasia,* ed. Chris M. Hann (New York: Routledge, 2002), 279–96.

20. Marlène Laruelle, "The Two Faces of Contemporary Eurasianism: An Imperial Version of Russian Nationalism," *Nationalities Papers,* March 2004, 115–36.

21. Yevgeniy G. Vodichev, *Yevropeyskiy soyuz i Sibir': Opyt realizatsii programm tekhnicheskogo sodeystviya v Sibirskom regione* (Novosibirsk: SibAGS, 2004).

22. Alex Pravda, "Putin's Foreign Policy after 11 September: Radical or Revolutionary?" in *Russia between East and West: Russian Foreign Policy on the Threshold of the Twenty-First Century,* ed. Gabriel Gorodetsky (London: Frank Cass, 2003), 39–57; the quotation here is on 41.

23. Anton Steen, "The Post-Communist Transformation: Elite Orientations and the Emerging Russian State," *Perspectives on European Politics & Society,* May 2002, 93–127.

24. On these points, see Lilia Shevtsova, *Putin's Russia* (Washington, D.C.: Carnegie Endowment for International Peace, 2003).

25. United Nations Development Program, *National Human Development Report: 2004,* available at http://www.undp.ru/.

26. Alexander Marcus, "Internet and Democratization: The Development of Russian Internet Policy," *Demokratizatsiya,* Fall 2004, 607–27.

27. D. J. Peterson, *Russia and the Information Revolution* (Santa Monica, Calif.: RAND, 2005).

28. E.g., see A. A. Kokoshin, *Natsional'naya bezopasnost' Rossii v usolviyakh globalizatsii* (Moscow: Institut Problem Mezhdunarodnoy Bezopasnosti, 2001).

29. The space sector is a major exception to the overall pattern of industry, inasmuch as it is closely linked to international states and firms for access to Russian research and development, services, and technology. This contrasts with the information technology sector, in which most Russian technology components are imported. United Nations Development Program, *National Human Development Report: 2004,* esp. 26–27.

30. The Kearney Report is available at http://www.atkearney.com/.

31. E.g., by 2004, the United States had already invested $6 billion in Kazakhstan, mostly in the energy sector, compared with only $20 million from Russia. See V. A. Vashanov, "Problems of Interregional Cooperation between Russia and the Commonwealth of Independent States," *Problems of Economic Transition*, April 2005, 9–17.

32. E.g., see Jacques Sapir, "Russia's Economic Growth and European Integration," *Post-Soviet Affairs*, January 2003, 1–23.

33. Georgiy Vel'yaminov, "Rossiya i globalizatsiya," *Rossiya v Global'noy Politike*, May–June 2006, available at http://www.globalaffairs.ru/.

34. George E. Hudson, "Civil Society in Russia: Models and Prospects for Development," *Russian Review*, April 2003, 212–22.

35. N. A. Moiseyeva, "Globalizatsiya i 'russkiy vopros,'" *Sotsialisticheskiye issledovaniya*, June 2003, 13–21; Yevgeniy Yasin, "'Russian Soul' and Economic Modernization," *Russia in Global Affairs*, July–September 2003.

36. Aleksandr Kamenskiy, "Rossiya i mir: Opyt istorii," *Kosmopolis*, Fall 2002, available at http://www.rami.ru/cosmopolis/.

37. K. Kholodkovskiy, "Konflikt 'zapadnichestva' i 'pochvennichestva' v kontekste drugikh linii razmezhevaniya," *Mirovaia Ekonomika i Mezhdunarodnye Otnosheniya*, June 2004, 38–48.

38. Celeste Wallander, "Global Challenges and Russian Foreign Policy," in *Twenty-First Century Russian Foreign Policy and the Shadow of the Past*, ed. Robert Legvold (forthcoming).

39. Aleksandr Zinov'ev, "Ideologicheskie zametki," *Svobodnaya mysl'-XXI*, 2005, available at http://www.postindustrial.net/.

40. Putin's address to the Federation Council, April 25, 2005, available at http://www.kremlin.ru.

41. T. D. Valovaya, "Postsovetskoe prostranstvo v epokhu pragmatizma," *Rossiya v global'noy politike*, March–April 2005, available at http://www.globalaffairs.ru/; Dmitri Trenin, *The End of Eurasia: Russia on the Border between Geopolitics and Globalization* (Washington, D.C.: Carnegie Endowment for International Peace, 2001).

42. Yevgeny Gavrilenkov and Wolfram Schrettl, "Integration into the World Economy: Russian Dilemmas," in *Russia and the West at the Millennium: Global Imperatives and Domestic Policies*, ed. Sergei Medvedev, Alexander Konovalov, and Sergei Oznobishchev (Garmisch-Partenkirchen, Germany: George C. Marshall European Center for Security Studies, 2002), 125–35.

43. Aleksey Arbatov and Aleksandr Pikayev, "Problemy novoy struktury mezhdunarodnoy bezopasnosti i Rossiya," in *Grani globalizatsii: Trudnye voprosy sovremennogo razvitiya*, ed. A. B. Veber (Moscow: Alpina, 2003), 513–55; the quotations here are on 537.

44. Alexander Sergounin, "Global Challenges to Russia's National Security," in *Globalization, Security, and the Nation-State: Paradigms in Transition*, ed. Ersel Aydinli and James Rosenau (Albany: State University of New York Press, 2005), 117–33; Nikita Lomagin, "Forming a New Security Identity in Modern Russia," in *Russia as a Great Power: Dimensions of Security Under Putin*, ed. Jakob Hedenskog et al. (New York: Routledge, 2005), 257–77.

45. Bratimov et al., *Praktika globalizatsii*, 316.

46. See Timofei Bordachev and Arkady Moshes, "Is the Europeanization of Russia Over?" *Russia in Global Affairs* April–June 2004, available at http://eng.globalaffairs

.ru/. See also Vyacheslav Morozov, "O kovarstve Zapada i ego razoblachitelyakh: Rossiyskaya vneshnepoliticheskaya mysl' i samoizolyatsiya Rossii," *Neprikosnovennyy zapas,* 2005, http://magazines.russ.ru/nz/2005/43/mo3.html.

47. Dmitrii Trenin, "Identichnost' i integratsiya: Rossiya i Zapad v XXI veke," *Pro et Contra,* 2004, 9–22.

48. Margot Light, "In Search of an Identity: Russian Foreign Policy and the End of Ideology," *Journal of Communist Studies & Transition Politics,* September 2003, 42–59.

49. As Molchanov suggests, "With the loss of its Ukrainian soul, Russia will cease to be the Russia we know and it will have to rebuild its identity practically from scratch." Mikhail A. Molchanov, *Political Culture and National Identity in Russian-Ukrainian Relations* (College Station: Texas A&M University Press, 2002), 246.

50. Boris Dubin, "Zapad dlya vnutrennogo upotrebleniya," *Kosmopolis,* Spring 2003, available at http://www.rami.ru/cosmopolis/.

51. Sergey Kortunov, *Stanovlenie politiki bezopasnosti: Formirovanie politki natsional'noy bezopasnosti Rossii v kontekste problem globalizatsii* (Moscow: Nauka, 2003), 123–44.

52. Ibid., 427–36.

53. Vera Tolz, *Russia: Inventing the Nation* (New York: Oxford University Press, 2001), 155–90.

54. Aleksandr Dugin, *Russkiy Revansh (*Moscow: Yauza, 2004). For an analytical review of Dugin's theories, see John B. Dunlop, "Aleksandr Dugin's Foundations of Geopolitics," *Demokratizatsiya,* Winter 2004, 41–57.

55. Denis Dragunskiy, "Krasnaya glina (ideya territorii-pochvy-rodiny v politicheskom diskurse," *Kosmopolis,* Winter 2002–3, available at http://www.rami.ru/cosmopolis/.

56. See Sergey Medvedev, "Rossiya: vneshnaya politika, bezopasnost', identichnost'," *MEiMO,* July 2003, 22–30.

57. Mikhail Delyagin, "Russia's Mission in the Age of the Second 'Gutenberg Crisis," *Russia in Global Affairs,* January–February 2004, http://eng.globalaffairs.ru/numbers/6/511.html.

58. Andrei Tsygankov, "Mastering Space in Eurasia: Russia's Geopolitical Thinking after the Soviet Break-Up," *Communist and Post-Communist Studies,* March 2003, 101–27; the quotation here is on 106. Tsygankov distinguishes among five schools of thought: Westernizers, Expansionists, Civilizationists, Stabilizers, and Geoeconomists.

59. Igor F. Kefeli, *Sud'ba Rossii v Globalnoy Geopolitika* (Saint Petersburg: Severnaya Zvezda, 2004), 153–56.

60. Vladimir Degoyev, "Apologiya mifa: Rossii obresti sebya, chtoby ne byt' obretennoy drugimi," *Druzhba narodov,* 2004, http://magazines.russ.ru/druzhba/2004/6/.

61. See Viktor P. Starodubov, *Rossiya—SShA: Global'naya zavisimost'* (Moscow: Molodaya gvardiya, 2004).

62. An example is the well-known journalist Mikhail Leont'ev. See Mikhail Leont'ev, "Po zakonam voyennogo vremeni," *Nezavisimaya gazeta,* September 9, 2004; and Mikhail Leont'ev, "Restoring Russia's Future," *Russia in Global Affairs,* October–December 2005, available at http://eng.globalaffairs.ru/.

63. On this point, see Bill McSweeney, *Security, Identity, and Interests: A Sociology of International Relations* (New York: Cambridge University Press, 1999).

64. Tuomas Forsberg, "The EU-Russia Security Partnership: Why the Opportunity was Missed," *European Foreign Affairs Review,* June 2004, 247–67.

65. Andrei V. Belyi, "New Dimensions of Energy Security of the Enlarging EU and Their Impact on Relations with Russia," *European Integration,* December 2003, 351–69.

66. Wolfgang Zellner et al., *Managing Change in Europe: Evaluating the OSCE and Its Future Role,* Working Paper 13 (Hamburg: Center for OSCE Research, University of Hamburg, 2005).

67. Natalya Narochnitskaya, "Russia in the New Geopolitical Context," *International Affairs: A Russian Journal of World Politics, Diplomacy & International Relations,* January–February 2004, 60–73; the quotation here is on 64.

68. Boris Mezhuyev, "Tupiki transnatsionalizatsii," *Neprikosnovennyy zapas,* No. 1 (2005), http://magazines.russ.ru/nz/2005/1/.

69. T. T. Timofeyev, "Protivorechiya globalizatsii i tsivilizatsionnye protsessy," in *Globalizatsiya: konflikt ili dialog tsivilizatsii?* ed. T. Timofeyev, Y. Yakovets, and E. Azroyants (Moscow: Novyy Vek, 2002), 9–22.

70. Sergey Karaganov and Vladislav Inozemtsev, "O mirovom poryadke XXI veka," *Rossiya v global'noy politike,* January–February 2005, available at http://www.global affairs.ru/.

71. Anatoliy Utkin, *Vyzov Zapada i Otvet Rossii* (Moscow: Algoritm, 2002).

72. Mikhail Titarenko, in the roundtable, "New Geopolitics for Russia," *International Affairs: A Russian Journal of World Politics, Diplomacy & International Relations,* March–April 2005, 67–82; the quotation here is on 77.

73. Vladislav Inozemtsev, "Globalizatsiya po-amerikanski kak al'ternativa vesternizatsii," *Kosmopolis,* Winter 2003–4, available at http://www.rami.ru/cosmopolis/.

74. Norrin M. Ripsman and T. V. Paul, "Globalization and the National Security State: A Framework for Analysis," *International Studies Review,* 2005.

75. "Gref: bez gastarbeyterov Rossii ne vidat' udvoeniya VVP," February, 25, 2005, Lentu.ru; for an analytical overview, see Yuri Andrienko and Sergei Guriev, *Understanding Migration in Russia,* Occasional Paper 23 (Moscow: Center for Economic and Financial Research, New Economic School, 2005).

76. See, e.g., Putin's address to the opening session of the Council for Priority Projects and Demographic Policy, October 5, 2006, available at http://www.kremlin.ru. For data on related social tensions, see Mikhail A. Alexseev, *Fortress Russia: An Overview of the 2005 Russian Federation Survey on Immigration Attitudes and Ethnic Relations,* Working Paper 139 (San Diego: Center for Comparative Immigration Studies, University of California, San Diego, 2006). A typical statement of such tensions is "Nashestviye," *Rossiya,* May 19–25, 2005, 4.

77. Mikhail A. Alexseev and Richard C. Hofstetter, "Russia, China, and the Immigration Security Dilemma," *Political Science Quarterly,* Spring 2006, 1–32.

78. An instructive analysis on this point is Robert Orttung and Louise Shelley, *Linkages Between Terrorist and Organized Crime Groups in Nuclear Smuggling: A Case Study of Chelyabinsk Oblast,* Program on New Approaches to Russian Security Policy, Memo 392 (Washington, D.C.: Center for Strategic and International Studies, 2005). See also Johanna Granville, "From Russia without Love: The 'Fourth Wave' of Global Human Trafficking," *Demokratizatsiya,* Winter 2004, 147–55.

79. Alex Cooley, "Globalization and National Security after Empire: The Post-Soviet Space," in *Globalization and National Security,* ed. Jonathan Kirshner (New York: Routledge, 2006), 202–29.

80. Victor Cha, "Globalization and the Study of International Security," *Journal of Peace Research,* May 2000, 391–403.

81. John O'Loughlin, Gearoid Ó Tuathail, and Vladimir Kolossov, "Russian Geopolitical Storylines and Public Opinion in the Wake of 9/11: A Critical Geopolitical Analysis and National Survey," *Communist & Post-Communist Studies,* September 2004, 281–318.

82. "V Gosdume podderzhivayut predlozheniya Gryzlova po bor'be s terroriz-mom," July 27, 2005, available at http://www.strana.ru.

83. John Berryman, "Putin's International Security Priorities," in *The New Security Environment: The Impact on Russia, Central and East Europe,* ed. Roger Kanet (Burlington, Vt.: Ashgate, 2005), 31–52.

84. With regard to soft power constraints on the exercise of hard power, see Sean Kay, "Globalization, Power, and Security," *Security Dialogue,* March 2004, 9–25.

85. L. V. Vardomskiy and S. V. Golunov, eds., *Prozrachnyye granitsy: Bezopastnost' i transgranichnoye sotrudnichecstvo v zone novykh pogranichnykh territoriy Rossii* (Moscow: Nauchno-obrazovatel'nyy forum po mezhdunarodnym otnosheniyam, 2002), 109–30.

86. Ibid., 134–38. See also Roxanne Doty, *Imperial Encounters: The Politics of Representation in North-South Relations* (Minneapolis: University of Minnesota Press, 1996).

87. Christopher Rudolph, "Sovereignty and Territorial Borders in a Global Age," *International Studies Review,* March 2005, 1–20.

88. See the overview of relevant scholarship in Julia Rozanova, "Russia in the Context of Globalization," *Current Sociology,* November 2003, 649–70.

89. This is perceptively discussed in Irina Isakova, *Russian Governance in the 21st Century: Geo-Strategy, Geopolitics and Governance* (New York: Frank Cass, 2005).

90. Tim McDaniel, *The Agony of the Russian Idea* (Princeton, N.J.: Princeton University Press, 1996).

91. Oleksandr Pavliuk, "Russia's Integration with the West and the States 'in-Between,'" in *Russia's Engagement with the West: Transformation and Integration in the Twenty-First Century,* ed. Alexander J. Motyl, Blair A. Ruble, and Lilia Shevtsova (Armonk, N.Y.: M. E. Sharpe, 2005), 185–208.

92. Vadim Medvedev, Yuriy Krasin, and Aleksandr Galkin, "Samoopredelenie Rossii v globaliziruyushchemsya mire," in *Grani globalizatsii,* ed. Veber, 447–512.

93. Andrew Linklater, "Citizenship and Sovereignty in the Post-Westphalian European State," in *Re-Imagining Political Community,* ed. Daniele Archibugi, David Held, and Martin Kohler (Cambridge: Polity Press, 1998), 113–37.

94. Karen Litfin, "The Greening of Sovereignty: An Introduction," in *The Greening of Sovereignty in World Politics,* ed. Karen Litfin (Cambridge, Mass.: MIT Press, 1998), 1–27.

95. Tatyana Shakleyna, *Rossiya i SShA v novom mirovom poryadke* (Moscow: ISKRAN, 2002).

96. See chapter 1 in this volume by Hedetoft; and see also Rodney Bruce Hall, "The Discursive Demolition of the Asian Development Model," *International Studies Quarterly,* March 2003, 71–99.

97. Richard Sakwa, "Russia and Globalisation: Concluding Comments," in *Russian Transformations,* ed. Leo McCann (London: RoutledgeCurzon, 2004), 211–23.

98. Emil' Pain, "Ksenofobiya—ekstremizm—terrorizm," *Druzhba narodov,* no. 1 (2005), http://magazines.russ.ru/druzhba/2005/1/.

99. On the general relationship between collective identity and state capacity, see Ersel Aydinli, "Conclusion: Seeking Conceptual Links for Changing Paradigms," in *Globalization, Security, and the Nation-State,* ed. Aydinli and Rosenau, 231–40.

Contributors

Douglas W. Blum is professor of political science at Providence College and adjunct associate professor of international studies at the Thomas J. Watson Jr. Institute of International Studies at Brown University. His general research interests center on cultural globalization, as well as the connections between globalization, identity, and security in the former USSR. He has published and spoken on a number of related themes, including Russian and American policy foreign policy, energy geopolitics, and environmental security in the Caspian Sea Basin. His most recent work is *National Identity and Globalization: Youth, State, and Society in Post-Soviet Eurasia* (Cambridge University Press, 2007).

Michael Bradshaw is professor of human geography in the Department of Geography at the University of Leicester in the United Kingdom. His research is on the economic geography of Russia, with a particular focus on resource development, the Russian Far East, and energy relations with Northeast Asia. He writes regularly for the *Pacific Oil & Gas Report* and

Oxford Analytica. His publications include *Russia's Regions: A Business Analysis* (Economist Intelligence Unit, 1995); *Regional Economic Change in Russia* (coeditor, with Philip Hanson; Edward Elgar, 2000); and *The Russian Far East and Pacific Asia: Unfulfilled Potential* (editor; Curzon Press, 2002).

Rick Fawn is senior lecturer in international relations at the University of Saint Andrews in the United Kingdom. His books include *The Iraq War: Causes and Consequences* (coeditor, with Raymond Hinnebusch; Lynne Rienner, 2006); *Global Responses to Terrorism: 9/11, Afghanistan and Beyond* (coeditor, with Mary Buckley; Routledge, 2003); and *Ideology and National Identity in Post-Communist Foreign Policies* (editor; Routledge, 2003). His articles have appeared in such journals as *Communist and Post-Communist Studies, Democratization, Europe-Asia Studies, European Security,* and *International Affairs.*

Alexey Fenenko is a senior research fellow at the Moscow Institute of International Security Studies of the Russian Academy of Sciences, an assistant professor in the School of World Politics at Moscow State University, and project coordinator at the Academic Educational Forum of International Relations. His recent publications include *The Notion of Nuclear Stability in Contemporary Political Theory* (URSS, 2006) and *The Theory and Practice of Counterproliferation in U.S. Foreign Policy* (URSS, 2007).

Sergey R. Filonovich is professor of management and dean of the Graduate Management School at the State University–Higher School of Economics in Moscow. He is a member of the Board of the Russian Association of Business Education. He has published several books and articles on cross-cultural management, organizational behavior, and education.

Ulf Hedetoft is professor and director of the SAXO Institute at the University of Copenhagen and director of the Academy for Migration Studies in Denmark. His works include *The Postnational Self: Belonging and Identity* (Minnesota University Press, 2002); *The Global Turn: Nationalist Encounters with the World* (Aalborg University Press, 2003); and *The Politics of Multiple Belonging: Ethnicity and Nationalism in Europe and East Asia* (Ashgate, 2004).

Alla Kassianova has taught at Tomsk State University and has also held visiting research positions at several Western universities, including Stanford University. Her research interests include Russian foreign policy and security policy, and the defense industrial dimension of international security relations. Her articles have been published in *Europe-Asia Studies; US and Canada: Economy, Policy, Culture* (in Russian); *Nonproliferation Review;* and *Contemporary Security Policy.* She has also contributed chapters to edited volumes on current international security issues.

Darya Khaltourina is research fellow of the Center for Regional Studies, Russian Academy of Sciences, and associate professor at the Russian Academy for Civil Service. She has written more than forty scholarly essays on topics ranging from complex social systems, crisis management, demography, and sociocultural anthropology to the mathematical modeling of social processes.

Gennady N. Konstantinov is professor of management at the State University–Higher School of Economics in Moscow. His fields of interest include strategic management, enterprise restructuring, corporate governance, and systems analysis. His most recent publications include the article "Intellectual Entrepreneurship" in the *Harvard Business Review* (Russia) and several works on recent trends in education.

Andrey Korotayev is acting director and professor of anthropology at the East Center, Russian State University for the Humanities, Moscow, as well as senior research fellow of the Institute for Oriental Studies and the Institute for African Studies of the Russian Academy of Sciences. He has written more than two hundred scholarly essays and books, including *Ancient Yemen* (Oxford University Press, 1995) and *Introduction to Social Macrodynamics: Mathematical Models of the World System Development* (URSS, 2006).

Vladimir Lamin is director of the Institute of History, Russian Academy of Sciences, Siberian Branch. He is a corresponding member of the Russian Academy of Sciences and is the author of more than a dozen books, including most recently *Zolotoy Sled Sibiri* (Golden Trace of Siberia).

Erik Noreen is associate professor and head of the Department of Peace and Conflict Research, Uppsala University. His research interests are foreign policy analysis and security studies, with a focus on the Baltic Sea and North Atlantic regions. His recent publications include an article in the *Journal of Peace Research* and *Security Strategies, Power Disparity and Identity: Applying New Perspectives on the Baltic Sea Region* (Ashgate, 2006).

James Richter is professor of politics at Bates College in Lewiston, Maine. He is the author of *Khrushchev's Double Bind* (Johns Hopkins, 1994) and has published works on foreign assistance and civil society in post-Soviet Russia.

Eduard Solovyev is a senior research fellow at the Institute for World Economy and International Relations in Moscow. His fields of research include international relations, national interests and national security, geopolitics, and democratic transitions. He has published more than fifty essays and books, including the book *Natsional'nyye interesy i osnovnyye politicheskiye sily sovremennoy Rossii* (Nauka, 2004).

Mikhail Troitskiy is assistant professor and deputy dean at the School of Political Affairs at the Moscow State Institute of International Relations, and deputy director of the Academic Educational Forum on International Relations. He has published works on U.S. foreign policy, European integration, U.S.-European relations, and U.S.-Russian relations. He writes regularly for Oxford Analytica. He is the author of *Transatlanticheskiy soyuz 1991–2004* (Institute for U.S. and Canadian Studies, 2004).

Evgeny Vodichev is vice director of the Institute of History, Russian Academy of Sciences, Siberian Branch. He is the author of five books, including most recently *Evropeyskiy Souz i Sibir': Opyt Realizatsii Programm Technicheskogo sodeystviya v Sibir'skom Regione* (The European Union and Siberia: Implementation of EU Technical Assistance in the Siberian Region); and *Ekonomicheskiye i Sotsiokulturnye Vzaimodeystviya v Uralo-Sibir'skom Regione* (Economic and Sociocultural Interactions in the Urals-Siberian Region).

Index

Abkhazia, 46, 48, 218
Abramovich, Roman, 17
Adzharia, 321
Afghanistan: antiterrorist campaign in, 298; opiate production in, 67, 78n57; threat of occupation of lands neighboring CIS, 314
AIDS epidemic, 330
alcohol consumption and alcoholism: anti-alcohol campaign (1985–87), 54; beer, wine, and vodka consumption by country, 55, 57; and economic surplus, 66; and globalization, 15, 330; and homelessness, 69; and male fertility, 77n54; and mortality rates, 38, 39, 53–57, 61, 63, 77n41; and suicide rate, 75n24; and vodka, 55, 61, 69–70
Alexeev, Mikhail, 351
Algeria weapon imports, 168
Alkhanov, Alu, 276, 278
Almaz-Antei, 178n38
Altay, 335
Alyoshin, Boris, 171
amphetamine-based drugs, 59
Amsterdam Treaty, 142
anti-Americanism, 298
Anti-Ballistic Missile Treaty of 1972, 224
anti-Western sentiment, 344
Arbatov, Aleksey, 217

"arc of instability," 118
Armenia: economic crisis in, 40–41; mortality rate in, 41, 44, 45, 48, 49
arms trade, 153–54, 167; reciprocal procurement between U.S. and its allies, 156; Russian defense industry presence in, 167. *See also* defense industry (Russian)
Asia, and Russian foreign policy, 112–14, 127–28
assembly, restrictions on, 356
Association of Crisis Centers, 193
Association of European Universities, 143
Astana Appeal (2004), 348
Autonomous District of Inner Mongolia, 128
autonomy, 31n12
axis of instability, 314
Azerbaijan, 218, 320

Babitsky, Andrei, 273
BAE Systems, 158, 176n16
Baltic Sea States, 233–51; human rights issues, 249, 250; NATO membership, 245; security policy development in, 245; socialization process in, 234, 235, 251. *See also* Estonia
Balzer, Harley, 195
bank crisis of 2004, 322

Bashkotorstan, 121, 334

Batalov, Eduard, 214

beer consumption. *See* alcohol consumption and alcoholism

Belarus: Belarusian "cross," 38; Belarus-Russian defense integration, 169; partnership with Russia, 218; U.S. criticism of elections in, 227

Berezovsky, Boris, 17

Beslan school siege of 2004, 263

Bindig, Rudolf, 273

bin Ladin, Osama, 243

birthrate decline, after collapse of USSR, 38

Blum, Douglas W., 30

Bogaturov, Aleksei, 298

Bologna Process: and globalization challenges, 143; and higher education, 26, 139, 142–48; reactions of professional community to adoption of, 144–47; Russian involvement in, 336

Bolshevism, 19

Boronoyev, A., 117

Bosnia and Herzegovina, 309

Bradshaw, Michael, 25–26, 123, 330, 333, 337

Bratislava summit, 318

Brezhnev, Leonid, 118

Budanov, Yuri, 273

Bulgarian "cross," 38

Bull, Hedley, 209

Bureau of the Presidential Envoy on Human Rights and Liberties in Chechnya, 272

Buryatiya, 336

Bush, George H.W., 297

Bush, George W.: and CPRF opposition to war policy of, 291; and NATO, 299; propaganda trip to Georgia (2005), 24; and Russian policy, 224

capital punishment, 270

Carothers, Thomas, 184

Center for Strategic Developments, 141

Center for the Analysis of Strategies and Technologies (CAST), 166

Chechnya: and international terrorism, 243–44; and Russian-U.S. foreign policy, 218; U.S. criticism of elections in, 227. *See also* Russian-Chechen conflict

Checkel, Jeffrey, 277

checks and balances, 290

Chernomyrdin, Viktor, 359

child mortality, 43–44, 75n14

China: economic revitalization of Inner Mongolia, 127–28; foreign direct investment in, 90, 91; industrialization of, 310; and nuclear fissile control, 318; refusal to negotiate on Xinjiang and Tibet, 315; and Russia, 220, 297; weapon imports, 167

Chubays, Anatoliy, 292

CIS. *See* Commonwealth of Independent States

Citizenship Law of 1992, 236

civil society, promotion of, 27, 181–200; disappointing results in, 182; new policy agenda, 182–84; and non-governmental organizations (NGOs), 181–83, 186, 189, 195–97, 338; organizational funding, 185, 186, 187, 194, 195, 199; Putin and *Gosudarstvennost,* 194–98; Russian associational life, 184–88; Russian state and society, 188–89, 338; Third Sector recruits, 189–94, 199; Western investment in, 267

Clash of Civilizations, The (Huntington), 302

Clinton administration, 264

CoE. *See* Council of Europe

coefficient of variation (CV), 102

collective identity. *See* political history/collective identity

Collective Security Treaty Organization (CSTO), 168

"colored revolutions": aftermath of, 348; American involvement in, 220; changes seen as threat to social stability, 351; funding of, 338; as ideological problem, 319; and international norms of justice, 28; as nationalistic movements, 320–21, 342; Orange Revolution, 196, 320; Rose Revolution, 320; and U.S.-Russian relations, 224; Western state support of, 338

Commonwealth of Independent States (CIS): Collective Security Treaty Organization, 168; Russia's position within, 297–98, 338

Communist Party of the Russian Federation (CPRF), 290–91

complex connectivity, 4

Comprehensive Test Ban Treaty, 24

Concern PVO "Almaz-Antei," 178n38

Condition of Postmodernity (Harvey), 82

Conference on Security and Cooperation in Europe (CSCE), 267

Consortium of Russian Women's NGOs, 186

containment strategy, 318

Convention for the Protection of Human Rights and Fundamental Freedoms, 272

Convention on the Prevention of Terror, 272

Cooley, Alex, 351

Council for Facilitating the Development of Civil Society Institutions and Human Rights, 196

Council of Europe (CoE): access to Chechen campaign, 272–73; influence of, 270–71; international requirements as domestic law, 271–72; membership in as expression of values, 268–70; membership requirements demanded of Russia, 29, 261–62; and Russian-Chechen conflict, 259–260, 266; Russian responses to pressure of, 270, 275–78, 315, 348; sanctions and suspension from, 271

counterterrorism: indiscriminate use of violence as, 264; U.S. policies, 218. *See also* war on terrorism

Cox, Michael, 2

CPRF (Communist Party of the Russian Federation), 290–91

creative intelligentsia, as Third Sector recruits, 190

crisis of authority, 339

Croatia, 309

CSCE (Conference on Security and Cooperation in Europe), 267

CSTO (Collective Security Treaty Organization), 168

cultural identity: European, 125; Russian contribution to world cultural heritage, 214. *See also* national identity

Cyprus: alcohol consumption in, 76n37; investment activity in Russia, 92

Czech Republic: ethnic foundation of, 309; as EU member, 219; foreign direct investment in, 90

death penalty, 270

decentralization, 313, 356–57

Declaration of the Heads of State of the Shanghai Cooperation Organization Member Countries, 226

decolonization, 20–21, 33n39

deep integration, 85

Defense Industrial Complex (OPK), 162, 177n28

defense industry (Europe), 160; European-wide national defense procurement, 161; French technological support programs, 160; reciprocal dependence in, 161; U.K. policies, 160

defense industry (Russian), 153–75, 337; budgeting of, 164–65, 178n45; CIS market interest, 168–69, 179n54; consolidation of, 163–64; coproduction and codevelopment partnerships, 169; dual-use technologies, 156; and economic globalization, 154; export production, 165–66, 167, 179n46; international/transnational dimension of, 167–70; licensed production and assembly, 169; nonstate investment in, 172; ownership pattern of, 162–64;

defense industry (Russian) (*continued*)
restructuring in globalization context,
171–73; state regulation of, 159–62;
structural characteristics and trends,
162–66; transnationalization of, 157,
159, 161, 167–70; U.S. and European
models, 155–59

defense industry (U.S.): acquisition and
procurement in, 161; import dependency in, 158; industrial exports,
176n14; military spending after Cold
War, 156; privatization and internationalization of, 157; protection
of domestic armaments production
base, 177n28; regulation of, 160; and
Russian contractors, 170; state
industrial base policy, 161–62

Degoyev, Vladimir, 346

Delyagin, Mikhail, 345

demographic crisis: comparative
demographics, 38–59; GDP and life
expectancy, 37–38; and globalization,
330; mortality rates, 38–59; statistical
analysis, 59–68

derzhava (great power), 290

Dicken, Peter, 85

disaggregation, 5–6

disease, threat of, 351

Djamaldayev, Shaid, 279

Dmitriev, Mikhail, 180n68

Dneprov, E.D., 141

domestic political affairs, rejection of
outside interference in, 315

domestic violence, 193

Donnelly, Jack, 275

Drachevskiy, Leonid, 332

drugs and illegal drug use: amphetamine-
based drugs, 59; globalization as factor
in, 330; heroin, 58, 67; and HIV, 61,
77n53; and mortality rate, 39, 57–59;
opiates, 58–59, 61, 67, 78n57

drug trafficking, 225, 322, 351

Dubin, Boris, 344

Dugin, Alexsandr, 289–90, 344

"Dutch disease," 322

Dzhabrailov, Taus, 279

"Eastern Shift," 114

EBRD. *See* European Bank for
Reconstruction and Development

ECHR (European Convention on Human
Rights), 272, 274

economic geography, and market
economy needs, 99

economy, of Russia: energy assets,
32n21, 80, 87, 93, 106, 300, 316–17,
348; energy export and high-
technology potential, 154; export
sales, 154, 175n2; financial crisis of
1998, 100; foreign trade, 80–81, 86–
90, 304; gross regional product, 95,
97; import of commodities, 87;
interaction with global economy,
85–98; Internet and economic
development, 337; neoliberal policies
of 1980s, 182; non-energy resources,
87; regional economic performance,
99–105, 107; transitional recession,
99–100. *See also* defense industry
(Russian)

education, higher, 139–51; and Bologna
Process, 26, 139, 142–48; and
Enlightenment ideas, 150; EU support
of Russian reform in, 145–46;
integration processes, 142; knowledge
economy and incipient trends in,
148–50; levels of and degrees
awarded, 140; modernization thesis,
141, 151; and policymaking, 336;
reform of, 139, 140–42, 356; trends,
150–51; university role, 149–50

Elementy magazine, 289

energy security concept, 317

environmentalists, 185

Erasmus Mundus, 145, 148

e-Russia program, 337

Estonia, 234–36; cohesive identity of
ethnic Estonians, 247; and Council of
Europe, 278; economic, societal, and
political consolidation of, 236–37;
economic crisis in, 42; Estonian
"cross," 38; and EU, 24, 237, 250;
human rights issues, 250; mortality

rate in, 43, 44, 45, 46–47, 49–50; national identity, 235, 236; NATO membership, 237; post–Cold War phases of, 236; relationship with Russia, 237–39, 252*n*9; Russian-speaking minority in, 28–29, 248–49, 250; State Integration Program, 237; terrorism concerns in, 238; threat images, 244–45, 250

ethnic nationalism, 312–13, 319

ethnic-social processes, 308

Eurasianism, 125, 335, 346

European Bank for Reconstruction and Development (EBRD), 91, 266, 283*n*22

European Commission, 149

European Convention on Human Rights (ECHR), 272, 274

European Court of Human Rights, 270, 274

European Defense Agency, 160

European Union (EU): Bologna Process, 26, 139, 142–48, 336; and "Europe" defined, 262; membership of formerly dominated countries, 21; and Russia, 24, 343. *See also specific countries*

Evangelista, Matthew, 274

Far East regional associations, 119

Fawn, Rick, 29, 124, 341, 358

FDI. *See* foreign direct investment

Federal District Council, 332

Federal Registration Center, 197

Fedulova, Valentina, 192

female life expectancy, 50–52

Fenenko, Alexey, 17, 30, 350, 352, 358

fertility rate: alcohol and drug use as cause of, 68; comparative demographics, 38; and excessive male mortality, 57, 63; general factors affecting, 65; and life expectancy, 52, 60, 62, 64, 66

Filonovich, Sergey R., 23, 26, 336

financial centers, 98

financial crisis of 1998, 100

fissile materials, control of, 318

Ford Foundation, 201*n*19

foreign direct investment (FDI), 90–98; geographical distribution of, 85, 94–95, 106; sectoral structure of, 91, 93, 330; statistics relating to, 108*n*24; top recipient regions, 94, 96

Foreign Policy Doctrine (2000), 225

Foreign Policy Framework of the Russian Federation, 217–18, 295, 296

foreign policy (Russia): and China, 220; cooperation with European Union, 121–26; demands for justice in, 354; East/West balancing act, 126; and globalization, 122–23, 224–27; international justice case studies, 220–27; mass media role in, 318, 328*n*67; and national identity, 334–35; NATO enlargement, 221–22; parallel planes of, 298; political action with China, 296, 297; power balancing, 213–14, 215; pressure to end imperialism, 261–62, 281*n*2; Putin emphasis on collaboration and competition, 342; role of justice in formation of, 208–9, 211; and Russian conception of justice in 1990s, 218; and Russian security policy, 311; trends, 228; U.S.-Russian relations (1992–2005), 222–24; U.S.-Russian security agenda, 226

foreign trade, 86–90, 160, 304

France: and nuclear fissile control, 318; and technological support programs, 160

free speech restrictions, 356

Fuller, Steve, 150

Gates, Robert, 267

Gazprom, 32*n*26, 128

GDP. *See* gross domestic product

Gelderblom-Lankhout, Hanneke, 285*n*52

"geographic situatedness," 84

geography, and globalization, 81–85; distribution of Russian exports/imports, 88–89; geography of foreign investment in Russia, 90–98; Russian foreign trade participation, 86–90 geopolitics, 287–304, 344–46; communist geopolitics, 290–91; idea of Russian liberal empire, 292; multipolar world concept, 293–301; and national identity, 301–4; neo-Eurasionism, 289–90; of Russian liberals, 291–93; shared assumptions, 288–89

Georgia: conflicts with Abkhazia and Southern Ossetia, 321; economic crisis in, 40–41, 42; life expectancy in, 51–52; mortality rate in, 42, 44, 45–46, 48–49; political turmoil in, 319, 343, 352; protests and regime changes in, 220; pro-Western course of, 218; and revoked autonomy of Adzharia, 321; and Rose Revolution, 320; Russian air raids in the Pankisi Gorge, 319

Germany: industrialization of German Empire, 310; investment activity in Russia, 92; reunification of, 212

Gil-Robles, Alvaro, 273, 280

globalization: "Atlanticist" image of, 233; challenges of, 2, 3–9; Communist Party attitude toward, 291; definition of, 2, 82; demographic change and public health, 330; and educational reform, 139; and existing Russian values, 260; fighting negative implications of, 226; financial, 330, 331; foreign investment in Russia, 90–98; globalizing processes in Europe after the Cold War, 260–63; identity and perceptions of, 349–50; of military-industrial complex, 338; national sovereignty vs. benefits of, 227; and the new security environment, 308–11; rebuilding power and identity in context of, 21–22; Russian participation in foreign trade, 86–90; Russia's evolving views on, 224–27; Russia's interaction with global economy, 85–98; seen as strategy to consolidate American power, 350; and sovereignty, 353–55.

See also economy, of Russia; geography, and globalization; international socialization; territorial cohesion, and globalization

"glocalization," 84

Glotov, Sergei, 277

Goldman, Marshall, 133

"good governance," 183

Gorbachev, Mikhail: on national identity, 120, 348; "new vision" military strategy, 313–14

Gosnarkokontrol, 57–58

Gosoboronzakaz (GOZ), 164, 166, 173

Gosudarstvennost, 194–98

Greater Urals, 119

Greater Volga, 119

Greece, alcohol consumption in, 76n37

Gref, German, 141, 171, 351

Gross, Andreas, 263, 273

gross domestic product (GDP): and foreign trade, 304; and life expectancy, 37–38, 60–63; redistribution of national income among regions, 105

gross regional product, 102–4; per capita, 102, 103, 104; regional variations in, 95, 97

Group of Eight, 24

Group of Seven–NATO complex, 314

Harvey, David, 82

Havel, Václav, 268

health care: deterioration of, and mortality, 53–57; and globalization, 330; investment in, 38

Hedetoft, Ulf, 329, 353, 355

Held, David, 82

Helsinki Accords, 267

Hemment, Julie, 202n33

heroin, 58

Herrera, Yoshiko, 135, 334

historical identities, 16

HIV, and drug use, 61, 77n53

Hofstetter, Richard, 351

homelessness, 69

homogeneity, 350

Hoon, Geoff, 175n16

human rights: in Baltic states, 249; European and Russian interpretations of, 124; international human rights norms, 264; Putin and European ideals of, 347

human rights organizations, in Russia, 185

Human Rights Watch, 270

human trafficking, 225, 351

Humboldt, Wilhelm von, 150

Humphrey, Caroline, 335

Hungary: alcohol consumption in, 65; Hungarian "cross," 38; as member of European Union, 219; mortality rates in, 57

Huntington, Samuel, 302

Hussein, Saddam, 218

identity: collective (social), 246–47, 357; in foreign policy and institutional membership, 347–49; fragmentation of regional and ethnic identity, 336; and geopolitics, 301–4; historical, 16; international socialization and development of, 245–48; local, 85; orientations, 339–47; and perceptions of globalization, 349–50; regional, 333–34; social identity theory, 247. *See also* national identity

IGOs. *See* intergovernmental organizations

Ikenberry, John, 218

imaginative geography, 344–45

"imagined economies," 135

IMF (International Monetary Fund), 80, 182

immigration: attracting immigrants, 351, 356; globalization and immigration phobia, 351; and resulting social tensions, 6–7, 333

imperial collapse, 33n39

imperialism, 291

Independent Women's Forum, 191

India: defense policy, 175; Indian–Russian Brahmos joint venture, 169–70; industrialization of, 310;

political and economic strength of, 297; Russian cooperation with, 317–18; weapon imports, 167

industrial centers, 98

infectious diseases, 225

Information Security Doctrine, 337

information technology industry, 156, 360n29

in-group, 246

INO Center, 152n16

"Integration of Knowledge" (Ryabov), 144

interethnic conflicts, 321

intergovernmental organizations (IGOs): Russian exclusion from, 342, 344; social norms and expectations regarding state intervention, 357

International Atomic Energy Agency, Additional Protocol of (1997), 318

internationalization, of defense industry, 157

International Monetary Fund (IMF), 80, 182

international socialization: communication, learning, and social identity in framework of, 234; and developing identities, 245–48. *See also* Baltic Sea States

Internet security, 337

Interregional Studies in Social Sciences, 152n16

Iran: and nuclear fissile control, 318; Russian cooperation with, 317

Iraq, Russian/U.S. disputes over, 226

Irkut Corporation, 163, 170

Irkutsk University, 140

Islamic fundamentalists, 248, 254n39, 311–12, 329, 332

Italy, industrialization of, 310

Ivanov, Igor, 16, 248, 268, 272, 278, 319

Ivanov, Sergei, 171

Jackson, William, 278

Jackson-Vanik Amendment (U.S.-Russia trade relations), 342

Jamestown Foundation, 271

Japan, industrialization of, 310
Joint Declaration on New Strategic
    Relations, 224
Judd, Lord Frank, 279
justice, 17–18, 207–28; definition of,
    209; in foreign relations, 354; as
    identity-shaping force, 212–16;
    "international justice" concepts, 208,
    219; the past as a moral guide to,
    209–12; principles, 209–10;
    relativistic drift of early 2000s,
    216–20; resource distribution, 210,
    211; and Russian culture, 208; Russian
    foreign policy issues, 220–27

Kádár, János, 57
Kalmykiya, 335
Karabakh war, 45, 48, 49
Karaganovym, Sergei, 325n28
Kaskol, 170
Kassianova, Alla, 27, 337
Kay, Rebecca, 191
Kazakhstan: mortality in, 75n18; U.S.
    investment in, 361n31
khalifate, 244
Khaltourina, Darya, 15, 25
Khodorkovsky, Mikhail, 17
Kissinger, Henry, 287
knowledge-based society, 336
knowledge economy, 139, 148–50
Konstantinov, Gennady N., 23, 26, 336
Korotayev, Andrey, 15, 25
Kortunov, Sergey, 212–13, 214, 344
Kosachev, Konstantin, 278
Kosovo crisis, 242, 348
Kozyrev, Andrey: on economic
    sanctions, 264; idealist policies, 219,
    227; on NATO and Western relations,
    241, 325n28; policy toward U.S.,
    222–23, 230n21; refusal to sign
    Partnership for Peace documents,
    254n27; and Washington, 297; and
    Westernization, 16
Kuzminov, Ya I., 141
Kyrgyzstan: military base in, 352;
    political uprisings in, 343; and "Tulip
    Revolution," 320

Lamin, Vladimir, 26, 27, 333, 334
Latvia, 309
Latvian "cross," 38
Lavrov, Sergey, 16, 222, 259, 280–81
Lebed, Aleksandr, 317
Lebed, Aleksey, 317
Lenin, Vladimir, 234
life expectancy: and alcohol
    consumption, 61, 77n41; calculation
    flaws, 77n47; female, 50–52, 62–64;
    and gross domestic product, 37–38,
    60–63; in Ingushetia and Dagestan,
    54–55; in Islamic countries, 55;
    Russian and British compared, 53;
    statistical analysis, 59–68
Likhachev, Vasiliy, 269–70, 276
"limited war" idea, 314
Lithuania, 309
living standards, 103, 105
local identity, 85
Lockheed Martin, 170, 179n57
Lomonosov, Mikhail, 113
Luxembourg, investment activity in
    Russia, 92

Maastricht Treaty, 142, 156
Macedonia, 309
MacKinder, Halford, 213
"Magna Carta of the University," 142
"managed democracy" notion, 335
managed pluralism model, 195
manufacturing, 92
mass/elite interaction, 4, 5–6, 8, 33n29
Massey, Doreen, 83–84, 85
mass media, and foreign policy, 318,
    328n67
Matvienko, Valentina, 269
Mavrodi, Sergei, 17
McAuley, Mary, 201n19
McDaniel, Tim, 353
medical care. *See* health care
Medvedev, Dmitriy, 213
megaterrorism, 225
Memorial (Russian human rights
    organization), 266
Mendelson, Sarah, 267

MIC (military-industrial complex), 27, 162

military: "Gorbachev's new vision," 313; "limited war" idea, 314; policy and strength, 309, 315, 326*n*42, 327*n*49; political-military elite, 316; "social weaknesses" of Russian army, 315. *See also* defense industry (Russian)

military-industrial complex (MIC or VPK), 27, 162

Ministry for Regional Development, 105

Mironov, Sergey, 144

Mitrofanov, Aleksey, 288

mobility of population, 356

modernization: and energy resources, 316–17; as model of economic development, 309

Molchanov, Mikhail A., 362*n*49

Moldova: alcohol consumption in, 55, 57; mortality rate, 77*n*39; post-Soviet conflict in, 352; pro-Western course of, 218

Molotov, Vyacheslav, 70

money laundering, 351

moral authority, 212

Morin, Edgar, 143

mortality rates, 38–59; and alcohol consumption, 38, 39, 53–55, 68; child mortality, 43–44, 75*n*14; and drug consumption, 57–59, 61–62, 68; economic collapse effect on, 39, 40–45; and fertility rate decline, 57, 63; and health care deterioration, 53–57; and organized violence, 45–53; psychological stress as cause of, 40; Russian working males and children compared, 75*n*26; and smoking, 77*n*52; social causes for, 39; stroke rates, 53

Moscow, and Siberian identity, 133–34, 136

Moscow State University Department of Economics, 140

multipolarity doctrine, 215–16, 223, 229*n*8, 299

"Muscovite subethnos," 133

Narochnitskaya, Natalya, 349

National Education Policy Project, 151

National Fund for Training of Scholars, 152*n*16

national idea, 308–9

national identity, 111–36, 247; and building of empire, 114; Communist ideals, 118; cultural and political traditions, 125; European cultural commonality, 341, 342; and foreign policy, 334–35; and geopolitics, 301–4; hybridization tendency, 339, 344; justice as a shaping force for, 212–16; and large-scale migrations, 309; modernization and territorial expansion, 112–14; in post-Soviet years, 120; relativistic drift of early 2000s, 216–20; Russian identity after loss of Ukraine, 362*n*49; self-identification processes, 111; Siberian regionalism in 19th and 20th centuries, 114–17; and social-status-based divisions, 334; sources of Russian identity, 340; "Soviet people," 118; and vodka, 70

nationalistic projects, 320

National Security Concept of 1997, 223

National Security Concept of 2000, 241

NATO: Baltic states membership, 245; cooperation needed for success and effectiveness of, 238; expansion of, 24, 221–22, 240–41, 253*n*19, 294, 296, 299, 312, 325*n*28, 342; former Soviet allies' integration into, 219; Group of Seven–NATO complex, 314; interoperability of NATO forces, 156; membership as safeguard to Russian encroachments, 21; operation in Yugoslavia (1999), 315; Russia's "equality" with U.S., 213–14, 217; Russia's view of as security threat, 239

Nazism, 19, 212

Nedoroslev, Sergei, 170, 179*n*59

Nemtsov, Aleksandr, 54, 61

Nemtsov, Boris, 189

neo-Eurasionism, 289–90

Netherlands, investment activity in Russia, 92

new military doctrine, 318–19

"new regionalism," 83
new world order, 291. *See also* globalization
NGOs. *See* nongovernmental organizations
Nizhnii Novgorod, 189, 190
nongovernmental organizations (NGOs): and "colored revolutions," 338; funding of, 181–82, 189, 195; Putin's idea of, 182, 183, 196, 197; social norms and expectations regarding state intervention, 357; women's organizations, 186
Noreen, Erik, 24, 124–25, 341, 358
North Bukovina, 321
North Caucasus, 121, 334
North Korea: and nuclear fissile control, 318; Russian cooperation with, 317, 318
Novgorod, 332
Novikova, Elvira, 200*n*11
NPO Almaz, 178*n*38
Nuclear Non-Proliferation Treaty (1968), 213
nuclear weapons and materials: and arms control measures, 213, 224, 314; black market for, 310; and defense production budget, 166; in Europe, 224; and national identity, 11–12, 19, 213; security challenges, 317–18, 322; and state sovereignty, 313–14; threat of, 225, 307, 318
Nukhazhiyev, Nurdi, 274
Nunn-Lugar initiative, 318

Odessa Jewish community, 321
Ögütçü, Mehmet, 90
OHB-System AG, 170
oil and gas resources, 80
Oldberg, Ingmar, 250–51
oligarchs, ethnic and populist agitation against, 15
"On Education" law, 140
"On the Introduction of a Multitiered Structure of Higher Education in the Russian Federation," 140
opiates, 58–59, 61, 67, 78*n*57

OPK. *See* Defense Industrial Complex
optoelectronics industry, 176*n*19
Orange Revolution, 28, 196, 320
Organization for Security and Cooperation in Europe (OSCE), 216, 269, 315, 348; Assistance Group in Chechnya, 273
Orthodoxy, 115, 118
outsiders, distrust of, 15

PACE. *See* Parliamentary Assembly of the Council of Europe
Pakistan, 318
Panarin, Aleksandr, 290
"parade of sovereignties," 120
Parliamentary Assembly of the Council of Europe (PACE), 263, 271; Recommendation 1444, "The Conflict in Chechnya," 270
Partnership and Cooperation Agreement (1994), 121
Partnership for Peace, 24
perestroika, 70
pilot regions, 332
Poland: European Union membership, 219; foreign direct investment in, 90
political history/collective identity, 4, 7, 246–47, 357
pollution, 330
Polyot, 170
Ponarin, Eduard, 2, 3
population decline, after collapse of USSR, 38, 128
populism, anti-immigrant, 6–7
"positionality," 84
Potanin, G., 116
"power geometry," 84
Pozdnyakov, Eduard, 213
Pravda, Alex, 335
Primakov, Yevgeniy (Evgeniy): and Council of Europe, 276; multipolarity doctrine, 223, 294, 297–98; national-interest-based approach of, 227; on NATO and Western relations, 241, 295–96, 325*n*28; ratification of Council of Europe treaties by, 268–69;

"Russia First" policy, 16; on Russia's role in international relations, 215

Primorye region, 132

privatization, of defense industry, 157

property rights, security of, 91

public activism, 189. *See also* civil society, promotion of

Public Chamber (Obshchestvennyi Palata), 196–97

public health, 330

Pukhov, Ruslan, 172

Pursianen, Christer, 272, 277

Putin, Vladimir: approach to civil society, 195–96; centralizing programs of, 353–55; on Chechen conflict, 265; control of nongovernmental organizations, 182, 196, 197–98; control of private defense firms, 337–38; on cooperation with NATO, 222; and cooperation with the West, 351–52; on diversity, 350; economic policy of, 331; on expansion of NATO, 240; foreign policy of, 127, 225, 281n2, 343; and funding of nongovernmental organizations, 339; globalization perspective of, 225, 335; and *Gosudarstvennost,* 194–98; on higher education, 151; and human rights ideals, 347; implementation of vertical power structure by, 134; policy toward U.S., 223; reform efforts of, 219–20, 313, 331, 353; relativistic vision of international justice, 217; Russian Communist opposition to, 291; on Russian identity, 341; and Russian state sovereignty, 199–200; and Single Economic Space, 226; and sovereign integrity of Russia, 17; tax reforms introduced by, 105; visit to Yakutiya in 2006, 327n55; and Westernization, 16

Putnam, Robert, 183

quality of life, 40

research and development, domestic investment in, 159, 337

"resource rent," 106

Richter, James, 23, 27, 338

Robinson, Mary, 272

Romanov Empire, 19

Rose Revolution, 320

Rosoboronexport, 165–66, 167, 172, 177–78n33

Rosvertol, 164

ruble devaluation (1998), 101

Russia: culture of, and globalization, 3; economic crisis in, 40–41; as Eurasian power, 213; and European Union, 24, 249, 250; foreign direct investment in, 90–95; geopolitics and identity of, 301–4; historical factors, 18–22; modernization of, 112–13; Muslim regions of, 311–12; nuclear disarmament in, 318; as nuclear power, 213; political action with China, 296, 297; relationship with Estonia, 237–39; Russian "cross," 38, 39; shared political history with USSR, 18; as spiritual authority, 214; strained relationship with globalization, 22–24; threat image agenda, 244–45, 250; Western view of reform in, 230n22. *See also* national identity; *specific topics*

Russia-EU Partnership and Cooperation Agreement (1994), 223

Russian Academy of Sciences, 152n4

Russian-Chechen conflict, 126, 259–81, 329, 332; human rights issues, 263–67, 272; impact of human rights norms on state practice, 265–67; and response to CoE pressure, 275–78; Russian accountability for, 273–75; Russian membership in Council of Europe, 268–70; terrorist atrocities, 263–65, 282n5

Russian-Chechen Friendship Society, 197

Russian Empire, industrialization of, 310

Russian Foreign Policy Concept of 1992, 221, 229nn10–12

"Russian Gaullism," 298

"Russian Idea," 353
Russian Justice Initiative, 197
Russian Mafia, 17
Russian Orthodoxy, 340
Russian School forum, 141
Russocentrism, 288
Rusyns, 321
Ryabov, Gennadiy, 144

Saakashvili, Mikhail, 320
Sadovnichiy, Viktor, 144
Sakha, 334, 335
Sakhalin Island projects, 95, 109n26
Sakha-Yahutia, 12
Sakwa, Richard, 234, 247
Schwimmer, Walter, 273
science and technology revolution (of
   1950s), 324n13
security, in Russia, 307–23; effect of
   globalization on security policy,
   350–53; energy factor, 310, 321–22;
   external military threats, 307; future
   challenges for, 317–22; globalization
   and the new security environment,
   308–11; modernization and energy
   resources, 316–17; new parameters
   and objectives for, 311–13;
   nontraditional security problems, 322;
   Russian adaptation to new security
   environment, 313–17
security, international, 310. *See also*
   terrorism
security and threat scenarios, 4, 7–8, 16,
   17
security community, 234
Security Council (UN), 216, 230n13
security environment: changing
   conception of, 308; and globalization,
   308–11; socialization of, 308
security scenarios, 16, 17
separatist movements, 319
sexually-transmitted disease, 330
Shakleina, Tatiana, 217
Sharandin, Yury, 279
Shelekhov, Irkutsk Province, 129
Sheppard, Eric, 84

Shevardnadze, Eduoard, 320
Shokhin, Aleksandr, 151, 276
Siberia: attitude toward Moscow,
   133–34; colonization of, 114–15;
   ethnic identity of, 334; export of
   resources from, 89; identity of, 335;
   mass colonization of, 116; population
   decline, 128; regional identity, 115–17,
   119, 121, 135; regionalism in 19th and
   20th centuries, 114–17; Russian
   expansion to, 112–13; self-
   identification issues, 112, 119,
   129–33; socioeconomic development
   of, 128; Soviet identity and self-
   identification archetype, 117–21
Siberian Accord, 317, 332
Siberian Compact, 119, 131
Siberian Curse, The (Hill and Gaddy),
   99
Sibneft, 128
"singing revolution," 236
Single Economic Space, 226
Slovakia, 55, 309
Slovenia, 309
smoking, and mortality, 39, 77n52
social capital, 149, 183
social disenchantment and distrust, 15
social identity, 246–47
socialism, 291
socialization: of Baltic Sea States, 234,
   235, 257; of Russia, 216, 227; of
   security environment, 308. *See also*
   international socialization
social pessimism, 76n24
social pluralism, 303
social stratification, 334
Solovyev, Eduard, 29, 243, 344, 358
Sorbonne Declaration, 142, 152n5
South Ossetia, 218
sovereignty, 4, 9–15; as autonomy and
   global institutions, 14–15; borders,
   9–11; and domestic conflicts, 12–14;
   and globalization, 4–6, 353–55;
   military factors, 313–16; military
   strength and economic weakness,
   11–12; role of nuclear weapons in

defense of, 314; Schmitt's definition of, 31*n*10; trust issues between leaders and citizens, 15
Soviet Bolshevism, 19
space sector, of Russian industry, 360*n*29
Space Transportation Inc., 179*n*57
Sperling, Valerie, 192
Stalin, Joseph, 69–70
State Armaments Program, 173
state defense orders, 164, 166, 173
Stockholm International Peace Research Institute, 157
Stoliarov, Mikhail, 333
Stolypin, Piotr, 116
Strategic Nuclear Potentials Treaty, 224
Strategy for Russia: Education, 141
stress, psychological, 40
stroke mortality, 53, 75*n*21
substance abuse, 15. *See also* alcohol consumption and alcoholism; drugs and illegal drug use
Sukhoi, 165
Swyngedouw, Erik, 84
Syria, Russian cooperation with, 317

Tajikistan: mortality crisis in, 75*n*18; post-Soviet conflict in, 352
Tarasov, Artyom, 17
Tatarstan, 121, 334
tax reforms, 105
technological development, 336–37
technological revolution, 309–10, 324*n*13
tempus program, 145
territorial cohesion, and globalization, 79–107; foreign investment in Russia, 90–98; geographical issues, 81–85; regional economic performance, 98–105; Russian foreign trade, 86–90; unsustainable energy resources, 106
terrorism: and conception of security, 351; and globalization, 311; international, 242–43, 254*n*39; megaterrorism, 225; and Russian-U.S. foreign policy, 218, 224; transnational

terrorist networks, 310, 322; war on, 17, 220, 225, 291, 319, 351. *See also* Russian-Chechen conflict
terrorist attacks of September 11, 2001, 298; effect on Russian security policy, 242; U.S. policy toward Russia following, 210
Third Sector professionals, 183–84; recruits, 190–91; Western ideals of, 191
threat scenarios. *See* security and threat scenarios
"time-space compression" concept, 82–83
tobacco use, and mortality, 39, 77*n*52
Tolz, Vera, 344
Tomlinson, John, 4
trade. *See* foreign trade
trafficking. *See* drug trafficking; human trafficking
Transcarpathia, 321
Transcaucasia mortality rate, 48
transfer payments, from donor regions, 105
transfer pricing, 88
transitional recession, 99
transnational crime, 351
transnationalization, of defense industry, 157–58, 159, 161, 167–70
Transnistrian Republic, 218
Troitskiy, Mikhail, 17, 28, 350, 354, 358
Tsygankov, Andrei, 346
Tulip Revolution, 320
Tuva, 335

Ukraine: energy trade pressures, 347; ethnic minorities in, 321; and gas prices, 32*n*26; Orange Revolution, 196, 320; political turmoil in, 319, 343; protests and regime changes in, 220; pro-Western course of, 218; Russian subsidization of economy of, 300; Russian-Ukrainian transport aircraft project, 170; Ukrainian "cross," 38

382 *Index*

"Ukrainization," 321
Union of Russian Women, 185
unipolarity, 291
United Kingdom investment in Russia, 92
United Nations, and international security, 216, 230n13
United States: anti-Americanism, 298; defense procurement and arms export controls, 160; foreign direct investment in, 90; information technology and foreign interfirm alliances, 156; investment activity in Russia, 92, 93; objection to Russian cooperation with nuclear proliferators, 317–18; perceived expansion of influence of, 329–30; perception of USSR, 19; Russian pressure to downsize military presence in Central Asia, 227; Russian-U.S. relations (1992–2005), 222–24; Russia's view of as unequal to task of unification, 214
United States of Islam, 244
university education. *See* education, higher
University of Maryland, 140
Ural region, 114
Uralvagonzavod, 171
U.S. Agency for International Development, 192
USSR, industrialization of, 310
USSR and collapse of, 19–20; and expectations regarding Cold War hostilities, 212; and fragmentation of national identity, 336; military and nuclear status of, 19; and "new policy agenda," 182; regional opportunities following, 120; Russian geopolitics following, 288–89; and Soviet identity crisis, 120; Western patronage of reforms following, 302
Uzbekistan: economic crisis in, 42–43; life expectancy in, 51; military base in, 352; mortality rate in, 43, 44, 45, 47–48; pro-Western course of, 218

violence, organized, 45–53
Virgin Islands, investment activity in Russia, 92
Vladivostok State University, 140
Vladychenko, A.I., 277
Vodichev, Evgeny, 26, 27, 333, 334
vodka and consumption of. *See* alcohol consumption and alcoholism
Volga-Urals resources, 89
voluntary associations. *See* nongovernmental organizations (NGOs)
VPK (military-industrial complex), 27, 162

war: Abkhazia war, 46, 48; global antiterrorist war, 319; Karabakh war, 45, 48, 49; transnational Islamic network threat, 314. *See also* "colored revolutions"
war on terrorism, 17, 220, 225, 291, 319, 351
Warsaw Pact, 213, 219
weapons and weapons production: government policies on, 159; market-driven, 158; weapons development, 156. *See also* arms trade; defense industry (Russian); nuclear weapons and materials
weapons of mass destruction. *See* nuclear weapons and materials
Wedel, Janine, 194
Weiner, Douglas R., 190
welfare benefits, 15
wine consumption. *See* alcohol consumption and alcoholism
Wolf, Alison, 150
women: domestic violence issues, 193; isolation of women's movement, 191–92; Russian organizations of, 185, 186; as Third Sector recruits, 190
Women's League, 192
World Bank: and "new policy agenda," 182; on regional economic performance, 100; regional inequality study, 101–2; and Russian economy and international competition, 80

World Health Organization, 54
World Trade Organization, 80, 338, 342
World War II sacrifices, 212

Yadov, V., 130
Yadrintsev, N., 116
Yeltsin, Boris: and Council of Europe,
   275–76; and economic liberalization,
   57; ethnic self-identification policy,
   120–21; and foreign assistance, 194;
   and justice in foreign relations, 354;

reform efforts, 188–89; and Russian
   identity, 332; and United States, 222,
   297; and Westernization, 16
Yugoslavia, 315
Yukos, 91, 338
Yushchenko, Viktor, 320

Zavtra (newspaper), 289
Zhirinovskiy, Vladimir, 288
Zvonosky, Vladimir, 334
Zyuganov, Gennadiy, 288, 290–91